Praise for
Storm on the Horizon

"A memorable study of a transformative battle . . . Lucid and well written; a worthy companion to Anthony Swofford's *Jarhead*."
—*Kirkus Reviews*

"David Morris has brilliantly recaptured a forgotten moment in American military history. We relive the battle of Khafji with the soldiers who fought it, and we discover what it means for our world today. One of the best books yet on the Gulf War."
—H.W. BRANDS,
author of *Lone Star Nation*
and *The Age of Gold*

"This is the story no one thought could be told about the Gulf War, but David Morris has done so magnificently—he is an engaging, dramatic storyteller. These Marines come alive as blood brothers, and their story becomes our story. Morris has breathed sharp life into an unknown part of recent history."
—DOUG STANTON,
author of *In Harm's Way:
The Sinking of the USS Indianapolis
and the Extraordinary Story of Its Survivors*

ublished by The Random House Publishing Group
lable at quantity discounts on bulk purchases for
n, educational, fund-raising, and special sales use.
ils, please call 1-800-733-3000.

"An intriguing account of the confusion and valor in the first battle of the Gulf War."
—BERNARD E. TRAINOR, Lt. Gen. USMC (Ret.),
coauthor of *The Generals' War:
The Inside Story of the Conflict in the Gulf*

"Part of the pleasure in reading this work comes from the way Morris tells the story from the war fighter's point of view. We come to know the characters and terrain through Morris's vivid detail. . . . [*Storm on the Horizon*] is rife with controversy and the raw emotion of combat, yet covers the national political aims and the operational and tactical objectives of the war. . . . Reads like fine literature."
—*Air Force Times*

"Morris has done yeoman work in finding and interviewing veterans of this battle, and tells their story with all the exhilaration, panic, bravery, and physical endurance that words can convey."
—*The Decatur Daily*

"[Morris's] narrative style is excellent, ma[...]
as if one were there. . . . Consider this on[...]
books on small-unit action in the first Gul[...]
—*Booklist*

"The real strength of [*Storm on the H[...]
portraits of the men on the ground. . . [...]
how the fog (and smoke, dust and san[...]
the people in it. While clarifying the [...]
reader, not something that most [...]
manage."
—*Publishers Weekl[y]*

"What is fresh about Morris's worl[...]
way the author captured the feel of [...]
all its fog, uncertainties, devasta[...]
quiet heroics, and then folded tha[...]
researched and well-documented [...]
significant ground fights of the Gu[...]
—*Marine Corps G[...]*

Book[...]
are a[...]
premi[...]
For d[...]

STORM ON THE HORIZON

Khafji—The Battle That Changed the Course of the Gulf War

DAVID J. MORRIS

BALLANTINE BOOKS • NEW YORK

Some of the names in this book have been changed.

2005 Presidio Press Mass Market Edition

Published in the United States by Presidio Press, an imprint of The Random House Publishing Group, a division of Random House, Inc., New York.

Presidio Press and colophon are trademarks of Random House, Inc.

Originally published in hardcover by Free Press, a division of Simon & Schuster, Inc., in 2004.

ISBN 0-345-48153-4

Printed in the United States of America

www.presidiopress.com

OPM   9   8   7   6   5   4   3   2

Khafji was the defining moment of the war.
—LIEUTENANT GENERAL BERNARD TRAINOR, USMC (ret.),
coauthor of *The Generals' War*

In my view, Khafji was a pivotal battle of the war. It was a turning point as significant as the Coalition's battle for air supremacy in the first few minutes of the air campaign.
—GENERAL KHALID BIN SULTAN AL SAUD,
commander of Arab troops during the Persian Gulf War

It really is a hell of a story and the trouble is the Army doesn't want it told because the Army wasn't involved. But it was the only ground battle that we fought in the war where the issue was in doubt.
—GENERAL CHUCK HORNER,
commander of U.S. air forces during the Persian Gulf War

I think Khafji sort of happened. We didn't really know how significant it was until after it was all said and done. And then after the war as we started to look into it, it became a larger evolution than I could have imagined.
—COLONEL JOHN R. BIOTY, USMC,
Marine air group commander

PREFACE

Why I longed to go grubbing into the deplorable details of an occurrence which, after all, concerned me no more than as a member of an obscure body of men held together by a community of inglorious toil and by fidelity to a certain standard of conduct, I can't explain. You may call it an unhealthy curiosity if you like; but I have a distinct notion I wished to find something.
—JOSEPH CONRAD, *Lord Jim*

A FEW DAYS INTO the melodrama of Officer Candidate School in Quantico, Virginia, in 1992, one of my fellow inmates pointed out a barrel-chested senior drill instructor from another platoon, saying, "That guy's fucking amazing. Everybody in third herd worships him. They say he was at Khafji too." I quickly looked the young staff sergeant over, a daring, possibly life-threatening move within the confines of OCS. He was a vision of soldierly virtue: fit, deeply tanned, and with gold naval parachutist's wings gleaming on his chest, identifying him as an elite reconnaissance Marine.

Then I thought about that other thing my buddy had mentioned: Khafji. I'd heard the name before, vaguely recalling images of Iraqi tanks careering through the shattered streets of some Middle Eastern town in the opening days of the Persian Gulf War. At that embryonic stage in my Marine career, I didn't know much of it beyond what I'd learned from CNN. But this Marine, like others before him who had been to Beirut and Somalia, had that look about him as if he were the sole proprietor of a secret that I longed to hear and yet whose essence was always somehow lost in the telling. Like most warrior wannabes, I viewed this guy as being somehow more than mortal. He had *been there*—he had seen the life beyond the veil.

The battle of Khafji is much like many crucial battles in recent times that briefly occupy center stage in the world theater and are then condemned to the dustbin of history. But among fighting men, engagements such as Khafji, Mogadishu, Haiti, Beirut, and Baidoa are endlessly recounted in hushed tones and with a reverence for the moment that would floor most civilians. Despite their surprising obscurity, these battles had an immeasurable impact on the lives of the men who fought in them. Being shot at and watching other men die violently is something that alters a man forever, regardless of how little the rest of the world happens to care. Being a party to the death of thousands and witnessing the dismemberment of a foreign army only enlarges this effect.

The battle of Khafji ushered in a new era in American military history. It was the first major U.S. engagement after Vietnam, and it became the de facto proving ground for a new generation of astonishingly effective tactics and technologies. The battle to retake the town largely prefigured the U.S. war in Afghanistan, with small, mobile U.S. teams providing fire support to motivated but unskilled indigenous forces. American soldiers and their allies saw up close and for the first time the staggering psychological impact of modern precision-guided munitions upon an outmoded Third World army. These same men were forced to learn in agonizing detail the devastating effectiveness of these new weapons as they were unwittingly unleashed upon their own comrades.

The conclusion of the Persian Gulf War is a matter of history that most are familiar with: the dispirited Iraqi army, pushed to the breaking point by a revolutionary precision-bombing campaign capitulated after a hugely anticlimactic ground offensive. Before Khafji, however, such an outcome seemed highly unlikely. The Iraqis were seen, in one Marine's words, as "ten-foot-tall giants" who were the undisputed masters of desert warfare. They possessed the world's fourth largest army and had fought Iran, a country four times its size in population, to a standstill in an eight-year slugfest. They had rolled into the Kuwaiti emirate, seizing it with a scripted efficiency that one can only compare to Hitler's conquest of the Low Countries in 1940, conquering it utterly in four days. Responding to the invasion, President George H. W. Bush in August of 1990 dispatched an advance force including the Army's 82nd Airborne division and the 7th Marine Expeditionary Brigade to protect Saudi Arabia and its flowing oil fields from further Iraqi aggression. By late October it was decided that the American forces in theater would lead a broad Coalition to take Kuwait back from the Iraqis.

Unlike the most recent conflict with Iraq, there was no reason to expect an easy victory in this first war. There was no Kosovo or Afghanistan to point to. The devastating effects of precision airpower were only a war-college professor's dream. The American military establishment, whose confidence had been greatly bolstered by the huge buildups of the Reagan years, had yet to emerge from Vietnam's long shadow. It hadn't produced a major victory since the Inchon offensive in the early stages of the Korean War. Most officers, unaware of the extent of the revolution in weaponry that was only just coming to fruition, expected a bloodbath in Kuwait.

On January 29, 1991, twenty-seven days before the Allied assault was set to roll, the Iraqis invaded Saudi Arabia, seizing the coastal town of Ra's al-Khafji, and everything changed. The fight to retake Khafji, the primary subject of this book, when taken in its full context, represents the passing of an era. At Khafji the Iraqi fighting man's true nature was revealed and a new epoch in war was introduced. Saddam was handed his first resounding defeat. Immediately following the battle, Marine commanders began reshaping their offensive plans to deal with what they expected to be the largest prisoner-collection exercise in American history.

The men who fought at Khafji were, for the most part, children of the 1980s and were raised on Ronald Reagan's vision of a nation born from the ashes of Vietnam. They possessed a seemingly boundless faith in both their country and a resurrected American military arm. They represented a new breed of American warrior, distinct in character from their grandfathers, who'd fought in World War II. They were elite professional soldiers who had enlisted by choice and endured years of arduous training. No one was drafted to fight in this new war. There were no volunteer masses; there was no high-minded Bush doctrine to justify its prosecution, no post-9/11 war cry. The war was not seen by the rank and file as a moral crusade or some sort of Homeric undertaking; most viewed it with an antiseptic, cause-and-effect detachment. Their cause, if it can be called a cause, was simple and circumstantial: Saddam had stolen a country and they were there to take it back as efficiently as possible.

Leading these men was a graying cadre of Vietnam veterans who were sworn to correct the mistakes committed nearly thirty years earlier. As Lieutenant General Walt Boomer, the overall Marine commander in the Gulf, recalled, "Vietnam hung over the Gulf War like a fog." Boomer, along with most of the senior Marine commanders in the Kuwaiti theater, had served as an advisor to the South Vietnamese Marine Corps and had experienced the trauma of the war in Southeast Asia with a striking degree of intimacy. They were determined to get it right this time around.

Later in my career, I served with other Marines who were at Khafji during the crucial four days that form the nucleus of this story, including then-Colonel John Admire, commander of the Third Marine Regiment. I remember well the late nights in the deserts of Twentynine Palms training base, when the war had become a well-whispered memory and these men would describe their days in Saudi Arabia. These stories inevitably began with, "Man, back in the desert . . ." I like to think of this story as a collection of the best of those late night tales, buttressed by the hard facts contained in the official histories and the over 100 veterans I have interviewed.

To remember and, in some way, celebrate men caught up in war is a curious enterprise. I realize that stories about war are what make young men, convinced of their immortality, join organizations like the Marine Corps in the first place. The mythology of battle inspired my youth and played a central role in my decision to enlist. And yet War, in all its monstrous cruelty and squalor, somehow retains its fascination. The melodrama inherent in war seems somehow to embody the very essence of the human condition in all its rage, bliss, and contradiction. To paraphrase the Greek philosopher Heraclitus, war is the father and king of us all.

CONTENTS

Preface   *xi*

Dramatis Personae   *xxi*

Prologue: 8:00 P.M., January 29, 1991,
Observation Post 4, on the Kuwaiti Border
50 Miles West of Khafji   *1*

PART I THE OUTPOST BATTLES

1 **The Persian Gulf Theater,** Winter 1991   *11*

2 **Camp Schwab, Okinawa, Japan,**
July–August 1990   *19*

3 **January 19, 1991,** Northeastern Saudi Arabia   *37*

4 **6:00 P.M., January 29, 1991,** Observation Post 4   *46*

5 **8:20 P.M., January 29, 1991,** Observation Post 4   *65*

6 **Approximately 8:45 P.M., January 29, 1991,**
the Berm, Observation Post 4   *73*

7 **9:00 P.M., January 29, 1991,** the Berm,
Observation Post 4   *80*

8 **Approximately 9:00 P.M., January 29, 1991,**
Observation Post 4   *89*

9 **Nighttime, January 29, 1991,** Riyadh,
Saudi Arabia, 250 Miles South of
Observation Post 4   *94*

10 **Approximately 9:15 P.M., January 29, 1991,**
Observation Post 4   *99*

11 **Approximately 9:30 P.M., January 29, 1991,**
Observation Post 4   *117*

12 **12:45 A.M., January 30,** Observation Post 4   *128*

13 **Dawn, January 29, 1991,** Just South of the
   Kuwaiti Border *136*

PART II THE BATTLE FOR KHAFJI

14 **6:45 A.M., January 29, 1991,** Observation Post 8,
   Six Miles North of Khafji *153*
15 **January 29, 1991,** Surveillance, Reconnaissance,
   Intelligence Group Forward Headquarters,
   Four Miles North of Khafji *171*
16 **9:00 P.M., January 29, 1991,** Khafji *190*
17 **Morning, January 30, 1991,** Khafji *203*
18 **Mid-Morning, January 30, 1991,** Khafji *214*
19 **2nd Saudi Arabian National Guard Brigade
   Headquarters,** Five Miles West of Mishab *220*
20 **11:00 P.M., January 30, 1991,** on the Coastal
   Highway Just South of Khafji *253*
21 **Nighttime, January 30, 1991,** Five Miles
   Northwest of Khafji *274*
22 **Dawn, January 31, 1991,** Khafji *287*
23 **7:00 A.M., January 31, 1991,** Khafji *293*
   Epilogue *324*

   Where Are They Now? *333*
   Roster of the Fallen *336*
   U.S. Marine Corps Key Words and Acronyms *337*
   Sources *339*
   Notes *346*
   Acknowledgments *358*
   Index *360*

MAPS

Iraqi Offensive, January 29, 1991   *10*
Observation Post 4, Evening of January 29, 1991   *47*
Al Khafji, January 30, 1991   *204*

DRAMATIS PERSONAE

Deep Reconnaissance Platoon, Charlie Company, 3rd Reconnaissance Battalion

1st Lieutenant Steven Ross	Platoon Commander
Staff Sergeant Greg Gillispie	Platoon Sergeant
Sergeant Mike Davis	Team Leader
Sergeant John Jestel	Team Leader
Sergeant Thomas Manney	Team Leader
Sergeant Luis Bench	Combat Engineer
Corporal Miguel Roche	Platoon Communications Chief
Lance Corporal Jeffrey Buffa	Team Member

Delta Company, 3rd Light-Armored Infantry Battalion

Captain Roger Pollard	Company Commander
1st Lieutenant Scott Williams	Company Executive Officer
1st Lieutenant Dave Kendall	Second Platoon Commander
2nd Lieutenant Glenn Sadowski	First Platoon Commander
1st Sergeant Alfonso Villa	Company First Sergeant
Corporal Bill Covington	Infantry Scout
Corporal Russell Zawalick	Company Forward Air Controller
Lance Corporal Ron Tull	Driver, "Blaze of Glory," a.k.a. "Red 2"

Alpha Group, TOW Platoon, 1st Light-Armored Infantry Battalion

Sergeant Nick Vitale	Alpha Group Leader
Sergeant Michael Wissman, Jr.	Alpha Assistant Group Leader
Lance Corporal Jason Brown	TOW Gunner
Lance Corporal Scott Pruett	TOW Gunner
Lance Corporal Joshua Brierly	TOW Gunner
Lance Corporal Derek Puterbaugh	Assistant TOW Gunner
Lance Corporal Dave Burrows	LAV Driver
Private First Class Benz Crosby	Loader

*Not everyone present in theater is listed.

DRAMATIS PERSONAE

1st Marine Expeditionary Force

Lieutenant General Walt Boomer   MEF Commander

1st Surveillance, Reconnaissance, and Intelligence Group

Lieutenant Colonel Rick Barry   SRIG Executive Officer

1st Marine Division

Major General Mike Myatt	Division Commander
Captain Joe Molofsky	Division Arab Liaison Officer

3rd Marine Regiment a.k.a. "3rd Marines"

Colonel John Admire   Regimental Commander

3rd Battalion, 3rd Marine Regiment

Lieutenant Colonel J. J. Garrett	Battalion Commander
Major Craig Huddleston	Battalion Executive Officer
Captain John Borth	TOW Platoon Commander

3rd Platoon, Alpha Company, 3rd Reconnaissance Battalion (Attached to 3rd Marines)

Captain Dan Baczkowski	Platoon Commander
Sergeant Bill Iiams	Team 1 Leader
Corporal Lawrence Lentz	Team 2 Leader
Corporal Scott Uskoski	Assistant Team 2 Leader
Corporal Scott Wagner	Team 2 Radio Operator
Lance Corporal Marcus Slavenas	Team 2 SAW Gunner
Lance Corporal Alan Cooper	Team 2 Member
Lance Corporal Jude Woodarek	Team 2 Member
Hospital Mate Carlos Dayrit	Team 2 Corpsman
Corporal Chuck Ingraham	Team 3 Leader
Corporal Jeffrey Brown	Assistant Team 3 Leader
Lance Corporal Harold Boling	Team 3 Member
Lance Corporal David McNamee	Team 3 Member
Lance Corporal Patrick Sterling	Team 3 Point Man
Hospital Mate 1st Class Kevin Callahan	Team 3 Corpsman

1st Air-Naval Gunfire Liaison Company

Lieutenant Colonel Clay Grubb	Commanding Officer
Captain Kris Elliot	1st MODA Brigade ANGLICO Team Leader
Captain Jim Braden	2nd SANG Brigade ANGLICO Team Leader
Captain Doug Kleinsmith	2nd SANG Brigade ANGLICO Team Leader (forward)
1st Lieutenant Paul Deckert	5th SANG Battalion ANGLICO Team Leader
Captain Mark Dillard	7th SANG Battalion ANGLICO Team Leader
1st Lieutenant Kurt Lang	Fire Control Team 9 Leader (Observation Post 8)
Sergeant Elisio Lozano	Fire Control Team Chief (Observation Post 8)
Corporal Mel Russell	Fire Control Team Communications Chief (Observation Post 8)
Captain Jon Fleming	Supporting Arms Liaison Team 5 Leader
Captain John Bley	Fire Control Team 12 Leader

Marine Light-Attack Helicopter Squadron-367 (HMLA-367)

Major Gary Shaw	Operations Officer/Cobra Pilot
Captain Scott Haney	Cobra Flight Leader
Captain Max Morton	Cobra Pilot
Captain Gary West	Cobra Pilot

Arab Coalition Forces

HRH General Khalid bin Sultan al Saud	Commanding Officer

Joint Forces Coalition-East (Arab Coalition Eastern Sector)

Major General Sultan 'Adi al-Mutairi	Commanding Officer

DRAMATIS PERSONAE

2nd Saudi Arabian National Guard Brigade

Colonel Turki al-Firmi   Commanding Officer

7th Saudi Arabian National Guard Battalion

Lieutenant Colonel Matar   Commanding Officer

PROLOGUE

8:00 P.M., January 29, 1991,
Observation Post 4, on the Kuwaiti Border
50 Miles West of Khafji

Our brains ache, in the merciless iced east winds that knife us . . .
Wearied we keep awake because the night is silent . . .
Low drooping flares confuse our memory of the salient . . .
Worried by silence, sentries whisper, curious, nervous,
But nothing happens.
          WILFRED OWEN, "Exposure"

D ARKNESS falls fast in the desert. It is this time, soon after the light has gone, that a man can feel most alone. The blackness envelops him, denying him sight, severing or diminishing his connection with those around him. Nevertheless, Lieutenant Steven Ross and his platoon sergeant Greg Gillispie were in good spirits as they sat improbably perched in brightly colored aluminum beach chairs atop a large earthen berm. They'd stolen the beach chairs from some rear-area types before striking out into the heart of the Arabian desert to occupy the border-police post that was their home, their fighting position, and their desert redoubt all rolled into one. They peered into the belly of Kuwait through high-tech night-vision goggles. An utterly desiccated sandscape, flat as a billiard table, stretched off as far as the eye could see.

They were happy because tomorrow morning they, along with the rest of their platoon, were going to be relieved and would finally get a chance to grab a shower and maybe a camel burger at the PX trailers that had been set up in the rear. They'd been out at Observation Post 4, one of the most remote outposts in the Marine sector, encircled by the sands, for nearly two weeks now and were running low on chow and water. OP 4 was one of those places in the war that Marines got dropped into that didn't really exist in the normal sense. You pulled out the map sheet marked "Umm Hjul," and it was just a bunch of empty grid squares with barely a feature or contour line on the entire page, devoid of even the most basic landmarks to orient yourself save the sun, the blank horizon, and the small cluster of spartan buildings that comprised the border fort.

Battalion headquarters had been putting them off for some time, saying, "Tomorrow you'll be relieved." So far there'd been three "tomorrow" calls this week. They'd been hung out there for so long that the cryptographic fills for their radios had expired, forcing them to talk "in the plain," leaving them perilously exposed to Iraqi eavesdropping—not a minor concern. Staff Sergeant Gillispie had been up and down the border to the other Marine outposts innumerable times on scrounging missions, trading what he could for field rations, water, and extra gear. But even for a crafty devil with beaucoup connections like Gillispie, karma eventually runs out. However, this most recent promise from Battalion seemed solid, and Ross had decided to consolidate his two northernmost positions in order to expedite the morning turnover.

Still, until they were relieved, they had a job to do. They were recon, the eyes and ears of the First Marine Division, there to provide early warning in case the Iraqis started acting up and to collect the deserters who had been crossing over through no-man's-land in increasing numbers since the air war started two weeks prior. In the words of a division staff officer, their mission was to "see, scream, and scram"; that is, they were to observe and report any enemy activity and if threatened by a large enough force, they were to evacuate with utmost haste. To this end, Lieutenant Ross had designated a fallback point in the event they were overrun. Should everything go to shit, a small, horseshoe-shaped berm 500 meters behind their position would be their safe harbor. From there they would regroup and make their way to friendly lines by whatever means necessary.

Ross and Gillispie had deployed the platoon in three teams each with a full complement of night-vision and spotting scopes, an M-60 machine gun, and stacks of disposable light antitank weapons known as AT-4s. Their position was centered around an old two-story Saudi police post that in better times had housed border guards and customs officials. Because of the expected relief in the morning, Sergeant Mike Davis's team had been pulled in from their bunker from the north into the building with Sergeant John Jestel's team. This move was as much for punishment as for any tactical consideration. Davis and Jestel, who detested each other, had somehow come upon a few cases of MRE (meals ready to eat) on their own and had neglected to share the booty with the rest of the platoon.

As reward for their selfishness, Gillispie made them hootch together their final night at the OP. Sergeant Thomas Manney's third team, along with Ross, Gillispie, a Marine lieutenant named Turk, their Arabic translator, and their communications chief, Corporal Miguel Roche, were 300 meters southeast of the house. When not on post up on the berm, they would sleep in the hastily constructed bunker, arranged out of some sandbags and plywood they'd found lying around the customs house. Roche worked out of his own small comm bunker, which kept the radios out of the cold and drizzly weather.

The platoon's situation was, on the one hand, completely insane. They were way out on the edge of the empire, miles from friendly lines, utterly exposed to an Iraqi attack, so far forward that even the American artillery couldn't reach them. It would take any attack helicopter that happened to be ready to launch over half an hour to reach their position. As if to reinforce the point, they'd been probed earlier in the week by some Iraqi sappers, who'd taken a wild RPG (rocket-propelled grenade) shot at their pos. On the other hand, they were merely a reconnaissance platoon, which meant they were under no obligation to pull some sort of die-hard Alamo move and fight to the last. If things got too hairy, they were free to retreat with their honor fully intact. Recon

Marines were trained to locate, identify, and lastly, to artfully dodge the enemy.

Although Ross and the boys would be loath to admit it, this mad exposure was part of the game, part of the recon Marine mystique. This is just how the grunt game is played, the way it's always been played: You make plans, set up security, coordinate for fire support, try not to get ambushed. But at some point you really just hope for the best. In the end there's no way to control what actually happens, to decide who lives and who dies, who gets a sucking chest wound and who walks away with a Bronze Star and a great story to tell the folks back home. The gods of war roll the dice, and the dumb grunts in the middle of it get to sort it out.

As it turned out, the whole thing began almost like a comedy routine as Ross and Gillispie settled into the first watch of their last evening at OP 4, the early shift, 2000–2200 in mil-speak, looking forward to another eventless night on post in the middle of nowhere.

Out of the cornerless expanse of cool night air, Ross's ear seized on a noise. A squeaking almost. Seconds ticked by. The noise emerged again. Ross thought, I *know* that sound. It was the sound of tanks, killer metal beasts lurching forward in the night. One could just imagine a perfect phalanx of them, their brutal iron tracks churning the sand. The chilling *clank-clank-clank-clank* of so much moving deadly metal.

"I think I hear something," Ross said.

"Ah, whatever, sir," Gillispie said.

"I'm serious, man."

"It's probably just another B-52 strike," Gillispie said, referring to the monstrous bombing runs that could be heard halfway across Kuwait.

The darkness plays its tricks. A few choice minutes into another of a thousand shifts and tanks appear as if by magic out of the night. This is exactly the type of apparition the mind searching for distraction would conjure on a night watch.

Yeah, right, Iraqi tanks coming straight for us.

The ominous noises grew.

"No, really, I think I hear something," Ross said. This back and forth was quickly becoming a case of the jumpy young lieutenant with an overactive imagination being admonished by the old salt.

Minutes passed.

"Yep, that's it. I *do* hear something."

"You know, sir, you may be right," Gillispie said, acquiescing at last.

Ross put his eye up to the aperture of the night-vision scope. There in the haunting green light of the scope was the proof. Three tiny black dots on the move. In and of themselves, these blips meant absolutely nothing, but when you've been looking out over the same horizon, the same stretch of dirt for a virtual eternity as Ross and Gillispie had, even the smallest new object sticks out like a tarantula on a wedding cake.

The black dots were enemy armored vehicles, and they were headed toward their position.

Things started happening fast. Ross hopped down to the foot of the berm to Roche's comm shed and told him to wake the boys up and to call battalion and let 'em know we got movement to our front. A minute later, he told him to raise the company of Marine light-armored vehicles that were to their rear. Ross looked back into the scope. The three vehicles had just turned into five. It was as if the vehicles were emerging out of a slight depression. With each passing minute another wing of their formation unmasked itself from the defile.

After trying on the local radio net to rouse Davis's and Jestel's teams, Roche started punching up a message to headquarters on the DCT, a small electronic pad that had numerous pre-formatted messages stored in it. All you had to do was fill in the blanks, and bam! the message went out in digitally encrypted bursts. But the messages weren't going through. Roche rebooted the whole system and tried again. Still nothing.

Ross popped his head back in the shed and said there were now five tracked vehicles approaching. After messing around for a few more minutes, Roche still couldn't figure out what was the matter. Gillispie ducked in and asked, "Did you get the message off to Battalion yet?"

"No."

"Well, keep working it. I gotta go wake everybody up."

Roche knew something was seriously fucked up. The other teams weren't even 500 meters away. He'd *always* had comm with them, loud and clear. At that moment Ross ducked back in and asked, "What did Battalion say?"

"Sir, something's up. I can't get comm with anybody." Ross looked at him for a second and shot back out to the berm.

Gillispie ran over to the bunker where the headquarters team slept and calmly told everyone inside that we got action to the front and to get your gear together and throw it in the three platoon Humvees. He'd always been a real stickler for having their gear all packed up and ready to go, so it only took them a minute before they were ready to rock and roll.

Things weren't looking good for Roche. He was the comm chief and had two other radio operators under him. He was supposed to be the platoon's radio guru, and yet he couldn't raise a soul. *What had he missed?* He sprinted away from the berm to go check on the long-range antenna farm he'd set up in order to reach back to the rear, some 50 miles distant. Intel had told them the Iraqis didn't have any jamming capability. *What else could it be?* Then, thinking back, he remembered that right as their watch began, the pitch of the radio static, the ubiquitous background *ssssshhhh,* had wavered ever so slightly. It seemed kinda weird at the time. Then he knew: They were being jammed.

Ross went in to the comm bunker and grabbed one of the radios to try to locate some aircraft to do bombing runs. He began by doing the standard Hail Mary radio routine to yank some air out of the sky: "Any station this net. Any station . . ." After several minutes, he came up dry. They had no air and no comm with anybody and they were about to mix it up with a company of tanks with peashooters.

Meanwhile, the vehicles, which had long since ceased to

be mere blips, were rapidly closing the gap to the police post. The growl of the tracks rolling in concert grew in intensity. The Marines of the Deep Reconnaissance Platoon prepared to engage, rechecking ammo, grabbing AT-4s, and sighting in with machine guns, fingers in trigger wells.

Ross counted the vehicles again and thought to himself only a number, a number that described exactly the state of their fortunes at the moment: 23.

PART I

THE OUTPOST BATTLES

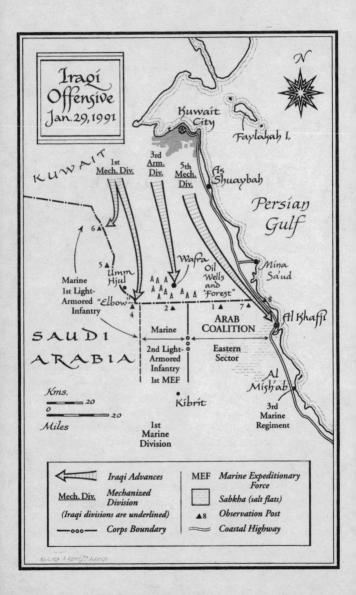

1

The Persian Gulf Theater,
Winter 1991

I calculated that it is only by a counterstrike that one can disrupt the enemy's preparation for a new offensive. To force the enemy to take the offensive earlier than at the time which he had set is more advantageous for us than to sit and wait until he is fully prepared.
—SOVIET GENERAL VASSILI I. CHUIKOV, remarks regarding the Soviet offensive at Stalingrad, October 1942.

EARLY ON the morning of January 17, 1991, the multinational Coalition arrayed against Saddam Hussein kicked off an air campaign the likes of which the world had never seen. Capitalizing on nearly two decades of unprecedented American techno-military advancement, the execution of such a wide-reaching surgical campaign signaled a revolution in warfare. Conceived by a top secret U.S. Air Force planning cell known as Checkmate and its iconoclastic leader, Colonel John Warden, this air assault made use of a ground-breaking new class of weapons technologies developed in the years after the Vietnam War. Unlike the comparatively crude carpet-bombing campaigns of World War II and Vietnam, this operation, portentously named Instant Thunder, was designed to systematically demolish Saddam's leadership structure without leveling Iraq's cities along with it. What made Instant Thunder unique, however, was not just the technology it exploited but the extreme discretion with which it was prosecuted: Rather than try to methodically kill off every arm of the vast Iraqi war machine, Instant Thunder zeroed in on the Iraqi central nervous system: its electrical grid, its telecommunications networks, its radar installations, its command-and-control nodes, leaving Saddam's vaunted armored divisions to die on the vine. Taken as a whole, Warden's audacious plan seemed as much an argument to prove the supremacy of airpower as it was an attempt to force Saddam out of Kuwait.

Handpicked to fire the opening salvos of this new war was a four-ship flight of Apache helicopter gunships from the Army's 101st Airborne. Piercing Iraqi airspace just after 2:00 A.M., they unleashed a volley of Hellfire missiles into a key battery of Iraqi radar dishes poised on the Saudi border, opening the door to flights of electronic jamming aircraft and Stealth fighters. Wave upon wave of American aircraft soon thundered over Baghdad, unleashing their deadly cargo, in some cases near waiting television cameras. And as CNN floated these images around the world, the war began to take on the queer character that has since become fixed in the public imagination, that of spectral bridges, buildings, and tanks being silently obliterated as if by magic on a million television screens, of antiaircraft fire arcing gracefully into the Iraqi sky. Thus the illusion of virtual war was born. After a week of round-the-clock bombing, Saddam was nearly blind, deaf, and dumb as his telecommunications and command networks were decimated.

Nevertheless, Saddam was far from defeated, and the air campaign, while strikingly effective, left plenty to be desired as far as ground commanders were concerned. The practical problem with this new war was that it was focused so intently upon the fat targets in central Iraq that it left much of the Iraqi army dispersed throughout Kuwait totally unmolested. Ten days into the landmark campaign, at which point American Stealth fighters were essentially operating at will over Baghdad, the Iraqi tanks and howitzers across the berm from the Marines were practically untouched. As Colonel Manfred A. Rietsch, a Marine air group commander noted, "We weren't able to concentrate on the areas that affected our Marines. There were certain areas where there was a lot of enemy activity that appeared to be untouched by the JFACC [U.S. Air Force headquarters in Saudi Arabia]."*

General Boomer, the head Marine in the Gulf, was particularly concerned about Saddam's III Corps, the most dangerous enemy unit in Kuwait. III Corps occupied Kuwait City and was arrayed in depth along the Saudi border with belts of conscript infantry divisions protecting the Corps's mobile reserve, the 3rd Armored and the 1st and 5th Mechanized Divisions. Although not the vaunted Republican Guard, these were some of Saddam's best divisions. The elite 3rd Armored, outfitted with Russian T-72 tanks, was far and away the best trained and equipped unit in the Iraqi army and was often lumped in the same category as the Republican Guard by intelligence experts. III Corps was commanded by Major General Salah Aboud Mahmoud, one of Saddam's most trusted field commanders, who had distinguished himself in the closing campaigns of the Iran-Iraq War. He was that rare Iraqi general who had been promoted by dint of his operational talent rather than his political connections.

Making matters worse, III Corps posed an unnerving artillery threat with Soviet-made howitzers that easily outranged their American counterparts. That artillery tubes were the preferred means for delivering chemical weapons only heightened Boomer's concern, which at times blossomed into near-paranoia. Indeed, Boomer once spoke to his staff of a dream where he "woke up at two or three o'clock in the morning . . . shaking, soaking wet . . . from a terrible bad dream where two divisions on line are attempting to go through two breaches . . . being bogged down in the minefields and obstacle belts . . . and in the middle of all that somewhere between 1,100 and 1,400 artillery tubes were raining a fiery death and destruction. My Marines are dying." After repeated appeals to JFACC, Boomer and his

---

*Indeed, on February 15, fully two weeks after the battle of Khafji, a U-2 overflight of the Tawakalna Division, the southernmost of the Republican Guard divisions, showed it at 74 percent combat effectiveness, well above Air Force estimates.

staff were eventually able to begin shifting more air missions onto targets inside Kuwait.

After nearly two weeks of round-the-clock bombing, Saddam was feeling pinched and was searching for ways to hit back. In a tactic reminiscent of the Iran-Iraq War, where an air "war of the cities" between Tehran and Baghdad had raged, Saddam launched a barrage of Scud missiles toward Tel Aviv, banking on Israel's tradition of swift retribution to drive a wedge between the Arab and Western members of the Coalition. However, aggressive Washington-led diplomacy headed off any Israeli revenge attacks with, among other things, the promise of commando raids on Saddam's mobile Scud launchers. This development further dimmed prospects for Marine commanders, as in order to placate the Israelis, critical air missions were diverted to what became known as the the Great Scud Hunt. This campaign was an illustrious failure, and in the end only a handful of missile launchers were ever confirmed as destroyed.

During this same time frame, Major General Mike Myatt, commander of the First Marine Division, began launching what he dubbed "ambiguity operations," designed to confuse Iraqi defensive preparations, Myatt declaring, "I want to fuck with the Iraqis' heads." This unorthodox deception effort consisted of widely scattered artillery raids along the Kuwaiti frontier and the creation of a highly unusual unit known as Task Force Troy. Troy, headed up by Myatt's deputy, General Tom Draude, was a bogus division composed of a handful of APCs (armored personnel carriers) jam-packed with radios and loudspeakers, which rolled along the border simulating the sounds and radio traffic of a full-strength Marine division, complete with fake call signs and operations orders.

Adding to the confusion along the border, just before midnight on January 21, a platoon from the Marines' First Force Reconnaissance Company was attacked at Observation Post 6 by a company of Iraqi infantry. That morning the Marines had gotten word from a captured lieutenant that an entire infantry company was preparing to defect in their sector. After conversing with an advance group of eight Iraqis, things quickly soured as the Marines heard rounds being chambered in the darkness. The Marines were soon enveloped by machine-gun and RPG fire, and after a disjointed hour-long gun battle, backlit by the phantasmal glow of Iraqi artillery illumination rounds, the Marines managed to extract themselves from the observation post and move to a predesignated rally point beneath a nearby bridge. They emerged unscathed, albeit confounded as to the Iraqis' intentions. No blood trails were found the following morning, although Iraqi defectors later confirmed that the attack had been conducted by a commando company from the 36th Division. The Iraqis suffered five dead.

By late January, the failure of the Scud attacks and air strikes, along with the bewildering situation near the Kuwaiti border, all added to the pressure on Saddam to act, to do *something.* As one Pentagon official put it, "Only an idiot would sit there forever while his military was being destroyed." On the twenty-seventh, the plan for the offensive into Saudi Arabia was approved by Saddam. Some reports assert that he in fact caravanned to the southern Iraqi border town of Basra to confer with his field commanders about the upcoming operation.

Saddam, who had once told his staff that "the air force has never decided a war in the history of war," seemed to have concluded that the time had come to draw the Allies into a slugfest where his tanks and artillery could slaughter the Americans. In September 1980, Saddam had done this very thing, launching a daring preemptive attack deep into Iranian territory that only bogged down after outrunning its supply lines. He hoped to do one better in Saudi Arabia.

Like Ho Chi Minh before him, Saddam was keenly aware of how impatient and irresolute the American public can be. He knew that if he produced enough body bags or POWs renouncing their country on the evening news, Americans would cry to their president to bring the boys back home. With a surprise thrust into Allied lines, Saddam would bloody the Americans on CNN and chop their resolve off at the knees.

Saddam's plan called for a three-pronged drive into northeastern Saudi Arabia by the 3rd Armored Division and 1st and 5th Mechanized Divisions. The exact military objectives of the offensive remain unclear. Iraqi knowledge of American unit locations and strengths during this time frame was spotty at best. It appears that the focus remained upon dealing a strong blow against the Coalition, striking at its weak points, primarily the Khafji region, which was manned by inexperienced Saudi and Qatari units, as well as lashing out against the American units that had for several weeks been taunting frontline Iraqi troops with artillery raids and psychological operations.

A major concern for the Coalition was the colossal Marine logistics complex at Kibrit. Located at an abandoned airfield 30 miles south of the Kuwait border, it was in the direct line of the Iraqi assault. Kibrit, the largest fuel and ammunition dump in the Marine Corps's history, had been erected on a previously unheard-of scale, sprawling over 25 square miles and at one point containing nearly two million gallons of gasoline. Kibrit had sprouted up practically overnight in preparation for the ground war and had been brazenly situated *forward* of friendly lines in order to maximize the attack's forward momentum.

Amid all this sound and fury, Boomer and his staff were focused inward, consumed with the preparations for the impending Kuwait offensive, set to roll in late February. The Marines had been given what many considered to be a suicide mission.* They were to attack due north into the teeth of the Iraqi defenses, breaching two major obstacle belts loaded with burning oil pits, elaborate tank traps, miles of barbed

---

*A British tank brigade initially attached to the Marines had, in fact, been reassigned to the U.S. Army because London was convinced that the Marines were walking into a killing field in southern Kuwait. The assumption of this type of mission seemed at the time to fit into the pattern of ill-considered Marine charges such as the controversial assault on the Tarawa atoll in the Pacific during World War II, which cost 990 American lives.

wire, and row upon row of antipersonnel mines. While a new age in warfare may have been heralded over the skies of Baghdad, for those on the ground it seemed as if nothing had changed.

The breach itself was expected to be an exceedingly complex operation, with two 10,000-man divisions leapfrogging each other, all while exposed to the fearsome Iraqi artillery corps. In the doomstruck atmosphere that dominated the preparations, nightmarish visions of mustard and nerve gas attacks swept through the ranks, driving some to request transfer stateside. It seemed to some as if the legion follies of World War I were about to be relived. One light-armored vehicle company was told by higher headquarters to expect 85 percent casualties.

As a result of the immense, elaborate efforts dedicated to the coming thrust, the border itself was left only lightly manned. The entire Marine command was so intent upon the attack succeeding, so obsessed with the grim prospect of mass casualties, that the only units left protecting Kibrit, the fattest target imaginable, were a few scattered companies of light-armored vehicles and Ross's platoon. This outward complacency extended all the way down to the enlisted-man level. As one Marine lance corporal put it, "The last thing we expected was for Saddam to invade Saudi Arabia."

The U.S. Army forces in theater were also distracted, caught up in the preparations for the far-western Hail Mary run set to crush the Republican Guard in southern Iraq. This armor-heavy thrust exacted an enormous logistical and psychological toll as millions of man-hours were expended getting the army's lumbering tank formations in place along with their extensive fuel and ammunition trains, all of which deflected attention away from the border and Iraqi activities in the here and now.

Adding to the Coalition's woes, the Iraqis were exploiting their knowledge of American reconnaissance satellite patterns garnered from when the U.S. had shared overhead imagery with Saddam during the Iran-Iraq War. This striking case of blowback allowed the Iraqis to begin surreptitiously staging vehicles and equipment in southern Kuwait without setting off any alarms at the Coalition high command in Riyadh. Rolling forward in brutally enforced radio silence, Saddam's legions slunk into their designated assembly areas while the mighty juggernaut, the largest American military force assembled since World War II, was looking the other way.

2

Camp Schwab, Okinawa, Japan,
July–August 1990

*For I am a man under authority, having soldiers under me; and I
say to this man, Go, and he goeth; and to another, Come, and he
cometh; and to my servant, Do this, and he doeth it.*
—MATTHEW 8:9

*In the big war companies, 250 strong, you could find every sort of
man, from every sort of calling. There were Northwesterners with
straw-colored hair that looked white against their tanned skins, and
delicately spoken chaps with the stamp of Eastern universities on
them. There were large-boned fellows from Pacific coast lumber
camps, and tall, lean Southerners who swore amazingly in gentle,
drawling voices. . . . And there were also a number of diverse people
who ran curiously to type, with drilled shoulders and a bone-deep
sunburn, and a tolerant scorn for everything on earth. Their speech
was flavored with navy words, and the words culled from all the folk
who live on the seas and the ports where our war-ships go. Rifles
were high and holy things to them. They were the old breed of American regulars, regarding the service as home and war as an occupa-
tion; and they transmitted their temper and character and viewpoint
to the high-hearted volunteer mass which filled the ranks of the volunteer brigade.*
—CAPTAIN JOHN W. THOMASON, *Fix Bayonets!*

IN ORDER for a platoon to work, it needs a mother and a father. The lieutenant, the father, must command the platoon
from a position of aloofness, secure in his authority and yet
deferential to those who know better than himself. The platoon sergeant, the mother, must shepherd and care for his
troops, picking them up when they fall, cleaning up after
them on occasion, admonishing them to better days and better duty. Most important, however, the mother and the father

must respect and trust each other: the lieutenant, the field commander, must be allowed to deploy his men as he sees fit. The sergeant, the caretaker, the traffic cop, must be allowed to discipline and harden his men when they err.

To believe in and practice this symbiosis is the Marine Corps way. Nevertheless, it is impossible to predict how this dynamic will work itself out in the individual platoon. In Deep Reconnaissance Platoon, Charlie Company, 3rd Reconnaissance Battalion, stationed on Okinawa, the Corps's Western Pacific island base, things arranged themselves in an extremely unusual fashion—that is, backward. It is a tribute to both men that they were able to adapt themselves to this odd circumstance and recognize intuitively the other's strength.

Young Lieutenant Steven Ross of Berkeley, California, fresh from the U.S. Army's Ranger school, had already spent two years as an infantry platoon commander and reported in to Charlie Company in July of 1990.

Staff Sergeant Gregory Gillispie, who had been with the Deep Recon Platoon (DRP) for some time before Ross's arrival, was the type of platoon sergeant who has over the years become an institution in the American military. Salty, hardbitten, omnicompetent, pragmatic to the point of impatience, Gillispie was among other things an exceptionally clear-thinking and seasoned reconnaissance Marine.

The reconnaissance community, or more simply, *recon,* is a special unit within an already elite Corps. Composed of volunteers who have passed an arduous day-long physical fitness screening, recon regularly operates forward of friendly lines, observing the enemy up close and reporting his designs to headquarters via radio. Due to its emphasis on parachute and scuba insertion techniques, recon has always occupied a certain romantic niche within the Corps. A fine example of this ethos, Gillispie was a recon Marine through and through and had graduated from nearly every commando-type school in the U.S. arsenal. He'd even been to a combat driving course that, among other things, instructed students in the finer points of hot-wiring automobiles. To hear Gillispie go on, you'd think the Marine Corps was a never-ending green-themed party with extreme sports attractions. There was always another jump to do, another dive rig to try out, another weapon to fire.

The platoon members themselves, the family, were of mixed heritage like their parents. They were, some would say, an "all-star team" pieced together from the various other platoons of Charlie when the word filtered down the chain of command that a single recon platoon from Okinawa would be deployed to the big show in Saudi Arabia. Competition for a spot in the platoon was intense. Among an elite crew like recon, there was a lot of bitterness when the selectees were announced and certain personalities around the company failed to make the cut. Gillispie, as the senior staff NCO (noncommissioned officer) in the company beneath the company first sergeant, was the logical choice for platoon sergeant. Among the remainder of the company, individuals were chosen based upon their time in service and the number of specialized combat training schools they'd attended.

The platoon itself was built around Sergeant Thomas Manney's team. Manney, considered one of the better team leaders in the company, had been with the 2nd Reconnaissance Battalion in Camp Lejeune, North Carolina, for some time. Sergeants Mike Davis and John Jestel, who had previously been platoon sergeants in Charlie, were also added as team leaders. Gillispie had worked with Manney's bunch for nearly two years, an extreme rarity for Okinawa Marines. Okinawa, the Corps's forward base for Asia, was usually staffed by Marines on one-year tours, and oftentimes the Marines who passed through 3rd Recon never fully matured into the seasoned bands of brothers that the Corps has long prided itself on.

From the beginning, the Deep Recon Platoon was a bit different. Gillispie had picked up the platoon when they were little more than a gaggle of boots, fresh from the School of

Infantry. They had never even been through a recon screening or "indoc," the fundamental rite of passage in recon. Gillispie, a senior buck sergeant at the time, had just completed a tour with 1st Recon battalion at Camp Pendleton, California, where he'd worked with more experienced operators doing building takedowns and oil platform raids in the middle of the Pacific Ocean. Gillispie recalls, "I show up to Oki and get put in charge of this platoon of like eighteen privates. I was *pissed,* like what did I do to deserve this shit? I mean, I hated those suckers."

In an instinctual move that is perhaps the key to the man, he decided to train up the privates to the level of a veteran recon platoon, reasoning that they'd either quit or become hard. He launched headlong into a grueling training routine designed to weed out the weak. "It was like eighteen hours a day. I would hold reveille on those fuckers at 4:30 and I was in their faces until ten at night. We'd do physical training every day for three hours before the sun came up. Then it was ambush patrols, movement to contact, machine-gun training, boat drills, you name it." At that time, recon on Okinawa was stationed at Camp Schwab, on the edge of the jungle on the remote northern end of the coral isle, far removed from civilization. It was about as distant from liberty as you could get. The local Okinawans even had a special name for Marines from the northern camps, *mangadai,* which roughly translated meant "barbarians from the north." Schwab Marines trained like mad just to pass the time.

Gillispie went to great lengths to school them in basic fighting skills, building upon what they'd learned at the School of Infantry. They learned the art of the ambush, patrolling deep into viper-infested jungles, humping thirty-pound machine guns along with the heavy tripods and traversing and elevation lugs that allowed the guns to be employed much more accurately. In the rarefied world of amphibious reconnaissance, whose elite membership is accustomed to fast-roping out of helicopters and conducting rubber boat raids from submarines, this type of training wasn't considered cool or "high-speed." But Gillispie realized that 95 percent of the operations they would ever do were basic scouting missions, which required a solid grasp of grunt 101 skills like land navigation, using hand-and-arm signals, and maintaining good noise and light discipline while on patrol. There wasn't anything magical about these techniques, but they were difficult and time-consuming to master.

In the end, only five of the Marines from the platoon ended up quitting after three months of Gillispie's abuse. But the dozen or so who remained became the nucleus of the platoon and proficient operators in their own right. All this hard training would later pay off in combat in the desert. Looking back, Gillispie reminisced, "The thing was, I formed 'em in my own image. Imagine if you have a captive audience of eighteen-year-olds and you could teach 'em whatever you wanted. That's basically what I did." By the time they deployed to Saudi Arabia in September of 1990, nearly every member of the Deep Recon Platoon had been to Ranger school and the amphibious reconnaissance course, and was airborne and scuba-qualified.

For better or worse, Gillispie's syllabus also included a section on extracurricular activities, which as with all crack infantry units, consisted of a strict regimen of drinking and fucking. Once the Marines began to click as a platoon, they moved on to more advanced training, including getting over on bar fines in the Philippines, forging liberty passes, dodging the shore patrol, and getting out of chickenshit working parties. It wasn't long before most of the guys had girlfriends in Olongapo, the village adjacent to the main Navy base in the Philippines, which Marines of that era universally describe as a "sexual Disneyland."

These intense common experiences helped forge an unusually strong bond between the men. Corporal Miguel "Pete" Roche, the platoon's communications chief, who joined the unit much later, right as they were about to launch out to Saudi, recalled, "They were born again hard. Recon was all they'd ever known. Most of those guys, even though they were young, had extended to stay on Okinawa. They were a tight bunch. I actually kinda dug my own grave with them. I remember we were sitting around when they were stacking the platoon, figuring out who was going to Saudi. A young lance corporal, Jeffrey Buffa, walks up to me and says, 'Hey, what's the matter, Corporal? You're not goin'? And I said, 'I'm actually mad 'cause I got picked.' Buffa was like, 'What's wrong, don't you wanna go to war?' I said, 'I don't want to go to war with you guys. I don't know any of you. I don't trust any of you.' Later another Marine walked up to me and said, 'I heard you don't trust us. What makes you think we trust you?' It took me *months* to dig myself out of that hole."

Under Staff Sergeant Gillispie's tutelage, the Deep Reconnaissance Platoon had grown from a collection of boot privates into a unit of salty nineteen-year-olds who would quickly have you believing that they'd seen and done everything. They cursed magnificently, kept their liquor. They had been master-schooled in all the profane arts of war, shadowboxing in the traces of their ancestors, the Old Breed: grizzled, cigar-chomping veterans of Iwo Jima and Guadalcanal, and although their combat would undoubtedly be of a different sort, they yearned for it still. Yearned for it because they had read about it in a thousand dime-store paperbacks, had seen Clint Eastwood in *Heartbreak Ridge,* had watched stirring medieval-themed recruiting commercials with men in Marine blues with swords. Foolishly perhaps, they pined for war, the worst thing that can befall a man because they knew with a certainty that surpassed all understanding that they could handle whatever the enemy might throw at them, whoever that enemy might be. They were, according to a Marine who was later attached to the platoon, a bunch of "beautiful lunatics."

About the same time that Roche was assigned to the DRP, Lieutenant Ross rolled in, fresh from Ranger school. In 3rd Recon Battalion, having been to Ranger school was a big deal.

The battalion commander, who had worked at the school, had decreed that everyone in a leadership billet had to go through Ranger. Captain Mike Bean, who had just taken over the company, hadn't been to Ranger school yet and seemed to take a disliking to Lieutenant Ross.

Bean had a strange reputation around the company. A fierce martial arts enthusiast, he was an incredible physical specimen with next to zero body fat. He took special pride in the fact that he could drop nearly every member of the company during unit runs. One day, he called the company out for physical training and began leading them through a traditional martial arts routine. What began for Bean as a serious exercise quickly devolved into a World Wrestling Federation Smack-Down, with the Marines tossing each other around like rag dolls. To the more field-minded noncommissioned officers in the company, things were never the same with Bean after that. Despite his conspicuous intensity and attention to duty, to Gillispie, Bean was "a complete buffoon who tried to make the company into kung fu fighters."

Soon after Ross's arrival in July of 1990, Bean took the company on a twelve-mile run with rucksacks as part of a "pre-Ranger" training sequence. Before stepping off on this run, however, the men had to complete a traditional Marine Corps physical fitness test, which consisted of a timed three-mile run, sit-ups and pull-ups, all in boots. About halfway through the run Bean collapsed, a victim of heat exhaustion and the stifling tropical climate of Okinawa. Ross was suddenly the senior man in the company. In the interest of safety Ross decided to call it a day and cancel the run. The next day, Ross found that his office had been moved to the common eating area of the abandoned chow hall that served as the company headquarters and was given an old-style student writing desk by the water fountain.

To Staff Sergeant Gillispie, it looked as if Ross was being punished and thought this was all good humor. "When you're an enlisted guy and you see an officer getting fucked over like that, it's pretty funny. We all laughed." But apart from the laughs, Gillispie saw Ross as being beyond the type of idiocy that infected Bean. "The men basically liked Lieutenant Ross because he saw Bean as an idiot too and stood up to him, which endeared him to the enlisted guys. Plus, Bean would always talk down to us, like we were enlisted swine. But Lieutenant Ross would talk *to* us, not *at* us." Ross and Gillispie would become great friends.

By mid-August the platoon had been stacked and they were ordered to proceed to Subic Bay in the Philippines to meet up with a naval task force that was bound for the Persian Gulf. A huge multinational coalition against Saddam was being formed and Headquarters Marine Corps, had ordered practically every available unit to the Gulf. Things were happening fast now and there wasn't time to do the traditional predeployment coordination such as arranging shipping, ground transportation and figuring out who exactly the platoon would be reporting to. Ross and Gillispie were simply instructed to link up with the task force and attach themselves to whatever ship had enough berthing space. They would simply have to figure things out on the fly.

The big push was on, and it seemed as if every Marine with visions of martial glory was jockeying for a place in the grand showdown with Saddam. Indeed, the mythology of the 1990s Marine Corps is rife with tales of action-starved Marines unceremoniously abandoning units that weren't going and showing up dockside with only a full seabag, asking around to see who was short on people.

True to their gypsy nature, the Marines of DRP raided Charlie's gear lockers before departing Camp Schwab ("gear adrift is a gift"). Gillispie saw to it that the platoon deployed with its full complement of amphibious reconnaissance gear as well as a more than generous loadout of radios, machine guns, and Humvees. They packed all this gear along with a liberal supply of parachutes, scuba tanks, and rappelling kit into two ancient semi-trailer-size shipping containers which had been rusting at Schwab since the Vietnam War. In all they ended up with enough gear to outfit the average Desert Storm recon *company*. This deluxe outfitting would come in handy later.

For the Marines of the Deep Recon Platoon, being *ordered* to the Philippines was like a child being commanded to go to the candy store; the PI was "home away from home." It was a sweet deal, they were going off to war, and en route they were hitting their favorite party spot in the whole world. The big hysteria at this point was that the Iraqi hordes would be pouring across the border into Saudi when the Marines arrived, so they figured they might as well start living large while they had the chance. It was an affirmation of the adage "Eat, drink, and be merry, for tomorrow we die."*

The problem was the New People's Army, the Philippines' homegrown Maoist insurgency, was once again on the warpath and the villages surrounding Subic Bay were living under a form of martial law. Just a few days prior to the DRP's arrival, a Marine gunnery sergeant had been shot in the back of the head in a local bar. As a result, no sailors or Marines were permitted off base without a specially produced liberty pass, no exceptions. After conferring on the matter, Ross and Gillispie decided that the men were going off to a potential wartime situation and that they deserved one last chance to get some beer in their bellies before descending into the land of no-fun-in-the-sun Muslim Saudi Arabia. Gillispie managed to get his hands on a copy of an example pass and forged twenty-two copies for the entire platoon.

Unfortunately, the big night on the town was not without incident. Two young lance corporals, Wright and McCracken, both stout, poster boy, Ranger-schooled Marines, decided to take a swing at the shore patrol on the way back to the barracks. They were swiftly bounced back to Schwab and weren't seen again until after the war. This incident was a blow to the morale of many of the Marines. Not only were Wright and McCracken great operators and certain to be

*A variation on Isaiah 22:13.

missed, but the episode seemed trivial and inane to Marines about to risk life and limb for their country. Marines are supposed to be fighters, so why shouldn't they be allowed to brawl once in a while?

The next morning they embarked on the U.S.S. *Ogden,* an old amphibious landing vessel with a small helicopter pad on the stern. In the great scramble to get as many Marines over to Southwest Asia as quickly as possible, the *Ogden* had been loaded with twice the authorized number of Marines. Jammed into already overcrowded berthing spaces, the men slept on the metal decks on their thin field sleeping pads. Quarters were tighter than any of the Marines had ever seen. Staff Sergeant Gillispie slept on the floor of Lieutenant Ross's officer stateroom. Compounding an already miserable situation, the *Ogden* broke down several times in the middle of the Indian Ocean, halting the entire task force. The Marines took this as a bad omen and couldn't wait to escape the old rustbucket, get ashore, and start figuring out how to survive in the desert.

As the *Ogden* neared the Saudi Arabian peninsula, the platoon was helicoptered off to Masira, a small island off the coast of Oman. From there they jumped on a C-130 to the Royal Saudi Naval Base at Ra's al-Ghar. After sitting on the forlorn landing strip at al-Ghar fermenting in the dull heat for several hours, Gillispie and Ross decided that there must have been a serious headquarters disconnect and that once again they were on their own, free agents in the largest Marine show in history, accountable only to themselves. In the mad rush to go to war, the chain of command had simply forgotten about them.

After snooping around the local tent city, they discovered they'd been dropped off at a Marine air wing base and set about carving out their own fiefdom out of the scraps and unattended provisions they could lay their hands on. For several weeks, they lived out of their shipping containers and some GP tents they'd liberated, reveling in their newfound freedom. However, after they'd spent numerous languid days swimming in the Gulf and dodging all adult supervision, the local sergeant major finally got wise to them after spotting the platoon on a walk-through inspection of the area. He told Gillispie to report to his command tent the following morning, presumably for mess duty and camp working parties.

This development called for drastic action. If they got earholed by this starched sergeant major, they would surely spend the war as his personal piss boys, up to their elbows in Palmolive, pulling KP or some other horror-show shit detail until their fingers bled. Employing all the stealth techniques they'd honed over the years, Gillispie and the boys packed up their kit in the middle of the night and hit the highway. They'd heard through the grapevine that there was a Marine recon unit up the road at an old oil field worker lodgment known as Camp 15. Gillispie figured they'd fare better if they at least were hitched up with their own kind.

Upon arrival at Camp 15, they were pleasantly surprised to discover that the 1st Reconnaissance Battalion was quartered there. Gillispie had only left 1st a couple of years prior and still had beaucoup friends in the battalion. The battalion commander, a well-regarded lieutenant colonel named Charles Kershaw, was sympathetic to their plight but was disinclined to simply add a vagabond platoon that had appeared out of the desert to the battalion rolls. However, when Ross happened to mention that they had a minor fleet of Humvees and two shipping containers chock-full of every recon toy imaginable, Kershaw's attitude suddenly changed. It seemed that 1st had somehow gotten hung out to dry in the lurching chaos of the deployment and been left with only a meager portion of its traditional complement of equipment. They had no parachutes to speak of. They got one look at the DRP's gear and started salivating.

They were assigned to Alpha Company under Captain Rory Talkington. Talkington, a mustachioed young recon veteran, was a cool head who had an odd, almost disinterested swagger to him. He wore his pistol belt low on his hips and loped around camp like he owned the place. To the

Marines, Talkington was more than just a good officer who they liked; he was just so fucking cool that they wanted to *be* him. To the point, the company executive officer looked like a little Talkington. The captain made a point of welcoming them aboard and assuring them that they wouldn't be treated as the red-headed stepchildren of the company. He was short two platoons and was glad to have them. It seemed to Gillispie that after all the Captain Bean madness and the shifting insanity of the deployment, they'd finally found a home.

Now that they had somewhat of a support structure to tap into, a place to get some chow, a shower and maybe some gear, they began making forays into the howling wasteland that surrounded the camp. They had to get out and stretch their legs a bit, they had to figure out how to survive out in the cornerless sandscape, how to move stealthily, how to use what precious little terrain there was to their advantage. They had to figure out how to disappear in a place where there was literally nowhere to hide.

For a crew that had essentially been raised in the triple-canopy jungles of northern Okinawa, this was a huge change of pace. Before they had looked at Humvees as mere administrative vehicles that got you to a drop-off point to begin the real work of a patrol. Now they realized that vehicle-mounted patrolling, like the famous British Rat Patrols of World War II, was the only sane modus operandi. So they stripped the Humvees down to their frames, removing the ribbing that covered the rear of the vehicles, taking out the glass and folding down the front windshields to further reduce the silhouette. They welded jerry cans to the tail to hold extra fuel and water. Sergeant Manney, the platoon gearhead and handyman, fashioned a rig to mount the machine guns out of metal plating lying around the camp. To complete this transformation, they garnished the whole vehicle with strips of camouflage netting to further break up the outline.

But the gear was only half the story. Next to no one in the platoon had ever operated in the desert before. The only time Bronx-born Corporal Roche had even seen a desert was getting lost once during Field Communications School at the Marine Mojave desert base at Twentynine Palms, California. They had to adapt their tactics and, more important, they had to adapt their mind-set. They were inured to the riotously vegetated jungles of the Far East, ideal territory for stalking a foe. Now they were caught in what seemed like the first genuine shooting match in decades enveloped by the perfect desolation of one of the world's great deserts.

Sometime later, teams from the DRP began lighting out on four- to seven-day patrols in two Humvees to conduct general area reconnaissance missions. One vehicle would advance slowly, while the other perched itself atop whatever rise in the terrain might be available to provide covering fire. Given the stunning lack of concealment and the furnace-like heat, the Marines came to prefer working at night. Humvees never operated alone. They learned how to navigate through the *sabkhas,* a quagmire-like salt marsh that stretches inland like octopus tentacles from the coast. During the winter rainy season the *sabkha* was completely impassable and became like the La Brea tar pits, studded with immobilized military vehicles in place of dinosaurs. On patrol, a fine talcum-like dust smothered and permeated everything. Marines returning to the rear looked like graying old men because of the windborne particulate that infiltrated their eyebrows and salted their hair.

Even basic land navigation proved surprisingly difficult. Due to the complete absence of traditional landmarks normally employed to orient themselves, the Marines fell back on the old nautical standard of dead reckoning, using the issue lensatic compass and the Humvee's odometer to measure distance traveled. Despite the Corps's traditional heavy emphasis on good compass work, some Marines still managed to get hopelessly disoriented. A shortage of quality topographic maps exacerbated the problem. Several units were issued maps formerly used by British Airways pilots with the warning "Not Suitable for Ground Use" stamped across the top. One patrol from the battalion woke up one morning to find itself in the middle of a live fire range. With rounds snapping all around them, they hastily evacuated the scene, abandoning their gear, a mortal Marine sin. The appearance of the celebrated Global Positioning System satellite navigation handsets helped reduce these embarrassing incidents, but staying oriented on the featureless sands remained a continuing challenge throughout the war.

As it became clear that the Iraqis weren't about to descend upon the oil fields of Saudi Arabia as had been feared, various reconnaissance units began making their way closer to the Kuwaiti border in anticipation of the grand offensive. On January 14, Deep Recon Platoon was split into three teams and sent to different observation posts on the frontier. Ross didn't like that the platoon was being split up, and the redistribution didn't seem to make much sense, as at each OP, Ross's teams were paired up with a recon team from another Alpha Company platoon along with a U.S. Army Special Forces A-team.

The Marines for their part loved being around the Special Forces guys because they always carried the wackiest new space-age gadgets and military toys with them. The Green Beret supply system was the paragon of opulence by Marine standards, and wherever they went, they always seemed to leave a trail of night-vision goggles, digitally encrypted radio sets, laser range-finders, and other cool gizmos like bread crumbs. The platoon, who at this point were scroungers nonpareil, quickly snapped up these high-tech goodies. Over the course of the next several weeks they acquired three new Humvees when Special Forces soldiers abandoned them due to mechanical problems that Manney was able to swiftly surmount with a little creative tinkering.

Relations with the Special Forces teams weren't always harmonious. To the DRP Marines, Special Forces soldiers, or "SF guys," sometimes came across like spooky, self-righteous mercenary wannabes, who at the end of the day were out to save their own skins, comrades be damned. Soon after occupying OP 7, the second fort inland from the coast, Corporal Roche noticed that the Special Forces team at the post had inexplicably disappeared. The Saudi border guards bugged out soon after, piling into the vehicles, grabbing whatever gear was within lunging distance. Captain Talkington, who was running Alpha Company from OP 7, put all the teams on 100 percent alert, suspecting that the soldiers knew something he didn't. The evening passed without incident, and when the SF guys returned the following morning, Talkington waded into them, pointedly asking them why, if they'd gotten word of an imminent attack, they hadn't bothered to mention this choice fact to their Marine colleagues. This bitter harangue continued for several minutes, with the Special Forces team leader finally offering up that they had indeed gotten word of an impending assault but that "our headquarters told us to leave you guys." The Marines watched their backs around the SF guys after that, and for Gillispie, who'd been charting the locations of their gear and food cache sites for some time, the temptation to dip into them must have been strong.

On January 17, the air war began. Thirty miles to the west, at OP 3, Lance Corporal Buffa had just finished building a hootch out of discarded lumber and old oil drums when Ross and Talkington rolled up to his position in a Humvee and announced that at three the next morning, the air campaign against Saddam Hussein would begin. The long months of waiting were over. A little over five hours later, Buffa watched from his hootch as "the night sky lit up like a Christmas tree and enemy antiaircraft fire tore into the night, looking for our airplanes. It was almost surreal to watch as streaking tracer rounds and burning missiles filled the night sky. As I peered out over the muzzle of the M-60 machine gun I was helping to man, I counted 42 missiles launched from a single site inside Kuwait territory. The antiaircraft fire and missile fire didn't let up for nearly three days." With the air campaign under way, the Marines knew their day was coming and began mentally preparing themselves for the prospect of combat with a seasoned foe.

Up on the border, the edge of the realm, the final stop before Indian Country, something strange always seemed about to happen, and a weird air of treachery and abandon seemed

to hang over the place. It was as if, now that the shadow of
real action and actual death was passing over, none of the old
rules applied anymore: Up was down, black was white, gravity was negotiable. There were so many straphangers and un-
knowns passing through, the only guys you could trust were
guys you knew. It was a reiteration of one of the most basic
laws of combat: Complacency was a gamble, paranoia a sure
thing. Gillispie began sleeping with a pistol and a grenade
inside his flak vest.

Guys who were wound a little tight to begin with suddenly
got real jumpy. During a particularly unnerving Iraqi artillery barrage, one Marine from 3rd Recon who'd always
been a tiger in training dove underneath a Humvee and
wouldn't come out until someone finally fired up the engine
and drove off. A rumor that the Iraqis were dressing up like
Bedouin nomads and crossing over to scout American positions and plant antipersonnel mines spread like a virus.*
This unconfirmed report, along with the presence of Saudi
military personnel, whom the Marines instinctively mistrusted, and the regular Iraqi artillery barrages kept everyone
on edge. As one DRP Marine remarked, "You just never
knew what to expect from one day to the next."

One evening, an odd-looking Marine captain approached
Ross and Gillispie while they were digging a bunker into the
berm to sleep in. As custom dictates when two unacquainted
officers meet, Lieutenant Ross began peppering him with
questions about his training, his time at Quantico, searching
for common buddies and mutually hated instructors from
The Basic School. However, this officer seemed put off by
the young lieutenant's entreaties and answered his questions
haltingly if at all. He departed the following morning. A few
days later they discovered that the "captain" was, in fact, a
counterintelligence staff sergeant who'd been snooping

---

*The Bedouin are a devoutly Muslim desert people who have wandered the deserts of
the Middle East for millennia. At one time Bedouin tribes dominated the Arabian
peninsula, and their culture is venerated throughout the kingdom.

around the frontier, impersonating an officer in order to get by easier with the Saudis.

On the afternoon of January 21, the Marines spotted a white, unmarked Range Rover approaching the OP from the south. For the Marines, who were accustomed to seeing only military vehicles, this seemed suspicious. The Range Rover pulled up and out popped Bob Simon, the CBS news reporter. He was greeted by Staff Sergeant Gillispie, who told him in no uncertain terms that he needed to depart the area most riki-tik. U.S. forces had only recently been given permission by the Saudi government to approach the frontier, and news media were strictly forbidden. Nevertheless, Simon persisted, requesting to interview Gillispie's men. Ever the diplomat, Gillispie ordered Simon and his crew "to un-ass the area before he killed them all" and had the two Marines he was with level their M-16s at him to drive the point home. He was in no mood to play public relations games with an errant reporter who was clearly on the lam from the powers that be. Simon eventually departed, and Gillispie watched through binoculars as they drove directly south for a few kilometers and then suddenly veered to the west, seeming to aim for the next observation post over. Gillispie called over to the OP and told them to take Simon into custody when he arrived, but inexplicably, the Range Rover took a hard right again and crossed over into no-man's-land through a gap in the berms. Simon and his crew were quickly snapped up by Iraqi soldiers and spent the remainder of the war in a Baghdad prison.

The Marines, who were already suspicious of the news media, thought this whole incident was hilarious. After the war, Simon described his capture, "What I did was a stupid mistake. It's not like we were after some fantastic story and got unlucky. We were just careless." Without an ounce of sympathy for his plight, Gillispie declared, "We thought it was fitting end for Simon and his band of idiots."

Although Simon's actions were seen by the Marines as the height of media buffoonery, proof positive that all reporters were morons, the episode served as a grim reminder of the high-stakes game being played out in the desert. This was no place for amateurs or war tourists. If you lost your head, it was gonna cost you and cost you big, and although the Marines came equipped with a gallows humor that scorched everything it touched, there were some things that weren't so easily laughed off in the hootch late at night.

3

January 19, 1991,
Northeastern Saudi Arabia

Some of the evil of my tale may have been inherent in our circumstances. For years we lived anyhow with one another in the naked desert, under an indifferent heaven. By day the hot sun fermented us; and we were dizzied by the beating wind. At night we were stained by dew, and shamed into pettiness by the innumerable silence of stars. We were a self-centred army without parade or gesture, devoted to freedom, the second of man's creeds, a purpose so ravenous that it devoured all our strength, a hope so transcendent that our earlier ambitions faded in its glare.
—T. E. LAWRENCE, *Seven Pillars of Wisdom*

EVENTUALLY the word came down for the DRP to occupy Observation Post 4. The Special Forces teams on frontier guard duty were being drafted for other operations, including hunting Saddam's elusive Scud missile launchers. This move initiated a rather large game of musical chairs along the border, with all the various recon and Navy SEAL units working in the region being shifted and rotated around. The upshot for the DRP Marines was that they were reunited as a platoon and ordered to assume OP 4 on the northwestern edge of the Marine sector. Ross was happy to have his guys back together and to be heading to a part of the Saudi wilderness where they'd essentially be out on their own. The logistical and fire support would probably be spotty out there, but at least they would know what to expect. They wouldn't have to second-guess the Saudis or the SF guys. The Marines at this point were becoming accustomed to life in the desert and were happy to have a little breathing room.

They made their way to OP 4, located in the vicinity of a

place known simply as Umm Hjul. Umm Hjul is an inconsequential depression in the earth that is noticeable primarily because someone from a British military survey team in the late 1980s had thought to include it on a map of the area.* It sits just over the Kuwaiti line at 179 meters above sea level. The highest spot in the area, an unnamed point twelve miles to the west, is a mere 60 meters higher. That Umm Hjul was considered a noteworthy navigational landmark by someone is stark testimony to the appalling desolation surrounding OP 4.† This wasn't *Lawrence of Arabia,* there were no graceful *ergs* stretching off to the kiss of the horizon, just a empty, echoless wasteland.

Travelers to the area are often struck by the near-mathematical perfection of the land, marked only by the regular interval of *arad* scrub brush and the imperceptible undulations of sand. These almost invisible micro-depressions, much too small to appear on any map, had the unsettling capacity to obscure small formations of military vehicles until one walked practically on top of them.

The site for the police post/customs house that would become the DRP's home was chosen because of its peculiar location along the Kuwaiti border. Known to the Saudis as Markaz az Zabr, it sat on a corner of the frontier where the border makes an almost 90-degree turn to the north, a monument to the frequently whimsical habits of the British cartographers who carved the nations of the Middle East out of

---

*Umm is a common Arabic prefix that also means "mother," an appellation that points to the pre-Islamic Bedouin belief that they emerged from the bowels of the desert to rule the Arabian peninsula. *Hjul* is a local name of unknown origin. I have chosen to use the British cartographer's spelling of this place-name. As with all Arabic words translated into English, innumerable permutations appear, including Umm Hujul, Umm Hajul, and Um Hjul.

†The numbering system used for the border observation posts seems almost deliberately confusing. They were originally numbered according to when they were occupied by the Special Forces. The Marines subsequently tried to create a new system beginning with OP 0 at the coast and increasing to OP 8 out to the west, but this arrangement never caught on. Adding to the confusion, the police posts where the OPs were located had corresponding Arabic names. OP 6, for instance, was also known as Markaz al-Hamaltyat, *markaz* being Arabic for "center," as in "police center."

the shifting sands shortly after World War I.* It was rumored that all of the police posts along the border had been erected to stem the tide of illegal drugs, chiefly heroin, flowing in from Saudi Arabia's more laissez-faire neighbor to the north.

The land gently slopes up and away from Markaz az Zabr in all directions. This seemingly immaterial geographic happenstance added up to a distinct disadvantage for the platoon. Any Iraqi forces approaching the OP would have the benefit of being just slightly higher than the Marines and in a position to rain fire down upon them. In the jungle or the mountains the difference of a few feet means nothing, but in The Great Sand Lot this ratio often dictated the tactical process. This effect worsens when one considers the immense ranges at which modern armor and anti-armor weapons can be employed. The main American antitank weapon, the TOW missile, has an effective range of almost two and a half miles. It is common knowledge that in a fight with tanks, he who sees first and fires first, wins. So, in addition to being well forward of any American firepower, they were also in a something of a fire trap.

The Marines had little choice in the matter. Sitting on top of the berm was the only way to see anything in the area. On one of his many trips up and down the frontier, Gillispie stopped at OP 6 one evening and hung out briefly with the reconnaissance platoon manning the post (a place he described as "really creepy," possessing "a weird graveyard-at-midnight feel to it"). He was aghast to see them deployed back away from the border, underneath a bridge where they couldn't see a thing.

In the infantry, being able to *see* is paramount. According to the Western conception of war, almost all fighting positions are selected based upon how well one can observe the likely avenues of enemy approach, the ideal position being a solitary, steeply sloped, uniformly graded hill with an escape route to the rear (such as Culp's Hill at Gettysburg). This ob-

---

*The borders of Kuwait, Iraq, and Saudi Arabia were established by the British-imposed Treaty of Uqair in 1922.

session with ground, with the peculiar ways that dirt arranges itself, refers back to the basic concept of ground combat, that of avoiding being surprised at all costs. Put simply, one cannot shoot what one cannot see. The berm, a fifteen-foot-high wall of sand, rocks, and marl was far from perfect, but it was the best they had.

The evening they arrived, it was raining, according to Gillispie, "like a cow pissing on a flat rock." He wanted to wait out the deluge inside the police post, and then move outside to begin improving the position, constructing bunkers, delineating fields of fire, and creating range cards and the like. Ross, however, had decided that the customs houses, which were the centerpiece of nearly every OP along the border, were also probably registered Iraqi artillery targets, i.e., concrete death traps. He wanted no part of this and ordered the men to begin preparing positions in the downpour. Gillispie was exasperated: "It was one of the only times when Lieutenant Ross and I didn't see eye-to-eye." It was one of those weird things officers would do sometimes: flatly overrule their noncoms and take a hard tack on some seemingly random issue to the complete bewilderment of the enlisted men underneath them. The invisible gulf between officer and enlisted seemed to yawn a bit wider in tense moments like these. To Ross, it seemed obvious. Lingering in the buildings was an unnecessary hazard, and if they'd taught him anything at all those officer schools, it was one thing: Bring all your men back alive. There was work to be done. They would dig in the rain.

After settling in for the first night, they set up the traditional observation post watch schedule. Observing was more their job than killing, and a no-bullshit watch had to be maintained twenty-four hours a day every day. Marines at each of the three positions at Markaz az Zabr would stand watch in pairs for no longer than two hours. The Marines had long ago learned that two hours was the practical limit of a man on post—after that he became drowsy and ineffective. At nighttime, they would do a sweep of the area with night-vision goggles every five minutes.

Over the course of the next several days, the Marines set about improving the position, modifying it to suit their tactical preferences. Gillispie and Sergeant Luis Bench, a five-foot-two, Peruvian-born combat engineer who'd recently been attached to the platoon, emplaced several Claymore mines and trip flares out in front of the berm.* Gillispie set the trip flares out in a U-shaped pattern around the position, personally ensuring that all the main approach routes the Iraqis could use were covered. Ross managed to get a back-hoe tractor out their way to cut a hole in the backberm that sat directly behind the platoon headquarters in the event they had to evacuate the scene in a hurry. Behind that, Corporal Roche set up a remote antenna farm to house the special field expedient antennas he'd created.† Ross found an eight-foot-high horseshoe-shaped berm directly behind the police post that he designated as the platoon's fallback position.

The berm seemed like it was custom-built as a harbor site, being large enough to hold the entire platoon without its small fleet of vehicles, which at this point included four Humvees and a five-ton truck. The mouth of the horseshoe faced away from the berm, providing a passably covered and concealed position that wasn't completely obvious to the enemy. They arranged for visual signals in the event that radio communications were lost. A green pop-up flare was the signal to open fire. A red flare meant for the platoon to fall back to the horseshoe. Small, disposable infrared light sticks were tied to the front grille of each vehicle with green cord so that the Marines would be able to distinguish between friendly and enemy vehicles in the darkness.

---

*Claymores are command-detonated devices that launch a deadly wall of 700 steel balls in a 60-degree arc out to 170 feet. To activate them, the user squeezes a handheld trigger apparatus three times in quick succession. Claymores are used in deliberate defensive positions to cover *dead space,* i.e., any part of a position that the defenders are unable to see or cover by machine-gun or rifle fire.

†Roche was a master of the complex art of high-frequency radio communications. To maintain this type of communication, the radio operator employs an in-depth understanding of electromagnetic wave propagation, atmospheric reflectivity, geomorphology, and consumer electronics. Roche used his skills to great effect, getting BBC news broadcasts from London, one of the platoon's major sources of intelligence.

The platoon occupied a 500-meter frontage along the berm. Despite considerable confusion to the contrary, the berm itself was not the actual border of Saudi Arabia. The berm simply delineated the beginning of a no-man's-land that extended for several miles to a corresponding earthen wall on the Kuwaiti side. Just inside Kuwaiti territory, an abandoned police post with a large radio mast faced Markaz az Zabr. The customs house itself was a spartan, two-story concrete structure complete with a Medieval-style parapet on the roof, which lent it a comical sand castle–like appearance. Numerous windracked trees stood inside a tortured and collapsing thin metal fence. Lurking behind the main house was a low white building that held an idle electrical generator used to power the police post. The main berm tapered off on both ends of this compound. The whole ensemble had obviously weathered a generation's worth of sandstorms and was decorated with years of litter, discarded lumber, metal piping, and bowling ball–size rocks.

The weather, which when they'd washed ashore in September had been furnace-like, had gone within the space of two weeks from unbelievably hot to wet, drizzly, and generally shitty, with temperatures dipping down into the 30s at night. Having gotten earfuls about the Dantesque climate of the Middle East, the Marines had deliberately left all their cold-weather gear back at Camp Schwab. Thus they were forced to double up on T-shirts and cammies, augmenting that with rappelling gloves, thin field jackets, and watch caps. Most of the men stood watch with their sleeping bags draped over their torsos. Some of the Marines, desperate to stay warm, took to sleeping in the Humvees. Roche, who couldn't stand the oppressive human stench inside the bunkers, racked out in the open, braving the long nights in the desert wind to stay close to the radios.

The absence of good cold-weather gear was one of the things that drove the platoon to its raucous scrounging, behavior that in peacetime would have gotten them in serious hot water. After surrendering their trailers of gear to Battalion, they'd received nothing material in return. As Staff

Sergeant Gillispie put it, "Anything that our platoon needed we either traded for, bought out of mail-order catalogs, or just flat out stole from other unsuspecting and clearly less-deserving units."

To stay clean, the Marines would take "air baths," stripping down and simply letting the cool desert air blow away some of the raw funk that clung to their bodies. The ever-fastidious Roche took canteen showers, stripping down to nothing, then washing himself with chilly handfuls of water. The men would shave in the rearview mirrors of the Humvees.

Seeing their images in the mirror was one of the few solitary moments the Marines had. To be sure, they were alone out there, enveloped by the world's loneliest desert, but they were always together, surrounded by their buddies, the closest friends they'd ever known. Inspecting their visages in the green-rimmed glass, they saw for the first time how tan they were, how much weight they'd lost. This regular morning ritual became part of the odd ascetic poetry of daily life in the field. It was trivial, commonplace routines such as these that made the days in the desert bearable.

On the evening of the 25th, the new battalion commander, Lieutenant Colonel Michael Rapp, paid a visit to Markaz az Zabr with an entourage of staff officers in tow along with the battalion sergeant major. As fate would have it, Iraqi infiltrators chose this evening to probe the OP, sneaking up within a few hundred meters of the customs house and firing off a fusillade of RPG rounds* (lending credence to the strange superstition that some grunts had about visits from the CO being bad luck). The rockets whizzed over the Marines' heads, impacting in the sand behind the customs house. Pandemonium swiftly ensued, with the colonel barking out orders up and down the line and screaming mysteriously for a toothbrush and a dogtag to gauge how far away the Iraqis were. One private, a recent addition to the platoon, jumped

---

*The RPG-7 is a Soviet-made rocket-propelled grenade. Along with the AK-47, the RPG is a ubiquitous piece of gear in former Soviet-client states.

into a Humvee and attempted to drive it over the berm. According to Roche, "He was in full-on spaz mode. He just wanted to get the fuck outta there and that was the direction the Humvee was facing, so he was just gonna *drive*. Lance Corporal Henderson managed to drag him out. After that, we never let that private have a loaded weapon again."

Showing marked restraint, the Marines managed to hold off from opening up on their attackers, and the Iraqis quickly beat feet. The Marines, of course, wanted to return fire but knew such ineffectual probing to be a common tactic for getting your opponent to open fire and reveal the location of his heavy weapons. In the cold calculus of grunt life, sometimes you had to fight the white-hot impulse to fire up the enemy and just sit on your hands and wait for him to slink away.

This was the first up-close, no-kidding encounter for the Marines, and even though it was far from a decisive engagement, it was enough to rid them of any illusions they might have retained about this all being some monumental exercise. There was no denying it now, they were in the shit; the enemy knew where they were and had taken a furtive jab at them, and although most of the Marines had been watching Iraqi movement across the border for weeks and were pretty philosophic about the whole deal, they were essentially in uncharted waters now.

The incident did have one positive outcome. Upon returning to the rear, Colonel Rapp ordered up an air strike on the Kuwaiti police post across the way, which the Marines had long suspected to be an Iraqi staging area. A pair of F-18s reduced the structure to rubble the following day.

A couple of days later, a wounded camel, which earlier in the week had set off one of the trip flares and seriously freaked out a couple of young Marines on watch, wandered toward Sergeant Davis's position. The trip flares, when actuated, bathed the area out in front of the position in a pulsing, unearthly light that was freaky enough without it being the possible announcement of a deadly enemy probe. (The heart-stopping *ksssh-ksssh* noise they made when tripped seemed the perfect noise with which to begin a symphony of fire.)

Gillispie had jokingly taken to calling Davis's position "Paranoia Point" because the young sergeant always seemed so amped up, so it was not a huge surprise when he heard an explosion and saw the camel in question limping away as fast as its legs would carry it.

The Marines, perhaps desperate for target practice or for something to engage, had shot the poor thing with a grenade launcher despite Gillispie specifically instructing them not to. (Knowing the devious sergeant well, he'd spelled out in detail what they were not to do: "Don't shoot at it, don't throw hand grenades at it, don't try to run it down and stab it, don't hit it with a Humvee, don't call a close air strike on it.") The stricken beast wandered north out of sight into Kuwait and was never seen again.

4

6:00 P.M., January 29, 1991,
Observation Post 4

*Our cards were speed and time, not hitting power. The invention of
bully beef had profited us more than the invention of gunpowder, but
gave us strategical rather than tactical strength, since in Arabia
range was more important than force, space greater than the power
of armies.*

— T. E. LAWRENCE, *Seven Pillars of Wisdom*

*A horse will carry a man in his first action where his legs may not
go; and a mechanized vehicle will carry him further than a horse
will go; but finally no mechanized vehicle is any better than the
heart of the man who handles the controls.*

— ERNEST HEMINGWAY, *Men at War*

IN THE DEEPENING winter dusk, Captain Roger "Rock" Pollard, the commander of Delta Company, 3rd Light-
Armored Infantry Battalion, set his vehicles in for the night.
He deployed his 19 light-armored vehicles, or LAVs, a little
over two miles back from Lieutenant Ross's position in a
loose screenline, taking advantage of the slight rise in the
ground to the northwest of the police post. It wasn't the
greatest terrain in the world, there were no clear commanding features, no hills with graceful fields of fire as in some
West Point textbook—just a dusty, naked plain that depressed slightly as one got nearer the police post.

Pollard had a section of TOW antitank vehicles to set in as
well, and as they were considered valuable assets and had
powerful nightscopes with which to pierce the darkness, he
took great care in their deployment, interspersing them
among the long line of Delta vehicles, tucking them in on
both sides with his lighter, 25-millimeter-armed LAVs. The

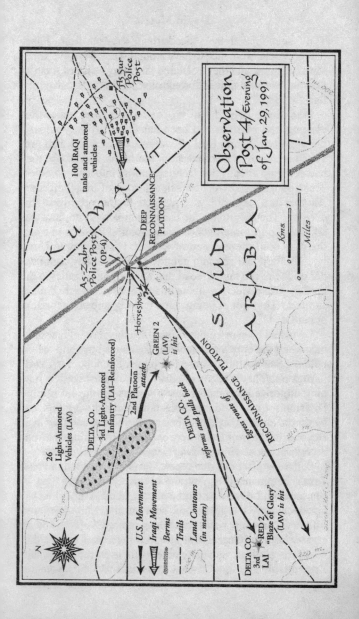

Observation Post 4/Evening of Jan. 29, 1991

As-Sur Police Post

100 IRAQI tanks and armored vehicles

KUWAIT

SAUDI ARABIA

As-Zabr Police Post (OP-4)

DEEP RECONNAISSANCE PLATOON

Horseshoe

GREEN 2 (LAV) is hit

2nd Platoon attacks

DELTA CO. 3rd Light-Armored Infantry (LAI-Reinforced)

26 Light-Armored Vehicles (LAV)

DELTA CO. reforms and pulls back

Egress route of RECONNAISSANCE PLATOON

DELTA CO. 3rd LAI ★ RED 2 "Blaze of Glory" (LAV) is hit

N

Kms

Miles

LEGEND
U.S. Movement
Iraqi Movement
Berms
Trails
Land Contours (in meters)

TOW section, led by a headstrong sergeant from Joisey named Vitale, were nice to have around. They were the battalion's big guns, and they bolstered the ailing sense of security that the Marines nursed through the long nights out on the line.

Like Ross, Pollard had no reason to expect action this evening; the Marines had been launching artillery raids in the vicinity of Umm Hjul all week, none of which had provoked so much as a sneeze from the Iraqis. It was like they had given up already, the frontier settling into a rough quiescence punctuated by the occasional troop of Iraqi defectors. Another artillery raid was planned to the northwest this evening. The only thing for Delta Company to do now was sit back, collect intelligence from captured Iraqis, and count the days until the invasion of Kuwait. On his way to Umm Hjul, Pollard had run into another LAV company commander on the paved tapline road that ran roughly parallel to the border. When queried about his new assignment, Pollard snorted, "They got us doing some fucking screening mission out at OP 4."

Delta had been in-country since the edgy days of late summer when the only thing between Saddam's boys and the oil fields of Saudi Arabia were a few jumpy Saudi border guards in pickups. They'd been cut adrift in the desert wastes, running motorized reconnaissance missions for the 1st Marine Division for nearly four months now, and although this was by far the closest they'd ever been to the border and the Great Beyond, the boys of Delta were expecting little more than another evening staving off sweet sleep inside their LAVs.

Pollard, a prior enlisted recon Marine from Wichita Falls, Texas, commanded a new and relatively untested type of Marine unit. Loosely patterned after the U.S. Army's mechanized cavalry, the heart and soul of the Light-Armored Infantry company was the Light-Armored Vehicle-25, an eight-wheeled, fourteen-ton armored personnel carrier that could run circles around any other vehicle on the battlefield. Armed with only light 25-mm cannons, LAV units were designed to serve as an advance guard for the slower-moving main body of the division, breaking up enemy formations, scouting and raiding in a manner not unlike Jeb Stuart's famed Civil War cavalry rides. What they lacked in raw firepower, they made up for in sheer feel-it-in-your-ribcage diesel velocity and unparalleled agility.

These hot new toys were sexy, fast, and fun. The troops loved them, calling them "hogs," "pigs," "beasts," or "ponies" and painting them up with shark's teeth on the front. Compared to their clumsy tracked brethren, LAVs were nimble eight-wheeled sports cars. They flitted about the battlefield, consuming wide swaths of earth at unbelievable rates. Whereas straight-leg grunts talked in terms of grid squares, puny kilometer-size bites of dirt, LAV guys spoke of map-*sheets* and joked about the foot-high stack of charts that they had to keep handy just to stay oriented from day to day. They chewed up terrain, screening brashly forward on a scale that was simply unthinkable to your average foot-mobile rifleman.

Perhaps because of the LAV's newness, Delta Company had developed a reputation within the division as somewhat of a bastard child. Since its foundation in the late 1980s, Delta and its parent battalion had been staffed by a mixed lot of officers and staff NCOs. Many of the young officers who found themselves assigned to the battalion were eccentric, outside-the-box thinkers weary of the grinding, linear grunt mentality that dominated many traditional Marine infantry units of the time, and yearned to be a part of an innovative, fast-moving, fast-hitting new unit. Nevertheless, many senior Marine leaders looked at the battalion as a backwater unit, a foundering experiment safely away from the mainstream and a fine place to offload their undesirables. It was this impression that often clung to the unit. More than one officer when assigned to the Light-Armored Infantry felt compelled to ask, "Who did *I* piss off?"

Before deploying to Saudi, Delta had languished under a lackadaisical captain who was clearly on his way out of the Corps and had allowed the unit to deteriorate into a depressing state of readiness. The company shambled along, revel-

ling in the languid rhythms of garrison life, rarely going to
the field to train, seemingly content in its mediocrity. Fortunately, by mid-summer 1990, a fresh new batch of leaders
began rolling into the company. A spirited, snap-and-pop
first sergeant named Alfonso Villa came aboard in July and
instantly set about whipping the company into shape, relight-
ing the fires of discipline and intensity that had somehow
wavered since the Marines had graduated boot camp. Villa, a
career Marine who had started out in the air wing, possessed
that odd, transcendent dignity unique to American noncommissioned officers. In his presence, enlisted men could be
seen standing up a little bit straighter, like Dad had just
walked into the room. Later that summer, a tanker lieutenant
and former general's aide named Scott Williams was given
command of Delta Company. An earnest, fresh-minded young
officer, Williams's energy and technical expertise were a
welcome change from the seemingly endless procession of
washed-up grunt officers that Delta had endured in the past.
A fresh burst of life and excitement seemed to infuse the
company.

On August 2, 1990, when Saddam invaded Kuwait, the
company was out on maneuvers in the Nevada desert when
the call came in to return to base at Twentynine Palms, California, and begin preparing for deployment to the Middle
East. The following day they launched into a battery of gear
inspections, predeployment lectures, and inoculations that
stretched into the next week. The Marines were issued their
first sets of light tan "chocolate chip" desert camouflage uniforms, a novelty item at the time. This thing looked to be for
real.

Nevertheless, despite all this predeployment commotion,
several pieces of the Delta puzzle were still missing. The
company had only a single commissioned officer in its ranks.
The three platoons, all of which rated a lieutenant, were
being led by enlisted Marines. Some of these erstwhile platoon commanders were just old salts who'd simply been
around the company longer than anyone else. First Sergeant
Villa was left to juggle much of the executive officer's tradi-

tional duties, adding to his already taxing workload as the senior enlisted man in a 100-man company. This marginal state of affairs might have been acceptable for garrison duty, but for a company about to go off to war it was unconscionable. To make matters worse, Delta had yet to receive its full complement of infantry scouts. These Marine riflemen, who rode in the back of the vehicles, were central to the whole concept of the LAV company. They provided security for the vehicles when halted and cleared trenchlines and buildings when operating in urban areas. Without their scouts, LAVs were little more than glorified Hummers.

Fortunately, down the road at Camp Pendleton—the huge Marine base on the California coast—there were numerous straight-leg infantry units not slated to deploy that had plenty of bodies available. A few days after Delta was given its marching orders, several Marine battalions called all their companies in from the field and began combing the ranks for volunteers. A few hours later, officers began pulling service record books at random and "volunteering" men. Anyone with more than six months left in the service was deemed eligible. The next day several hundred of these men were packed into white school buses and sent up to the high desert purgatory of Marine Corps Base Twentynine Palms.

On one of these buses was a newly minted second lieutenant from Yonkers, New York, named Glenn Sadowski. Sadowski had initially been assigned to First Battalion, Ninth Marines. When he was checking in at 1/9, the battalion executive officer mentioned that they were looking for volunteers to head out with the first Marine units who were shipping out to the Gulf. "Could be a good career move," the major added without a hint of irony. Sadowski, still in his dress Alpha uniform, asked him where he could store his car while he was away, and got on the bus. He hadn't even unpacked his seabags from basic training yet.

At Twentynine Palms, they lined up the new lieutenants and began assigning them to various units. Sadowski was the lone second lieutenant in the bunch, in reality just a glorified college senior. He had been on active duty a grand total of nine months. Every other officer there had already commanded an infantry platoon for at least a year and completed an overseas deployment. The first few officers were assigned to a tank battalion. Sadowski and the two men standing next to him, Dave Kendall and a first lieutenant, were sent off to Delta Company, 3rd Light-Armored Infantry Battalion.

Sadowski, who had been trained in the grand Marine Corps tradition, had always expected to be a regular rifle platoon commander. At The Basic School, the Marine Corps' lieutenant academy, he'd received a single one-hour class in light-armored vehicle tactics. He'd never even seen the inside of an LAV before. He knew practically nothing about armored doctrine, anti-armor operations, screening formations, or basic vehicle maintenance.

When Sadowski arrived in the Delta Company area in mid-August 1990, he overheard a group of enlisted Marines talking. One of the Marines piped up, "Hey, Corporal, can you believe it, you know who our vehicle commander is? Some fucking boot lieutenant who doesn't know shit about LAVs!"

Sadowski figured now was as good a moment as any and introduced himself: "How you doing, Lance Corporal Rodriguez? I'm Lieutenant Sadowski, your new platoon commander."

Also arriving with the 1/9 crew was a lance corporal named Bill Covington. Covington, a pugnacious young squad leader, had just returned from a six-month deployment to the Western Pacific, where the naval task force he was with had stopped at every port in the Far East: Thailand, Hong Kong, mainland Japan. To the extreme joy of everyone aboard, they'd hit the Philippines three times. He hoped to make the Marine Corps a career. When they initially asked for volunteers to go to the Middle East, Covington was one of the first to step up. "I was young, and I thought to myself, Hell, this is what I've been training all my life for. Let's rock and roll."

Covington and his 1/9 compadres rolled into Twentynine Palms late the following day. They were greeted at the battalion area by the jeers and catcalls of the Delta Company Marines, who assumed that the new guys were all boots, fresh meat direct from the School of Infantry. The 1/9 Marines, many of whom had several overseas tours under their belts, weren't having an ounce of this, and several fistfights broke out on the spot.

In the few days that remained before shipping out, the two groups were able to tentatively bridge this rocky start, knocking back a few beers at the enlisted men's club and getting to know one another. There wasn't any time to get things ironed out operationally, but the Marines were at least familiar with the guys they'd be fighting alongside, and the 1/9 crew was seasoned and enjoyed a fine reputation among West Coast Marines. However, it would take several months of exile out in the desert before the division between these two disparate groups of men truly dissolved, and in the meantime the company still had the feel of an ad hoc organization, still in the throes of a collective adolescence. Nevertheless, all the elements appeared to be in place for a solid, spirited fighting unit.

To everyone's dismay, shortly after arriving in Saudi Arabia, there was a reorganization within the higher echelons of the battalion and Delta found itself with a brand-new company commander, a salty, big-talking Texan named Roger Pollard. Because Pollard had a traditional infantry background, Lieutenant Williams, the former tanker, was kept on as the company executive officer to provide some tactical expertise. The enlisted Marines had grown fond of Williams, and many were bitter about this seemingly senseless change in leadership. Things had been going just fine, and they failed to understand why they had to break in yet another new commander who probably knew next to nothing about LAVs.

Pollard was an unusual officer. He had served in recon for nearly a decade before earning a commission. Finally in command of his first company, he played up the trail-weary cowpoke bit to maximum effect, drawling raucously, seeming to start half his sentences with, "Shoot . . ." or "Boy, I tell ya . . ." He frequently addressed his colleagues as "pardner." As a young sergeant he had earned the nickname "Rock" after he began porting a small boulder that had been painted fire-engine red during formation runs in order to motivate his platoon mates. The sobriquet stuck, and throughout his career he introduced himself high and low as "Rock Pollard." He incessantly referred to the enlisted Marines as his "war dogs." The words he would later scrawl across the turret of his vehicle spoke volumes about the fervent confidence he retained in himself and his affected larger-than-life persona; with a large indelible black marker he had written, "The American Hero."

Beneath this florid exterior, Pollard was an exacting commander who was infamously hard on his lieutenants and demanded an unusual degree of commitment from his Marines. As a young sergeant he had suffered under several marginally competent officers and felt strongly that he owed it to the Marines to ride his young officers. Pollard reflected, "I have always believed that most Marines die because of stupid mistakes and stupid lieutenants. Every Marine we lost in recon was due to a lieutenant's mistake. So I was a real pro-enlisted, pro-noncommissioned officer guy." A staff tour at Officer Candidate School prior to his assignment to LAI only deepened Pollard's disdain for fresh-faced college boys. When he met Glenn Sadowski, Pollard informed him matter-of-factly, "I hate second lieutenants."

When Pollard assumed command in late September, the floggings began. While he sensed that Lieutenant Williams had begun to turn the company around, he was convinced that Delta still lacked the tactical proficiency that it would need to survive in battle. Pollard recalls, "They still had no idea how to employ these things in combat. They just raced around like they were in go-carts. They had no concept of vehicles supporting each other or the capabilities of the 25-millimeter main gun." He immediately set out on a series of training exercises in the Saudi wasteland. The grueling work included mounted and dismounted attacks, setting up moving screenlines, hand-digging defensive positions for the vehicles, vehicle camouflage, and long-range gunnery with the LAV's 25-mm Bushmaster chain guns. Pollard was especially adamant about their gun drills and was convinced that the company had failed to exploit the maximum effective range of the Bushmasters in training. He'd learned that in trials, armor-piercing 25-mm rounds had been measured traveling far beyond the manufacturer-specified maximum range of 3,700 meters and was determined to capitalize on this little-known fact when they finally had their date with Saddam.

Pollard could also be a holy terror when it came to safety and would hammer his Marines incessantly about not making dumb mistakes while out on patrol. Several Delta Marines recall one particularly dark and foggy night when a lone LAV had gotten lost out in the barrens and had to be talked back into the company position through a combination of tentative radio calls and yelled voice commands. Lieutenant Williams had for some time been trying to corral the errant vehicle, and at one point when he thought he'd called the vehicle in close enough, he instructed several adjacent LAVs to kill their engines and then yelled out into the chilly night air, "Hey! Can you hear me?" Sure enough, the lost Marines heard Williams's voice and began approaching the center of the company's lines. In the process they rambled right over the company shitter, completely demolishing it. Pollard came barreling right out of his LAV and chewed the vehicle's commander up one side and down the other. Failing to see any humor in the situation, he was convinced that it was only through sheer dumb luck that a Marine hadn't been killed.

The Marines for the most part loved Pollard and instinctively responded to the big-daddy cowboy figure now at the helm. Under Pollard's regime Delta earned an unusual reputation around the battalion as a scrappy outfit with a rough, dog pound–like charm. Pollard enjoyed wrestling with the men and would often throw down during lulls in training just for grins, which some enlisted Marines found strange at first. Most of the other companies in the battalion affected a more polished, strictly business professionalism, so it wasn't hard for Delta, with its flamboyant commander, to stick out. After several months in Saudi, Marines from other companies were shocked to learn that Delta Company had begun opting out of the normal battalion R&R rotation, forgoing the all-too-rare chance for a hot meal and a shower, choosing instead to kick back in the desert in the hogs, sitting around the fire, playing spades or pickup games of tackle football. Marines from the other companies began referring to them as "Delta Battalion."

Nevertheless, Delta was far from a happy family. Within a few weeks of coming aboard, Pollard had relieved one of his lieutenants and had him transferred out of the company after he'd observed him take his platoon on a killer formation run immediately after returning from a particularly taxing six-week spate of division screening duty. Pollard refused to allow a lieutenant who held his men's welfare in such low regard to remain in his company. With the loss of this officer, Pollard was thus forced to modify the traditional company structure of three platoons plus a headquarters contingent, paring it down to two subunits, an arrangement that Pollard found to be tactically preferable in the long run.

Scott Williams, who had had a fleeting taste of the king-ship prior to being supplanted, struggled under Pollard's heavy yoke as well. The two possessed completely opposing leadership philosophies. Williams was studious, unassuming, and circumspect; Pollard brash, animated, dictatorial. After butting heads over just about everything for weeks on end, they stopped talking, a leadership catastrophe within a small infantry unit. Pollard spoke to the battalion operations officer, a close friend named Jeff Powers, about having Williams replaced. Then, through some invisible miracle of self-deprecation, Williams backed down, acquiescing to Pollard's will. He pledged to do what needed to be done to get the company up to speed.

Lieutenant Sadowski also felt slighted by his boss's my-way-or-the-highway approach and held Pollard in dismally low regard due to his persistent habit of belittling and openly contradicting him in front of his men. Sadowski often felt isolated and alone in his vehicle out on screenline night after night and, because he refused to complain about the captain in front of his men, had essentially no one to commiserate with. This situation worsened when, in an attempt to balance out the leadership within Sadowski's platoon, Pollard replaced his platoon sergeant with a more experienced NCO, Staff Sergeant Conner. Within the confines of a forward-deployed Marine company, a mid-course roster change such as this is often viewed as a vote of no-confidence in a young lieutenant. In fact, Conner, while technically senior to his predecessor, was not nearly as tactically gifted and seemed at odds with Sadowski from the get-go. He quickly proved to be a liability, contradicting all of Sadowski's operations orders behind his back, instructing the junior Marines to ignore Sadowski's directives and issuing his own separate sets of orders.

The deranged atmosphere in Delta Company crossed the threshold from bad to unthinkable when on Christmas Day, 1990, it was discovered that Conner had for some time been harboring a secret plot, code-named "Plan Purple," to kill Captain Pollard and the other officers in the company when given a clean opportunity. Pollard caught wind of the plot when Conner approached the command tent to collect up the special Christmas tray rations that the company had received. The staff sergeant began tossing aside some of the trays that he didn't feel like carrying to his platoon's position out on the screenline. Pollard reflexively confronted him, ordering him to take all the rations out to his platoon.

After this curious encounter, several of the headquarters Marines cryptically suggested that Pollard avoid pissing off Staff Sergeant Conner in the future. When queried, the Marines informed him that Conner was planning to assassinate the company's officers, with Pollard as the prime target.

The rare and reprehensible phenomenon of purposely killing one's comrades is known in the ranks as "fragging." Thought by most to be an extinct Vietnam-era depredation, its unheralded appearance in Delta Company took the entire

chain of command by surprise. And while several of the
Marines in Delta had caught wind of the plot weeks prior, no
one was quite sure what to make of it.

The following day Pollard summoned Conner to his command tent and began the parley by reading Conner his Article
41 rights, the military version of Miranda. When confronted
with the charges, Conner backpedaled, accusing Pollard of
being overly aggressive and reckless with the lives of the
Marines in his charge. Under Pollard's intense questioning,
Conner subsequently admitted that he thought Sadowski incompetent and confessed to contradicting his orders and
generally undermining the lieutenant's command.

Staff Sergeant Conner, whose career had apparently been
tarnished by a series of poor fitness reports while on recruiting duty before reporting to Delta, was swiftly removed
from the company and banished to the rear to await a court-
martial. But the staggering breach of trust that this event
represented was not easily covered over. The episode and the
somber atmosphere that it generated was far beyond most
Marines' ability to comprehend. One can only surmise that
Conner was buckling under the intense pressure of living
week after week far away from home in a combat unit that
was expected to take heavy casualties in the upcoming offensive. At one point during a battalion formation, some
officers had driven this grim reality home by having one-
quarter of the company sit down, saying, "Everyone still
standing will be dead by the end of the war."*

The dark swirl of events turned a tone weirder when
Conner was subsequently killed during a combined LAV-
artillery raid with Bravo Company a few weeks later. The
staff sergeant had mysteriously been left unguarded at some
rear-area cantonment and went AWOL, jumping on one of
Bravo's vehicles without even the pretense of authorization.

---

*Scott Williams recalls going to staff meetings and listening to the battalion surgeon
complain of a body-bag shortage. Apparently 600 wasn't enough. Initially, the battalion was given only one set of objectives for the Kuwait offensive. Third LAI wasn't
expected to survive long enough to warrant any follow-on objectives.

He was killed when the LAV he was riding in was struck in the rear at full speed by another LAV.*

When news of Conner's death reached the company, several Marines at first thought it was some sort of sick joke. Men in war are a notoriously superstitious lot, so it is unsurprising that some viewed this event as merely the gears of karma turning. With his fragging plan, Conner had, in some strange way, challenged the whole constellation of primal, us-versus-them beliefs that hold a fighting unit together. Yeah, Rock was a self-described stubborn ass, but you didn't tempt the fates by openly plotting his murder. The bonds tying a company together are sacred in a way that runs counter to all in our latter-day world and Conner was on nobody's hit parade after his hare-brained scheme hit the airwaves.

In the wake of these inexplicable events, the fraternal bonds forged between the men seemed to grow stronger. Ron Tull, an LAV driver and dedicated Christian from Dallas, who had nicknamed his vehicle "Blaze of Glory"† after the popular single by Bon Jovi, recalls that Pollard appeared chastened by the turn of events and the increasingly bleak reports emerging from higher headquarters. At one point Tull and another Marine were shuffling around the company area, Tull with an old Vietnam-era LAW anti-tank rocket, slung over his shoulder. They began horsing around with the captain, saying, "Sir, why don't you let us poke on up to the border and get this show started?"

Pollard's response was chilling: "I look around and watch y'all and y'all probably have some pretty good friends around here and you think you're pretty bad. Lemme tell you

---

*Staff Sergeant Conner was killed with Bravo Company near OP 4 on January 24, 1991. He had reportedly written a letter to his sister instructing her to press for an investigation into his death if he was killed in Southwest Asia, claiming that his officers had it in for him. No one interviewed has been able to advance any theories as to why Conner went rogue or what his motivations might have been during this time frame.

†"Blaze of Glory" was an appellation given in addition to its official designation as "Red 2." In order to reduce confusion I have chosen in this instance to omit Delta Company's call signs because they often duplicate other unit designations.

something: If this thing gets as ugly as its supposed to, a lot of y'all aren't coming back."

Sergeant Nick Vitale, head of the TOW section cross-attached to Delta Company, was hardly worried about being fragged. A cocky, silver-tongued new sergeant, he was singularly blessed to command a unit of talented young Marines who practically worshipped him. Vitale had served with an elite antiterrorist company during the 1989 invasion of Panama, and despite the fact that when he reported to the battalion he knew next to nothing about LAVs, he quickly picked up the rudiments and won the young Marines over, regaling them with rich tales about life on the Corps' fringe and stories of Manuel Noriega's ouster. Vitale was a natural raconteur and to an impressionable group of fresh enlistees this was powerful stuff. They ate it up. A few of the Marines began acting like little Vitales.

Given the TOW's awesome capabilities, the men chosen to crew them were of a slightly different caste. Usually selected because of their high aptitude-test scores, TOW gunners had a reputation for being bookish and slightly more mature than your average grunt. Because they were expected to be able to distinguish between hundreds of NATO and Warsaw Pact vehicles, they frequently had their noses buried in field manuals and the latest edition of *Jane's Armor and Artillery.* There were bitter ongoing rivalries within the section over the ownership of the armor identification flashcard championship. They spent countless hours learning to discern the Rorschach-like heat signatures of scores of friendly and enemy vehicles. Before deploying, Vitale's crew had established a near-monopoly on the battalion meritorious promotion boards, which were conducted in a panel format that played right to their strengths.

Lance Corporal Jason Brown, who had attended an elite private Jesuit high school in St. Louis, remembers, "I gave everything I had to being a TOW gunner. I wanted to be the world's best. I just didn't care about anything else. If I saw a book about tanks or armored tactics lying around the company area, I picked it up and read it. On weekends, I was either in my room studying armor or doing physical training. In high school I'd always been written off as a goof-off and most of my friends had kinda given up on me. But in the Marine Corps I could start over again. I didn't have three years of legacy bullshit dragging me down."

Scott Pruett of Broken Arrow, Oklahoma, was the TOW gunner for Green 4 (Vitale's group was subdivided into the Red and Green sections. Numeric values were assigned to each vehicle based on the seniority of the vehicle commander. Pruett's vehicle commander, Corporal Bryan Smith, was the junior VC in his section and was thus number four.) Pruett had come to LAI after completing a one-year tour at Guantánamo Bay, Cuba, pulling sentry duty along the infamously fortified fence line that separated Communist Cuba from the U.S. Naval Base. One day on post he watched as two defectors swam over from the Cuban side, hoping to be reunited with their relatives living in the United States. Spending a year on the ragged edge of the realm had given Pruett a sense of urgency in training and an intensity that was often lacking in stateside Marine companies. Still, Pruett thought Vitale a fine leader and mentor and thrived on the competition that coursed through the TOW section.

The TOWs were the heavy-hitters of the LAI battalion and were armed with one of the most brutally effective antitank missile systems ever conceived. The Improved Tube-Launched, Optically-Tracked, Wire-Guided missile, or TOW, was developed by Hughes Aircraft Corporation in the mid-1980s. It capitalized on a half-century of American Cold War research and development, employing cutting-edge aerospace technology to defeat the cold, rolled steel of Soviet armored vehicles. It was rumored that the tank hadn't been built that the TOW couldn't kill.*

---

*The supremacy of the TOW was more than a rumor. Several reports of TOWs in combat during the invasion of Kuwait shocked even the engineers who designed them. In one instance a TOW missile went right through the tank it was aimed at and penetrated the solid steel hull of another parked next to it. Another TOW passed through a six-foot dirt berm and knocked out an Iraqi armored personnel carrier on the other side.

The LAV-ATs, such as the ones Vitale's Marines piloted, performed a pivotal role in the functioning of a Marine Light-Armored Infantry unit. The LAV-25s, while faster than any extant armored vehicle, were also perilously thin-skinned and largely dependent upon their raw speed and mobility for survival. Their 25-mm cannons, designed to kill trucks and certain types of armored personnel carriers, were essentially useless against the brutishly thick armor of 1990s Warsaw Pact tanks, which, in some instances, ranged up to ten inches of solid steel. Thus, Vitale's crew provided the only real means by which Pollard could expect to keep any sizable Iraqi force at bay before the vaunted American air armada appeared.

The antitank variants were also equipped with the most effective night-vision devices at the time, the A/N-TAS-4A, a thermal imaging system capable of piercing the darkness out to distances of over four miles. This sight, which translated variations in heat levels into a surprisingly precise view of the nocturnal world, also penetrated smoke, dust, and practically any battlefield obscurant the Iraqis could throw up. The sum total of these myriad capabilities was to invest the nineteen-year-old gunners who manned the TOW with an almost God-like power to reach out and annihilate their fellow man across vast stretches of material space. The upshot for Vitale was that because the vehicles he commanded were so capable and deadly, he was often treated like royalty wherever he went. He was the commander's eyes, informing him of his fortunes developing out on the horizon, his night lifeline. People loved having him around because he brought the fire with him.

Because Vitale's TOW vehicles, with their powerful armament and thermal sights, were central to the plan for the evening, they were offered pride of place within Delta Company's defensive position. Vitale spread out his vehicles for maximum observation within the middle of Delta's lines. Pollard's LAV-25s then collapsed in staggered positions around them to provide flank security. Each vehicle was arduously dug-in by hand in order to create some protection from enemy fire and to reduce its heat signature. To ensure against any Iraqi infiltrators, some of Pollard's Marines, including Bill Covington and Dion Stephenson, a scout from Ron Tull's vehicle, began digging individual fighting holes in the sand near the LAVs. Nearly half of the men would spend their nights this way, the old Marine way: counting the hours of a lonely watch out in the cold.

Within the TOW group itself, Vitale's Red section occupied the right half, with Sergeant Michael Wissman's Green section holding the leftmost portion. They trained all their potent thermal sights to their direct front toward the border.

Because of the near-Cartesian perfection of the terrain surrounding Umm Hjul, the company, with its various attachments (Vitale's group was a battalion asset and was only attached to Delta Company for a single evening) and logistics trains, was able to cover a staggeringly wide area. With its mission to screen as large an area as possible, Delta Company occupied a frontage inconceivable to most straight-leg Marine commanders, well over four kilometers from end to end. Some LAVs were more than 500 meters from their nearest wingman. The incredible separation between vehicles made for an eerie nightfall. Before dusk practically the entire company could be taken in with a single sweep of the eye. Now, as darkness descended, enveloping each individual vehicle like a shroud, the evening took on an almost Gothic tone, with every LAV in seeming isolation from its brethren. The only thing connecting one LAV to another was their single-channel VHF radios.

Within each vehicle, the Marines were further cloistered: Drivers could only see forward through their night-vision periscopes, gunners were fixed to their sights, vehicle commanders, standing halfway out of their cupolas, could see only the veiling blackness in front of them. It was an eerie way to go into battle, alleviated only by the miracles of American science in the form of revolutionary night-vision technologies and communication gear. Jason Brown described the inside of a buttoned-down LAV as "like being in a four-man submarine."

As the night pulled in tighter, Vitale jockeyed his vehicles up and back and side to side a few dozen meters, just in case Iraqi artillery forward observers had marked their original positions in the daylight. Every vehicle settled into its night-watch schedule, with 25 percent up in Delta and 50 percent for the TOWs which, because they carried no scouts with them, were cursed with only four men with which to spread the watch load. There was a full moon that evening, and the light reflected off the desert floor like a busy ocean caught in freeze frame.

5

8:20 P.M., January 29, 1991,
Observation Post 4

The mass did not arrive for an hour or more, when the wind had altogether died away, and the evening, calm and black and full of stars, had come down on us. Auda set a watch through the night, for this district was in the line of the raiding parties, and in the hours of darkness there were no friends in Arabia.
—T. E. LAWRENCE, *Seven Pillars of Wisdom*

Lance Corporal Derek Puterbaugh, assistant TOW gunner for Red 4, was just about to lie down when the call came. Lance Corporal Dave Burrows, Red 4's driver, had the first watch of the evening.

"Red One, this is Red Four, spot report, over." Burrows was calling Sergeant Vitale, indicating that he had a contact to report.

"Send it, Red Four."

"Roger, three Victors, twelve o'clock, six thousand plus meters, moving north to south, over."

"Are you sure, Red Four?" Vitale was incredulous. He figured Burrows was seeing a mirage. It wasn't the first time he'd gotten a call pregnant with expectation in the middle of the night.

"Roger, Red One, three Victors."

"You sure they're not civilian, Red Four?"

"They ain't roller-skating out there, over."

In Vitale's vehicle, Jason Brown, the TOW gunner for Red 1, was just about asleep when he heard Burrows's report echo over the LAV's intercom. Brown was accustomed to hearing spot reports all the time. It was a regular evening ritual designed to keep the gunners sharp and to ensure that no one fell asleep on watch. The reports ranged from dogs at 3,000 meters to food stains on a Marine's shirt right in front of an LAV. This, however, was the first time he'd heard anything about vehicular traffic. Burrows might be seeing things, but just being this close to the border was cause enough for concern. Burrows, who could be a real smart-ass, seemed adamant about his call, and his roller-skating joke hinted at an undercurrent of deadly serious intention.

Vitale tapped the intercom. "Hey, Jason, get up there and tell me what you see."

"One step ahead, as usual," Brown replied as he brought his hydraulically powered TOW turret to life and spun 180 degrees to the direct front of the LAV. The gunner's seat was connected to the turret on a large swivel, and Brown, perched just below and inside the vehicle, peered into the apparatus, which bore a more than passing resemblance to a submarine's periscope. His left hand worked the turret's directional controls, while his right hand brought the eyepiece into focus. After he spent several seconds getting oriented to the red-toned netherworld of the TOW's thermographic sight, five blips quickly came into view, moving from left to right.

"I count five Victors, Sergeant V., but the rest is dead on."

The contacts were still too far away to deduce what type of vehicles they were or even if they were Iraqi. They could be Kuwaiti scavengers out wandering the wastes or a lost patrol of some sort.

"Red One, this is Green Four." It was Lance Corporal Smith, Scottie Pruett's vehicle commander, checking in from the southernmost vehicle in the section. He was well over a kilometer distant, giving him a markedly different perspective on the situation. "Roger. Same spot rep, only we got seven Victors and counting, over."

"Roger, Green Four, I copy seven Victors and counting." There was a slight pause and then, "All Red and Green vehicles stand to. I say again, all vehicles stand to."

Extricating himself from the turret, Brown reached down and grabbed a full canteen from his pack. He popped his head out of the top hatch of his LAV, nicknamed "Hammer of the Gods," as the remainder of the section checked in.

"Red Two, roger."

Brown threw the canteen at the first sleeping bag he saw.

"Red Three, roger."

"What the fuck?" Brown's driver, Jason Boileau, hollered as the canteen bounced off his sleeping bag. The zipper burst open.

"Stand the fuck to, motherfuckers. We got enemy movement on the other side of the berm," Brown yelled, spinning around, sinking back into the queer ruddy warmth of the TOW.

"Green One up."

Boileau sent Brown's canteen flying over to Lance Corporal Crosby's bag.

"Green Two, roger."

"I heard him the first time, you oversized fuck," Crosby replied, having weathered the rude blow of the canteen.

"Green Four, roger."

With Green Four's call, the whole section of seven LAV-ATs were up, centered, and observing the contacts as they came into view. Vitale seemed to pause for a bit to collect himself and then, flipping the master switch that controlled all the radios in the vehicle, announced, "Alpha Group, this is Red One. Keep all Victor counts off the net. I'll be on the company tac talking with Delta Six. Will be back on the net soon. Red One out."

Vitale had been through this before. He was about to ring up a company commander in the middle of the night and tell him that he had bogeys outside the wire and that he didn't really know who they were, where they going, or what their intentions were. At times like this, officers tended to play twenty questions with Vitale, expecting a crystal ball–like prescience from the young sergeant, as if he really knew any more than they did. LAV companies at this stage in the war were equipped with first-generation passive night sights, which were practically worthless in this type of situation. So before switching over to Delta's net, Vitale jotted down some notes in his small green notebook. Pollard was relying upon him for a lot at this point, and he wanted to have his ducks in a row.

For his part, Vitale remained unconvinced that this contact would develop into anything significant. At first he'd thought Burrows and Brown were just seeing buildings on the horizon and had somehow convinced themselves that these tiny red blocks were moving. Thermal image interpretation is an inherently tricky business. Any old grunt could look into a TOW sight, spy a bunch of rats clustered in front of an LAV, and declare that an Iraqi armored regiment was bearing down upon them. And if a school-trained 0352 TOW gunner were jumpy enough, he could talk himself into seeing just about anything. They'd never been out to Umm Hjul before, so it was possible that the boys, sharp as they were, were just white-knuckling the deal here. And even if there were Iraqis out there, they were headed south, essentially away from OP 4 and therefore not their problem. The contacts were still so far out that they wouldn't be a threat for a long time yet.

Nevertheless, the number of contacts appeared to be growing, and Captain Pollard needed to know about it. He rolled over to Delta's tac net and began briefing him in clipped tones. Pollard asked if they were tanks or just armored personnel carriers. Vitale had no idea. Pollard reminded him of the recon team in OP 4 that was at least three or four kilometers closer to the situation than they were and in a much better position to make the call. If this thing were for real, they could expect to hear from recon soon.

Vitale clicked back over to his vehicle's intercom. "How's it looking, Jason?"

"Just hit two-niner, make that three-zero. They just keep coming, Sergeant V."

Vitale radioed this number to Pollard. It was becoming difficult for Brown to keep track of all the vehicles pouring through his crosshairs. With each vehicle that rolled into view, the palpable tension ticked up another notch. That much firepower running amok in the middle of the night, even if it wasn't blazing right down on them, was a bad, bad thing.

Brown reached down into the zippered thigh pocket of his crewman's suit and pulled out a plastic can of Copenhagen. Beating the can against his thigh, he packed the chew and kept counting. He took a lipful of chew and put the can back into his pocket, zippering it shut. His loader, Private First Class Benz Crosby, moved in behind him.

Crosby whispered, "What the fuck's going on, man?"

"A shitload of Iraqi vehicles, bro, single file, north to south."

"Aww shit, man. Think we're gonna engage?"

"Hell if I know," Brown admitted. "Although I doubt it—there's too goddamn many of 'em. But get the next two missiles ready just in case."

Pollard had just finished briefing his headquarters section and was climbing into the back of his hog to take his boots off when the radio crackled to life. He had just spent the better part of the last six hours organizing the company plan for the evening and was looking forward to relaxing for a spell, so this was not a welcome call. Pollard, along with the rest of the Marines, was dog-tired. They'd been on the move all day and then scouting and digging the vehicles in throughout the afternoon.

He threw his boots back on, then his crewman's headset, and clambered up into the commander's hole in the turret. As he climbed in, he reminded himself that every vehicle in the company would be able to hear him over the tac net and that he had to be cool.

Vitale informed him that they had numerous vehicles on the far side of the berm moving south. After quizzing him briefly, Pollard said, "Roger that," and ended the transmission.

Pollard then called over to battalion headquarters and requested permission to engage. They were still in that odd twilight part of the war where everyone was still hesitant about simply unleashing the dogs of war without some form of authorization. After giving the battalion commander, Lieutenant Colonel Cliff Myers, a detailed situation report, he was told to sit tight and wait for the situation to develop. They would try to get some air out to them as soon as possible.

Soon after talking with Colonel Myers, Vitale came up again, reporting that there were now 50 vehicles across the berm and that they were leading with main battle tanks. This last bit of information was particularly disconcerting, as Soviet doctrine to which the Iraqis woodenly adhered, dictated that they lead with lighter reconnaissance vehicles, something akin to LAVs. No armored commander in his right mind would lead with tanks; it was like sending your star tailback straight up the middle without any blockers. It made absolutely no sense. These Iraqis were either radically disoriented or were just trying to rattle the Americans with a naked show of force.

Then, out of nowhere, a new factor in the equation presented itself. A steady stream of red tracer fire appeared from recon's position. It took several seconds for the hollow popping sound of the fire to travel to Delta's position.

What the fuck was recon thinking opening up with machine guns? Were they totally insane?

Over at First Platoon, which occupied the northern one-half of Delta's screen line, Ron Tull was sitting in the driver's seat of Blaze of Glory when the calls of Iraqis across the berm began pouring in. When Tull first picked up the story, it was 15 vehicles. The 15 quickly grew to 20, then 25, then 50, then 70 with no end in sight. Tull's vehicle was equipped with only feeble passive night sights, and the Marines inside were, for all intents and purposes, completely blind to the situation building on the horizon. Tull had tried scanning repeatedly with his binoculars to the east but was unable to make out a thing. Unsure of what else to do, the Marines were relegated to merely listening in as the situation was called like a distant baseball contest by the eagle-eyed TOW gunners. Every transmission that came in left the Marines more confused and tense. Tull himself was mystified. *Where could all of these vehicles be coming from?*

Suddenly red tracers lit up the night in front of him. He had no idea that there were friendly troops in front of them, and he wondered who was firing. As Tull watched, green-colored tracers started hammering back from the far side of the berm. The Iraqis were firing now.

This was the first time Tull had ever seen anything like this. *You gotta be kidding me.*

Then he remembered that his best friend, Dion Stephenson, was in an open fighting hole 20 yards to his front. Tull hopped out over the nose of Blaze of Glory and sprinted out to get him.

Stephenson was an unusual recent addition to Delta Company. He was raised in an all-American family from Bountiful, Utah, and his father was a decorated Marine Vietnam veteran. Dion had spent several years in the Corps' elite First Force Reconnaissance Company until he was busted down in rank and reassigned after being caught with alcohol on his breath after a parachute jump. He had come to the company as a conspicuously seasoned and enthusiastic lance corporal. He seemed to thrive on the unbridled rhythms of Marine field life.

Tull dropped down into Dion's hole and began shaking him vigorously, yelling, "*Dude,* we gotta get going. You gotta get up!"

Stephenson, annoyed at being so rudely disturbed and still mostly in the throes of a deep sleep, looked up at Tull coolly, "What, man, *what?*"

Tull, at a loss for words, yanked Stephenson up roughly, shoving his head toward the berm, yelling, "Look, dude, they're fighting!"

For a long, deep moment Stephenson gazed absently over at the tracer fire, now in full bloom, just taking it all in, as if a dream. Then, like a man opening his eyes underwater for the first time, a look of recognition swept over him. A vengeful energy seized the young man, and at once Stephenson was all motion, snatching up his gear, rolling up his sleeping bag, then throwing on his H-harness and his Kevlar helmet.

When the pair jogged back to Blaze of Glory, all hands were abustle, stowing loose gear and preparing to move out. This virus of activity, which began with Dave Burrows and the TOWs, had spread fitfully at first but was now clearly infecting the entire company. All hands were fully engaged, readying themselves for the coming fight. Throwing everything inside the LAV and buttoning up all the troop hatches, the crew of eight Marines were soon ready to go, the LAV's turbo diesel V-6 idling roughly in the background. Through the jangling din of the company radio traffic, Tull heard Stephenson yell, "This is it, Tully!" They were the last words he would ever hear from his friend.

6

Approximately 8:45 P.M., January 29, 1991,
the Berm, Observation Post 4

*It struck me as I saw them from the corner of Leuse Wood how sym-
bolic of all war they were. Then one saw them creeping along at
about four miles an hour, taking all obstacles as they came, sputter-
ing death with all their guns, enfilading each trench as they came to
it—and crushing beneath them our own dead and dying as they
passed. I saw one body on a concrete parapet over which one had
passed. This body was just a splash of blood and clothing about two
feet wide and perhaps an inch thick. An hour before this thing he
had been a thinking, breathing man, with life before him and loved
ones awaiting him somewhere in Scotland, for he was a kiltie. Nothing stops these cars, trees bend and break, boulders are pressed
into the earth.*
—BRITISH OBSERVER *of one of the first armored attacks
during World War I*

ROSS STILL couldn't raise a soul on the radio. He'd been
trying for almost twenty minutes to find an aircraft to
run a mission for him and had come up dry. The platoon had
been more or less abandoned, left out at the observation post
for so long that the cryptographic data for their radios, which
normally allowed them to talk encrypted to other units, had
expired. This allowed them to transmit to aircraft orbiting
over Saudi Arabia, but when the pilots tried to talk back,
their transmissions were hopelessly garbled. Even their radio
frequencies, which were rotated every twelve hours to prevent enemy eavesdropping, were out of date. It was one of
those stupid, utterly preventable situations that drive even the
cynical old salts crazy. They had probably ten radios spread
throughout the platoon, and because Battalion had left them
out at the OP for so long, they could no longer perform their

mission. Without the use of radios to talk to the rear, a reconnaissance unit is nearly worthless and becomes just another
rifle platoon lost in the desert.

Compounding this already aggravated situation was the
Iraqi jamming, which was preventing Ross from talking to
his other teams who were practically within shouting distance. Ross couldn't talk to anyone, and a growing force of
Iraqi armored vehicles was bearing down upon his position
and his Marines. They were for all practical purposes all
alone out there.

Ross knew they would have to evacuate soon, but he
couldn't leave without telling some higher-ups what was
brewing. The Iraqis were coming, and commanders back in
the rear needed to know about it. The vehicles lurching in the
sand out in front of them were the very reason the platoon
had been sent up to the border in the first place.

There were other murkier concerns as well. Twentieth-
century military history is replete with epidemic outbursts of
what is known in the business as tank fright or tank terror.
This mass psychological phenomenon was first observed in
World War I, when German troops, faced with the dread
prospect of tracked iron beasts bearing down upon them,
broke ranks and ran. And while Ross had no reason to expect his men would run off screaming into the night,
the sheer awesome fear that tanks can produce in even seasoned troops is undeniable. There are few things that put the
scare into grunts quicker than a platoon of tanks running
amok.

All the training Ross had been through, all the years with
a pack on his back, the never-ending patrols, the endless
classes on combined arms warfare and integrated air-ground
force packaging, and he had been reduced to pleading over
the net, searching for some airplane somewhere to heed his
calls. It could have been a scene right out of the North Africa
campaign in World War II. All their incredible technology
had been negated by simple negligence and a half-baked
Iraqi electronic warfare plan. He'd even taken to openly ex-

plaining his predicament to whoever might be listening—a total procedural taboo—saying simply, "This is a recon unit. We are at an OP on the border. We have Iraqis tanks coming at us and we need help."

By this point, not knowing really what else to do, Ross just started rolling from one frequency to another, channel-surfing. He'd do a few calls on one freq and then roll to the next one and start all over again: "Any station this net, any station this net. We are a Marine recon unit out front. We have Iraqi armored personnel carriers approaching our pos. Request immediate air support." It was impossible to know if he was completely off track or if someone had answered his calls after he'd changed to a new freq. He was pissing in the wind.

Back at the antenna farm, Roche was feverishly working the problem as well. One of the radio operators who worked for him, Lance Corporal Babski, was up at the comm shack at the foot of the berm, double-checking Roche's work. While they labored, they talked over a small green microphone-speaker set, which because it was wire-connected, was completely unjammable. Hands flying now, Roche checked the batteries, switching out the old ones, putting in new rectangular green ones, shaking them, calling upon every comm trick he'd ever learned: using a pencil eraser on the contact points, double-checking all the slash wire connections, disconnecting and reconnecting all the components. He was fairly certain that they were being jammed, yet he had to keep trying. He was the radio guy. He made magic with the green metal boxes. No one talked to anyone else unless he made it happen.

While all the other Marines were scrambling around, prepping for the fight, he was immersed in the comm, enveloped in all the various radio sets and wires. He could hear the Marines screaming at each other up on the berm, steeling each other for the big dance that was coming. The guys were nervous. He looked up and saw one Marine pointing an AT-4 antitank rocket downrange with another Marine directly behind him, a major no-no because the AT-4 had a killer backblast to it. It was almost as dangerous to be behind an AT-4 when it went off as it was to be in front of one.

Over at the customs house, Sergeant Luis Bench had the watch. A recent addition to the platoon, he had come over to the desert with a combat engineer unit several months prior. One day his company commander pulled him aside and informed him that he'd been "volunteered" to go out with a recon unit to survey the Iraqi obstacle belts in southern Kuwait. Recon needed some engineering expertise to help locate and mark the assault lanes that the main Marine force would go through. Bench was glad to do the job but was disappointed to be leaving his Marines behind. He'd never worked with recon before and was unsure of what to expect. Recon had a mixed reputation. The Humvee trek out to recon's position was the longest ride of his life. He was told to tell his platoon that he was going away on a mission but not to say with whom or where.

Sure enough, when Bench rolled up to recon's position, Sergeant Mike Davis, whom the Marines strangely referred to as "Strike," was out there to greet him. Davis, a zealous, effusive recon veteran, seemed on fire. "Hey, man, how's it going? We got some awesome shit coming our way. Man, this mission, shit, I tell ya . . ."

This seemed to fit right in with Bench's perception of recon Marines as self-absorbed, Oakley sunglass–wearing prima donnas. Seeing Davis, his first thought was, "Oh, God, here we go." The platoon, however, wasn't like any he'd encountered. They seemed to be an entity unto themselves—they were the DRP. They looked down on everyone else, and within the platoon the feeling was, "We're the Okinawa platoon. This is who we are." As he began working with Davis's team and doing rehearsals for their breach patrol, Bench was blown away. His young lance corporals were serious. When they got together to talk over the patrol plan, these nineteen-year-olds began briefing their schemes like they were generals. They knew their stuff and readily shared their ideas about stalking and patrolling with Bench.

Bench, a bantam young NCO, quickly reciprocated, proffering his vast knowledge of military obstacles, specialized demolitions, and mines. Through this earnest give-and-take Bench was able to establish an excellent rapport with the platoon. When they finally made the move up to OP 4, Bench helped them design their bunkers and even constructed a Dutch oven out of rocks for the Marines to cook their chow in. Bench, who'd been born into the grinding poverty of Peru, was one of those rare Marines who'd grown up in an utterly foreign culture and been drawn to the Marine Corps after emigrating for reasons he couldn't fully explain. The Corps was his home in a way that most other Marines didn't comprehend. Perhaps because of his hardscrabble upbringing, he brought an unusual sort of intensity and resourcefulness to whatever unit he was assigned.

Bench heard the sound of the tracks out in the night and yelled over to Davis, "Hey, Strike, we got something out there." Davis woke up and came over to Bench's position on the berm. He pulled out his night-vision goggles, and after seeing what he thought to be fifteen vehicles coming on line, he and Bench went around and starting rousing everyone. Bench woke up Lance Corporal Buffa. Buffa rose quickly, grabbed his M-249 squad automatic weapon, put his helmet on, and went upstairs to check in with Sergeant Jestel, his team leader.*

Between them, Bench and Strike Davis had a small arsenal of AT-4s lined up against the berm. The sound of the vehicles was getting louder and louder. Bench could hear the tracks with their dreadful squeaking, metal grinding against metal. Bench realized that he was just along for the ride. The Marines around him were Davis's men, his to employ. Al-

---

*The M-249 squad automatic weapon, or SAW, is the standard light machine gun issued to U.S. forces.

though Bench was one of the senior men at the position, he—along with the rest of the Marines—was just waiting for Davis's command for them to engage. He thought, *Anytime . . . c'mon, Strike.*

While Ross was trying to pull some air out of the sky, Gillispie was up on the berm with his night-vision goggles keeping an eye on the approaching Iraqis. They were about a kilometer out. He'd already gotten the headquarters element Marines up and ready to evacuate back to the horseshoe. Initially, he hadn't been overly concerned, thinking it was probably just a gaggle of Iraqi reconnaissance vehicles poking around that they could scare away with a few well-aimed AT-4 shots. The Iraqis always seemed to be up to something weird and never really had a solid tactical plan for anything they did. Gillispie didn't consider them a professional army. Not like the Koreans or the Thais he'd seen. He watched through the goggles as the vehicles got closer and closer.

Just then, one of the lead vehicles turned, and Gillispie could see the long barrel of the tank's main gun sticking out. He yelled back to Lieutenant Ross.

"Sir, I think we fucked up 'cause those are tanks right out front!"

The Iraqis were coming at them with a battle force of T-62s, mid-grade Soviet-produced tanks with ten inches of rolled steel armor on the front. A direct hit by an AT-4 would bounce right off these things. Gillispie knew this because they'd shot at a few old tank hulls when they'd first arrived in Saudi Arabia. About the only way to stop these monsters was to call a close air strike right on top of 'em. Even then, only certain munitions would have the desired effect.

It was time to go. They'd made a valiant effort to develop the situation, to get air and report back to headquarters, but now the Iraqis were coming with the Sunday punch.

Ross told Gillispie to hit the red pop-up flare, the platoon signal to move back to the horseshoe. Gillispie pulled out the silver, cigar-shaped pyrotechnic and fired it into the night. It was a clear evening with a full moon and the flare rose well above the entire position like a errant firework, adding a pale red light to the night sky.*

*According to the U.S. Naval Observatory, the moon was 99 percent illuminated on January 29, 1991. The moon had risen at 4:34 P.M. local time, which meant that it would have been high in the sky by the time the engagement started. Additionally, some accounts of the battle have mentioned the intense lunar light reflecting off the pale-colored sand. Even though the Marines were far from the lights of any city, the area was surprisingly well lit that night.

7

9:00 P.M., January 29, 1991,
the Berm, Observation Post 4

These voices, these quiet words, these footsteps in the trench behind me recall me at a bound from the terrible loneliness and fear of death by which I have almost been destroyed. They are more to me than life, those voices, they are more than motherliness and more than fear, they are the strongest, most comforting thing there is anywhere, they are the voices of my comrades.
    —ERICH MARIA REMARQUE, *All Quiet on the Western Front*

THEY WERE OUT. Throwing their gear into the back of the five-ton and the Humvee, Ross, Gillispie, Roche, Babski, Lance Corporal Abkins, and Lieutenant Turk, the translator, pulled away from the berm and began covering the 500 meters back to the horseshoe berm. Roche had had to disconnect all the radios and just leave the antenna standing there. Nevertheless, all was going more or less according to plan. Ross had somehow even managed to get hold of an airborne command-and-control bird orbiting far overhead. Did they have anything they could send his way? he asked. The command bird said affirmative, and before he knew it, Ross was talking to *Blaze 71,* a Marine A-6 Intruder attack aircraft out of Shaikh Isa, a Marine base located on the Persian Gulf island of Bahrain. They were inbound to OP 4. It would take them a few minutes, but help was on the way.

They still couldn't get hold of the light-armored vehicle company to their rear, but they at least had air inbound. This would buy them precious time and allow them to collect themselves before striking out to the south to find a harbor site to wait out the night. *Blaze 71* would also be able to relay the message to headquarters to begin waking up the sleeping giant and getting some more air out this direction. The situation seemed to be sorting itself out.

Then, unexpectedly, pops of green tracer fire from the second story of the customs house punctuated the seeming peace, the rounds pulsing down at the lead tank. It was Sergeant Jestel's M-60 machine gun. *What the fuck were they doing? Did they think the red pop-up flare had meant to open fire?* As if to answer the question, the M-60 spoke again, followed by several resounding AT-4 shots like horizontal lightning in the night sky.

The Iraqi tanks returned fire with their 115-mm main guns, virtual artillery pieces versus the DRP's peashooters. It was beyond David and Goliath. The tanks were now only a few hundred meters away, practically point-blank range for armored combat. The tank rounds seemed to go in slow motion, to almost float across the battlefield.

Due either to confusion over the meaning of the red pop-up flare or a desire for a simple fuck-you shot before leaving, Strike Davis and Jestel's teams had decided to engage the enemy tanks to their front.* As the force of somewhere between ten to fifteen tanks approached, Davis finally gave the signal to engage, and Sergeant Bench, who'd been counting the pregnant seconds, unleashed, rapidly expending all the AT-4 launchers within his reach, scoring one direct hit. He noticed that Lance Corporal Anderson, the team's SAW gunner, had thrown down his weapon to grab an idle M-60 nearby. The rule at this point seemed to be the more firepower, the better, so Bench discarded his M-16, picked up Anderson's SAW, and began engaging the tanks to his front.

Strike yelled to Lance Corporal Mercer to go get the Humvee ready. Running the few yards back to the vehicle, Mercer jumped in and tried the starter, desperately cranking

---

*There is a fundamental disagreement among the Marines on this point. Jeffrey Buffa and Thomas Manney both recall the flare being fired *after* they began engaging the tanks, while Ross, Gillispie, and Roche all insist that the Marines inside the customs house had confused the meaning of the red flare.

the engine for several minutes. The Humvee was dead. *How could this be happening?* Bench thought. Mercer kept at it. Finally the vehicle's diesel V-8 caught and thrummed to life.

Up above in the customs house, Lance Corporal Jeffrey Buffa knew that because the police post was the only break in the berm for miles around, the Iraqis would be drawn to their position as if by some invisible tractor beam. Just as one of the vehicles moved into his sights, Jestel and the other Marines unleashed a fusillade of antitank rocket fire. One of the Marines, Mike McAvoy, struggled with a LAW rocket, the predecessor to the AT-4, which had failed to fire. He proceeded to pick up another LAW, which also misfired.

After this first volley, Buffa unleashed a long burst from his SAW, pinging an Iraqi vehicle to his direct front. The others joined in. Their fire flourished, building into a hail of bullets which obliterated the darkness. It was like a Godzilla movie with everyone aggressively mashing triggers, firing on full-auto at the crawling beasts for minutes on end. Red tracer rounds ricocheted off the tank hulls at chaotic angles. What Iraqi return fire there was seemed to be totally ineffective, impacting well behind the Marines.

Lance Corporal Blackwell popped off an illumination round at one of the tanks with his M-203 grenade launcher. The grenade rebounded off the tank's front glacis plate and wedged itself in between the turret and the hull, still burning brightly. This unbelievable shot lit up the behemoth, creating a perfect aiming point for the Marines and illuminating the entire fantastic scene. Another Marine loosed a rocket at a nearby Iraqi tank. The missile struck the tank, rebounding harmlessly into the blackness.

After what seemed like several minutes of frenetic blasting, an odd pause developed; the Iraqis amazingly appeared to be breaking off their attack. *Could it be? Had they blunted the assault?* Exploiting the brief lull, Sergeant Jestel yelled for his team to advance on the tanks. They sprinted out to a small clump of sand mounds in front of the house and hastily organized a defensive position.

*   *   *

Back at the horseshoe, Ross and Gillispie watched Jestel's salvos in stunned disbelief. They knew full well the futility of trying to stop tanks with machine guns and failed to understand why Jestel was shooting at them. Nevertheless, as Gillispie put it, "there was this unwritten thing, if one of our teams was going to stay and fight, then we were *all* going to stay and fight." Piling into their vehicles, they made their way back to their original position on the berm. They were back in the fight.

Then, without explanation or warning, the Iraqi jamming, which had so frustrated Ross's efforts and thoroughly stymied the platoon, lifted like a fog in the afternoon. Ross suddenly had comm with Davis's team. He told Davis to go and get Jestel's team and have them fall back to the horseshoe.

Rocketing far overhead, First Lieutenant Michael Kies, the bombardier-navigator of *Blaze 71,* a Marine A-6 attack jet, got a radio call from the air-support center informing him that a ground unit on the border was in trouble and needed close air support. Behind the stick was Kies's squadron commander, Lieutenant Colonel Beaman Cummings. Cummings, a Vietnam veteran with scores of combat missions over Hanoi under his belt, was possibly the most experienced Marine aviator airborne that evening. The bird they commanded, the Grumman A-6E Intruder, was one of the most capable night attack aircraft ever produced. Packed to the gills with the most advanced precision bombing avionics and night-vision technology available at the time, the Intruder lacked the *Top Gun* panache of an interceptor but was a superlative weapons delivery system. The DRP was getting the deluxe package. It was like dialing 911 and having Dirty Harry pick up.

Cummings and Kies had been headed into Kuwait to do bombing runs but quickly diverted when they realized that there were Marines under fire. They had a full tank of gas and were ready to rock and roll. The air-support center instructed them to roll to the ground radio frequency and make contact with the ground unit commander.

Kies contacted Lieutenant Ross and informed him that they were inbound but that it would be a few minutes before they reached their position. As they drew closer, Ross attempted to pass the traditional nine-line close-air-support brief to Kies. The nine-line brief, standardized throughout the Marine Corps, elucidates in fine detail the myriad factors related to an impending mission, including such things as attack headings, friendly locations, suggested egress routes, in addition to a detailed target description. This tedious, frequently maddening process is designed to maximize the effect of the munitions on hand and to prevent friendly fire, a problem which has plagued the U.S. military since the advent of close air support in the 1930s. An aggressive young bombardier, Kies didn't really need any of these formalities, and after conducting a single high-speed pass, asked Ross simply, "Where do you want the bombs?" Relieved to catch a break for once, Ross adjusted Kies off an Iraqi tank that had just discharged its main gun, an event clearly visible to both men.

Descending out of the gloom, the Intruder began its run roughly perpendicular to the Iraqi formation, releasing its deadly cargo almost directly on top of them. An immense shower of blazing sparks issued from the sky, enveloping the tanks. Following on the heels of this exquisite visual display, a staccato of thunderous pops echoed off the desert floor as if Thor himself had spoken. They were dropping cluster bombs on the tanks. *Blaze 71* continued this staggering demonstration for two more runs, unleashing two cluster bombs on each pass. One of the bombs looked like it smacked right into a tank.

To the Marines on the ground, it was the greatest fireworks show they'd ever seen.

Having dropped their load, Cummings and Kies headed back to base. As they were egressing, Kies pointed the aircraft's infrared scope to the rear to try to get a sense of the destruction they had just unleashed. The Iraqi vanguard appeared in disarray, with numerous vehicles breaking off the attack and careening through the gloom in random directions. Peering deeper into Kuwait, Kies spied a huge line of vehicles stretching off into the darkness. He stopped counting after he'd reached 100 vehicles.

Back at the horseshoe, Ross finally had the family back together again, and while he worked the radio talking to *Blaze 71* and Delta company, Gillispie went around making sure that all the men and gear were accounted for. Bench and Davis made it back. Bench the émigré was all smiles, claiming now that he'd taken and returned fire, he'd for sure be granted American citizenship. When Jestel reached the crescent-shaped berm, Gillispie confronted him: "What the fuck happened? Why did you open up?"

Jestel, equally enraged, fired back, "Why the fuck did you leave us?"

There was no time to sort all this out. There had a mission to focus on, and Gillispie dropped it. They all turned and watched the A-6 Intruder work its magic. He didn't seem to be hitting anything, but the gross, almost supernatural, display was scattering the Iraqi charge. You could almost see the Iraqi tankers eyeing the destruction to their front and yelling, Whoa! It was a huge relief to the Marines to see that kind of firepower at work even if it wasn't 100 percent accurate.

They felt comparatively safe in the horseshoe. The walls, although composed entirely of sand, were ten feet high and fifteen feet deep, probably not thick enough to stop a tank round, but good enough. In combat, any fold, any slight declivity in the earth where one can hide becomes unspeakably precious. When the rounds start flying, the dirt is your best friend.

Bench's head was on a swivel, looking around, peering over the berm, staring incredulously at the other Marines, thinking all the while, *What the fuck are we still doing here?* He looked over at Jestel, who had found a lone tennis shoe in the hollow of the berm and was strangely fascinated by this fortuitous discovery. He was walking around showing it to the other Marines, "Check it out, man, *a tennis shoe*." Bench thought, *What the fuck is going on?*

Bench gazed over the berm and saw an enormous muzzle flash from one of the tanks. Yelling, "Incoming!" he ducked beneath the sand wall. Inching back up to the lip of the berm, he returned fire with his SAW.

The Iraqis, stunned initially by the volume of machine-gun fire and the cluster-bomb strike, had regrouped and were pressing on with their attack. They began blasting away at the small generator building behind the customs house and grinding toward the Marines.

With *Blaze 71* outbound and more air sure to follow, Ross began focusing on getting the light-armored vehicles up to his position so they could conduct a battle handover. Rather than surrender ground without a fight, he wanted to have the LAVs, with their heavier armament and antitank missiles, link up with his platoon and begin attriting the Iraqi armored formation in preparation for the coming air strikes. But what Ross was really hoping was that they would be able to suppress the Iraqis, take off some of the pressure, and allow him and his Marines to escape.

Ross had had a brief meeting with the LAV company commander just after sundown that evening. The liaison had been less than ideal. The LAV commander, a tough-minded mustang captain named Pollard, had seemed distracted and wasn't particularly concerned with what recon was doing up at the berm. Pollard had just been assigned to the Umm Hjul area and was absorbed with getting his company, which had just been reinforced with a section of antitank vehicles, situated for the night. He'd been ordered to occupy OP 4 the following morning. Nevertheless, they did trade frequencies and if Ross needed to find Pollard, he knew where to reach him.

Ross grabbed another radio from Roche and began conversing with Pollard's second-in-command, Lieutenant Williams. The LAV guys seemed to just be waking up to the situation. To Ross, Williams didn't seem to fully appreciate the gravity of their predicament. The company was several kilometers back from the berm and really had no way of seeing how close the Iraqi vehicles actually were. The Iraqis were always up to some mischief in Kuwait, and Williams had no reason to believe that this night would be any different. It was probably just a lost Iraqi platoon banging around out there. He called back to Ross and told him that the tanks didn't appear to be an immediate threat.

Ross was apoplectic: "No immediate threat? *Fuuuuuckkk!*"

All radio protocol broke down at this point, and Ross began screaming expletives into the handset, "No threat? I know what a fucking threat is. I'm staring right at one, motherfucker!" The tanks were firing through the berm gaps, the rounds thundering over the Marines' heads. Machine-gun rounds were slowly but surely beginning to find their way to the horseshoe.

After several minutes of this heated exchange, Ross managed to coax the LAVs forward. They had some ground to cover, so it would be a little while. En route, Williams requested that Ross mark his position with an infrared strobe. This was a nearly universal control measure, and the LAVs, which had night sights mounted on their hulls, would be able to pick up the infrared flashes, thereby designating the DRP's position and forestalling any intramural fire between recon and the LAVers. Further, Williams informed Ross that as the company got closer, they would fire their 25-mm chain guns over recon's heads to cover their escape.

Ross sent Lance Corporal Pacheco out with a wallet-size infrared strobe light to the mouth of the horseshoe. As soon as Pacheco activated the beacon, tank rounds began impacting all around the Marines. One of the T-62 rounds whizzed right over the five-ton truck. Noticing the increasingly accurate barrages, Pacheco quickly snapped off the device. It appeared as if, contrary to all intelligence, the Iraqis had night-vision scopes after all. They would have to attempt to talk the LAVs in via radio, a challenging proposition at the moment.

Gillispie, meanwhile, fed up with all this apparent inaction, began collecting up Marines to go strike at the converging tanks with their remaining AT-4s. He saw that the AT-4s weren't doing any damage, but they at least had the benefit of rattling and confusing the Iraqis and, anyway, anything was better than sitting around and waiting for some raghead to get lucky. He figured they could hide in the buildings, crank off a few rockets, and maybe knock off some of their treads, immobilizing them. Something had to be done; just sitting around was making the Marines apprehensive, and Gillispie could see it in their faces. As this hastily assembled patrol began to move out, Ross spotted them, pointedly asking the staff sergeant, "Where do you think you're going?"

"To go kill some some tanks, sir."

The last thing Ross wanted was for the platoon to get split up again or for half of the platoon to get decisively engaged right as the other half was preparing to evacuate, imperiling both. It was the old mantra again: *Bring all your men back alive.* Ross told him to stand fast.

8

Approximately 9:00 P.M., January 29, 1991,
Observation Post 4

*There are many shades in the danger of adventures and gales, and
it only now and then that there appears on the face of facts a sinister violence of intention—that indefineable something which forces
it upon the mind and the heart of a man, that this complication of
accidents or these elemental furies are coming at him with a purpose of malice, with a strength beyond control, with an unbridled
cruelty that means to tear out of him his hope and his fear, the pain
of his fatigue and his longing for rest: which means to smash, to destroy, to annihilate all he has seen, known, loved, enjoyed, or hated;
all that is priceless and necessary—the sunshine, the memories, the
future; which means to sweep the whole precious world utterly away
from his sight by the simple and appalling act of taking his life.*
—JOSEPH CONRAD, *Lord Jim*

THE FIRE emerging from recon's position was a sight to behold. As Pollard watched, stitches of red tracers arced
gracefully into the black sky and were quickly answered by
the thunderous rushes of the Iraqi tanks. Like lightning their
fire came out of the night against recon's puny machine guns.
It was inconceivable that they might actually hurt the tanks,
but the small bore fire, crimson and irregular, persisted
nonetheless. The Iraqis were shooting Sabot rounds, which
because they were designed to pierce the thick laminate steel
of American tanks, were punching straight through the
buildings of the observation post and emerging like blazing
evil comets out the other side. The rounds would skitter
across the desert floor before finally detonating in the sand.
In the desert, at night, such strange symphonies of fire can be
beautiful; beautiful and deeply dreadful, especially when
one arrives at the cold realization that it is exactly these
things that will end a man.

Now Lieutenant Scott Williams came up on the company tac, telling the captain that recon was under fire and requesting Delta's immediate assistance. To Williams, Ross sounded panicky and he seemed to have lost control over his men. They clearly weren't responding to his flares, and he was desperate for Delta to come up and provide covering fire for them, which would take some of the pressure off and allow them to effect their escape. Ross apparently thought it was no big deal for LAVs to go head-to-head against the much heavier Iraqi tanks.

Pollard was now caught in the quandary of his life. Scared, tired, mad, confused, frustrated, and with a balefully incomplete understanding of the situation, he now had to decide whether to take his LAVs, which were never designed to lock horns with tanks, into the attack against the largest Iraqi armored force he'd ever heard of. He had no idea what recon's true disposition was, didn't know what had transpired at the police post, didn't know what had caused recon to open up, didn't know what else the Iraqis had in store for them. Earlier that afternoon, he had watched Lieutenant Ross drive up in a single Humvee to coordinate with him, but in the rush to get his company deployed before the light failed, he had neglected to ask Ross if he had enough transportation for all of his Marines. He didn't even know if Ross had an entire platoon up on the berm or if it was just a single five-man team. And because Ross's platoon was equipped with an older type of radio set, the only way Pollard would be able to talk to them was by relaying his calls through Lieutenant Williams. This relay ate up precious time, and inevitably messages got distorted as they passed from one end of the chain to the other like a child's game of Operator.

Still, Pollard couldn't simply ignore recon's pleas. He had to do something. Before, he had planned to square off a safe distance away from the border and, capitalizing on the incredible range of Vitale's TOWs, simply destroy any Iraqis that tried to cross through the gap in the berm adjacent to the police post.* He knew that without an intense engineering effort, the Iraqis would be unable to cross over the berm at any other point. Thus, controlling the berm gap became the decisive element to defending OP 4. Pollard figured that while he fought that fight, Lieutenant Williams could work on getting them air support. They were miles and mapsheets beyond the reach of any friendly artillery, but once some American air arrived, their troubles would be over.

This prim, elegant plan had been rendered totally irrelevant by recon's incomprehensible machine-gun volleys. Now the Iraqis knew where they were and were coming to the fight with knockout force. Delta would now be forced to abandon the safety of their dug-in positions and launch into the fray with friendlies caught between them and the enemy. Recon had screwed up, and now they were paying the price, caught in a slow-moving vice with Delta on one end and the Iraqis on the other. It was a shitty situation and Pollard hated every bit of it.

Pollard called over to Vitale and informed him that he and Lieutenant Kendall's Second Platoon were punching up to the border to go get recon and that he would need half of Vitale's TOW vehicles to follow in trace to provide protective long-range fire. Pollard stressed that he wanted a solid overwatch set up so as to allow his LAV-25s to sprint up and snatch recon before things got too hairy and mixed up. It would be a tricky operation but hopefully one that could be brought to a swift conclusion. They would be safely back from the border and under the umbrella of the American air armada before they knew it. As a final preparatory measure, Pollard ordered his logistics trains, the fuel truck, the recovery vehicle, the drinking water trailer, and the headquarters

---

*TOWs had the capability to destroy vehicles out to 3,750 meters (2.33 miles). The longest range of any Soviet-produced tank was just shy of 3,000 meters. This far from accidental circumstance allowed American gunners to employ "standoff" tactics, i.e., simply destroying enemy vehicles while staying out of range of the Iraqis' main gun rounds. As the Iraqis advanced, American forces could simply retreat incrementally, plinking enemy tanks all the while.

Humvees, led by First Sergeant Alfonso Villa, to displace safely back a ways from the fight.

The voice of Sergeant Nick Vitale, fresh from the Jersey shore, crackled over the net: "Alpha Group, stand by for bounding overwatch. Green section will lead. Red One will be their fourth Victor. We're goin' in for a better look, over." There followed a few moments of chatter as Vitale switched over to Delta's tac net and talked with Pollard about the coming movement. "Okay, Green element, stow your turrets, let's move." Sergeant V. released the radio controls. Jimmy Boileau, Red 1's driver, floored it, giving the hog a quick burst of horsepower to wrench its 14 tons up out of the hole in the sand where it rested.

Vitale switched over to the intercom. "Brown, you better be the first one on target and giving me a report."

"Aren't I always, Sergeant V.?" Brown said. He sat in his turret, going over his controls as they bounced across the desert floor toward Kuwait. "Hey, Crosby," he whispered, "you got the next two missiles ready?"

"Yeah. You think we'll need 'em?"

"I hope not, but if I fire off the two in the turret, I sure as hell won't feel like waiting for the next two."

"Gotcha. Just gimme the word and I'll have you loaded in a heartbeat."

"You'll know when I'm ready, don't worry." Brown redirected his attention down to the turret controls, which looked disturbingly like a popular arcade game apparatus. *Anytime now . . .*

After they had rolled forward a few kilometers, Sergeant V. clicked back over to the TOW net, "Green Element, Icecube! Say again, Icecube!" Icecube was the code word for all TOW vehicles to halt, erect and stabilize their turrets, and begin scanning the horizon for targets. Brown had his turret up and moving in no time.

Leaving Sadowski's platoon of six LAVs to hold down the fort, Pollard, along with 2nd Platoon, launched up to the border and the uncertainty that lay with it. Pollard rolled up immediately after delivering the attack order. He had been behind at his traditional commander's position, perched several hundred meters back from the main company screen line to better observe the night's events. Leading the charge, Pollard zoomed right through the company lines, pointing the way with his hog to the southeast.

Soon after they crossed the start line, things began to get disorganized. Standing halfway out of the gunner's turret hatch, Sergeant Gilmore, who had begun referring to himself Pollard's "bodyguard" after the Plan Purple affair, was hollering into the company tac, trying vigorously to get all the surging vehicles back on line. They weren't running hell-for-leather, but somehow everyone had managed to get out of true. What was supposed to be a reinforced platoon on-line attack now looked more like a lazy wedge, with Pollard as the point vehicle. This seemingly trivial misalignment, within the context of a fluid nighttime armored engagement, was not a minor concern. With nerves and adrenaline running at an all-time high, it would be shockingly easy for one of the hogs to get turned around, separated, or cut off from the company in the smothering blackness and find itself and its crew with shaky comm and fighting against the world to make it back in. As T. E. Lawrence once remarked about a similar ominous evening in the Arabian desert, "It was a night to despair of movement."

While they were en route, Vitale updated the enemy count to 75 vehicles.

9

Nighttime, January 29, 1991, Riyadh, Saudi Arabia,
250 Miles South of Observation Post 4

> *Octavius: Now, Antony, our hopes are answered.*
> *You said the enemy would not come down,*
> *But keep the hills and upper regions.*
> *It proves not so. Their battles are at hand;*
> *They mean to warn us at Philippi here,*
> *Answering before we do demand of them.*
>
> *Messenger: Prepare you, generals.*
> *The enemy comes on in gallant show.*
> *Their bloody sign of battle is hung out,*
> *And something is to be done immediately.*
> —WILLIAM SHAKESPEARE, *Julius Caesar*

AT THE tactical air command center in Riyadh, the Coalition air headquarters for the war, it was business as usual. Warnings of a major Iraqi incursion had been filtering in for days, but General H. Norman Schwarzkopf's air planners, under the command of Air Force Lieutenant General Chuck Horner had other concerns.* Schwarzkopf had ordered that the Iraqis' vaunted Republican Guard divisions be degraded to 50 percent of their original combat strength before the invasion of Kuwait, and there were literally thousands of air missions to attend to if this goal was to be achieved. Consumed with this and intent upon solving the persistent Scud missile problem, Horner's jets had left Kuwait and the Iraqi III Corps untouched. A mere three

---

*On January 22, a powerful experimental radar plane, the Joint Surveillance Target Attack Radar System, or JSTARS, had detected 320 Iraqi armored vehicles entering the al-Wafra oil fields in Kuwait, a mere eight miles from the Saudi border. No action was taken by the Air Force in response to this discovery.

hours before Ross and the Deep Reconnaissance Platoon came under attack, Horner sent off a message to Schwarzkopf: "We're well into our attack on the Republican Guards. It is not going to be spectacular. It's going to be a lot of work. We'll fight the weather the next couple of days but keep the pressure on the Republican Guards. It's the target. When we have the Republican Guards in the bag, *then we'll turn our attention to the ground forces in Kuwait* [italics added]."*

Horner went to bed before the reports from OP 4 reached Riyadh. Sometime after midnight, one of Horner's deputies, Brigadier General Buster Glosson, checked in at the air operations center to see how the night's sorties were shaping up. He was stunned to hear reports of Iraqi tank columns attacking into Saudi Arabia. It looked to be a major effort, encompassing most of the border region from OP 6, in the west, all the way to the town of Khafji on the Persian Gulf coast. Nevertheless, judging by the mood in the command center, it was difficult to tell that a major battle was being fought; a strange complacency prevailed over the air controllers, as if this were all just another exercise.

Air strikes were being directed toward the border but only in a piecemeal fashion. Horner's air controllers were responding to Marine requests, but no larger battle plan had been put together. No decisive action had been taken for over three hours. None of the air controllers on duty that night had even bothered to warn Horner or Glosson that a major Iraqi offensive was under way. Virtually every airfield on the Arabian peninsula was jammed with Coalition aircraft, four carrier battle groups were poised in the Gulf, and no effort was being made to mobilize them. The greatest air force in the history of warfare was sitting idle while Marines battled Iraqi main battle tanks with rifles.

Glosson called Horner immediately and told him that the Iraqis had charged into Saudi Arabia.

---

*After seizing Kuwait, Saddam's Republican Guard had been repositioned just north of the Iraq-Kuwait border to act as a strategic reserve.

* * *

Over at the Light-Armored Infantry battalion command post, twenty miles south of Observation Post 4, operations officer Major Jeff Powers heard Delta's Company's frenzied radio calls of "Tanks! Tanks! Tanks!" and thought, *Aw, fuck, the only thing between them and Kibrit is us.* Pollard and he were good friends, and as Delta became more and more engaged, Powers radioed over to try and get a handle on the situation, calling Pollard by his nickname: "Hero, Hero, this is Wolfpack. How you doing, buddy?"

After getting an update from Pollard, Powers, the battalion commander's right-hand man, ordered his staff to break down the command post tent and prepare for a fight. He didn't know where the Iraqis were coming from. For all he knew, they could be behind them already. This whole thing had caught everyone off guard, even the Air Force with all its powerful surveillance aircraft and satellites. It seemed odd to Powers that it was the Marines on the ground with nothing but their bare eyeballs who were putting the picture together. *If all the intel geeks had missed this one, who the hell knew what else they had coming their way?*

This was what he'd come to expect from higher headquarters. Most of the "intelligence" they received was simply repackaged information that they had forwarded up the chain several days prior. As far as Powers was concerned, whatever the Marines out on the screen line were reporting was the latest intelligence.

Soon enough, Powers started receiving spot reports from his other company commanders. Bravo Company to the south was reporting enemy movement to their front. Charlie Company, in transit from Khafji to OP 6, also had Iraqi tanks on their horizon. Powers had a full plate, but he was ready. A scrappy, rough-tongued officer, Powers was born for the fight. Considered tactically gifted by many of his peers, he was the consummate operations officer, always in command of the relevant facts, ready to brief the CO at a moment's notice. He was beloved by the Marines of Delta Company for the battalion pit wrestling matches he organized and for his rugged, frequently profane sense of humor. He often ran around the battalion area sporting a plastic Viking helmet with fake purple hair cascading out the back.

Powers told the Bravo Company commander to spread his vehicles out. They had a lot of ground to cover and gaps to fill if they were going to save Kibrit. A single tank leaking through would wreak havoc on the supply dump. He gave the Alpha Company commander an update and told him that he'd be in reserve, in the bullpen until his company was needed to plug whatever gaps developed or to exploit the Iraqi flank.

Meanwhile, in the 2nd Marine Division sector, 15 miles east of OP 4 at OP 2, the recon Marines manning the police post watched the flashes from the fight at OP 4 on the horizon and decided to get out while they could.

Much as at OP 4, there was an LAV covering force south of the berm positioned to blunt the advance. With the exit of recon, the 2nd Marine Division force, led by Lieutenant Colonel Keith Holcomb, became the first line of defense. As the reports of Iraqi penetrations all along the border reached Holcomb in his command vehicle, he ordered his companies into a horseshoe-shaped defense oriented to the north, a move that enabled him to cover the border as well as his flanks. The Marines could hear the Iraqi tanks moving on the horizon, but no one could get a visual. The Marines sat looking through their nightscopes waiting for the Iraqis to appear.

General Chuck Krulak, the head Marine logistics officer in the Gulf, had been worried for some time that the Iraqis would learn of Kibrit and attack the exposed supply base, demolishing the Marines' offensive plans. When he learned of the Iraqi mechanized assault, Krulak was convinced that Kibrit was the objective. He immediately ordered the base to 100 percent alert, marshaling clerks, typists, and truck drivers to man a hastily formed defensive line north of the sprawling supply hub. The Saudi and Qatari armored units that had been tasked to protect Kibrit had cut and run earlier that evening, leaving the poorly outfitted support Marines to fend for themselves. Armed with only disposable rocket launchers and small arms, every Marine, male and female, responded to the crisis.

Reflecting on the depth of his predicament, Krulak radioed over to the Second Marine Division and requested that a tank force be dispatched immediately. Bill Keys, the division commanding general, radioed back personally to inform Krulak that he could have a company of M1A1 tanks out his way in an hour. Help was on the way, but it would take some time.

Around midnight, a detachment of Marines from Kibrit, who had been erecting a prisoner-of-war camp for Iraqi soldiers to the north, put all the shotguns, rifles, and machine guns and several sets of night-vision goggles into a pile and blew them up with plastic explosives, falling back to Kibrit to avoid capture.

Back at Kibrit, the Marines were ordered to don gas masks. They watched, tensed behind a defensive berm, as bright flashes from OP 4 reflected in the night sky to the north.

10

Approximately 9:15 P.M., January 29, 1991,
Observation Post 4

Cyrus took Adam to walk with him one late afternoon, and the black conclusions of all his study and his thinking came out and flowed with a kind of thick terror over his son. He said, "I'll have you know that a soldier is the most holy of all humans because he is the most tested—most tested of all. I'll try to tell you. Look now—in all history men have been taught that killing men is an evil thing not to be countenanced. Any man who kills must be destroyed because this is a great sin, maybe the worst sin we know. And then we take a soldier and put murder in his hands and we say to him, 'Use it well, use it wisely.' We put no checks on him. Go out and kill as many of a certain kind of classification of your brothers as you can. And we will reward you for it because it is a violation of your early training.
—JOHN STEINBECK, *East of Eden*

ZOOMING IN rapidly after the Icecube call, Joshua Brierly,* the TOW gunner for Green 1, had an Iraqi tank in his sights almost immediately. Ranging away from Green 1 at just under 3,000 meters, this singular vehicle presented a grave dilemma for the Marines. The original thought had been to move up to the border and lie in wait for the Iraqis to approach just outside of TOW range. The Iraqis, blundering in the darkness, would wade right into the Marine engagement zone and be cut to ribbons by a missile ambush from vehicles they would never see. The Delta boys would watch as one by one the Iraqi tanks were pulverized by Vitale's TOWs. But now, in defiance of all reason and topography, Brierly was reporting to his vehicle commander that an Iraqi main battle tank rested squarely in his crosshairs less than two miles away. This was just under the range of a Soviet

---

*Not his real name.

T-80 tank. The Marines were exposed, and something had to be done immediately. Silently and without warning, the tables had been turned.

Brierly's vehicle commander, Sergeant Michael Wissman, who was also the TOW group's second-in-command, called over to Vitale, "My gunner has a tank at three thousand meters. Request permission to engage, over."

"Roger, wait one."

A few hundred meters away, in Red 1, Nick Vitale sat in the vehicle commander's cockpit thinking. He knew Brierly well. Brierly had been his gunner for some time before breaking his arm changing an LAV tire immediately prior to deploying. Because of the broken arm, Brierly was unable to deploy with the main body of the battalion over to Saudi Arabia. To his dismay, when Brierly rejoined the TOW group several weeks later, he was reassigned to another vehicle, away from the much-admired Sergeant V. A ferocious competitor, Brierly had always been one of the best in the group at armor identification and was a quick shot, rapidly scoring kills in the TOW simulators that the Marines trained with. He had a few years of college under his belt and was a confident, even brash young operator who was held in high esteem by both officer and enlisted.

It seemed that it was always Jason Brown, Scottie Pruett, or Brierly vying for perceived title of Best TOW Gunner, struggling ever upward on the invisible pyramid that all the gunners carried with them inside. Who could have their turret up, stabilized, and with a target in their sights the quickest? Who knew the most armored vehicles? Who had more thoroughly mastered the quirks and idiosyncrasies of the turret's hydraulic system?

Vitale mulled this strange contact over. *How had the Iraqis rolled up so close on them without them knowing? Were there other Iraqis lurking? How had they missed this lone tank?* Vitale knew that Brierly saw something. *He was a good Marine. He wasn't just making this tank up.*

Still, Vitale felt compelled to double-check the young gunner, and despite the mounting pressure to get the shot off, he ordered Brown and Pruett from nearby Green 4 to conduct a thorough search of the immediate area to confirm Brierly's distance to target. Both traversed their motorized turrets a full 360 degrees in search of the tank.

"Whatcha got, Brown?" Vitale demanded.

"I got nothing, Sergeant V. There isn't anything within four thousand meters of us."

"What the fuck is Brierly seeing, then?"

"Fuck if I know."

"Bullshit, Brown. Find it or I'll rip you right out of that turret and find it myself."

Wissman repeated his call: "Red One, this is Green One, permission to engage, over."

Following Vitale's orders, Brown did another 360 with his turret. Still nothing.

"Green One, Red One, wait one . . . break-break . . . Green Four, Red One, over."

"This is Green Four," Pruett replied.

"Roger, Green Four, whatcha got over there?"

"Negative on Green One's target. The only targets we have are way outta range, over."

Pruett had also been unable to locate Brierly's tank. His vehicle commander, Brian Smith, had even had him zero in on Green 1 in an attempt to divine what direction Brierly's hammerhead-shaped turret was facing. Pruett knew it was real easy to forget to look down at your bezel ring and see which direction you were pointing. Brierly's call just didn't sound right. It was way too close.

Over at Green 1, Sergeant Mike Wissman's patience was running out. He thought the entire evening up to this point had been a total clusterfuck. When he'd first heard that there were tanks across the berm, he'd expected that Captain Pollard would simply call in some air strikes and the Marines would get to watch a cool fireworks show. *Why the fuck were they going up to the berm only now? Why hadn't they moved up to the berm in the daylight?* They were outgunned and outnumbered four or five to one. To attack under these circumstances was insanity, like taking a knife to a gunfight. As they approached the berm in the dark, everyone seemed to be falling off-line. Vehicles were going all over the place. It was all he could do to maintain visual contact with the two LAV-25s nearest him.

When Brierly first reported the tank, Wissman had had his doubts. The Iraqis were at 6,000 meters one minute and then somewhere under 3,000 the next? It just didn't add up. Nevertheless, it would have taken a virtual eternity for Wissman to yank Brierly out of the turret, get oriented to the TOW sight picture, and acquire the target himself, so that wasn't an option. And throughout the endless deliberation over the net, Brierly hadn't wavered; he remained emphatic about his call. After interrogating Brierly several times, Wissman concluded that he must be on the money. Brierly was one of the best. He'd never been wrong before. It was time to go with this thing. "Red One, this is Green One, request permission to fire, over," Wissman said, his voice rich with adrenaline.*

Vitale came back, "Roger, Green One, break-break . . . all Green Victors . . . prepare to volley fire . . . I will contact Delta Six, so stand by. Red One out." Vitale switched over to talk with Pollard, who, after listening to him describe the situation, cleared him to fire. He switched back over to the TOW net, "All Green Victors, stand by." Brierly, Brown, and Pruett, each with his own target, waited, their fingers tensed over triggers for Vitale's command. They didn't have to wait long.

The missiles roared over the desert plain.

Meanwhile, over in Lieutenant Dave Kendall's 2nd Platoon, Bill Covington was standing out of his vehicle's rear scout

---

*It is imperative to note here the fundamental discrepancies between the various accounts of this event. Both Brown and Pruett claimed to have been unable to locate the tank Brierly had acquired. However, Vitale insists that both Brown and Pruett confirmed Brierly's target and agreed with his call. When pressed, Wissman was unable to remember if any other gunners confirmed Brierly's target. Joshua Brierly declined to be interviewed. Vitale also recalled that Brown had fired and missed an Iraqi tank prior to the Icecube call. Vitale therefore thought it plausible that an Iraqi tank had indeed rolled up on them and that Brierly's sighting was accurate.

hatch, watching the TOW section move toward the berm through his binoculars. Covington had listened in on the radio exchange as the first TOW gunner came over the net saying he had a tank within range. Prior to the movement he'd seen recon's tracers burning bright in the blackness and saw several Marine AT-4 rockets blaze off toward the Iraqi tanks. He'd listened in as recon reported being engaged at point-blank range and to Pollard's response saying, "Recon needs help up there. We need to get up and engage for recon now."

Covington's hog was the leftmost one in the platoon screen line. As they deployed southeastward toward the police post, he watched the LAV-TOWs come up alongside them, racing toward the melee. The Iraqi fire was so intense as they bounded forward that Covington assumed that the Iraqis must have blown past recon in the gap in the berm and were now gunning for him and his comrades. It came as no surprise when Pollard cleared the TOWs to fire.

Covington's wingman, the TOW vehicle Green 2, led by Corporal Ismael Cotto, had just moved forward of his LAV by about 25 meters. Covington watched as Cotto's hog and another TOW behind him fired. Then he heard a noise behind him, and as he turned toward the noise, he saw a fireball rocketing over the desert floor. Blasting furiously across in front of him, the missile missed his vehicle by mere meters before slamming straight into the back of Green 2.

Covington was knocked down by the heat and force of the explosion. *Oh fuck oh fuck oh fuck oh fuck. How had the missile not hit him? It was so damn close.*

After watching Green 2 erupt, Covington was convinced that a TOW had just destroyed it. Straight away he jumped back down into his hog, buttoned up all the hatches, and waited for the next missile to come blasting through the rear troop door.

Covington listened in on his headset, the sounds of combat flooding the company net. Staticky panic and confusion buzzed in his ears. "We got a vehicle destroyed! The Iraqis just destroyed one of our vehicles! The Iraqis just destroyed one of our vehicles!" Then to his horror he heard, "I have another Iraqi tank in range. Am I cleared hot?"

There was no doubt in Covington's mind that his vehicle was going to be the next to die. He screamed into his headset, "Check his fire! Check his fire! He's gonna kill us! He's gonna kill us!"

Rock Pollard saw the whole thing. He and 2nd Platoon were heading to go get recon when he saw Green 2, to his left rear, stop and raise its turret. If the LAV-TOW vehicle had a fatal flaw, it was that owing to the delicate optics contained in the turret, it was unable to move and acquire targets at the same time. Pollard passed right by the halted vehicle, and as he passed, the vehicle fired off a TOW. At the same moment Pollard saw several large muzzle flashes across the berm.

As Pollard turned back, there was nothing but glitter as Green 2 was ripped apart. There was no fire, nothing, just a blinding flash. Pollard reported back to Battalion, "I think I just lost a TOW." Pollard knew then that an Iraqi tank had destroyed Green 2.

Jason Brown depressed the trigger and began counting to himself after his missile left the tube. After the initial thermal whiteout from the TOW's hot exhaust, he began tracking his missile's progress. *One . . . two . . . three . . . BOOM!— What the fuck—five . . . six . . .*

"Red One, this is Green One. Target destroyed, over."

Vitale was timing the missile tracks as well. When Brierly's missile impacted so soon, he knew something was amiss. The missile hadn't even gone for three seconds. Even for a tank that close the missile's flight should have been several seconds longer. All the other missiles were still rocketing off toward the horizon. At eleven seconds, Brown and Pruett's missiles were still going. Finally at 23 seconds, Brown's missile impacted. Pruett's exploded soon afterward. Brown hoped he'd hit something but knew that at that range he couldn't be certain. They had probably just scared the crap out of some Iraqis. They were simply too far to expect to get any confirmed kills at this distance.

Seconds later, Vitale heard a Marine over Delta's tac net say, "Hey, I think one of the TOWs just blew up!" Vitale knew then what had happened. He jumped back on the radio: "Alpha Group, report, over."

All the vehicles in the group started checking in:

"Red Two, roger."

"Red Three, roger."

"Red Four, roger."

"Green One, roger."

Silence.

Then after a long pause, *"Green Four, roger."*

The vehicle named Green 3 had been down for maintenance for some time and hadn't made the trek up to OP 4. The only vehicle unaccounted for was Green 2. Vitale started calling over to Cotto's vehicle.

"Green Two, this is Red One, over."

"Green Two, Red One."

"Green Two, Red One."

More silence.

It soon became apparent to everyone what had happened. Green 1 had just killed Green 2.

Over in Red 1, Jason Brown rolled his head back. Closing his eyes, he thought about his best friend, Daniel Walker, on Green 2. That Christmas Eve, Walker had given Brown a tin of Copenhagen tobacco from the States that his grandparents had sent him. Stateside Copenhagen or simply "stateside" was prized for its freshness over the plastic can tobacco carried in the PX, which tasted like sawdust. As far as the Marines were concerned, stateside was worth its weight in gold. Walker had also passed along a blue, bonded leather King James Bible sent by his grandparents, saying simply, "What am I gonna do with this thing? I never believed any of it." Brown and Walker had talked about God before, but mostly they had talked about fixing up Walker's 1973 Camaro. The car was pure white up front and bled into black as you went toward the rear. The California license plate said it all: "FAD2BLK."

Also on Green 2 was a scrappy young lance corporal named Dave Snyder. Snyder had been with Vitale's group for only a few weeks. He'd originally been assigned to another section, but after his vehicle was deadlined with mechanical problems, Vitale approached him in the battalion area one day and asked him if he wanted a job. One of the most popular Marines in the company, Snyder had been doing chicken-shit details for weeks. To Vitale's way of thinking, Snyder was way too good a gunner to be sitting in the rear handing out water jugs. Vitale snatched him up, using him to replace a lackluster gunner who'd been with Green 2 since they came to the desert. Private Scott Schroeder, also on Green 2, was brand new to the group as well. Corporal Ismael Cotto, Green 2's commander, was married with two children.

Brown hadn't known Cotto well, but once he'd shown him a picture of his young daughter wearing his dress Alpha uniform. She was swimming in it, of course, and the round green cover drooped over her ears. It was one of those painfully cute snapshots that under normal circumstances might mean really nothing, but cut off in the desert, months and thousands of miles away from everything you loved, it somehow encapsulated the warm totality of home in all its innocence and perfection.

Brown had to stop his vehicle's medical corpsman from jumping out to go help Green 2. It was no use, Brown told him, and explained what happens when a TOW missile hits an LAV. A TOW was designed to kill the most heavily armored vehicles in the world and would probably rip right through an LAV-TOW, detonating each of the 14 individual TOW missiles stored inside. Each missile contained 6.8 pounds of Octol, one of the most explosive substances known to man. Not only were Cotto, Snyder, Schroeder, and Walker all dead, but there probably weren't any pieces of them larger than a baseball left.

Then, within the minds of all of them, came the questions. Vitale, Wissman, Brown, Pruett, Puterbaugh, all the TOW

Marines thought: *How could this have happened? Did Brierly not have his eyepiece correctly focused? Had he selected the wrong magnification setting? Was his image-transfer assembly out of whack? Had Brierly been sighted in on a tank all along? Had the missile malfunctioned? How could Brierly not have seen that it was an LAV? How? How? How? The bootest gunner in the world could distinguish between a tank and an LAV. It was so obvious that it didn't need to be taught.*

Then Brown remembered the last call he'd heard from Green 2. They were in a bad spot and were moving up to get in a place with better observation. After that, nothing. Perhaps their radio had died. It had happened before, Vitale thought. The vehicles had been having problems with their batteries. Maybe their whole electrical system had died. Or maybe just their radios. Maybe they had been able to receive but not transmit. It was possible that Green 2 had heard the entire dialogue and knew that Brierly was disoriented and were powerless to prevent it. Maybe they had been preparing to abandon their stricken hog before the missile impacted. The possibilities swirled and spun, generating new permutations of theories as the seconds ticked by. But there wasn't time to think of these things now. Recon was still in trouble and the Iraqis were still coming.

Brierly, in shock, was no longer responding to Wissman's commands. Wissman told his loader to pull Brierly out of the gunner's seat and take over as gunner.

Over in Blaze of Glory, Ron Tull was buttoned up inside and looking through his three night-vision blocks. First Platoon hadn't gone up with the captain, so he, along with the other eight vehicles in the platoon, watched as half the company advanced toward the police post. He could hear the radio chatter as one of the Marines called over to Captain Pollard requesting permission to fire. Both Lieutenant Williams and Pollard came up now, asking, "Are you sure? What's its location? Are you sure it's an enemy vehicle?" Tull, along with every other Delta Marine, had sat through endless hours of armor identification classes and figured the Marine requesting to fire must know what he was talking about.

Tull just happened to be looking through his rightmost vision block, and as he watched, the one vehicle he happened to have laid eyes on went up in a ball of flames. Tull and everyone else inside "Blaze of Glory" were jubilant, screaming and hollering in celebration. Scratch one Iraqi tank!

A strange, deathly silence followed. Tull had been watching the LAV-TOWs advance toward the border and had at first wanted to believe that it was an Iraqi, but deep down he knew otherwise. He flipped the switch to the intercom to talk to Sergeant Garett Mongrella, his vehicle commander. "That wasn't an enemy tank, Mongo."

"Shut up, Tull."

"No, I'm serious, that wasn't an Iraqi! They just shot one of our freakin' TOWs!"

There was radio traffic still going, and Sergeant Mongrella, who had concerns of his own, didn't have time to listen to his driver just now. "Don't freak out on me, Tull."

"I'm telling you, dude, they just shot one of our TOWs!"

Then, perhaps having heard reports from Vitale over the radio, Mongrella came back, "I got it, Tull. I got it. I got it."

As Miguel Roche listened to Lieutenant Ross's pleas for relief being ignored by the LAV commander, the reality of how truly alone they were began to sink in. No one in a position to assist them seemed to understand how desperate the situation had become. They had managed to squeeze an airstrike in but the Iraqis looked to be shaking off the blow and pressing on with their attack. It almost seemed as if the A-6 attack which had struck behind some of the tanks was in fact driving the Iraqis into the recon Marines. Radio communication with outside units was still spotty. Some Harrier jump jets were inbound but incredibly the pilots were holding off and asking for bomb damage assessments, a request which would have required the Marines to leave the horseshoe to survey the damage that Cummings and Kies had inflicted, further exposing themselves to fire just so the pilots, safely ensconced at 10,000 feet, would have a warm and fuzzy about the mission they were about to run.

Lieutenant Ross was feverishly trying to get the situation sorted out but in the meantime the platoon was immobile and impotent, practically cowering behind a mound of dirt that offered at best fleeting protection from the Iraqi fire. Completing their misery, the Marines were beginning to hear the LAV's 25-mm rounds falling near them. The LAVs were still so far to the rear that Roche figured the coke-bottle-size projectiles were probably running out of momentum and plunging into the sand. Several Marines were now looking over at the lieutenant, saying, "We need to get the fuck outta here, *sir.*"

Sergeant Luis Bench looked over and to his great relief saw that Delta Company's antitank vehicles were moving up. Apparently, their antitank section was leading the charge ahead of the LAV-25s. One of the vehicles was several hundred meters ahead of the others and appeared to be trying to flank the advancing Iraqis. The Marines watched in grateful awe as the LAV-TOWs launched a thunderous volley at the Iraqis. Immediately following this barrage, an enormous white explosion from behind the horsehoe fractured the night in two, lighting up the darkness. This great luminous cloud generated so much light that Gillispie could see his shadow flickering dead against the wall of the earthen berm. Pacheco, who had remained at the mouth of the horseshoe to track Delta's progress with his night-vision goggles suddenly exclaimed, "Holy shit, I think one of the LAVs just shot the other one!"

Roche, who was monitoring the LAV radio nets, listened as a wave of frenetic chatter rose and built, flooding the airwaves. The Marines were stepping all over each other, cutting each others transmissions off, desperately groping for answers as to what had just transpired. The Marines in Delta's command vehicle were convinced that Iraqi tanks had flanked the company and would soon be pressing their attack into the main body of the company. They called over to recon and asked them to help spot the converging Iraqis.

To Roche, this theory seemed highly unlikely. He knew for a fact that no Iraqi tanks had gotten past them and that they didn't have a clear shot over the berm. The DRP was so far forward of Delta Company that they would have easily seen any tanks within striking distance of the LAVs. As Roche listened, Captain Pollard, responding to the rising confusion, halted the company's advance until things could be sorted out.

The DRP's prospects for getting out of this thing in one piece seemed to be rapidly dwindling. The LAVs, the supposed rescue squad, had just shot themselves up and were now frozen in place. Since abandoning their position at the police post, no effective fire had been launched downrange for several minutes. The incoming Iraqi fire seemed to be building in both volume and accuracy. After the infrared strobe fiasco, the Iraqis knew exactly where they were. It was only a matter of time before they zeroed in on the platoon's partially concealed vehicles and blasted them to kingdom come.

Lieutenant Ross was thus presented with a staggering dilemma. Did he and his platoon remain in the relative shelter of the horseshoe, try to put the Harriers to work and hope that the LAVs would come up to take the pressure off? Or did they cut bait and clear out of this spiraling scene, pile into a clutch of laughably thin-skinned vehicles, brave the Iraqi fire and then attempt to pass through a screen line of spooked LAV guys? The 5-ton truck alone was cause for concern. It was so tall it practically had a "please shoot me" sign painted on it. They would be utterly exposed once they left the horseshoe, naked on the coverless plains southwest of the berm. This was the hardest decision Ross had ever had to make but in the end he knew what had to be done: *they had to get the fuck out of there.* The mood of the platoon at this stage was such that they probably couldn't have tolerated further inaction. In combat, sometimes action, any action, be it hasty or flat-out nuts seems preferable to just sitting around doing nothing. Ross didn't have any answers but the rock in his gut seemed to be telling him something.

He told the men to load up. The Marines and Gillispie in particular seemed to be waiting for exactly this call. They were instantly full of life, firing up the vehicles and breaking open the infrared chemlights on the vehicle's front grilles to activate them.

Yelling, "Go! Go! Go!" Ross was the last man out, dragging the thirty-pound radio by its carrying handle as he jumped on the back of the last Humvee in line just as it was pulling away from the horseshoe.

Gillispie was in the lead vehicle with Lance Corporal Abkins at the wheel. For some reason, Abkins seemed incapable of driving in a straight line and the scene quickly devolved into the Laurel and Hardy show with Gillispie yelling, "No no no no. Left left left left . . ." Red Iraqi tracers stitched the night above them as they vacated the area. The LAVs were still a few kilometers back from the border but the recon Marines quickly consumed the ground, knowing that every yard traveled was a yard closer to safety.

Roche was all over Delta's frequencies trying to get comm with them to let them know they were inbound. He'd just seen an LAV get blown away and he didn't want he and his buddies to meet the same fate. As they got closer, the LAVs began firing their 25-mm cannons at them. *Those idiots thought they were the Iraqis!* Abkins and Gillispie banged a hard left, making a beeline to the south to get as far away from the LAVs as possible. They cautiously skirted Delta's lines for several minutes and eventually were able to make their way around the flank of the company near some low gravel hills. They hastily formed a 360-degree perimeter. They appeared to be safe. The Marines breathed easy for a bit, realizing they probably weren't out of this thing yet, but they were at least out of the line of fire.

Sometime around 11:00 that evening, Roche managed to contact the battalion headquarters to update them on all that had transpired. They'd been out of radio contact for nearly three hours and the watch officer proceeded to read Roche the riot act. Battalion had gotten word that something was

amok up at OP 4 and because of the DRP's cowboy reputation assumed that they had been out making mischief and
blowing off the required radio calls. This harangue lasted for
several minutes until Roche blurted out, "We were being
fucking jammed!" The watch officer on the other end got real
quiet after that.

After the death of Green 2, Pollard and Kendall's group of
LAV-25s pressed on with their attack, leaving the wounded
TOW group behind. Someone had to go get recon, and the
fire down at their position wasn't showing any signs of easing up. They began engaging the tanks with their 25-mm
cannons down near the berm. They were less than a kilometer away from OP 4 now. The battle had been raging for
nearly an hour. It was 9:30 P.M.

Lieutenant Kendall could hear American airplanes circling
overhead. As he watched, the first aircraft began making runs
on the advancing Iraqis. Captain Pollard remembers, "It was
strange fighting at night—tracers flew overhead in continu-
ous lines, tanks were silhouetted by their muzzle blasts, and
rounds impacted into the buildings of OP 4. Lead fell everywhere, but you could not see the enemy, just his fire."

As they continued bounding forward, Pollard looked up
and saw something he'd never forget. A sinister black dot
ringed by fire appeared on the horizon and seemed to grow
larger with each passing second. It looked just like a solar
eclipse. Pollard switched over to the intercom and screamed
at his driver, "Mitchell! Left hand down and punch it!"
Lance Corporal Marcus Mitchell whipped the vehicle's
steering bar over and stomped on the gas, shooting the LAV
backward and to the left. As he was turning the hog, an Iraqi
Sagger missile passed down the right side of the vehicle, impacting in the distance behind them. Pollard's gunner came
up, yelling, "What the fuck was that?"

After this close call, Pollard got back on the horn, frantically yelling over to Lieutenant Williams, "What do they
[recon] have for transpo[rtation]? How many of them do we

have to pick up? How close to the buildings do we have to go? Can't they just meet us halfway?" He'd already lost one vehicle, the air armada was still en route, and now they were under heavy missile fire. As he watched, a multitude of Saggers rose in the air.

Pollard by this point was simply furious. In order to get to the police post as rapidly as possible, they'd been forced to advance at an angle perpendicular to the Iraqis' axis, leaving their left flank horribly exposed. In their current posture, Kendall's platoon was every tank gunner's dream. One well-aimed barrage of tank fire could have wiped out their entire formation. All this to save recon.

Fortunately, the Iraqi fire wasn't terribly accurate, although the sheer volume of it was unbelievable, their blue-green tracers forming a nearly solid arc over the OP. As the moments slipped by, the Marines were able to discern the shapes of the Iraqi tanks skulking a few hundred meters beyond the berm, making their run for the breach. The Marines began putting a steady stream of 25-mm fire downrange. Initially, because of their poor night-vision sights, their fire was largely ineffective. The company procedure had always been to have gunners and drivers fully buttoned up, which greatly limited their depth perception, and the vehicle commanders, who were positioned halfway outside their hatches, exposed to enemy fire, would work adjusting them on target using their night-vision goggles. The steady, distinctive sound of the Bushmasters echoed between the hogs—*bop-bop-bop bop-bop-bop*.

But pinging the Iraqis with the 25 millimeters, while gratifying as hell, wasn't solving anything. Pollard needed to resolve this recon question, pull back to the main body of the company, and wait for some serious air to start leveling the playing field.

After several agonizing minutes, Lieutenant Williams came back with an answer to Pollard's query, saying, "Recon has a five-ton and a few Humvees."

"Well, tell 'em to get the fuck outta there!" Pollard responded, incredulous.

"Roger, they're heading back for pickup."

Pollard had everyone lay down cover fire to help recon escape, and the mad moment of fire grew as recon popped off another red firework into the air to signal their position to Delta. Eventually, the Delta Marines were able to discern the dun-colored recon vehicles emerging from the darkness as if from behind a stage curtain. As recon's convoy got closer, Pollard ordered everyone to shift their fire away, giving the recon Marines a safe corridor through which to pass. As Pollard watched with his night-vision goggles, recon exited the scene and bore off to the west toward Quwayrat al-Mashba on the same dirt track that he'd seen Ross approach on that afternoon. Pollard called and informed Battalion that recon was out.

One question had been resolved, but there was still the Iraqi juggernaut to contend with, and Delta was sitting squarely in its path, a situation ripe for further calamity. A full-flushed tactical retreat, the commonsense solution, was out of the question. Pollard knew there was nobody behind him. What they needed right now was a gross wave of good old-fashioned American airpower to start blasting these tanks to Mars. They needed B-52s, A-10s, F-18s, Harriers, Cobra attack helicopters, everything. And they needed it yesterday.

Meanwhile, as recon was making their escape, Lieutenant Williams began shifting Glenn Sadowski's 1st Platoon south to a new position 3,000 meters due west of OP 4. This superior locale allowed them to better suppress the Iraqis and provide cover for Pollard's withdrawal back to Delta's main line of resistance. More and more Allied aircraft were beginning to filter in, and Lieutenant Williams, along with the company's air controller, Corporal Russell Zawalick, began to direct these planes onto OP 4. The Marines, comforted and encouraged after the evening's debacle, could hear the planes wailing overhead. Pollard began a steady retrograde, keeping a regular line of fire on the Iraqis. The ricocheting 25-mm fire looked like distant fireworks as they danced off the iron hulls of the Iraqi tanks.

Eventually Pollard was able to rejoin 1st Platoon and Lieutenant Williams. Pollard then backed the entire company away from the border a couple of thousand meters farther to buy them time and space to maneuver in. His intention was to continue surging air over the police post and develop the situation with the eventual goal of reestablishing their original screen line.

Standing off a good ways from the border, the Marines were able to breathe a little easier. After the throes of first combat and the burning uncertainty, they seemed to have survived this dark encounter in reasonably good style. There had been some tense moments; a few of the Marines driving into the fight found themselves strangely absent, in an odd sort of mind-movie and demanding answers: *Is it time to be scared yet? Shouldn't I be shaking? What the hell am I doing here?*

Tull, who had remained in reserve with 1st Platoon, found the opening shots to be just like training at first. At once, they were moving, shooting, and communicating just as they'd been told. He was frightened, definitely away from his normal state, but the moves and the ease just came to him and those around him as they advanced. It was like muscle memory. There was adrenaline and the distinct awareness of danger, but there was also a distance in every man, a God's-eye camera, watching, as if to record the evening's events for future study. Efficiently, they moved, not knowing what they were doing and yet knowing it completely.

For the Marines of Delta Company proper the night's contest hadn't fully hit home yet. Because the TOW section had only been assigned to the company that evening, they didn't know the men in Green 2 and consequently didn't feel the loss directly. Owing to the seemingly arbitrary administrative divisions between these two units, the grief was isolated to Vitale's crew. Then, as more and more aircraft gathered overhead, forming a towering stack of fast-movers reaching thousands of feet upward, some of the jets began to have trouble finding the Iraqis. The pilots loitering in these first few waves began to get impatient, their fuel gauges hounding them. Imperceptibly, the illusion of cover and safety began to evaporate. In the odd, yawning silence between bombing runs, the evening shifted subtly beneath the Marines' feet.

Approximately 9:30 P.M., January 29, 1991,
Observation Point 4

As a writer who has spent ten years in the Balkans, Angola, and Afghanistan, I am recurrently astonished by the moral dilemmas, the metaphysical weight of the moral dilemmas, placed at very low levels in the chain of command. I owe my life to the fact that a Canadian peacekeeper in Croatia made a particular value choice at a crucial moment. What interests me is how you train people to make these judgment calls in real time, when you have a quarter of a second to do the right thing and a lifetime to live with the wrong thing.
— MICHAEL IGNATIEFF, "Handcuffing the Military?"

T HE FIRST flight to arrive at OP 4 after *Blaze 71* was *Zip-gun 65,* a two-ship formation of Air Force A-10 Thunderbolts, responding to a request from the LAV battalion. The battalion air officer, Captain William Wainwright, had heard reports of tanks at OP 4 and tried to call over to higher headquarters but was stymied when he ran into a blunt wall of Iraqi radio jamming. Eventually he was able to relay a request for aircraft through an airborne command-and-control plane flying near the Gulf coast. As with everything this evening, things were being done on the fly, using methods and means invented one minute and then executed the next.

The Marines watched in awe as the A-10s flitted over the battlefield, the jets seeming to command everything that passed beneath their wings. Without even firing a single shot, they had an enormous effect, bolstering the spirits of everyone on the ground. The A-10, an ugly, straight-winged workhorse designed expressly to kill tanks, was just what the doctor ordered. However, Wainwright was unable to reach Corporal Zawalick through the normal air-support net, and was forced to brief him up over the company's tactical radio network, a vexing and dangerous arrangement that resulted in vital company battle commands being intermixed with instructions to the loitering aircraft. Eventually, through the din, he was able to turn control of the *Zipgun 65* flight over to Zawalick, stationed two feet away from Lieutenant Williams inside Delta's antenna-studded command-and-control LAV, a few hundred meters behind the main screen line.

It didn't take long for another glitch in this scheme to emerge. As Zawalick began to direct *Zipgun 65* onto the Iraqi columns, he was dismayed to learn that unlike the Marine A-6 Intruder aircraft, the Air Force jets lacked potent night-vision equipment with which to acquire targets. And although there was a full moon that evening, there wasn't nearly enough ambient light to distinguish between friend and foe with only the naked eye. The pilots were thus reduced to squinting into a tiny television screen in the cockpit that was wired to an infrared-guided, air-to-ground Maverick missile.* It was a poor ad hoc solution that transformed what could have been a complete rout into an agonizing ordeal for the Marines on the ground. In a war that was being heralded by the Air Force as the beginning of a technology-inspired new age in airpower, the A-10, the Air Force's primary close-air-support platform, had somehow been left behind.

This unfortunate circumstance certainly wasn't making Zawalick's life any easier. A bright and capable young Marine, Zawalick was a rifleman from the 1/9 crew who had been pressed into service as a forward air controller, a billet normally reserved for pilots who have completed a four-year tour with a squadron. Prior to arriving in the desert, he had been tutored in close air support procedures by Captain

---

*The AGM-65D Maverick is the most widely used precision-guided munition in the world. The Maverick carries an electro-optical seeker in its nose that produces a television-like image on a cockpit display. In combat, the pilot selects a target on the display, marks it with a set of crosshairs, and launches the missile. The Maverick then autonomously guides itself to the target, allowing the pilot to safely evacuate the scene. Over 5,000 Mavericks were fired over the course of the Gulf War.

Wainwright, but had not yet had the opportunity to attend the extensive training courses reserved for Marines in his billet. Prior to January 29, he had controlled only a dozen or so simulated training missions at Twentynine Palms. He was just trying to make the best of a shitty situation.

As *Zipgun 65* checked in, Zawalick attempted to orient them, asking if they could spot the police post buildings, the virtual center of the action. He didn't have time to spell it all out for them in the traditional nine-line brief format. This was combat, and Zawalick was just trying to get the pilots generally aimed, give them the enemy's coordinates, and let them know where the friendlies were. However, owing to the breathtaking absence of landmarks around OP 4, the pilots struggled with this seemingly rote assignment. After conducting several passes, *Zipgun 's* flight leader radioed back to Zawalick, informing him that they were unable to locate their mark. Captain Wainwright had briefed the A-10s as they arced inbound to OP 4, so it should have been a relatively simple task to get them spun up on a few particulars and then unleash them on the Iraqis. Zawalick had no other available means to orient them. He didn't have a laser to designate with, and there wasn't a Marine artillery battery within ten map sheets of Umm Hjul to fire a spotting round. He was running out of tricks.

Once again, Delta found themselves on the short end of the stick. They were locked into a mismatched engagement with an invisible foe, and now, even though they had friendly aircraft orbiting overhead, they lacked the proper equipment and personnel and the plain dumb luck to see them through. The Marines had heard rumors that Air Force pilots were dangerous. Hell, the first Purple Heart in the war had been handed out to a corpsman who'd been hit by shrapnel from an errant A-10 strike.* Marines within the company raged at their incompetence. *How could they not find the enemy? Couldn't they see the tracers? Anything southwest of the bor-*

---

*U.S. Air Force A-10s were implicated in several high-profile fratricide incidents during the war, including three involving U.S. Marines.

*der was friendly. Anything northeast of the border was
enemy. What could be simpler?*

For Russell Zawalick this was a tough roll of the dice. He
could just give in, point the pilots in the right direction, and
hope for the best, knowing that they would, in all likelihood,
blast some Iraqis to kingdom come. The temptation to tell
Zipgun 65 to go for it must have been overwhelming, but Zawalick also knew that if he did so, he ran a serious risk of one
of those freewheeling zoomies mistaking one of Delta's LAVs
for an Iraqi tank. And it was exactly that type of thing that
keeps a young forward air controller up late at night. His
buddies would be dead, and it would be his fault.

Then someone in the company came up with the bright
idea of trying to direct the A-10s using the brilliant flashes of
the LAV's 25-mm rounds as they ricocheted off the tanks.
One of the pilots had mentioned that he could see their
rounds impacting and Lieutenant Williams thought that if
they could coordinate their fire, then they could adjust their
aircraft off the flashes and bring them to bear in short order.

Williams quickly turned to, ordering the company to train
their weapons on the tanks nearest the breach. He then ordered one vehicle to fire and coordinated with Vitale's eagle-
eyed TOW gunners to zero in that vehicle's fire onto an Iraqi
tank. The LAV-25's sights weren't powerful enough at that
range, so once again the TOWs played a crucial role in
Delta's continued survival. After getting the first vehicle on
target, Williams would then have the entire company open
up on the lone Iraqi, creating a dazzling shower of sparks
that Zawalick could spot from. After a series of such bursts,
Zawalick would radio the A-10s and ask, "Do you see that?"
and direct them accordingly. It was a crude and laborious
means of arranging close air support, and it forced the A-10s
to peel in from behind the company's screen line and then
follow the tracers in, a violation of established procedures,
but it worked. Zawalick milked three solid runs out of *Zipgun 65* before they were forced to head for the barn. One of
the runs had caught a pair of tanks blitzing for the berm
breach. The A-10s cut into them with their Gatling guns,

their sinister growl reverberating in the chill night air. Along the entire screen line the Marines stopped and watched the secondary explosions as one of the tanks erupted in flame, its Sabot ammunition cooking off inside like a colossal book of matches.

A second pair of A-10s, call sign *Hitman 75,* checked aboard. Zawalick tried to bring the flight around for a Maverick missile run. After several high passes with Williams synchronizing 25-mm fire for them, they still couldn't locate a target. Working as a team, Zawalick and Williams redoubled their efforts. Williams served as an extra set of eyes and ears for Zawalick, standing up outside the vehicle, craning his neck to spot the bird as it whipped over the desert floor. He was just waiting to rope the plane in and clear it hot to fire. He'd seen it a hundred times before—a pilot would be buzzing overhead, casting about to get eyes on the target, and then in a flash he would see it, get his weapon locked on, and then it was lights out for one enemy vehicle.

But this night knew no master and was aggravated by the Iraqi jamming and the fact that Delta and its enemies were now only hundreds of yards apart. At first they had been able to guide the fliers to targets without too much difficulty, but now as the forces converged, the pilots struggled to make sense of the swirling ground clutter. They would come around after completing a dry pass, and Zawalick would try again to describe the Iraqis' position to them. The pilots would then come up and tell Zawalick what they saw. Neither could reconcile the other's descriptions. It was maddening work, like a nightmare game of pin-the-tail-on-the-donkey, with each participant yelling instructions at the other through blistering radio static.

Williams sensed that the battle was entering a new phase. They'd already made contact with the Iraqis, a prime LAV mission; it was now time to begin extricating themselves from the fight and let the air arm work its magic. They were only in the way at this point. Williams had a million things running through his head, but amid the wash of discordant radio calls, he started yanking out maps to figure out where they were going to fall back to. Captain Pollard seemed to him to be in shock ever since Green 2 exploded and was just narrating the play-by-plays to Battalion, almost like a baseball game. Pollard hadn't been talking on the company tac net for a long time.

Time itself seemed to have taken on new meaning as the evening wore on, the seconds compressing themselves into previously unheralded spaces. What seemed like an hour was actually four hours and although Williams had lost all track of time, he knew that something needed to change. Decisive action had to be taken. He knew it was his job to figure out Delta's next move and soon.

Hitman 75 came around again and told Zawalick that he was going to drop a flare, hoping that Zawalick would be able to direct him from the bright marker. A huge, blazing cylinder soon dropped from the sky and lay menacing in the sand. It was the most blatant mark a pilot could hope for. The only problem was it was lying smack in the middle of Delta's screen line, silhouetting their entire position for every Iraqi tank for miles around. Quick as fire, Pollard was on the net, barking out orders for vehicles to displace away from the flare. Thinking that someone had accidentally popped off one of the LAV's smoke grenades, he admonished the Marines over the net. The Iraqi fire, wild and undisciplined before, fastened upon them as never before.

Over in 1st Platoon, Tull noticed that all of a sudden it was daylight outside. He looked over and saw a large, human-size flare. It was the brightest thing he'd ever seen. Sergeant Mongrella told him to start backing up to get away from it. He'd backed the vehicle up 50 or 60 yards when he saw one of his buddies, Jason Baumgardner, out in the desert trying to extinguish the flare. He was out there like some maniacal ditchdigger, furiously hurling sand over the thing with a shovel he'd grabbed off the side of their LAV.

Tull sat there idling for maybe thirty seconds before his vehicle was consumed by fire.

* * *

Zawalick told *Hitman 75* that he'd just marked Delta's position with his flare. He then radioed for him to engage targets 6,000 meters away at an azimuth of 126 degrees magnetic. He hadn't heard back from *Hitman* yet when Lieutenant Williams looked up and said, "There's the launch!" A dumbfounded look spread over Zawalick's face. As Williams turned to look toward the Iraqis, the missile streaked over to "Blaze of Glory," Sergeant Mongrella's vehicle, which erupted in an enormous ball of flames.

Williams was stunned that the missile had landed so close. He grabbed Zawalick and told him to shut *Hitman* down. Zawalick told him that no one he was controlling had fired yet. Williams told him to figure out who had fired the Maverick. Zawalick began spinning to all the air frequencies asking to know who had just shot. No one answered up.

Pollard had watched the A-10s following the tracers in and thought that the night seemed to be winding down. Battalion had informed him that reinforcements were on the way. Alpha Company, commanded by Captain Mike Shupp, was inbound along with a company on Marine tanks from Task Force Ripper off to the east. All he had to do now was delay and keep killing some ragheads and everything would be cool. The situation had calmed down enough that he had just leaned over the side of his hog to heed the call of nature when Blaze of Glory exploded with a fiery flash.

Pollard hopped back into the turret, wrenched his headset back on, and was overwhelmed by the storm of radio traffic buzzing in his ears. People had no idea what the hell was going on. He'd been proud of his Marines all night because of their outstanding radio discipline. Nobody talked unless they had to. No one interrupted anyone else. Suddenly every vehicle was on the net, flooding it with calls: *"Mongrella's been hit! Mongrella's been hit! What the fuck's going on? Where are the fucking Iraqis? Goddamn, sir, goddamn!"*

It took Pollard several minutes to get the net clear, screaming, *"Get off the net! Get off the net! Get off the net! Get off the net!"*

Pollard's first thought was that the Iraqis had flanked them. As the calls gushed forth demanding a withdrawal, he ordered everyone to just fucking hold on while he sorted things out. He thought that because of the flare, the Iraqis had zeroed in on Delta's position, but seeing as how they were still outside of tank range, he had no idea what they could have hit them with. He had Vitale scan their flanks to see if there were any Iraqis lurking in the darkness. The sergeant came back reporting that there were no tanks approaching. Pollard radioed Alpha Company to see if possibly one of their TOWs had fired. This inquiry also came back negative; Alpha was still twelve kilometers away.

Several of the recon Marines noticed the distinctive whine of a different type of jet orbiting overhead. It was now around eleven, the full moon was still shining brightly, and Gillispie spied the unmistakable twin tails of two Air Force A-10 Thunderbolts as they flashed from south to north. These tank-busting bad boys were just what they needed. The beast was rising and higher headquarters was beginning to surge all kinds of attack aircraft out to OP 4. One could just imagine avenging echelons of Allied aircraft lifting off from distant airfields all over Saudi Arabia, rising in spectacular formation with every type of killer high-tech munition dangling beneath their wings.

The A-10s were being controlled by Delta Company, and the DRP Marines watched as they circled overhead several times, attempting to get oriented before making their deadly runs. A few minutes later, the lead A-10 flew along the axis of the company's main screen line, appearing to almost survey it, to take it all in. It then swooped down, dropping a large and powerful flare in the middle of the LAV formation. To Gillispie it all seemed to make sense. The pilot had just designated the location of friendly lines and intended to use the flare as a reference point for his run-in. Nevertheless, this huge flare, much more potent than any the Marines had ever seen, had backlit Delta's entire screen line, making their position plainly obvious to the Iraqis. A Marine from the vehicle nearest the flare hopped out and frantically started shoveling sand over it, trying to snuff it out. The DRP Marines watched in puzzlement over these proceedings.

As the Marine continued to shovel, a violent explosion rocked the desert floor. The explosion was so massive that the DRP guys could feel the full flush of heat against their skin from several hundred meters away. It appeared to everyone as if the A-10 had just shot one of the LAVs near the flare. Roche had watched in horror as the missile struck the rear of an LAV. The vehicle's turret was pitched skyward, landing twenty meters away from the initial impact. To Roche, it looked like a textbook shot.

Full-blown pandemonium seized the company. The Delta Marines were going crazy over the radio, asking again if anyone had seen any Iraqi tanks nearby and checking frantically to see if any other LAV companies had fired. One of the Delta Marines started screaming into the radio, *"The Iraqis are behind us! The Iraqis are behind us!"*

Back at the Humvees, the recon Marines got the command to evacuate the vehicles. Everyone took off sprinting into the desert, desperately trying to get away from any vehicle that the A-10s might zero in on. The situation seemed to be spiraling out of control. What had begun as a relatively simple escape and evasion exercise was quickly turning into a nightmare of mistaken identity, miscommunication, panic, and fratricide as the avalanche of errors gained momentum. They were on the run from the Iraqis, they were on the run from the LAVs and now, completing the circle of misery, they were on the run from their own airplanes. It was every man for himself.

Gillispie was convinced that the Delta Marines had no idea what they were doing and were a danger to themselves and everyone around them. He'd heard of Captain Pollard from when he was an enlisted man and was happy to have a former recon bubba backing him up at first. Now as things continued to go south, he realized he'd been sadly mistaken. He started grabbing Marines and loading up the Humvees. They evacuated the area at top speed, plunging westward into the darkened wasteland. As he watched, Delta's vehicles scattered to the four winds, each one bailing off in a different direction. It seemed as if all command and control had broken down.

First Sergeant Alfonso Villa, back with the logistics vehicles and Humvees, radioed Pollard asking if there were any survivors from Blaze of Glory. Villa had several corpsmen back with him, and if they were going to mount a recovery effort, they needed to get started immediately. Pollard told him emphatically no. The explosion had been too intense. No one had survived that fireball.

Several LAV-25s pivoted around and, spying a separate cluster of vehicles out in the sand, requested permission to open fire. The company gunnery sergeant, a crusty old salt named Dell, came up on the net saying, "That's me you're looking at, you idiots. Don't open fire! I say again, do not open fire!"

It was then that Lieutenant Williams came up and said that he thought friendly air had killed Blaze of Glory. He added that they now had aircraft stacked up from OP 4 to Riyadh and that they should probably evacuate the area and let the air wing do its thing. With so many aircraft overhead he was no longer convinced he'd be able to control them safely. It was only a matter of time before tragedy struck again. They'd just suffered a catastrophic blow, they were horrendously silhouetted by the flare and the burning hulk of Blaze of Glory. The wisest thing for them at this point was to quit the field and make for the west.

Everyone was down and Pollard could hear it in their voices on the radio. It had been a real sour deal when the TOW vehicle had augured in, but no one in the company really knew the Marines on board. But this, this was altogether different. There had been eight of their own in Blaze of Glory. The vehicle commander, Garett Mongrella, was a hard-charging cook who was so motivated that he'd repeatedly asked for a transfer to a combat unit and had wound up in Delta Company.

Pollard thought, *These were good men. Proud men. Brave men.* His *men.* He knew he'd let them down. In training he'd always been such a disciplinarian, such a demon for procedure, harping on the men to not make stupid mistakes, to use their heads, to look out for each other, to be *safe.* He'd always known with a certainty that surpassed all understanding that Marines die because their officers fuck up, and now he pointed the blade of accusation back at himself. *What had he done wrong? How could he have kept his Marines alive? Where had he lost his way?*

Pollard had no answers. He called over to Battalion, who quickly gave him permission to evacuate OP 4. It was 11:30 P.M.

12

We rode across a sombre land. The rocks beneath our feet and the broken scattered fragments were darkened with age, sepia-colored. They looked as if they had been scorched by the sun and polished by the wind ever since they first emerged from beneath the sea. It was difficult to think that this stark land had ever been other than it was, that flowers and crops may once have flourished here. Now it was dead; the earth's bare bones lay around us, sand-scoured beneath a glaring sky.

The Arabs talked of death. They named men who had died in recent raids and pointed to low ridges where they had fought. I thought of the blood that had splashed on the ground and darkened for a while the colouring of the stones. Round us were the graves of the ancient dead: tumuli, grouped together on high places. Immensely old, they had grown into the desert floor; only their shapes indicated that they were once the work of men.

—WILFRED THESIGER, *Arabian Sands*

WHILE DELTA Company limped back to an assembly area, Sergeant Vitale and the TOW group linked up with Alpha Company to continue the fight. They'd worked extensively with Alpha and their commander, Captain Mike Shupp, before. They were happy to be back with Alpha. It felt like home. Several of Vitale's Marines had reservations about Delta Company. Some of them thought the company was cursed.

The night's adventure for Sergeant Vitale had only just begun with the death of Green 2. Delta had started to withdraw, but as far as he was concerned, he still had a missing vehicle out there. He couldn't just walk away. He was hoping against hope that somehow Cotto and his boys were still alive, that their radio was dead or that they'd experienced a total electrical meltdown and were just waiting for a pickup, waiting for Vitale to bring 'em home. He lit out from Delta's lines to go get them.

Out there cruising the barrens alone, it was Vitale and his vehicle against the world. He had no wingman to cover him. Easy prey for any switched-on Iraqi. After cutting circles near the border for some time, searching the invisible hollows and dips in the sand, Vitale was unable to locate the stricken LAV. It made no sense at all—Green 2 should have been afire, blazing like a Roman candle in the night. *Where had Cotto gone?*

Because he was trying to canvass as much ground as possible in the hunt for Green 2, when Vitale finally decided to head back to friendly lines, he discovered that he had become totally disoriented. The company screen line had shifted and morphed and he had no idea where his guys were anymore. It had been a long night, and Vitale had lost all track of time. It was just plain crazy out there. It was all you could do not to get lost and killed by your own.

After several abortive attempts to re-enter friendly lines, Vitale gave up, scrambled atop his hog, and began swinging a blue-colored chemlight on a piece of cord to attract the company's attention, hoping that they would spot the ring of blue light it created and guide him back in. He felt stupid out there on top of his vehicle, futilely whipping the chemlight around. But if he did nothing, he was certain some amped-out LAV-25 gunner would light him up. He'd seen one of them earlier in the evening just go rogue, popping off rounds between the other vehicles. No coordination, no crosstalk between vehicles, nothing, like it was a day at the range back at Twenty-nine Palms. Right before he'd broken out the chemlight, he'd heard someone from Delta report vehicular movement near the berm: Vitale thought, *Holy fuck, that's us!* Vitale had a clear image inside his head of what it would look like when they started taking 25-mm fire. The distant pops, the sharp impacts, the hot pinging as the rounds found their mark. Eventually, Lance Corporal Brian Smith from the

TOW section saw the chemlight and he and Scott Pruett talked Vitale back in.

As they continued the withdrawal, Sergeant Wissman's hog mysteriously died, losing all power as if someone had flipped a light switch. Vitale was forced to cram all Wissman's men into his other already tightly packed vehicles, an awkward arrangement for all hands. Jason Brown remembers seeing Brierly come aboard and not saying a word to him. The silence spoke volumes. He looked spooked for sure, but breathed no apologies and tendered no explanations. Vitale had Wissman zero out all his radio's frequencies and crypto data, hitting a switch with the words "Z-ALL" scrawled across it. He requested permission from Captain Pollard to destroy Wissman's hog and was denied.*

Soon after, Vitale got word that Alpha Company had officially turned over with Delta and was preparing to take the field. The time was 12:55. A new day had begun. Vitale briefed Captain Shupp as he approached and they integrated into his screen line. Shupp's vehicle pulled in directly behind Vitale. It gave Vitale a novel sense of confidence and security knowing that one of his favorite officers was right behind him. Things were going to be all right now.

Captain Shupp starting pumping Vitale for information, asking him for a detailed account of the evening's events. He then addressed Vitale directly, inquiring if he was okay, if he was feeling all right. For about twenty minutes he asked the young sergeant over and over if he was okay. It was almost as if Shupp sensed that Vitale needed to ease up for a minute, to take stock, to start thinking again and not just reacting. Later Vitale would chain-smoke a pack of cigarettes with a pilot lieutenant colonel who was his friend.

Given all that had transpired, the evening ended on an anticlimactic note. Stung by the Marines' fierce resistance,

---

*Virtually every TOW Marine interviewed hypothesized that Ismael Cotto's LAV experienced a catastrophic electrical failure similar to Sergeant Wissman's. All of the hogs in Vitale's group had struggled with temperamental batteries, and it was not uncommon for a vehicle to simply die out of the blue. This would account for Green 2's seeming disappearance and the lack of distress signals prior to the missile volley.

devastated by American airpower, the Iraqis seemed to be breaking off their attack. Shupp had been getting updates from Battalion and, after assuming Delta's old position, simply hung back and let the airplanes do their runs. There was mopping up to do, prisoners to be taken, men to be accounted for, but Shupp was in no hurry.

As Sergeant G. J. Michaels, a vehicle commander from Alpha Company recalls, "We spent a great deal of time just sitting there that night. We surveyed for any signs of enemy movement, and we watched as the Marine Corps Cobra helicopters lofted flares into the air in an attempt to find the targets. It had gotten incredibly dark, and we were not having any success finding the enemy. We crept forward and scanned; we crept forward and waited."

Wounded, burned, and bleeding, Lance Corporal Ron Tull awoke in the desert. Rolling onto his stomach, he looked over and saw his vehicle Blaze of Glory on fire and thought, *It really happened. We got hit by an Iraqi tank.*

He had been lost from himself for a time, adrift in a sea of night sky, and had no idea where he was or what time it was. Although the darkness persisted, Tull sensed that it was a new day. Through a carapace of memory he thought of how he'd pulled himself out of his driver's hatch using the winch cable guides near the nose of the vehicle. Then the falling to the earth. He lay there some ways away from the vehicle, apart from his body, drifting, unsure if he was alive. He was aware only that *something* existed. The world had not gone away, and he, whoever he was now, was still caught up in it. Nevertheless, his actual body, his corpse, remained a mystery, although he sensed that he was uncomfortable and felt his flak jacket twisted and bunched up underneath him.

On his back again, a voice reached out to him. He tried to lift his head to look toward the voice and failed. Weakness washed over him. With a struggle he somehow managed to look over and see the turret of the vehicle as it was: torn off, flipped upside down, blackened by the fire. He heard another faint cry and thought, *Is that me crying? Is that my voice? Oh, God, am I crying?*

Comically, he recoiled. *Man, I better shut up.* He knew they'd been hit by a tank but didn't know enough to deduce if there were Iraqis about and figured he should keep quiet until he knew for sure. More thoughts came to him in the desert: *Am I going to die? Why am I lying here?*

The voice came again. It was Linderman, one of the vehicle's scouts. Finally, with much effort, he got back onto his stomach and began crawling toward the turret, the origin of the voice. It was yelling, "Help me!" Tull had to get there. He began to low-crawl on his stomach, using his elbows, making three or four arm lengths before passing out. He did this three or four more times. This way, he would inch himself forward haltingly before being overcome.

After passing out several times, he rolled onto his back. The voice had stopped. The turret was still ten yards away. It was still dark. He had no idea how much time had passed. His eyes began to move around, searching, hunting. Then, as if to offset the lack of physical activity, squalls of thought began to develop within and he thought, *How long am I going to have to lie here?*

Then aloud, "This sucks!"

Just then Tull heard something approach and thought, *Oh, great, a vehicle.* He still had no idea where the Iraqis were. *What is it? What do I do?*

It had started to get light, the sky an uncertain shade of blue, the ground still black. In the weak, patchy light he discerned shapes moving toward him. Like hawks in a row they came. These shadows, black as the earth they emerged from, were wearing what looked like dull German helmets, their webgear and canteens chinging as they ran.

Somehow he breathed, "Hey, I'm over here."

He heard the reply: "We got a live one!"

More bodies came over, and he felt hands touching him, lifting him before he fell into the well of blackness again.

*   *   *

As Alpha drew closer to the berm, one of Michaels's comrades, Sergeant Sweeny, spotted some movement near the burning hulk of Blaze of Glory through his night-vision scope. It looked like a Marine crawling out there. Michaels's platoon commander told him to cover Sweeny's vehicle while they went up to investigate. Sweeny found Ron Tull crawling in the sand in front of Blaze of Glory, mumbling about saving his buddies. They snatched him up and transported him to the company rear, where several corpsmen began working on him.

Despite his horrific ordeal, Tull appeared to be okay. Apart from some flash burns, a concussion, bruised kidneys, and a few lacerations, he was fine. To the Marines who'd found Tull, the entire scene was difficult to believe. The Maverick had pulverized the LAV: the 2,000-pound gun turret had been launched thirty feet through the air, every weld in the vehicle had buckled, every metal hatch had been blasted off. That Tull had survived essentially unscathed was nothing short of a miracle. Tull, still unconscious, was loaded up on a logistics LAV, where he awoke next to Jason Baumgardner, who had been wounded by the blast. Baumgardner told him, "Hey, Tully don't worry, you're gonna be all right." Tull didn't learn the fate of his friend Dion Stephenson and the rest of his buddies until he was evacuated to a U.S. Army hospital in Wiesbaden, Germany, a week later.

When the sun finally came up over OP 4, several flights of A-10s and Marine Cobra attack helicopters were poised to finish off whatever Iraqis had survived the long night. Two T-62s sat smoking near the chain-link fence that encircled the police post. A half-dozen tanks were scattered across a wide area on the Kuwaiti side. Most of the enemy seemed to have slipped away in the night. Perched on the rise 1,500 meters back from the berm, the Alpha Company Marines watched for a half-hour as the A-10s made their runs. Marine Cobras came next.

Shupp, cognizant of what had happened with Delta Company, wasn't messing around with the air wing. He ordered the company's forward air controller to demand that the pilots count all of the LAVs before being cleared to fire. They had to call off several missions because the pilots came up one vehicle short. Even after all that, a TOW missile fired from a Cobra narrowly missed taking out Sergeant Michaels's vehicle later that morning.

That next day, after recovering their dead and collecting several dozen prisoners, the Marines from Delta Company began writing their Social Security numbers in permanent ink across their backs, their calves, and their hips. There hadn't been enough left of the Marines from Green 2 to fill a ziplock bag. They figured it was the only hope of being identified after a killing blast. A few Marines requested transfer out of the company. Those who remained never slept inside their vehicles again.

Eventually the recon platoon made its way to a safe position well away from the insanity on the border and circled the wagons. It was bitterly cold and windy, and the bone-tired Marines were looking to just harbor up and hold out for the dawn, so when trains of Delta's vehicles began appearing on the horizon, they were less than ecstatic. However, the groups of LAVs just kept coming and had brought their logistics and fuel trucks with them. Gillispie and Ross were pretty weary of the LAV company at this stage and were of half a mind to just ditch them, but for some reason chose to remain. They were soon enveloped by LAVs.

They watched on the horizon as the Air Force began dogpiling on the Iraqis. Several flights of Cobra attack helicopters arrived, multiplying the slaughter. Slowly, by degrees, it seemed as if the tide was turning as flight upon flight of attack aircraft came and went and the Iraqi thrust was progressively contained. Dawn began to break, and both units headed back east to the border to survey the destruction.

They approached the frontier, a scene that, according to Gillispie, "looked like the night of the living dead." Scores of dazed and wounded Iraqi soldiers and tank crewmen were wandering about the battlefield like boats cut adrift. The ground was charred black in places and pocked with shell fragments. Wreckage and debris littered the area. On the far side of the berm near an abandoned Iraqi tank, the Marines found two Iraqis in black overalls who'd been shot in the head, as if executed at close range.

Collecting up the Iraqis was surprisingly easy. Gillispie recalled, "It was like herding schoolchildren. There was clearly no fight left in these guys." Gillispie and Sergeant Manney managed to find the LAV that had been struck by the A-10. The dead and destroyed bodies of the Marines were inside. The turret, some ways away, was flipped over and had the upper half of the gunner's body smashed into it.

Later that morning they took an Iraqi colonel prisoner. He told them he thought he'd run into the main body of a Marine division.

13

Dawn, January 29, 1991,
Just South of the Kuwaiti Border

*No great dependence is to be placed on the eagerness of young sol-
diers for action, for the prospect of fighting is agreeable to those
who are strangers to it.*
—VEGETIUS, Roman military writer, fourth century A.D.

IN ACCORDANCE with the Iraqi grand scheme, three heavy
divisions struck at four major points along the Saudi-
Kuwaiti frontier. While the Iraqis moved toward Observation
Post 4, another large covering force was moving toward Observation Post 6 on the western edge of the Marine sector. On
the morning of January 29, Delta's sister unit, Charlie Company, was en route to screen this portion of the border.

Captain Thomas Protzeller, who'd been at his present rank
less than two months, drove Charlie Company west along the
tapline road, charting a course roughly parallel to the border
from the coastal town of Khafji toward the battalion headquarters in the pale morning light. There he expected to be
tasked out to support one of the artillery raids and so-called
drive-by shootings that the LAVers had undertaken in recent
weeks, pushing up to the berm, firing off a volley of well-
scouted rounds, and then waiting with counter-battery radars
at the ready for the inevitable Iraqi response. It was a mar-
velous harassing tactic, which exploited all of the Marines'
strong suits of detailed planning, aggressive execution, and
a raiding mentality, making use of the distinct technological
advantage that had followed Americans into battle since the
latter half of World War II.

The preceding evening had been a wearying one for
Protzeller and the Marines of Charlie Company. The 1st Ma-

rine Division staff, heeding the scattershot rumors of an impending Iraqi assault, had ordered Charlie to set up a heavy screen line along the coastal highway, which ran through Khafji.* Khafji, the likely focal point for an Iraqi invasion of Saudi Arabia, was an ideal first objective. It was a modestly sized, lightly defended town; a place to occupy, resupply, and reorganize before launching headlong again into the belly of the Kingdom of Saudi Arabia and the precious oil fields that lay within it. The now-abandoned burg of 20,000 was a mere dozen miles from the frontier and, given that it sat astride the main coastal artery, was easily located by the Iraqi tankers, who were notoriously poor navigators. Nevertheless, the promised assault failed to materialize, and the Marines spent the tense evening watching the road in an inky darkness deepened by the smoke of scores of Iraqi-lit oil fires across the way in Kuwait.

The night had not gone all well for the young company commander. One of his vehicles had nearly shot up a battalion commander, who had unwisely approached his position in the darkness without radioing ahead. The lieutenant colonel, who had been out on a reconnaissance with his staff, was recognized only after Charlie's executive officer, Lieutenant Tom Walsh, screamed out at the top of his lungs, "Stop, you motherfuckers, or I'll kill you!"

The sleepless night in town had been a taxing one, and there was a palpable sense of disappointment after the evening had passed with only a rumor of combat. Charlie Company had been specially tapped for the assignment, and the Marines had expected Khafji to be their baptism of fire. Now that they were being sent away, that familiar, unwelcome feeling of no-action-expected and "all quiet at the front" crept back in. The Marines, having endured the long, hot fall training for the promised Armageddon, were anxious

---

*The CIA had forwarded information to the Marines, gleaned from an Iraqi defector, that an offensive was imminent. The Iraqis, whatever their other operational shortcomings, were masters of subterfuge and frequently dispatched "defectors" to mislead their enemies. As a result, the Marines took these warnings with a grain of salt.

to know how they would measure up against their storied foe. It was the old axiom at work yet again: Young men who know nothing of actual combat often desire it in a way that runs counter to every born instinct.

After giving the word to redeploy to Lieutenant Walsh, Protzeller went straight to sleep, resting his head against the sight eyepiece inside the commander's hatch as his hog rambled westward. He was beyond tired, having been up for nearly 60 hours, and given the weight of command (he was only 27 years old) felt the adrenaline crash more than most. En route they were redirected by Major Jeff Powers at Battalion to screen between Observation Posts 5 and 6, the two westernmost outposts in the Marine area of operations, keeping an eye out for any Iraqi activity or armored vehicle concentrations. On the way to the battalion command post, Protzeller ran into Rock Pollard, and they compared notes on their respective missions. Neither had been given any specific intelligence about Iraqi activity in their sectors.

Reaching their assembly area sometime before sundown, Protzeller set his vehicles up in a wagon wheel ten kilometers off the border near OP 5, soon after lighting out to reconnoiter the berm and figure out how to defend the patch of sand that headquarters had seen fit to give him dominion over. An officer accustomed to quick thinking and hard action, Protzeller rapidly identified the dominant features of the ground. Amazingly, everything seemed to be working in his favor. The berm, built by the Saudi border police to control smuggling, was massive enough that a tank would never be able to surmount it and was exactly the right height so that an LAV-TOW variant could erect its turret and see over the sand wall. He would thus be able to dispose his company in a perfectly covered and concealed position with only a few TOW turrets exposed. If they remained there long enough, slits would be cut out of the berm, providing firing ports for his lighter LAV-25s. Taking into account that there was a singular break in the berm at OP 6 and two such apertures at OP 5, Protzeller concluded that his lot in life had become elegantly simple: Deny the Iraqis the use of the three breaches.

Thus a large stretch of the frontier could in theory be sealed with merely a handful of Marine light-armored vehicles.

After conferring with his platoon commanders, who agreed with this assessment, Protzeller brought his company, which had been augmented with a section of eight TOW variants and two 81-mm mortar vehicles, right up next to the berm. As they settled in, he thought that this was one of the simplest tactical problems he'd ever solved.

Further coordination was made when a nearby reconnaissance company commander stopped by to inform him that there were no recon teams in either of the two observation posts, a fact that further streamlined Protzeller's prospects. The two captains traded radio frequencies and call signs just as Pollard and Ross had done several hours earlier. Protzeller then called in a request to Battalion to emplace hasty minefields in both of the breaches using land mines that they carried with them, a petition that was denied. Apparently, if any land mines were to be laid, it was to be done only with the express permission of a general officer. After another leaders' conference, which was the norm in his company before any course of action was firmly decided upon, Protzeller turned the simple plan over in his head. If he saw any movement in Kuwait, he'd simply blast away with his TOWs and call for air support. The berm made things even easier: Anything east of it was enemy; anything west of it was friendly. It was a total no-brainer.

Sometime after darkness fell, Protzeller got a report from 1st Platoon that someone was watching them with binoculars from atop the Kuwaiti police post opposite OP 5. Ever the impetuous young officer, Protzeller's philosophy had always been to shoot first and report it to headquarters later. He ordered the mortarmen to drop some rounds on their Iraqi stalkers to rattle them. To his supreme disgust, the mortar Marines assigned to Charlie were unable to execute what Protzeller considered to be the rudimentary fire mission. After several abortive attempts, he abandoned the problem, figuring that while they hadn't scored a direct hit, they had at least shaken up their pursuers.

After scolding the Marines for their poor weaponeering, Protzeller called back to Major Powers to report the contact. Big Jeff proceeded to chew Protzeller's ass in high style. "Don't you realize that you're well within range of *at least* twelve Iraqi artillery batteries?" Powers inquired acidly. "What were you thinking?"

In Protzeller's mind, by firing on the Iraqi forward observers, he was conducting counter-reconnaissance, a primary LAV mission, and was well within his orders. He yearned for contact and thought, *If we saw 'em, why shouldn't we kill 'em? If we weren't sent up here to engage the enemy, then why were we sent at all?*

This was the first time he'd ever been admonished by Major Powers, and the reprimand stung far beyond what might have been expected for such a seemingly minor transgression. Powers had always treated him with the utmost respect and fraternity, which was not always easy, given that Protzeller was by far the most junior company commander in the battalion and was considered by some to be an impulsive upstart who'd simply lucked into a choice command. Their relations spoke volumes about Powers' respect for competence over rank and his predilection for unorthodox but effective solutions to problems.

After arguing the point to no avail for several minutes, Protzeller was ordered to pull his company back ten kilometers to a laager site in order to protect against any Iraqi barrages that might have been in the works. The screening mission would have to wait.

Back away from the border and coiled into a 360 once again, Protzeller put the company down to 25 percent alert, hoping to rest his men after their Khafji excursion and the dusty daylong road march that had followed. No sooner had he and Walsh settled down than they began to hear tank and small-arms fire emanating from OP 4. Charlie at present was angled off from the border, approximately equidistant from OPs 4 and 5, and although they believed that the developing tempest was fixed to the east near OP 4, they couldn't be sure. As they continued to monitor the battalion tac net, no reports were forthcoming. The small-arms fire continued to grow. Protzeller, who had never visited OP 4, was unaware that there was a dismounted reconnaissance platoon manning the police post, and because the buildings clustered in his sector were conspicuously vacant, he had assumed that OP 4 was abandoned as well. *Why the hell was Delta banging away with machine guns out there?*

Lieutenant Walsh, seated next to him inside his vehicle, asked, "Should we wake the Marines or do you wanna let 'em sleep?"

Protzeller, who in truth had never held his sister company in particularly high regard, replied, "You know what? I'll bet you they're shooting at camels or something. It's nothing. Let the boys sleep. They're tired and they need some rest." For nearly an hour, Charlie Company snoozed on. But the night was not to be denied, and after a time, scattered reports of Iraqi tanks at the berm began to crackle across the wire. It wasn't long before Protzeller heard the distinctive pop of the LAV's 25-mm chain gun off in the distance. He directed Walsh to rise the men.

Protzeller deployed his Marines, rolling them out of the coil into a linear defense oriented on OP 5. First Platoon was on the left. Second Platoon, led by Staff Sergeant Scott Sampson, was on the right. Protzeller remained in the center of his formation, his precious TOWs at hand. If the Iraqis attacked, he planned to use his LAV-25s to strip away the smaller, light-skinned vehicles and then pound the Iraqi main battle tanks with his TOWs.

The information emerging from OP 4 was poor and disjointed, but after a time Major Powers rolled up to Charlie's tac net with a frag order: "Charlie Six [Protzeller], this is Wolfpack. Stand by to occupy and block OP 5." The screen mission had just been transformed into a blocking mission; it was no longer a matter of furtively jabbing and reporting it to the rear, it was *get your ass up there and kill anything that comes through*.

Despite the boldness of the order, which was in accord with Protzeller's basic nature, the young captain was unhappy. He'd already been up to OP 5 and was now being forced to retake the very ground that he'd been ordered to surrender against his better judgment. Worse yet, the reports from OP 4 were so cryptic and fragmentary that he had no idea what the overall situation was. For all he knew, he could be walking into a battalion-size ambush at OP 5. Iraqi tanks could have already breached the berm and been rolling to exploit his flank. The battalion staff didn't appear to have any idea what was going on. Given the absence of any useful intelligence, the enemy situation was, as far as Tommie Protzeller was concerned, completely unknown.

Pressing forward into the uncertainty, Protzeller ushered his men ahead at a creeping pace, in no hurry to blunder into an ambush. Shortly after 10:30 that evening he received word that enemy tanks had indeed penetrated into Saudi Arabia. Upon receipt of these ill tidings, Protzeller tasked Staff Sergeant Sampson, a seasoned and cool-headed staff NCO, to orient his platoon to the south to refuse the flank should any tanks be bearing down upon them. He felt confident in dispatching Sampson, who while perhaps over-quiet, gave no counsel to his fears and would not imagine tanks where there were none. To further bolster Sampson's position, Protzeller turned over to him three of his treasured TOW vehicles.

With his most trusted subordinate guarding his flank, Protzeller began playing out the various scenarios in his head and, anticipating that Powers would soon call and order them up to plug the single remaining gap in the line, began orienting the remainder of his company—a single reinforced platoon—toward Observation Post 6. Sure enough, minutes later orders came down to proceed to OP 6 to prevent further Iraqi penetrations.

En route, Protzeller listened in as Delta Company began taking casualties. Given the absence of vital information and intelligence, the disparate, often conflicting reports patching ever inward, the only clear thought that presented itself was, *What the fuck is going on down there?*

Nevertheless, Protzeller was not one to worry and possessed an almost preternatural confidence in his men, his plan, and his equipment and reasoned simply, "If the Iraqis are stupid enough to come at us, then I'll just hammer the shit outta them."

Powers came up again, instructing Protzeller to hasten his movement to OP 6 as spotter planes had detected 70-plus vehicles moving from the al-Wafra oil field in the east toward OP 6. It was now a race against time to see who could seize the border station first. Protzeller proceeded north, using his TOWs in alternating bounds to cover his movement. This drive, roughly parallel to the border, which, after hanging a 90-degree turn at OP 4 ran nearly north–south, was a tricky geometric equation, with TOWs alternating between peering up over the berm to the east and scanning northward as they advanced on the OP.

During one bound, the TOWs acquired several thermal signatures across the berm and were quickly given permission to engage. Casting their deadly cargo downrange, they rapidly expended eleven missiles, killing an untold number of Iraqi tanks and armored personnel carriers. One by one, the Iraqis succumbed to Charlie's gunners. As they continued to bear northward, one TOW vehicle experienced a misfire; the quick-thinking NCO in charge extracted the live missile, placing it in a hastily dug trench and marking the site with glowing chemlights.

Staff Sergeant Sampson radioed, saying he had six vehicles approaching in formation from the vicinity of OP 4. Protzeller gave him permission to engage, but then thought better of it and called over to Battalion, asking if there were any friendlies moving to the south. The reply came back negative, but Protzeller wasn't convinced. He called over to Alpha Company directly, inquiring as to their whereabouts. Sure enough, his buddy Lieutenant John Manza, Alpha's second-in-command, confirmed that they had a platoon on the move. In an effort to double-check the contact, he inquired if Manza could have his LAVs briefly turn their headlights on. This highly unorthodox and possibly dangerous request was granted, and bright as day, the Alpha vehicles lit up the desert plain, thereby avoiding a tragic encounter the likes of which had bedeviled their Delta comrades earlier that evening.

As he continued north, Protzeller was relieved to learn of this outcome. A contact of six vehicles, given that that was the traditional LAV formation, just didn't sound right, and the fact that he and his Marines had expertly avoided a deadly exchange bolstered his spirits. There was precious little time for congratulations. As they neared the police post, the Iraqis began to pound it with artillery smoke rounds, enveloping the post in a thick haze. This same border fort, which in reality was more akin to a small village with over thirty buildings of various shapes contained within its perimeter, had been smoked by Iraqi cannoneers eight days prior, and it was clear they had their target zeroed in. Illumination rounds began wafting overhead, almost comical as they swung lazily on their parachutes. As the Marines looked on, the Iraqis seized the post with a dozen tanks and armored personnel carriers. Iraqi soldiers scurried out and occupied the buildings. The Iraqis had won the race.

Protzeller was unfazed by this acute reversal. His concerns at the moment passed from his immediate situation onto larger, more ominous matters. During the opening days of the air war, he'd watched as Saddam ordered the al-Burqan and al-Wafra oil fields in southern Kuwait lit afire and marveled at the savage cunning of this new enemy. To Protzeller, it seemed like a masterstroke; by completely obscuring the battlefield with choking black smoke, Saddam had cut the Americans off from their vaunted air arm, completely negating their technological advantage. He watched as they reenacted the same maneuver on a smaller scale over OP 6 and wondered what else the Iraqis had up their sleeve. *Were they attempting to draw him into a fight, enticing him to charge headlong into the labyrinth of the ville where his LAVs would be exposed to close-in Iraqi RPG fire? Would they press their attack through the miasma, pushing into Saudi Arabia?* The billowing haze muted several of Protzeller's aces, including his TOWs, who could see through just about anything save thick smoke. Further, the smoke made calling for air support inordinately more complex, as if it weren't difficult enough in the middle of the desert at night.

The situation deepened still as reports of Iraqi tank columns heading their way continued to pour in, seeming to almost redouble in their insistence after receipt of the initial bad news. What had begun as a no-brainer was turning into a straight fight.

Nevertheless, Protzeller decided that he wasn't taking the bait, electing instead to surrender the ville to the Iraqis and let Lieutenant Walsh, who doubled as the company's air controller, call down some jets from the bustling stack of attack aircraft that had been collecting overhead for some time. This course of action had its limitations as well. Although Protzeller was unaware of the Delta Company double tragedy, he had long been concerned by the threat of friendly air attacks and deployed several Marines forward of the company position to emplace bright road flares in the sand. Working swiftly in the night, they placed one road flare 50 feet to the direct front of each vehicle. White magnesium flares were subsequently placed on the far right and left edges of the company frontage, effectively outlining Charlie's entire position. It was a move considered rash and silly by some officers, but with scores of trigger-happy flyboys zooming overhead, Protzeller thought it best to not take any chances. It was yet another working example of the Marine axiom "If it's stupid and it works, then it isn't stupid."

The multitudinous challenges of attack aircraft control were thus reduced to a simple air-ground radio exchange: Walsh would inquire, "Do you see the flares?" If the pilot responded with a yes, he was directed to bomb anything north of the flares. Anything south of the flares was friendly and therefore off-limits. If the pilot was unable to locate the flares, he was simply waved off.

Several Harrier jump jets began their runs, and the battle entered a new phase, one that worked itself out much as OP 4 had: The Marines watched in awe as American airpower took command of the field, eviscerating the Iraqi formation, which after having disgorged their infantry had inexplicably egressed behind the village into the open desert plain.

While the smoke wasn't making the pilots' jobs any easier, the Iraqis had strangely backed away from their smoke screen, leaving themselves starkly exposed. It wasn't long before several resounding eruptions filled the night. The Marines watched as secondary explosions consumed the Iraqi formation. The rough noise rolled and dropped up to Charlie's position in great rippling sheets, filling the rank and file with a soaring confidence. They were physically apart from the fire and the dust and the death, safe and protected for the moment, but the fire on their horizon was their doing.

The only matter of concern was that the command-and-control LAV, which contained Lieutenant Walsh, had begun doing Sagger drills, vigorously zigzagging and hooking to avoid incoming Iraqi missiles. Protzeller didn't see any Saggers and watched bemused as his XO cut erratic circles in the sand. He could see only the TOWs as their turrets discharged and the Harriers' 500-pound bombs as they detonated near the border fort. Through his binoculars he witnessed numerous secondary explosions as tank after tank was destroyed.

Because of the slope of the ground, the Marines were unable to determine how many Iraqis had been killed, but they knew the attacks had had a mortal effect. Whatever momentum the Iraqis had possessed was stolen from them as the planes swooped in. Protzeller decided to maneuver the company around to the north to try and get a better look at the breach and figure how best to manage what by all appearances was a rout in the making. His orders to seal the gap had not changed, and he needed to get his eyes on a different part of the OP to see if any vehicles had leaked through.

Moving to within a few hundred meters of the fort, Protzeller told his scouts, "Time for you guys to go in and see what's up." He planned to have his infantry dismount and conduct a close-in reconnaissance of the village to root out whatever Iraqis had survived the bombardment. It was a textbook move: Protzeller's hogs would be gravely vulnerable in town, and the last thing the captain wanted was to roll into the fray without infantry covering his dead space. The situation in and around the OP was still confused, bombs were detonating all over the place, smoke shrouded everything, obscuring the air and the minds of men who tried to peer through it. Protzeller looked down through his commander's hatch at one of his senior scouts. The sergeant asked, "Sir, do we really gotta go in there? We're all fucking scared. Can't we just wait till morning to check it out?"

It was nearly 4:00 A.M. and the young captain looked down at the sergeant. It was a nervy moment, one that young officers dread, and the thought had to cross the captain's stressed mind: Do I order this man to what may be his death against his will? As the fight buzzed on around him, Protzeller thought, *You know, I wouldn't wanna go in either.* He knew that it was going to be light soon. *What would they accomplish by going in now? They could stand to wait a couple of hours.*

He said, "Yeah, that's probably a good fucking call." The dismount would wait.

Dawn came, bringing more problems in its wake. Protzeller realized that he had completely overlooked one thing: He had never schooled his men in house-to-house fighting. With the enormous amount of time and energy required to deal with the Iraqi armored threat and the many challenges of desert warfare, he had never thought to include a section on urban operations in their already crowded combat syllabus. Unfortunately, there was no getting around it. The village had to be cleared, and he'd delayed the move into town as long as he possibly could. They had to go in.

As the scouts emerged from the vehicles and moved into the village, searching for Iraqi holdouts, he cursed himself for overlooking this eventuality. Marines could die and it would be because he hadn't trained them well enough. As he watched from atop his hog in the weak morning light, he was so disgusted with his Marines' performance that he began screaming instructions at them, trying to school them in urban tactics as they wen: about clearing the buildings. He couldn't believe this was h ppening.

With the LAVs covering them, the Marines began their clearing, busting down doors and throwing grenades into the abandoned houses. A few die-hards were discovered, and the Marines, jumpy after the evening's ordeal, were in no mood to ask questions and quickly dispatched them. They took no prisoners. After completing a hasty search of all of the thirty-odd buildings, the scouts reached the far edge of town. Protzeller knew their work was almost done. He'd inspected the actual border causeway and saw that there were no vehicle tracks leading into Saudi Arabia. No Iraqis had slipped through.

The rest of the company moved through town, emerging on the far side. Just then, one of the Marines spotted a white pickup truck racing across the desert a few thousand meters away. After several near misses, a gunner finally got the right lead on him and the vehicle erupted in a shower of sparks. A few minutes later, Protzeller looked over and noticed an unidentified vehicle off in the distance. "That looks like a fucking tank!" Sure enough, after instructing his gunner to look through his sights, the vehicle turned out to be an Iraqi T-62. After lasering it to measure the distance, he called over to Staff Sergeant Catchings, his TOW section leader, to have him blast the lone tank.

After locking his TOW turret up, Catchings fired off a missile that struck the tank right between the hull and its rounded turret, launching it thirty feet into the air. Immediately after the explosion four Iraqis sprinted out from behind the blazing hulk into the open desert. Protzeller dispatched Sergeant Hernandez, one of his best vehicle commanders, to capture them. Driving out into the forbidden land of Kuwait for what was probably the first cross-border incursion of the war, Hernandez collected the four miscreants, along with a fifth Iraqi who had the misfortune to be lying underneath the tank when the missile impacted.

The five were the first Iraqis the Marines had ever seen. They were a miserable lot—filthy, in shock, and clearly petrified. Several of the Marines came up to get a look at them and were stunned at the sad state of their supposed adversaries. These characters looked more like Third World famine victims than hardened desert warriors. As Protzeller took all this in, he saw a profound change wash over his men. Whereas ten minutes before they had been trying their damndest to annihilate these guys, now they were coming up to the captain asking, "Sir, do they really need to be blindfolded? They look pretty cold—can we build them a fire?" After a few minutes, the Iraqis, who when they discovered they'd been captured by U.S. Marines were convinced that they would be executed on the spot, were sitting around a fire eating MREs with blankets draped over them.*

For Protzeller, as he watched these scarecrows shivering in the shadow of his hogs, the war took on a completely different aspect. He and his Marines had seen a face of war they'd never expected. After the noise and rage they'd just passed through, the future seemed impossibly bright. To the young captain it was evident that the Iraqis, who had always been held up as the masters of the defense, saber-wielding Saladins who'd fought the Iranians for eight years, clearly lacked the skill and spirit he saw in his Marines. As the smoke of the long morning dissipated, revealing the oblivion of the desert once more, Protzeller saw the war in miniature parading before him, saw the future billowing on the horizon. He knew that they could beat these people.

---

*A widespread rumor on the Iraqi side was that in order to be a U.S. Marine, you had to kill a member of your immediate family.

PART II

THE BATTLE FOR KHAFJI

First Lieutenant Stephen Ross (above) and Staff Sergeant Gregory Gillispie (below). The unusual bond between these two men made a strong platoon even stronger. Gillispie is holding a 40-millimeter M-203 round. Ross is standing in the rubble of the Kuwaiti police post, opposite Observation Post 4 which was bombed by American F-18s.

Deep Reconnaissance Platoon Marine (unidentified) at the platoon headquarters position on the berm. It was here that the lightly armed Marines first spotted the massive Iraqi assault force bearing down on them. Note the border fort in the distance. The headquarters bunker is located on the left edge of the frame at the base of the berm.

Courtesy of Gregory Gillispie

After the storm: Lieutenant Ross in front of one of the Iraqi tanks destroyed during the battle for OP 4.

Courtesy of Gregory Gillispie

Captain "Rock" Pollard and his crew. Pollard was a hard-bitten former enlisted man whose leadership style inspired both hatred and respect from the men under him.

Courtesy of Roger Pollard

Dave Snyder standing in the commander's hatch of his LAV-TOW. Dave was one of the most popular Marines in the company and was assigned to Sergeant Vitale's TOW group only days before the battle for OP 4. He, along with three other Marines, was killed when another TOW vehicle confused their LAV for an Iraqi tank.

Courtesy of Ken Lieuwen

Bill Covington just prior to Khafji. The assemblage to the right is a shelter he constructed to keep out the disgusting swarms of flies common to the Saudi desert. One of the Marines dubbed Saudi Arabia, "the filthiest place I have ever seen."

Courtesy of Bill Covington

Courtesy of Ken Lieuwen

Major Jeff Powers (left) and Captain Rock Pollard (right). Powers and Pollard had been good friends before the war. Both found themselves assigned to the fledgling 3rd Light-Armored Infantry Battalion, a new and untested mechanized unit whose concept of employment had been only crudely worked out.

The wreckage of the light-armored vehicle known as "Blaze of Glory" that was accidently destroyed by a U.S. Air Force A-10 attack jet on the night of January 29, 1991. The lone survivor, Ronald Tull, was violently ejected from the vehicle and somehow emerged with only minor injuries.

Courtesy of Ken Lieuwen

Chuck Ingraham (standing) and Lance Corporal Franks (kneeling). Ingraham, a young Corporal from an all-Marine family, led one of the Marine reconnaissance teams that played a key role in the recapture of Khafji.

Courtesy of Charles Ingraham

Corporal Lawrence Lentz, a thirty-two-year-old Citadel College graduate, led another Marine reconnaissance team that was cut off by the sudden Iraqi advance.

Courtesy of Charles Ingraham

Doc Callahan, an unusually experienced Marine medic, was the linchpin of Ingraham's team.

Captain Dan Baczkowski, Ingraham's and Lentz's platoon commander, found himself living every young officer's worst nightmare: his men were cut off behind enemy lines and he was powerless to protect them. He led a patrol into Khafji to recover his men but expected that they would be dead by the time he arrived.

Sergeant Bill Iiams, a level-headed NCO, accompanied Baczkowski on the rescue patrol.

Pat Sterling, an exceptionally mature and poised young Marine, was point man for Ingraham's team.

David McNamee, Ingraham's in-house anti-armor guru, and Lance Corporal Franks dig in preparation for a pre-invasion reconnaissance patrol.

Jeffrey Brown, Ingraham's assistant team leader, riding in Lentz's team Humvee, which was badly damaged by American artillery fire during the recapture of Khafji. The Humvee, inoperable after the battle, is being towed into Kuwait.

The building that Ingraham's team hid inside during the battle. Note the fire damage on the third floor.

(Left to right) An unidentified Navy liaison officer, Captain Doug Kleinsmith, Captain Jim Braden, and Captain Joe Molofsky. These men played a crucial role in the recapture of Khafji—a battle that was largely organized and directed by a small cadre of American junior officers from a previously obscure Marine unit known as ANGLICO.

Captain Doug Kleinsmith's ANGLICO team, a.k.a. Wild Eagle 3–2 forward. An obviously tight crew that thrived "out on the edge of the empire," living among Arabs for months on end in a forgotten corner of the Coalition. (Left to right) Captain Douglas Kleinsmith, Corporal John Calhoun, Corporal Steve Foss, and Corporal Ed Simmons.

Saudi V-150 armored car destroyed by Iraqi RPG fire on the morning of January 31, 1991. The lion's share of the Saudi casualties resulted from two killed V-150s in which all aboard perished. The Saudis euphemistically referred to this as "martyrdom."

Artist's rendering of Arab armored vehicles at the gates of Khafji. The lead vehicle is a Qatari AMX-30 of French manufacture. The wheeled vehicles are Saudi Arabian V-150s, thin-skinned armored cars which were egregiously vulnerable to Iraqi RPG fire. The Saudis suffered ten dead and thirty-two wounded recapturing the city. The building that Ingraham's team hid out in can be seen on the left edge of the drawing underneath the arches.

14

6:45 A.M., January 29, 1991,
Observation Post 8, Six Miles North of Khafji

The closer you get to the front, the better the people are.
—ANONYMOUS MARINE

THE DAY of the 29th had started strangely for Sergeant Elisio Lozano, a forward observer and close-air-support specialist with the Marines' 1st Air-Naval Gunfire Liaison Company (ANGLICO) stationed along the coast at Observation Post 8. At around seven that morning three Iraqi soldiers had sauntered across the border, emerging from the crepuscular light practically on top of his team's hilltop position. Lozano had been asleep down by a pile of rocks he'd been using for cover when Corporal Mel Russell, the team's comm chief, had yelled, "Stop!" in Arabic. It was strange seeing them suddenly there, and for a moment the two groups of soldiers had just stared at each other in shock. Lozano couldn't believe that Russell had just yelled at them and thought if he hadn't yelled, that he would have shot them all. The Iraqis threw their weapons down and looked at them.

The team of four Marines pounced on their uninvited guests, kicking weapons away, and digging through their gear. Looking over their new captives, Lozano was amazed. He'd never seen an Iraqi up close before. They were clean-shaven and wore fresh tanker crew suits, in stark contrast to the ragged Marines, who'd hadn't seen the inside of a bathroom or a chow hall in weeks. Adding to the disparity, the Marines were sporting ad hoc zarapes fashioned out of thick wool blankets because they didn't have any sleeping bags. They looked like whiskery Clint Eastwood doubles in tan camouflage.

153

Lozano and Russell found several marked-up maps of the area on the Iraqis. On one map they saw their position at OP 8 clearly plotted. They also noted a maze of Iraqi positions inside Kuwait and quickly set about transferring this information to their own maps. Lozano began thinking about all the missions he could call in with this new data.

Shortly after searching the Iraqis, some Navy SEALs, posted just east of them along the beach, caught wind of the Marines' capture and quickly ambled over, collecting up the Iraqis and spiriting them rearward. Lacking the manpower to process the prisoners, the Marines let the SEALs take them. The Marines weren't up on the border for prisoner exploitation duty. They were there to call in air strikes.

On January 27 Lozano, along with the three other ANGLICO Marines currently at OP 8, had been detached from his normal team, which provided fire support for a Qatari tank battalion, in order to orchestrate the air effort against various Iraqi units known to be jockeying around inside Kuwait. Colonel Clay Grubb, commanding officer of the 1st ANGLICO, a highly specialized fire-control and coordination unit that operated in dispersed four-man teams, had organized a rotation up to the border forts in order to get all the Marines in the company experience in handling live missions and to acclimate them to the sinister rhythms up on the bleeding edge of the war. The Iraqis, while not mounting any real offensive efforts, were always up to some form of indecipherable mischief, constantly shifting troops, vehicles, and artillery pieces around like a jumpy high school football coach; clumsily probing along the entire frontier; randomly firing haunting illumination rounds into the sky like votive fireworks. Army Special Forces teams, also working the line, were glad to have ANGLICO up there as well. Wherever ANGLICO went, airpower was quick to follow. And lots of it.

Moving up to the border, Lozano had noted the odd, transient cast of characters cycling through the area, each with a separate mission in life. Spooky signals intelligence guys; Navy SEALs dressed like harlequins; quiet, round-spectacled men in unmarked cammies. Each looking for a piece of the action. Each looking for quick war fix, a passing encounter before the main event looming on the horizon. At OP 8, a couple of hundred meters east of Lozano's position, a SEAL team was set in near the waterline, there to provide early warning for long-range missile launches toward the rear. Unlike the ANGLICO Marines, whose primary armament was the airplanes that they called in, the SEALs appeared to have brought some heat with them: a few .50-caliber heavy machine guns. Lozano was glad for that.

An unsettling World War I–like atmosphere had descended over the cluttered eastern portion of the border near OP 8. Less than a kilometer to the north, Lozano and his compadres could clearly see a line of Iraqi trenches in the undulating ground. The Iraqis seemed to know exactly where the Americans were as well, and to that end the Marines had long ago abandoned the conspicuous two-story border fort that dominated the OP, setting up shop in a lightly shrubbed sand rise 100 meters behind the ridiculous-looking fort. While abandoning the building was clearly the tactically sound thing to do, being out in the open didn't provide the Marines any peace of mind. The only modicum of cover the area behind the fort offered were some scattered rocks, which they promptly heaped together into meager foxholes.

The uncanny appearance of the morning Iraqis got the Marines' blood up. After briefly reviewing their predicament, they decided that they needed better security to their front. First Lieutenant Kurt Lang, the ANGLICO team leader at OP 8, called back to their higher headquarters and arranged for some reconnaissance Marines to establish a listening post in a shallow defile fifty meters to the north. Lozano realized that they had begun to get complacent. ANGLICO teams had been raining air strikes into Kuwait for weeks and the Iraqis seemed to be absorbing the blows, offering only token Astro missile barrages in response. In situations such as this where one can observe the seeming omnipotence of intelligently applied American airpower up close, it is easy, almost natural, to begin to feel a casual invincibility about it all. To believe oneself untouchable. Lozano realized that the Marines had wavered slightly off the hard tactical mantra of security, security, security and had paid the price. Their position had been compromised.

The tableau darkened a shade further when soon after the prisoners were collected up, a tank round thundered into their midst, missing the Marines by only 100 meters. Their hearts banging, the Marines scanned the horizon looking for the telltale muzzle flash. They came up empty but watched as some of the SEALs down by the water gathered up their gear and hit the road, bound for safer points to the south.

After establishing the forward post with the recon Marines, Lozano and company began preparing for another day of orchestrating bombing runs. A few hours before the Iraqis had rolled up, they'd directed a section of Harriers down on a low-slung building that the Iraqis seemed to be using for a barracks. Lozano was keen to follow up on it and begin working over the targets he'd derived from the captured Iraqi maps.

The bulk of the day passed without incident, and as per routine at eight in the evening two of the Marines bedded down in the team's Humvee in preparation for the long night of radio watch shifts ahead.

At around 8:30, Lozano sensed a disturbance in the system. Radio handsets were being shifted around at the various border OPs. Staticky chatter rising perceptibly. A commotion clearly brewing. Other ANGLICO teams dispersed across the frontier burbled about long mechanized columns approaching and about abandoning their positions. Talk about executing escape-and-evasion plans, which had always seemed like an exotic, unnecessary precaution, the SEAL plan being to swim out into the clear waters of the Gulf and radio inflatable boats to recover them.

It was a time to double-check the chambered round you had in your 16 and pull your personal stack of hand grenades in a little tighter.

Lozano roused Russell and Corporal Courtnay from the Humvee where they had sacked out and began gathering up the various pieces of team gear strewn about their living area. As the Marines wakened to the gathering malevolence, lines of flares began popping up far to the west along the border, seeming to conform to some prearranged sequence. As if to signal something.

Lozano, excited now, declared to Lieutenant Lang, after he got off the radio with their headquarters element—located in an abandoned water desalinization plant four kilometers to the south—"Sir, this is crazy. The Iraqis are moving around out there and we're right on a major avenue of approach."

Lang replied, "Lozano, you're spooking me. Just chill out. We'll get some aircraft out here and everything'll be fine."

The two worked the team's cluster of arcane-looking, olive drab–painted radios, hoping to rope whatever air they could find spiraling far above. Directing air was second nature to ANGLICO Marines, so much so that they prided themselves on their ability to sweet-talk pilots off whatever mission they might be flying to come bomb for them. ANGLICO teams would regularly steal aircraft working with their sister teams just for the sheer harassing fun of it. Over the course of the months leading up to the air war, the Marines had become master manipulators of the tactical air nets, like bond traders on the desert floor—juggling numerous missions, stacking the atmosphere with loitering airplanes, perfecting their choreography of the gross destruction with a cocksure, acronym-laden amalgam of cardinal directions, obscure buzzwords, and aviation terminology. The pilots all knew ANGLICO, knew that they were the best controllers in theater and would often roll up on their local frequencies asking for "Wild Eagle," the company-wide call sign.

As the clipped radio jabber grew, Lozano began hearing mechanized road wheels and tank tracks creaking out in the chill night air to the north. Grabbing his night-vision goggles, Lozano scanned the area where the noises were emanating from, an extended semi-urbanized swath of resort complexes along the Kuwaiti coast, and came up dry. Changing over to the team's ground-mounted night sight and laser-designator apparatus, known enigmatically as the MULE*, he again found nothing. It was the damndest thing. Everyone in the team could hear mechanized vehicles moving to their front, but try as they might, they couldn't get a visual. None of the planes they talked to wanted to waste bombs on phantoms, so the Marines watched disconsolately as the ribbons of air, signaled by the siren-screech of turbine wash, began flowing westward toward OP 7 and OP 2. It was maddening.

Lozano was agitated. They had an Iraqi mech force of unknown magnitude poking around out in front of them and no air assets to deal with them. They were like baseball announcers out there, doing the play-by-play, totally defenseless. Talking back to the officers at the desal plant, Lieutenant Lang got the order to remain in place until the position became untenable.

A few minutes later, around 10:00 P.M., they received an unexpected radio call saying, "Be advised, General Boomer has dedicated all close-air-support assets to you."

Now they were talking! Lozano and the other Marines, who in response to the noises had begun collecting all the non–mission essential gear into the Humvee in anticipation of leaving, turned right back around and began unloading it and setting it up on their little hill for a full night of raining death down on the Iraqis. It took several minutes to get the various radios and crypto gear back on line again.

The ratcheting tank track noises grew louder.

Despite the promise of air from on high, the team back at the desal plant didn't seem to be passing off any jets to them or forwarding them any contact frequencies for nearby formations. Mel Russell recalls, "I was so pissed off. We had a shitload of movement out front, and they wouldn't give us the fucking air to probe the area."

Suddenly one of the recon Marines from out front of the OP came running carrying an M-60 machine gun. His gear was all bouncing off his body, clanging like a one-man band.

*modular universal laser equipment.

The ANGLICOs watched in disbelief as this figure raced past them, screaming, "Tracks!" Moments later, a second recon man jogged up out of breath, huffing the same word, indicating that there were tanks coming right for the Marines.

No sooner had the second man gotten this out than rocks and dirt began kicking up in front of Lozano. Turning, he saw an Iraqi T-55 main battle tank less than 100 meters away, its 12.7-mm machine gun raking the Marine position. The jig was up.

Lieutenant Lang, groping for whatever gear he could locate in the darkness, snatched up the bulky MULE, and as he began to make his way down the hill, tripped, tumbling down in front of Lozano.

An enormous artillery illumination round burst over the landscape, skylining the Marines with its secondhand sunlight.

Lang somehow made his way down the hill to the Humvee, where Corporal Courtnay had the truck running and ready to go. This left Lozano and Russell trapped under the heaviest machine-gun fire either of them had ever seen. Lozano recalls, "There was literally a ceiling of bullets above us. It was solid as a roof."

Over to the west at OP 7, Captain Doug Kleinsmith, team leader for the ANGLICO team positioned there, had been watching the scene at OP 8 unfold and described it as "a sheet of green tracers. I mean a solid fucking sheet. You could've walked on it."

Somehow the Marines survived this initial barrage unscathed, and Lozano, sensing a brief pause opening up, popped up and squeezed off an M-203 high-explosive grenade at the Iraqis. According to Lozano, "I didn't expect it to do anything. It was really just a 'fuck you' shot."

Looking over at Russell, Lozano screamed, "Let's get the fuck outta here!"

Taking full advantage of the lull, both Marines alternately scurried and low-crawled down to the Humvee and jumped into the bed of the truck, kicking out all kinds of gear to make room for themselves. As the truck pulled away under heavy fire, Lozano and Russell both realized that they had left nearly all the radios and, most important, several pieces of invaluable encrypting gear back at the OP. Lozano had no idea what happened to the recon Marines. It was literally every man for himself.

Corporal Courtnay, the driver of the Humvee, could barely see through the windshield, which somehow over the course of the night had become obscured by mud and grime. The wildly zigzagging Humvee, a much more lucrative target than the scampering Marines, began taking direct fire from the tanks.

As they rolled at top speed, Lozano noticed that the only piece of comm gear they had was a broken PRC-77 VHF radio with a tag marked "Will Not Transmit" on it. He listened in as everyone began calling in reports about OP 8's demise. Everyone thought they were dead.

Everyone was yelling directions at Courtnay. The young corporal pointed the nose of the vehicle toward the desal plant and floored it. The tanks had clearly overrun their old position, and as the race southward continued, the fire closed in on the lone Humvee. Loud green tracers punched through the air all around the vehicle.

Unwilling to simply sit on his hands, Lozano ripped off the right side passenger door, so that he could better aim, hung his leg out, and cranked off another 203 grenade round. As he watched, the tracers inched closer. As if in slo-mo, Lozano watched as a single tracer walked its way up toward his leg. He thought, *Fuck, this is gonna hurt.*

The round zipped by.

A single tank round howled by on Russell's side of the vehicle. Lozano, who as a newly promoted sergeant and the senior enlisted man present, felt responsible for Russell and yelled over to see if he was okay.

"I'm all right, boss!" came the reply.

After several minutes of this chaotic zigzagging, the Marines managed to cover the four kilometers back to the walled desalinization plant compound, where a large detachment of the Marine Corps 1st Surveillance, Reconnaissance, and Intelligence Group, led by Lieutenant Colonel Rick Barry, was camped out.

Eight kilometers to the west at Observation Post 7, Captain Doug Kleinsmith, ANGLICO team leader for "Wild Eagle 3-2 Forward," was talking with his buddy Kurt Lang at OP 8 about the Iraqi tanks moving around to their front. Fingers of darkness were just beginning to seep in. Both officers were concerned but not overly worried. Kleinsmith, a promising, boyish captain, could see Iraqi artillery pieces being set in north of the border fort his team shared with twenty Green Berets. As aircraft began to circulate overhead, he directed two A-6 Intruders onto them. Lang was so close to the jumbly, urbanized stretch of the Kuwaiti coast that he couldn't get a visual on any of the Iraqis maneuvering to his front, and because Kleinsmith had actual targets in sight, all the air on station that night went to him. Kleinsmith began raining missions down on the Iraqis attempting to dig in.

All of the indications and warnings were now present. The battle was about to be joined, although no one at OP 7 or OP 8 or the desalinization plant or anywhere else along the border seemed to be able to sense the dimensions of the coming fight and formulate a coherent plan of action. Each individual American participant, while vigilant and well trained, knew only what was happening to his direct front and was responding accordingly, each reacting symmetrically to circumstances as they emerged from the darkness. Only in hindsight, as the overwhelming momentum of organized facts are taken into account, does a discernible picture begin to emerge.

Captain John Bley, who had handed control of OP 7 over to Kleinsmith earlier that evening, had had a field day on the evenings of January 27 and 28, calling down mission after mission on the Iraqis lurking in the deceptively undulating earth to the north of the border fort. Bley had noted the increased activity north of the border, which he assumed to be in response to the cross-border artillery raids that the Marines had been launching, designed as they were to poke and jab at the Iraqis, coaxing them into betraying their positions. At 3:15 A.M. on January 29, Bley observed a large enemy armored convoy moving westward off the coastal road to their direct front, heading toward the sparsely wooded al-Wafra forest. Bley requested air support and was passed a section of Air Force A-10s, which proceeded to destroy over a dozen Iraqi vehicles. The secondary explosions continued for two hours. At sunrise the Marines could see the Iraqis attempting cleaning up the carnage. The Iraqis were obviously up to something, and Bley had managed to catch them mid-stride.

After changing over with Kleinsmith, Bley had headed for the rear to check in with one of the Saudi Arabian National Guard brigades, headquartered near Ra's al-Mishab, that ANGLICO was attached to. Talking over the situation with two other Marine officers, one of them, an impetuous first lieutenant named Paul "Bubba" Deckert jokingly mentioned, "Christ, John, it looks like the Iraqis are setting up for an attack."

Bley replied, "You know, Bubba, you may be right."

This prophecy never reached the men up at OP 7, and shortly after working the strike package of A-6s, Kleinsmith hit the rack in one of the smaller offset rooms of the prominent Beau Geste fort. He figured he'd grab a bit of shut-eye before the next Iraqi probe, which was sure to come later that evening. After trailing off for a time, Kleinsmith was woken by Corporal John Calhoun, who exclaimed excitedly, "Sir, you need to get up on the roof right now. These Army guys are freaking out!"

Groggy, Kleinsmith replied, "Well, do you think you can handle it?"

"No, sir. I think you better come up."

They piled up onto the parapeted roof of the fort. To Kleinsmith it seemed as if the entire horizon was filled with the sound of rumbling tank engines. Kleinsmith couldn't see a thing, but a solid wall of rough noise extended all the way from the coast to the al-Wafra forest in the west. Scanning with his night-vision goggles and the team's thermal sights, he still couldn't spot any vehicles. He surmised that the Iraqis were hiding in the hollows and the dead space out in front of the OP, making maximum use of the cover, which remained invisible to the men on the roof. Soon flares and illumination rounds appeared, mixed with spurts of Soviet-style green tracer fire.

Shortly after Kleinsmith made his way to the roof, the feeble evening peace collapsed entirely. Lang was suddenly on the radio going fucking crazy. Looking east, OP 8 suddenly disappeared under a solid green arc of tracers, the land and coast covered by the fantastic iridescence. Lang's team was somewhere under the solid wall of lead.

All Kleinsmith or anyone else atop the fort could manage was, "Fuck!"

The initial American response to the attack coalesced with surprising quickness. Captain Jon Fleming, attached to Lieutenant Colonel Rick Barry's headquarters element at the desalinization plant, began plucking aircraft coming back from bombing runs deep inside Kuwait and offering them up to the ANGLICO teams dispersed along the border. The planes were all flying on vapors, most of them having just a few bombs dangling underwing, extras from the carnage up north.

At first Fleming attempted to hand over control of the aircraft to Lang, who was already hopelessly intermixed with the Iraqi tanks that had sallied across the border. Realizing his folly, he next tried to take some of the pressure off the OP 8 crew, targeting the tanks bearing down on his comrades. As Kleinsmith listened in, Lang screamed over the radio, "No! Don't drop anything! I don't know where we are!" Lang's team was clearly running for their lives.

Kleinsmith was stunned that they had survived the initial onslaught at all, remarking, "I have no idea how they made it out of there."

Because of the obvious disarray at OP 8, control of the aircraft circling over the Khafji region soon devolved to Kleinsmith's team, who guided a nearly-out-of-gas Harrier onto an artillery piece that had been missed in the earlier A-6 runs. It was dicey work because he didn't have a laser that would designate that deep into Kuwait, but after directing an A-6 Intruder onto a target using its unique on-board radio beacon system, Kleinsmith simply directed the Harrier off the brilliant explosions caused by the A-6's run. In a burgeoning era of precision weaponry, both aircraft were still using dumb 500-pound "Rockeye" cluster bombs. Nevertheless, the Rockeye, while not mathematically precise, scared the hell out of the opposition. The A-6 had unleashed six Rockeyes on one pass alone, illuminating half of the horizon. "It was just sheer intimidation," Kleinsmith recalled.

Another section of Harriers rolled in, which Kleinsmith directed onto OP 8, now clear of U.S. forces. Not long after, Fleming came up on the radio and told him that Colonel Barry had ordered the evacuation of the desal plant. Fleming, Kleinsmith's primary lifeline was being forced out of the picture by the rapidly advancing Iraqis. To Kleinsmith, who could hear most of the radio traffic along the border, it seemed as if OP 7 were the only U.S. position still bucking the tide. To cover his colleague's withdrawal, Kleinsmith began marshaling Cobra missions along the coastal road north of town, guiding off the Iraqis' telltale green tracer bursts.

With Fleming gone, Kleinsmith, the most junior captain in 1st ANGLICO, was left to coordinate the fight for a huge swath of territory with only his team of four Marines. Soon a propeller-driven OV-10 spotter plane appeared, and Kleinsmith and the pilot of the aircraft, Captain Dave Neely, attempted to piece together where all the various Coalition forces screening along the border had disappeared to. It was vexing work trying to locate everyone. Kleinsmith knew that he couldn't expect to control air effectively unless he had a positive location on all of the various teams, and yet he knew that practically everyone near Khafji was running away fast and therefore incommunicado. He sat atop the fort working the radios, realizing that it was only a matter of time before the Iraqis came for him and his team.

As if on cue, a heavy section of four Cobra gunships turned up. Directing them toward the sound of the engines, the helicopters thundered across the border, firing several salvos of 2.75-inch rockets toward the Iraqis. The sound of the four menacing birds, loitering noisily around the border fort, seemed for a time to stem the tide. Kleinsmith called over to them, "Hey, guys, can you just keep hovering around us? I think we're next." As long as the Cobras stayed, no Iraqis advanced on the fort.

To Kleinsmith the atmosphere on the night of the twenty-ninth seemed surprisingly clear, the normal soupy ceiling of clouds unusually high, the moon full and bright. High in his stone redoubt, Kleinsmith was able to monitor much of the opening moves of the battle. The tableau of war splayed out around him like the Bayeux Tapestry. He watched off to the east as the Iraqis motored into Khafij, the overexcited gunners spraying tracers wildly into the air. To the west he saw the reflected explosions and gunfire at the OPs as the light-armored vehicle Marines collided with the Iraqis. By midnight, OP 7 was an island in an Iraqi sea.

After running several missions and hovering near the fort to keep the Iraqis at bay, the Cobras' section leader told Kleinsmith, "We're out of gas. We'll be back in thirty minutes."

"You're what?" This was the last thing Kleinsmith wanted to hear, but he knew that there was really nothing he could do to make the Cobras stay. If they were out of gas, they were out of gas. The four gunships departed, seeming to take the final hope of the men at OP 7 with them.

Dave Neely, high overhead in the OV-10, informed Kleinsmith that no more aircraft were inbound. Shortly after receiving this word, Kleinsmith got a radio call from Jon Fleming saying that he was in a tower in southern Khafji but that he couldn't stay. Kleinsmith's team and the squad of Green Berets were now completely isolated.

The senior Special Forces soldier present, a staff sergeant whom Kleinsmith had worked with before and liked a lot approached him and said, "Sir, I think we need to get the fuck outta here."

Kleinsmith, whose focus up until that moment had been

almost exclusively on the air fight, looked back at the Green Beret and asked innocently, "Well, what's your escape-and-evasion plan?" referring to the standard allocation made by forward troops in the event of being overrun.

"Well, sir, our primary route was to skirt eastward along the border until we hit the coastal highway and then head south through the city."

"I guess that one's out. What's your alternate?"

"To head west until we hit the next observation post and then head south."

"That obviously ain't gonna work."

Kleinsmith realized then that their only means of escape from the Iraqis, surrounded as they were, was to strike out into the *sabkha*—a marshy quagmire that serpentined in from the Gulf to the south of OP 7—and wait out the night. Kleinsmith recalls, "We decided to just go straight into this badland, figuring that the Iraqis' heavier tanks would get bogged down before we would, and then if need be, we could abandon our vehicles and make it out on foot. That was really the only way we were gonna make it out of there. The Iraqis were well south of us on the right and the left." The ANGLICO Marines had been fooling around and getting vehicles stuck up to the axles in the *sabkha* for months. It was like their own briar patch. Kleinsmith figured they could leverage this knowledge against the Iraqis' brute firepower and hopefully navigate through the *sabkha* without getting stuck. Kleinsmith, who had been attached to Arab forces in the Khafji region for six months by this point, hoped to lead the mixed Army-Marine team to safety through a well-trafficked infiltration point into Saudi lines. It was the only place along the Saudi line where they stood a chance, given the notoriously jumpy Saudi troops.

The Special Forces guys, while first-rate soldiers, hadn't had the benefit of living and working with the Arab forces in sector and as a result didn't didn't know the area around OP 7 nearly as well as Kleinsmith and the ANGLICO Marines. Their prearranged escape plans had been rendered irrelevant within the first hour of the attack. To attempt to stand and fight or conduct a running withdrawal in open terrain was lunacy. The Iraqis with all their heavy armor would run right over them. After talking things over, the Special Forces staff sergeant agreed that descending into the *sabkha* was the thing to do.

It was a comical moment heading out from the rooftop as Kleinsmith, in truth a very young captain who prior to Operation Desert Storm had never completed an overseas deployment, made it a point to walk slowly down the stairs and make his way toward the contingent's collection of Humvees. He was trying to do as he'd been lectured at Quantico: to keep cool, to radiate calmness and serenity in the midst of a desperate situation. Iraqi rounds were flying all over the place, and as far as he knew, they were the sole remaining Coalition team within fifty miles. His Marines were starting to get jumpy, and Kleinsmith realized that if there was ever a time to play it cool, it was now.

With the Marine Humvee at the head of the convoy, the group headed south away from OP 7. Corporal Steve Foss, the well-muscled and tattooed Marine driver, knew the *sabkha* as well as Kleinsmith and tried to stay away from the larger lakes, worming his way through the archipelago of saline puddles and sucking mud pits. Prior to shoving off, Kleinsmith had instructed all the drivers, "Drive where I drive. Don't veer off."

After proceeding for several minutes, the column came across an abandoned Saudi V-150 armored personnel carrier, most likely from the 5th Battalion of the Saudi National Guard, whose mission it was to screen along the eastern portion of the border. Trash and military gear were strewn about the area, the fire for evening tea still flickering, the soldiers clearly having left in a hurry. As the Humvees moved south, Kleinsmith would update Dave Neely orbiting in the OV-10 overhead, supplying him with position reports every few minutes, saying, "Everything north of us is enemy. Blast it." The Iraqis didn't seem to be in hot pursuit, but he didn't want to take any chances.

At one point Kleinsmith checked behind him and saw that

the next vehicle, the staff sergeant's Humvee, was trailing far to the rear. Thinking that the soldiers might be having difficulty keeping up, Kleinsmith stopped to allow the second vehicle to catch up.

"Hey, Staff Sergeant, am I going too fast for you?" he asked.

"Oh, no, sir. We were figuring if the Iraqis or the Saudis are gonna hit anyone, they're gonna hit the lead vehicle, so we're just hanging back."

Kleinsmith just shook his head. "You fuckers!" Pissed off, he added, "Let's go. And fucking floor it!"

Kleinsmith told the three corporals in his team, "Okay, guys, if you see a muzzle flash, just roll out of the vehicle. Just roll out and let the vehicle take the hit and we'll make it." Craning into the darkness, the four Marines inside were on pins and needles, just waiting to see an Iraqi tank—or worse, a Saudi V-150—looming in front of them. Kleinsmith knew that if they surprised a Saudi vehicle, they'd buy it for sure.

The convoy was continuing along in the *sabkha* when all of a sudden a blinding flash from a Saudi multiple-launch rocket system battery lit up the darkness in front of the Humvee. Foss exclaimed, "What's that? What's that?" and without any further ceremony, dove out the driver-side door into the wet sand. Corporal John Calhoun, in the seat behind Foss, had the presence of mind to grab the steering wheel after Foss's rapid departure and kept the vehicle heading straight until it rolled to a halt.

Running up, Foss whined, "Well, you said to roll out if I saw a big flash!"

"Get in here, Foss!" Kleinsmith yelled.

After rolling along in the mucky wastes for several hours, Kleinsmith finally decided that they were far enough away from any Iraqis or friendlies to be safe until sunrise, now only a few hours away. They were in the middle of nowhere, completely isolated from any major lines of communication or landmarks. Kleinsmith halted the Humvees and told the Green Berets, "This is your area. Set up a defensive position for the night," adding, "Get some rest. It's gonna be a long fucking fight."

Kleinsmith was concerned because his high-frequency, long-range radios—his primary mode of communication with the rear—had gone out. Somehow in the course of their hegira, the HF antenna had been broken in half. The only means of communications the team had now was the UHF, with which they could talk to the OV-10s. No one in the rear had heard from Kleinsmith for several hours, and he was concerned that they would think that they'd been wiped out at OP 7. Talking to the OV-10s high above, he told them to try to relay the word to ANGLICO headquarters that they were still alive and that they were on their way back in.

Near dawn, Kleinsmith was woken by some of the Special Forces soldiers, who thought they saw tanks coming toward their position. To Captain Kleinsmith, this didn't add up. *What would the Iraqis be doing way out here?* But after jumping on top of a nearby Humvee to get a better view, he acquiesced; it appeared as if the Iraqis had followed them after all. The men quickly packed up, abandoning their harbor site and heading southwest toward the Saudi infiltration point in the feeble morning light. As they decamped, Kleinsmith tried to call some air strikes down on the Iraqi tanks, but every aircraft seemed to be committed to other parts of the battle.

It was like a Mexican standoff when the caravan finally reached the Saudi infiltration point. Kleinsmith, who knew the Saudis' preferred method of operation—fire like mad at first, ask questions later—was as worried as he'd been all through the long night. That was the sole reason for selecting this point 40 kilometers south of the border to re-enter friendly lines. He knew full well that if they attempted to cross anywhere else along the screen line, the Saudi gunners, their nerves frayed after the longest night of their lives, would kill them all.

Saudi patrols had been using the transit point for weeks, and the pickets who manned the area were accustomed to seeing mixed groups of vehicles crossing over. The checkpoint he'd selected was their best chance for re-entry, but knowing the Saudis as he did, he nevertheless feared for his life and the lives of the men under him.

Parking just outside of small-arms range, Kleinsmith popped several red smoke grenades to indicate to the Saudi guardsmen that they were friendlies. Figuring that the pyrotechnics had at least gotten the guards to relax their trigger fingers, Kleinsmith began the nerve-racking walk over to Saudi lines. Kleinsmith, who had always enjoyed an unusually informal relationship with the Arab troops, was greeted by several soldiers who immediately recognized him: "Oh, Captain Doug. You are lucky. We almost shot you!"

Yeah, I know, you stupid motherfucker.

Kleinsmith waved the rest of the column forward, and they made their way past the first pickets and to the major east-west thoroughfare that connected Mishab to the interior of the Arabian peninsula. The Green Berets broke off to rejoin their unit, and Kleinsmith and his three Marines proceeded toward the coast for a homecoming with his unit, the 2nd Saudi Arabian National Guard Brigade, where his boss and best friend, Captain Jim Braden, was located.

15

January 29, 1991,
Surveillance, Reconnaissance, Intelligence
Group Forward Headquarters,
Four Miles North of Khafji

*The firing woke us up. It was about three-thirty, four in the morning,
January 31, 1968, which I think of now as a kind of birthday; the
first day in the rest of my life, for sure. Sergeant Benet and I hustled
outside and saw the flares going up all over the town. Soldiers from
the battalion were running past us, carbines in hand, heading for
the perimeter. I said I didn't like this. I could hear myself say it: "I
don't like this."*
—TOBIAS WOLFF, *In Pharaoh's Army,* discussing the start of
the Tet offensive in Vietnam

LIEUTENANT COLONEL Rick Barry, the executive officer of
the Marines' 1st Surveillance, Reconnaissance, and Intelligence Group and head of the special operations effort
on the border, had seen the Iraqi offensive coming a long
ways off. His hodgepodge team of signals collection men,
ANGLICO spotters, Navy SEALs, and Green Berets, who
had been in Khafji since Christmas, had been watching the
signs for weeks, intercepting a flood of cryptic Arabic messages over the radio, things like "The fist of Allah strikes
soon." The morning after the air war began, his men had captured the first prisoners of the war, four soldiers with perfect
stories, telling about how all the men in Kuwait were starv-
ing and that all their officers had abandoned them. Their stories had seemed just a bit too practiced to Barry, who thought
the Iraqis were trying to lull them into a false sense of security. He figured the Iraqis would take a poke at them at some
point.

171

Earlier that week Barry had relayed his suspicions back to General Walt Boomer's headquarters, but the message had been largely ignored or merely absorbed by the tent-dwelling staffers down at Safaniya, who likely added Barry's hunches to the swelling constellation of inscrutable military data collecting in the headquarters. Barry recalls, "I told 'em, 'This is it. The Iraqis want Khafji.' "

On January 28, Barry had listened in on the radio traffic as a line of Harrier jump jets struck an Iraqi heavy equipment transporter moving along an east-west road five kilometers north of the border, blocking a major artery that ran from the coast toward the al-Wafra forest in southern Kuwait. "The Iraqis put probably 150 sappers out there to try and clear that road. We sensed that they really wanted it open. They were obviously using that road as a sort of interior line like at Gettysburg."

At around four on the afternoon of the twenty-ninth, Barry's radio intercept men told him, "These guys are ready to go. They have their engines idling and we're getting a ton of throat mike chatter."

These clues, along with the increasing number of artillery shells and Astro missiles being launched toward Mishab, pointed to a large Iraqi operation brewing in northeastern Saudi Arabia. "A blind man could've seen it coming," Barry recalls.

Nevertheless, for reasons that have never been fully explained, these warnings went unheeded, and as the Iraqis overran OP 8 and charged down the coast toward Barry's safe house at the desalinization plant, he appealed to Boomer's headquarters, the 1st Marine Expeditionary Force, to surge airplanes to his position. His pleas fell on deaf ears, the planners at MEF having long ago concluded that any Iraqi thrust into Saudi Arabia would run along the Wadi al-Batin— a large gully that formed the western boundary of Kuwait and a natural invasion route that led straight to Riyadh, the Saudi capital. As the fight at OP 4 developed, MEF diverted all available aircraft to the west in line with this schema. From their perspective, the Iraqis were doing exactly what they'd always predicted—the force at OP 4 was surely a supporting effort for the main attack coming down the wadi—and they'd responded accordingly. Everything was going according to plan.

Ensconced inside the desal compound, Barry attempted to disabuse MEF of their preconceived notions: "Khafji is the Iraqis' main objective. Everything in theater points to it. They have Palestinian spies in town with a direct line to Baghdad. We've been trading licks with them for weeks. They're coming for us hard." MEF remained undeterred.

Barry's counterintelligence men had informed him of the presence of the Palestinians several weeks prior to the assault. It had been hairy knowing they were there at first. Barry recalls, "There was a certain fate aspect to it. I'm not saying we were being hung out to dry; we were doing some valuable collections. I thought that by remaining in town, we might be able to suck the Iraqis into some sort of offensive action. I was just disappointed with MEF's response when they actually did attack."

In the pixilated green light of his night-vision goggles, Barry could see the tanks charging past the border fort. He called "Buzzsaw" over the local net, which meant for all of the various teams to gather at the safe house and prepare to withdraw to the south. Barry had long felt as if he and his men, while they were performing a vital mission, were in a sense just bait for an Iraqi assault. Therefore, he'd forced the motley group to rehearse the evacuation plan throughout the month of January. All hands were to gather up all their mission essential gear and classified materials, muster at the safe house for a head count, and then proceed south in a tight convoy.

Lozano was confused when he and his team pulled into the desal compound sometime after 9:00 P.M. After abandoning OP 8, he'd assumed that they would stand and fight it out at the desal plant. As they rolled up, he could tell that Barry's crew had other ideas; a mass exodus was clearly under way, a long line of five-ton trucks and Humvees racing out of the compound toward the coastal highway and downtown

Khafji. To Lozano, it looked as if no one knew what was going on. The consummate noncom, he was worried because he couldn't account for the two ANGLICO Marines, Captain Jon Fleming and Corporal Cruz, who had been attached to Barry's team. It was like a Chinese fire drill—everyone was running around, dead set on bailing from the scene. No one would stop to tell Lozano what the plan was or where his Marines were.

Lozano searched the compound but couldn't locate Fleming or Cruz. At some point, Lieutenant Lang approached him and told him the two missing Marines had left in the main body of Barry's vehicles on its way south. Lang and Lozano piled back into their Hummer and chased after the southbound convoy.

Mel Russell couldn't believe how many vehicles had piled out of the compound. *Where the fuck did all these guys come from?* The whole movement seemed like total chaos. He thought, *This is the wrong thing to do. We have all these guys now. Why are we retreating?* As they joined the convoy headed south, it seemed like every 500 meters they would halt and a bunch of officers would get out of their vehicles, look around confusedly, then get back in and begin heading south again. It didn't look as if anyone was in charge. It was just a bunch of Special Forces guys and SEALs running amok.

Not long after exiting the desal, Barry stopped the convoy in order to get a head count to make absolutely sure that no one had been left behind. One of the Special Forces teams had been having trouble getting their five-ton truck started, and Barry was worried that they might still be in the compound. The men spread the vehicles out in a half-moon facing north across the breadth of the highway and out into the dunes by the beach. As they waited anxiously, the lone five-ton came trundling up.*

---

*In the confusion, some of Barry's men accidentally left several classified maps and cryptographic equipment. The highly sensitive nature of the abandoned gear far outstripped the cryptographic loss by Lang's team and the communications plan for the entire theater had to be reconfigured to guard against Iraqi eavesdropping.

Lozano recalls the convoy stopping and watching as Barry's men began breaking out a ton of AT-4s and LAW antitank rockets, looking like they were going to take on the Iraqi force coming down the highway. About this time a flight of Cobra gunships rattled overhead, and the ANGLICO Marines started breaking open chemlights and throwing them up on top of their Humvees so that the Cobras wouldn't light them up. The thin helicopters sped over the convoy and began engaging the Iraqi column to the north. Barry's men got off several AT-4 and M-203 shots at the Iraqis, who at this point were only a few hundred meters away. Responding to either the Cobras or Barry's men, the Iraqi attack seemed to pause briefly, buying the harried convoy a few precious minutes.

As the Cobras continued to shoot, Lozano heard Colonel Barry yell, "Mount up!" Lozano still didn't know what their ultimate destination was, but he hopped back into the Humvee and chased after the long convoy as it headed into the heart of Khafji. They had almost reached the southern limits of town when the convoy halted near the base of a huge concrete water tower. Lozano heard Barry holler, "We're not retreating one more fucking step!"

Barry recalled, "I thought that the Iraqis would be content to capture the desal plant and the northern part of Khafji."

With the consent of Colonel Barry, the two ANGLICO officers present, Captain Jon Fleming and Lieutenant Kurt Lang, decided to find a way to get up into a large water tower, which afforded a commanding view of the city. Circling around the tower looking for an entrance, Fleming discovered several Saudi soldiers in a basement area, barefoot and drinking tea, obviously unconcerned with the chaos unfolding around them.

"Don't you know the war's started?" Fleming asked, gesturing toward the sound of the distant gunfire.

One of the Saudis shrugged. "The Marines are here to protect us," he said.

After locating a metal door leading up to the top of the

tower, Fleming and Lang rushed up eight flights of stairs. Adrenalized and out of breath, the two peered north out a small window. A dozen round-turreted T-55s and a like number of Iraqi armored personnel carriers appeared to have transited the main causeway connecting the northern part of town to the downtown area. The Iraqi gunners were wildly spraying the upper stories of every building in an apparent effort to kill any lurking snipers. It wasn't long before green tracer fire began to make its way toward the tower.

Down below, Barry got the message from Fleming: *The Iraqis are coming hard.*

Lozano was livid. He had been thrown into this roving band of gypsies, none of whom wanted to take charge of the situation. When he learned the two officers had gone up into the tower, he was aghast. As an experienced artillery observer, he knew that you never picked the tallest building in a given area to use as an observation post, as it would be too obvious a target for the enemy. It was for this very reason that the ANGLICO Marines had elected not to use the warmer, more comfortable border fort up at OP 8. "When I heard that Colonel Barry had sent the two ANGLICO officers up into the biggest fucking tower in Khafji, I was pissed. I voiced my concerns saying, 'Hey, sir, there are plenty of other buildings we could observe from. Why are we going to that one?' It was the biggest target in town."

No one seemed to hear Lozano's logic. In a way, it was totally predictable: Officers were always getting wrapped up in big tactical issues and not thinking through the immediate ramifications. As Lozano saw it, sending Fleming and Lang up into the tower was dividing an already splintered force and making his job unnecessarily difficult. Not to mention that it was only a matter of time before the Iraqis spied the huge tower and blasted it, killing both of his officers. While Fleming and Lang were poking around the tower, Lozano was running around trying to locate them and keep track of Russell, Courtnay, and Cruz.

After about twenty minutes of this, it looked as if someone

on Barry's team had decided that it was time to quit Khafji for good. People were piling back into vehicles. Lozano ran over to the colonel's Humvee, saying, "Sir, we gotta get our guys down from the tower!"

He seemed confused and asked, "Who's up in the tower?"

"Fleming and Lang, sir."

"Why the fuck are they up in the tower?"

"Because you told 'em to go up there!"

"Well, go get 'em."

Lozano had no idea how to get up into the tower, and as Barry's Humvee, the trail vehicle in the convoy, began to move out, he jumped in front of it to stop him. "Hey, sir, we gotta get my officers down from the tower!"

"Well, goddamn it, follow me," Barry responded, hopping out of the vehicle and running off toward the tall lookout.

Reaching the tower, the colonel went inside, yelled up to Fleming and Lang, and took off back to his idling Humvee. Not satisfied, Lozano hollered up, "Hey, Marines! C'mon, we gotta go!"

Bullets sang off the tower as the pair bounded down the stairs. Joining Lozano on the ground floor, the three sprinted off to their Humvee and chased Barry's shrinking taillights south toward Mishab through the grand dual archway greeting visitors to Khafji.

The Iraqis owned the town, or so they thought.

10:00 P.M., January 29, 1991,
Jubail Port Facility, 125 Miles South of Khafji

CAPTAIN MAX MORTON sat behind a desk at the squadron headquarters in Jubail answering phones when a call of another sort came. Morton had just returned from Mishab, the forwardmost Marine position, where he and the aircrews from three other Cobra attack helicopters had been on strip alert for the past day, waiting to fly for any ground troops that needed air support. The pilots had sobered up out of this routine duty when soon after their arrival the Iraqis began lobbing Brazilian 300-mm Astro rockets at the Marine compound. Always on the hunt for a good joke, the fliers began referring to this day-long detail as "catching rockets." The Astros were wildly inaccurate, but the mere thought of the potentially chemically armed projectiles hurtling in their general direction unnerved everyone, and when the rockets came in the night, the pilots would pile like mad into sandbagged bunkers to wait out the barrage.

Upon his return to Jubail, Morton discovered that nearly everyone in the squadron had been sent to a planning conference in the rear, leaving the young captain to man the phones in the duty hut, logging administrative messages as they came in. It was humbling duty, in marked contrast to the adrenaline-laced chasm he'd been toeing up at Mishab. Mishab was, in the context of the war, almost like the last outpost of civilization, and although the dangers there were generally knowable and infinitesimal, just being there provided you with a sense of The Thing that was totally unavailable even ten miles to the south.

Shortly after Morton began his phone watch, the squadron operations officer, Major Gary Shaw, an old hand and former test pilot, stepped into the duty hut to inform him that they'd just launched the standby division up at Mishab. The Iraqis were coming hard and fast, and Shaw couldn't find his copilot and needed someone to fly in the front seat of his Cobra. Morton, a qualified flight leader himself, usually rode in the back seat, the senior man's position, but this was no time for quibbling. Shaw was a good soul, one of the leading minds in the squadron and somewhat of a mentor to Morton and the other captains. Morton was happy to go up with him. Abandoning the phone, he grabbed a "bullet bouncer"—a heavy Vietnam-era flak vest—and his night-vision goggles and headed out to the flight line in Shaw's footsteps.

The Iraqi thrust had caught the squadron flat-footed. Virtually every pilot in the unit had been sent to Riyadh to a frag conference to sort out the distribution of attack missions, a process that had become increasingly complicated, given the large number of air units and personnel flooding the theater. As he and Shaw powered up their Cobra gunship, he realized that he hadn't flown in the front seat since they'd deployed to Saudi Arabia, several months prior. He couldn't remember the last time he'd been up with Gary Shaw.

The Cobra had already been gassed and loaded with TOW missiles, so it was only a matter of firing up the bird's twin jet engines and launching to the north. They would light out with another Cobra, commanded by Scott Haney, a senior pilot and graduate of the Marine Corps's prestigious Weapons and Tactics Instructor Course, a Marine version of *Top Gun* run out in the Arizona desert. Whoever happened to be available to fly that evening was being sortied to wherever reports of Iraqi tanks were coming in, which at this point was practically everywhere. Heading out, steeling themselves for the fray, they hovered noisily out from the field at Jubail, the wide rotor blades of the sinister-looking bird chopping thickly at the humid air like an angry insect. Once airborne, they were instructed to proceed to "the elbow," where the Kuwait border banks 90 degrees to the north near Observation Post 4. There they were to link up with the four-ship division that had sortied from Mishab and await instructions from an LAV company that was under attack by an Iraqi armored column.

Morton and his comrades were professional close-air-support specialists and had trained for years, decades in some cases, rigorously preparing for battle. Because of their scrappy, nap-of-the-earth modus operandi, they prided themselves on their close, fraternal connection to the grunts they fired for. They weren't above landing next to a company's position, flipping open the canopy, and yelling over to ask the Marines where they needed fire put down. A former infantry officer himself, Morton was an art-of-the-possible operator who viewed the prospect of combat with a boyish simplicity, a place where clear thinking and quick action inevitably won the day. He detested the politics of higher headquarters and thought that the overly centralized Marine command structure often failed to serve the grunts to whom he was so dedicated.

This headquarters tunnel vision seemed to be in full effect tonight. Even though Iraqi tanks were breaking out like locusts all along the border, the air controllers who were orchestrating the battle were strangely fixated upon the elbow portion of the border battle, resulting in every available aircraft being diverted to OP 4 in the far west. Adding to the enigma, as they lifted off, word was passed that Iraqi tanks were threatening Khafji, and yet not a single aircraft was being sent to defend the town.

To Morton it seemed as if the command-and-control apparatus was completely overloaded. There was all kinds of intelligence floating around the theater, but nobody seemed to be willing to pause for a moment and let the big picture come into focus. It was like a French Impressionist painting: All the little points of color didn't amount to anything until you stepped back for a minute, tilted your head, and let the pieces slip into place. He personally knew that there was an unmanned aerial vehicle company up at Mishab that had been tracking Iraqi movements for days, but the information had never been acted on or synthesized in any significant way. The first big reports of the offensive had originated from OP 4, and the powers that be seemed to be reacting in a mechanical fashion, simply corralling everyone off to the far west. While this was great news for the lads out there, it left the remainder of the border, including Khafji, virtually undefended. It was as if the generals had decided to forfeit the town to the Iraqis.

After the half-hour transit from Jubail, they checked in with a forward air controller, call sign Bunny. The scene on the ground was all jumbled, and although there were probably a dozen jets ready to do bombing runs for the Marines, no one seemed to be organizing the air effort, which resulted in most of the planes idly cutting circles overhead. In harried, plaintive tones, the young-sounding Bunny explained to them that there had been a lot of casualties and that they were in dire need of air support. Judging by his voice, the kid was in way over his head. To Morton it sounded as if someone had handed the radio handset to an idle rifleman. The guy didn't give the impression of being a trained forward air controller or even of being generally apprised of the larger tactical picture.

The Cobras began looping over the target area in a wide racetrack pattern waiting for directions from Bunny. It was against regulations, not to mention downright dangerous, to pick off targets independently, so they bided their time, hoping the LAV guys would get their act together and start calling them in on the Iraqis. After some time it became apparent that the guys on the ground were overwhelmed by the burgeoning engagement. Sometime around midnight Morton looked down at his instrument panel and noticed that they'd hit their "bingo" fuel state, which gave them just enough gas to make it to Mishab with 300 pounds of fuel left in reserve. Morton reported this grim news to Bunny.

A series of transmissions ensued with the obviously desperate Bunny asking the pilots to stay on, hoping that by coaxing them into remaining, the Iraqi tide might be turned. In a locked-in fistfight like OP 4, where the action often pivots around invisible moral influences like the gentling calm of an officer's voice on the radio or the sight of a buddy firing next to you, the mere presence of friendly aircraft overhead can have a profound effect, and it is easy to imagine that the young Marine was casting about for any sign of encouragement, however fleeting. Bunny pleaded with them, "We really need you. Can't you just hang out for a few more minutes?"

This was a tough call for Morton and their flight leader, Scott Haney. They had prepared most of their careers for just such a moment, and now with a Marine in dire need practically begging them to stay on, it would be hard to just brush him off and fly back to the comfort of the rear. Yet the laws of physics to which all aviators are beholden are nonnegotiable. If they exhausted their fuel supply, they would be forced to crash-land in the middle of the world's starkest desert during an armored engagement of unprecedented scale.

It was a vexing dilemma exacerbated by the grim prospects for surviving a forced landing in a modern rotary-wing aircraft. When jet pilots lost power, they at least had the luxury of commanding a piece of machinery capable of actual lift. In contrast, an out-of-fuel attack helicopter had the rough flight characteristics of a bowling ball dropped from the top of the Empire State Building. Everyone aloft that night had buddies who'd experienced just such an event, known in the business as an "auto-rotation," and knew that when you attempted to land a Cobra with no power, you were gambling with your life.

Conferring between the two airplanes, Morton, Shaw, and Haney elected against their better judgment to remain on-station as long as possible, rationalizing that they could always dart down to Kibrit and sneak some gas from a fuel truck down at the oversized supply dump.

Leaning over his knee to the left wall of the cramped cockpit, Morton punched Kibrit's coordinates into the loran navigation system console and calculated a new "bingo" fuel state, figuring out to the minute how much longer they could remain on-station and still safely reach Kibrit, roughly thirty miles to the south.* They continued their low orbit of the battlefield, waiting for Bunny's call. By and by the time floated away and Morton discovered that they had hit their revised bingo fuel state. This time there was no negotiation. They bade Bunny farewell, and while the issue on the ground was clearly in doubt, they were secure in the comfort of knowing that they had done their best to aid their brothers caught in the melee below.

However, it quickly became apparent to Morton that something was seriously wrong. After recalculating their route to Kibrit, he discovered to his dismay that their new course was taking them over the tail end of an Iraqi armored

*Loran stands for long-range navigation and works by triangulating a position from a minimum of three low-frequency radio signals from around the world.

column. It wasn't long before they were enveloped by 23-mm antiaircraft fire. As they dodged the fire, Morton puzzled over how the Iraqis had managed to strike so deep into Saudi Arabia without them knowing it. Morton thought, *Shit, Kibrit has been overrun. This is really bad news.* Not only had the Marines' primary logistics base been seized but the fliers were out one gas station. Kibrit had been their refuge of last resort.

The two crews conferred. Given their rapidly dwindling options, they elected to try for Mishab, on the coast, reasoning that if they ran out of gas, they could land in the desert and walk the remainder of the way. Morton reprogrammed the loran again, this time aiming for Mishab, a mere twenty miles down the coastal highway from Khafji, double-checking the math between the two aircraft to ensure that their estimates were correct.

As the Cobras approached Mishab, Haney called over to the makeshift tower at the Mishab airstrip, saying, "We're a section of Cobras coming in on fumes. We're heading directly to the fuel pits." As Morton listened in on the landing frequency, the tower began hustling a pair of CH-53 cargo helicopters out of the pits. The tower came back and reported, "We don't have a visual on you, but you're cleared to land." Everything seemed to be coming together. They had dodged a bullet.

As they continued their final approach, Gary Shaw looked over and exclaimed, "Damn, the oil refinery's on fire!"

This made no sense to Morton. "There's no oil refinery at Mishab," he replied. As the four processed this news, the harsh truth settled in on the lost flight like a bad dream: They were in Khafji! Apparently, their navigation had been off, and now they were in the path of the Iraqi juggernaut.*

Hard on the heels of these ill tidings, Shaw announced, "Max, we've only got twenty-five pounds of fuel left! Do you see any place to land?" They were flying on vapors.

---

*Morton would later learn that the loran transmission stations in the Kuwaiti theater were malfunctioning on January 29.

Morton quickly spotted an empty lot on the northern edge of town, and after Shaw relinquished control of the bird, he eased the Cobra down in what appeared to be a large, abandoned parking lot. Haney quickly followed suit.

Without skipping a beat, Morton—along with Haney's front-seater, a former infantry officer named Gary West—jumped out of their birds, snatched up the M-16s in the ammo bay underneath their cockpits, and began clearing the buildings adjacent to the parking lot. There were two single-story structures, and Morton, after surveying their surroundings, decided they had to eliminate anyone inside the buildings, lest the Cobras be sitting ducks. It was a bizarre moment; in a matter of minutes the flight crew had been transformed from disoriented naval aviators into riflemen busting down doors in an abandoned Middle Eastern town.

The pair conducted a detailed clearing of both buildings, crashing violently into all the rooms. In one room it appeared as if they had interrupted someone's evening tea. There were teacups and a pot spread out and a traditional Muslim prayer rug lying on the floor. On their way out, Gary West grabbed the rug.

West and Morton headed back to the helicopters. Haney was over in his Cobra trying to raise a command-and-control aircraft to let them know they were trapped in Khafji. He wasn't having any luck. The city was clearly under siege. A-6 Intruders were dropping 500-pounders nearby; mortar rounds were impacting all around. As the pair traversed the lot, two Cobras raced right overhead, simultaneously launching all of their 2.75-inch rockets to the north. Listening to the sharp crack of Iraqi fire, Morton thought, *So this is what mortars sound like up close.*

Morton reflected that it was only a matter of time before the Iraqis rolled up and captured the lot of them. When they were still airborne, he'd mentally written off Khafji. Given how the night was shaping up and the fact that Kibrit had already fallen, he assumed that the coastal burg had been seized as well. His mind strangely unmoored, Morton won-

dered what it was going to look like when they paraded the
two Cobras through downtown Baghdad with a Coke bottle
jammed up his ass.

Morton decided that there was no way in hell he was going
to allow himself to be taken prisoner. In the back of his mind
he gave Shaw exactly twenty minutes to get this shit sand-
wich sorted out or he was heading for the coast, where he
would wade out to where the water was chest deep and *swim*
back to Mishab. Over the course of his career, Morton had
endured a battery of simulated prisoner-of-war exercises and
had long ago decided that under no circumstances was he
going to be taken alive. He didn't give a shit about his aircraft. He didn't give a shit about being court-martialed.

Gary Shaw was in curiously high spirits. Looking at Morton with a sly grin, Shaw asked coyly, "Do you know where
we are, Max?"

Well, that's a stupid fucking question, thought Morton.
"We're in Khafji!"

Shaw chuckled and said, "No, you dumb ass, we're in an
oil refinery!"

Morton looked around, and sure enough, they had landed
in the parking lot of the local ARAMCO oil facility.*

"What do they make in oil refineries, Max?"

Tilting his head around, assessing the situation, Morton
wondered if his boss had gone around the bend. Then the light
bulb came on. *Gas! They make gas in oil refineries.* By an
amazing stroke of luck, the open spot where Morton had put
them down turned out to be the very source of their salvation.

"Go find gas!" Shaw barked, adding, "Find anything that
looks like it'll burn, throw a match on it. If it burns we're
throwing it in the aircraft."

Morton and company began feverishly rummaging for
something resembling a gas container. Morton was hoping to
find a tanker truck or something, but after a hasty search discovered that there were no obvious gas receptacles nearby.

---

*ARAMCO stands for Arab-American Oil Company, the parent company for the mul-
tifarious joint American-Saudi petroleum operations.

After a few more minutes of hunting, Shaw happened upon an odd pump assembly powered by a Briggs & Stratton lawn mower engine with a green garden hose sticking out of it. As they fumbled around in the dark trying to get the thing started, Iraqi small-arms fire began cracking nearby. They got the pump started and splashed out a small puddle on the ground. One of the pilots put a lighter to it and watched as it flamed up. They were back in business.

Shaw looked over at Morton and said, "Max, start the bird up and hop it on over here," adding ominously, "Be ready for a flameout."

After hovering over to their newfound gas station, Morton leapt out and popped open the small gravity-fed fuel nozzle over the Cobra's winglet, jammed the garden hose in, and began pumping the mystery fuel into the bird. He managed to get 600 pounds into each of the helicopters, just enough to slip back to Mishab.

After they lifted off, they couldn't even tell that it wasn't good old JP-5 jet fuel in the tank. The Cobras ran like tops.

They proceeded south, flying directly to the fuel pits at Mishab. Less than a half-hour later they were gassed up and heading back up to Khafji to look for trouble. They didn't even bother checking in with the air-support center. They had up-close, first-hand knowledge about where the Iraqis were; they didn't need some weenie air-traffic controller in a building with no windows telling them where to go. During the brief inbound flight, Morton checked in with the commanding officer of their sister squadron, who was directing his piece of the fight from an airborne Huey helicopter. He mentioned that there were friendlies somewhere in Khafji and to be careful of the northern end of town, as there was a battery of Iraqi ZSU antiaircraft guns in the area.

To Morton the night thus far seemed like a bizarre dream. They'd just emerged from a harrowing scrape and here they were, out in the mix again, looking for more. Nevertheless, the raw physical shock from such a jarring episode seemed to hang over the flight, throwing off the men's rhythm. They were deadly serious professionals, men trained to evince serenity in the face of dangerous work, but nothing really could have prepared them for this wild ride.

It was obvious to Morton that he and his compatriots weren't operating at the top of their game when upon reaching the southern end of Khafji, they narrowly averted colliding with a large, unlit water tower. They'd been gunning hard to get to the fight, and a split-second before both Cobras would have struck the tower, they both whipped outboard, defying the laws of physics in the process. Both planes had been less than 100 feet apart, and the tower split the flight in two. After this second close call Morton began to get sick to his stomach.

The flight was quickly rejoined and the fliers pressed on, looking for bad guys. Breaking to the left, they soon happened upon a company of Iraqi tanks paused for a navigation check in the town. Morton peered down and found himself staring into the red-lit interior of one of the tanks; it was bright like a gigantic stoplight calling out to the pilots. They were only a couple of hundred feet up, and he could see Iraqi soldiers milling around. Morton was looking down at them, and they were looking up at him. The Iraqis looked as lost as Morton had been just an hour prior. Over the intercom he called to Shaw, "Hey, we're right on top of 'em." Unfortunately, there was a miscommunication with the other Cobra, and for some reason Haney, who was technically still the flight leader, wanted to begin their attack run from out over the water. Morton thought this was a terrible idea and further evidence that Haney was still a bit rattled.

Out over the water they had trouble getting oriented; they were flying on night-vision goggles, which at this point in the war were still relatively new. Due to the high humidity and the persistent ground haze, flying in the Persian Gulf with night-vision goggles is exceedingly difficult. Over the waters of the Gulf the task of maintaining level flight becomes even more challenging, and because there were no landmarks, Morton for a brief period lost all perception of forward motion. It was like they were just floating there.

This vertiginous effect worsened as they attempted to engage the tanks with TOWs from long-range. Because the Cobras weren't yet outfitted with proper night-vision targeting equipment, the pilots were forced to launch an illumination rocket toward the Iraqis, hoping to be able to acquire a tank for a hasty missile shot in the fleeting artificial light. It was a lamentable, ad hoc solution to nocturnal combat. After one such shot, Morton peered into the TOW sight and noticed that the city was coming up quickly toward them. They were falling out of the sky! Morton quickly grasped the controls, saving them from piling into the ocean. Even Gary Shaw, the old salt, was feeling the worse for wear.

A minute later Morton and Haney were able to get some TOW shots off, but the Iraqis, wise now to their presence, were artfully dodging in and out of the dark streets and were putting out a thick cloud of smoke to obscure their movements. Both missiles arced off harmlessly. Frustrated, the fliers shifted off to the north of town searching for other targets. After firing off another barrage of illumination rockets, the back of Morton's rocket pod suddenly burst off in a shower of sparks. The ordnance men back at Jubail had apparently mounted the wrong type of pod on the Cobra. They had been foiled yet again.

Stymied, the flight bent back around to return to Mishab to get new rocket pods. En route, Morton located some Iraqi supply trucks on the beach and was able to squeeze in a few strafing runs employing the 20-mm Gatling gun located on the nose of the Cobra.

After reloading back at Mishab, they made the mistake of checking in with the Marine air-support center, who flatly forbade them from returning to Khafji, telling the fliers, "There's friendlies up there."

"I *know* there are friendlies up there. But I also know where the Iraqis are," Morton replied.

"Doesn't matter. You can't go up there."

Morton was apoplectic. This rigid mentality represented everything that was wrong with the Marine air-support apparatus. They had two fully loaded Cobras ready to rock and roll, and some colonel with no sense of the situation was telling them to go pack sand. Khafji was being allowed to fall because of command incompetence. It was unbelievable.

Too exhausted to argue, the fliers acquiesced. They landed and turned the birds back over to the squadron. It was a decision Morton lamented the rest of the war.

16

9:00 P.M., January 29, 1991,
Khafji

The youth was in a little trance of astonishment. So they were at last going to fight. On the morrow, perhaps, there would be a battle, and he would be in it. For a time he was obliged to labor to make himself believe. He could not accept with assurance an omen that he was about to mingle in one of those great affairs of the earth.
—STEPHEN CRANE, *The Red Badge of Courage*

THE YOUNG MARINE poked his head up over the edge of the roof and looked out over the empty city. The fire had been building for some time now to the north of town, and he and his teammates were worried. It was night in the city, and the dim dun-colored sprawl yawned silently out before him. An entropy-like quiet enveloped the southern part of town where the Marines were hiding. The town—Ra's al-Khafji, an austere jumble of cinderblock and concrete that had at one time housed 20,000—had been evacuated and the electricity cut several weeks prior; it was like someone had dropped a neutron bomb, vaporizing all the inhabitants but preserving perfectly the architecture and the appliances.

The clamor up north had begun as small cracks of rifle fire, but it wasn't long before the Marines could discern the unmistakable sound of mechanized vehicles and main battle tanks on the move. Interspersed between long bouts of heavy machine-gun fire they heard what seemed to be enormous chain saws at work. Like the rumble of a distant thunderstorm shielded by mountains, the combat developed at a distance, far from them yet certain in its path.

Soon a line of Humvees and five-ton trucks came roaring down the main road through town heading south, hell-bent for sanctuary. They had all their lights off and drove with a headlong abandon that needed no explanation. They were running away from the fire. It was Colonel Barry's crew, a motley conglomeration of special operations soldiers and radio snoopers that had been camped out in town since Christmas.

The Marine picked up the black handset of the radio and called back to his platoon commander, "What do you want us to do?"

There was a long pause at the other end, and then through the crackling static came a most unexpected reply, "You're in a better position to make the call than I am. You are the intelligence. If you feel like you're in a secure position, then go ahead and stay in town. It's your call."

The bespectacled Marine, whose name was Chuck Ingraham, was tired and cold and scared, and although he would never voice it to his comrades, deep down he felt like they should go. He knew they had no support in the city. There were no artillery batteries in place to fire for them, no air assets that they could call upon—they didn't even know the radio frequencies of any nearby units. Their platoon was so strapped for gear that they didn't have any vehicles to escape in. If they wanted to get out of town, they were going to have to do it soon while they could still make a clean getaway on foot. All Chuck Ingraham and the five other Marines that made up his recon team had to defend themselves besides their rifles were their radios and a few handheld rocket launchers.

They were perhaps the greenest Marine reconnaissance team in all of Saudi Arabia. In truth, they weren't even really recon Marines. Their team, along with the other two teams that comprised 3rd Platoon, Alpha Company, 3rd Reconnaissance Battalion had been cobbled together from a section of small boat drivers at their home base in Hawaii. The boat section had been under the loose cognizance of Alpha Company, so when the balloon went up, the decision was made to absorb the coxswains and begin training them as recon Marines. As a result of this hurried vetting process, they were never fully accepted by the other members of the company. The old salts, the "dual cool" guys who had been to jump and scuba school, derisively referred to them as "the boat people."

Ingraham, a trained reconnaissance Marine who had been given command of the team only a few months prior, jokingly called them "The Bastards of the Bastards"—nobody wanted them. While the remainder of the company had deployed to the west in early January to begin preparing for the breach patrols that would precede the big push into Kuwait, 3rd Platoon was left behind in the backwater of the coastal sector running missions into the ghost town.

Ingraham looked around at the faces of the five of them and asked them what they wanted to do. Among the troop was Kevin Callahan, the team's U.S. Navy medical corpsman, known universally as Doc. A fourteen-year recon veteran with a walrus mustache, Doc was far more than the team's patch-'em-up guy, he was their big brother, their sober sage, a moral force, the lone cool head in the storm. The Marines felt better just having him around. He didn't even have to say a word.

Doc Callahan regarded Ingraham, and in his calm, almost drowsy, Floridian drawl settled the matter: "Ingraham, we're recon Marines. This is what we're trained to do. If we remain behind, we can wreak havoc on these guys. We should stay."

Fifteen hundred meters to the northwest, Corporal Lawrence Lentz was poised on the horns of the same dilemma. Lentz, team leader for one of the other 3rd Platoon teams, had been in and out of Khafji for weeks on missions for their parent command, the 3rd Marine Regiment, based out of Mishab. They'd been sent into town right after the air war began when the Iraqis started lobbing Astro rockets into the 3rd Marines area, six-o'clock-Charlie-style every evening, thoroughly freaking out everyone. Ensconced in a large unfinished house a few blocks east of the main boulevard, Lentz and company were supposed to give the rear a heads-up on any incoming rockets and to keep an eye out for Iraqi armored movements. As the missions continued, they helped coordinate cross-border air strikes against the mobile launchers responsible for the attacks. The raids dropped off sharply after the teams got to work, and Regiment was pleased with the results, extending their mission indefinitely in hopes that the Marines would be able to provide early warning for any other tricks the Iraqis might have up their sleeve.

On an earlier mission, Lentz had linked up with the storied Lieutenant Colonel "Ravishing" Rick Barry, who was honchoing the surveillance and reconnaissance group working in Khafji. Some of his Marines had noticed other Americans skulking around town, and when Lentz approached one of them, he immediately recognized him as a Marine master sergeant from a secretive electronic surveillance unit in Hawaii. He'd done a few jumps with the guy and asked him what was up.

The master sergeant in turn delivered Lentz to Barry's safe house on the northern edge of town. To Lentz it looked like the final reel of *Apocalypse Now*. There were five-gallon gasoline cans rigged to explode in the corners of every room. Clusters of exotic-looking radios and electronic gear were strewn throughout the house. A gigantic wide-screen television dominated the living room. The men in the team moved about the commandeered residence with a detached swagger that Lentz instinctively responded to. It was a total military safari.

The master sergeant announced, "This is Colonel Barry."

Lentz looked around confusedly and then saw down near his feet a cammie-clad figure with a cap pulled down over his eyes leaning against a wall.

"Sit down, son," the figure said without moving. Lentz did.

Barry proceeded to brief Lentz on the larger tactical picture. There were Navy SEAL and Marine ANGLICO spotter teams strung out in outposts all along the border. It seemed that Lentz's and Ingraham's teams were just faces in the crowd.

Barry declared matter-of-factly, "You're staying with me tonight."

"Oh, no, sir, I got my own thing going on. I'm new to this whole business. I don't think I can just stay here," Lentz replied coyly.

"Who you with?" Barry asked.

Lentz told him, and Barry got on the horn with 3rd Marines and in a matter of minutes had it sorted so that Lentz was cleared to spend the night at Club Barry away from his usual observation post.

Lentz felt strangely comfortable there. Barry seemed to know what was going on and had assets at his disposal that Lentz had only dreamed of. His men, although clearly not pressed from the crew-cut Marine mold, seemed focused, switched on. That afternoon Lentz watched *Rain Man* on the wide screen.

At around ten on the evening of the 29th, Lentz was roused by one of the patrol who had been on watch on the roof of the house that served as their observation post. "You guys need to get the fuck up here," the Marine said.

The entire seven-man team piled upstairs and watched as one of the buildings near Barry's safe house was pummeled by concentrated tank, machine-gun, and small-arms fire. Lentz recognized the structure, a tall telephone exchange building that served as the local Saudi National Guard command post. Lentz thought, *Someone knew exactly which building to hit.* Sometime after that they observed several of Barry's blacked-out vehicles blazing down the causeway that separated the northern quarter of town from Khafji proper. The vehicles continued on through the main concourse and out through the ornate, green-arched gates that delineated the southern reach of the town. The high-speed, low-drag operators were gone. Lentz and Ingraham were the only game in town now.

The team's lone squad automatic weapon gunner, Lance Corporal Marcus Slavenas, remembers watching the firefight on the northern edge of town drawing closer and closer and seeing a Saudi Arabian border police truck race southward on the main drag. One of the guys in the truck was on a .50 cal blazing wildly to the rear. As if to complete the battle tableau, several red flares swung lazily from parachutes overhead. Slavenas said to himself, *This is it. This isn't some fantasy anymore. I can't be imagining this.* Slavenas, along with several other Marines present in Khafji that evening, spoke of a strange, almost cinematic atmosphere settling in, the lights dimming, the main feature about to begin.

Talking on the radio to their platoon commander, Captain Dan Baczkowski, who was back at Mishab, the issue of whether to remain in town or not seemed like a moot point to Lentz. *This is what we're trained to do; we're staying,* he thought.

Lentz, known in the platoon as a shrewd, low-key team leader with a deliciously weird sense of humor, already had more than a dozen close-air-support and artillery missions for Khafji planned out on paper. After several forays into town, he'd gotten bored one afternoon and started scripting them out, writing them on notebook paper complete with compass azimuths and ten-digit grid coordinates. He even had the latitude and longitude coordinates figured out for any pilots unfamiliar with the standard military grid system. He took out the team's GPS receiver and figured out their location down to the foot.

After the decision was made to remain in town, Lentz radioed back to the rear to try and get some fire support queued up for the inevitable Iraqi thrust into downtown Khafji. The equation of staying or going or what to do at this point was abruptly clear to the thirty-two-year-old corporal. So long as they didn't lose their cool or do something to draw attention to themselves, the Iraqis would never know they were there. Further, Lentz reasoned, if they could maintain some sort of air cover over the city, he could rain artillery down on the Iraqis' heads all day and they would think it was the airplanes calling the fire in.

After poking around on the net for a few minutes, Lentz was dismayed to discover that no one would fire for them. Higher headquarters, awash in the hazy mental twilight of the rear, couldn't account for several Saudi National Guard battalions in the Khafji area. In addition, several of Colonel Barry's teams had been overrun and were missing in action. Higher-ups were denying any fire requests into Khafji until these units were located. It was a fucked situation.

"I know exactly where the Saudis are—they're getting blasted by the Iraqis!" Lentz had replied.

Frustrated but undeterred, Lentz dipped into his rucksack and produced a copy of the theater master communications chart that a buddy in the regiment intelligence shop had slipped him, in naked violation of virtually every security regulation in the book. Possession of such a sensitive and valuable document—it listed the radio frequencies of every Coalition unit in the Persian Gulf region—so far forward of friendly lines flew in the face of common sense and everything recon Marines were taught. Lentz had been hoarding it for just such a situation, and it proved to be a godsend. Lentz began rolling through all the air-support frequencies on one of the team's radios, hunting for any nearby aircraft with spare ordnance. If he couldn't get any help from the powers that be, he'd simply go right to the pilots and talk them into flying for him.

After scanning the airwaves for some time, Lentz came across what appeared to be a flight of jet crews talking among themselves. He broke in: "This is Echo Four Lima, I'm a recon team caught in Khafji right now. I can't get artillery to fire for me, the town's being overrun, can I put you to work?"

"Roger that, Four Lima, we're catching parts of the convoy that's coming into Khafji right now."

This was exactly what Lentz was hoping to hear, and for a moment he was able to breathe easy. Even though he knew that the noose around his team was tightening, just talking to those pilots and knowing that they weren't alone was tremendously comforting. Still, those birds, although they were heading the bad guys off at the pass, weren't doing anything for Lentz's immediate prospects. He kept dialing higher in search of more aircraft.

After two or three hours of no luck on the radio, Lentz noticed that the battle seemed to ratchet down a few notches. An invisible threshold of some kind had been crossed, the obscure forces involved regrouping. A tense, churchlike calm settled over the concrete maze of the town.

Around 1:00 A.M. Lentz began to hear tanks creaking around to the north. It was unnerving listening to them edging down the hollow streets. This wasn't at all like he'd expected: The Iraqis were supposed to blaze down the road at 100 miles an hour under a solid umbrella of artillery shells, shooting at everything in sight.

The Marines had night-vision goggles and began scanning the scene, trying to make some sense out of the dark distance, but because the Iraqis were still a ways off, the goggles revealed little. In contrast to the relative lack of visual stimuli, sound soon began to appear everywhere, channeled and amplified by the alleys and buildings, making it seem as if the Iraqis were right on top of them. The sputters and clanks of the dreaded vehicles pierced the cold night air, stabbing at the Marines' ears. They were like children poking around a haunted house in the middle of the night. Lentz, for one, was "scared shitless." Straining at this foul noise, he could just make out the sound of the rubber treads slapping the ground as one of the Iraqi vehicles crept along. He thought, *Do they know we're here? The Iraqis seemed to know right where to hit the Saudis. What were the chances they knew our position?*

After several more hours of this aural torture, the dead alien silence returned, leaving the Marines alone with their thoughts. In the space of this reprieve Lentz began reconsidering their options. *Should they execute their escape plan and get out of town while they had a shadow of a chance?* Previously, Lentz had broken the team down into two-man evasion teams; they knew the drill. Lentz, one of the company's strongest swimmers, figured they could abandon their two Humvees, dart through the streets, and make for the waters of the Gulf, telling Mishab to send a boat out for them. It was a shaky plan but Lentz knew that they could pull it off.

At around 4:00 A.M., Lentz received an unexpected radio call from an American identifying himself merely as "Coyote." Coyote, apparently a U.S. Army liaison officer attached to a Saudi battalion in the Khafji area, informed Lentz that help was on the way. Lentz listened in amazement as Coyote talked straight to him like a human being, using no brevity codes or military lingo: "Son, we're gonna pull back and regroup. We're gonna try and mount an attack to get you boys out as soon as we can, so hold tight." This came as a huge relief to Lentz. He had no idea who this Coyote was, but he sounded like he knew what he was doing, and clearly he was in the thick of the situation along with Lentz.*

Lentz shelved the swimming plan and told his team to prepare to stay for the long haul.

Ingraham had been watching the very same show from atop their building in the southwestern part of town. The Iraqis would pop off illumination rounds to see and creep forward in the vehicles. It wasn't long before the entire northern quarter, the neighborhood where Max Morton and his crew had scooted out, was in Iraqi hands. By watching and listening to the Iraqi artillery muzzle flashes, Ingraham was able to determine the position of the firing tubes. Counting "one thousand, two thousand . . ." as with the approach of thunder in an electrical storm, he could roughly compute their distance from him. He relayed this information back to Mishab, but no one would fire for them. It was unbelievably frustrating.

He and Lentz had conferred over the radio and after some drama had agreed that staying in town was the thing to do. The two teams wouldn't be able to support each other with fire, but they would at least be able to relay critical information and encourage each other. Just knowing there were other Marines nearby was comforting in a way not easily explained.

---

* "Coyote" was Lieutenant Colonel Michael Taylor, a Vietnam veteran assigned to the 7th Battalion of the King Abdul Aziz Brigade of the Saudi Arabian National Guard.

Examining the lay of the land again, Ingraham couldn't figure out why the Iraqis were just sitting there. Clearly they owned Khafji. After the Saudis and Colonel Barry had bailed, there was no resistance of any kind in the city. *What were they waiting for?*

10:30 P.M., January 29, 1991, Mishab, Twenty Miles South of Khafji

B<small>ACK AT THE</small> 3rd Marines Combat Operations Center, Captain Dan Baczkowski was swimming in the moment, unsure who or what to believe. A conscientious, Annapolis-trained officer, Baczkowski had been married just days before deploying to the desert, and although he never betrayed the truth to his men, he no more wanted to be in this war than be on the moon. He'd always been an exemplary officer: stoic, driven, consumed with his duties, but the prospects of marriage and the soft song of family life had changed him. For the first time in his life he'd had thoughts of a life outside the big green machine.

He had been given command of the Boat People shortly before deploying. Since he knew that they were essentially ignorant of reconnaissance work, he had embarked the platoon on a whirlwind of basic patrolling, reporting, and communications exercises in the Saudi wastes. It was, he thought, a tough hand to play. He felt like he was schooling these kids in the very basics right before they were about to launch into what looked to be Armageddon in the sand.

He did, however, have a few aces up his sleeve. The Alpha Company commander had given him a few of the unit's stellar noncommissioned officers, guys like Sergeant Bill Iiams, who had been in recon for nearly a decade, and Corporal Lentz, a sagacious thirty-two-year-old graduate of The Citadel military college. By leaning heavily on them, he was able to get his platoon up to what he considered an acceptable level of field proficiency. Nevertheless, 3rd Platoon remained an exceptionally raw recon unit. During the long months leading up to the air war, Baczkowski had had to relieve two team leaders, one for gross incompetence (the man could barely operate a compass) and another for lying to him (the sergeant had been joyriding while on patrol, pulling a squad of Marines behind their Humvee on camouflage netting at high speed. When Baczkowski inquired why all his Marines were scraped and bruised up, he'd told him that "they'd taken a hard turn out in the desert"). Thus, Chuck Ingraham, a diligent albeit unseasoned young corporal, was slotted into a team leader billet, a position normally reserved for Marines who had attended a bevy of reconnaissance and special operations–type schools. Ingraham, while studious and dependable, hadn't been to any courses and was known by some in Alpha Company as the guy who had flunked out of the pre–scuba school screening. But Baczkowski had had his fill of recon cowboys, and as far as he was concerned, he trusted Ingraham and therefore the job was his. As he listened to Ingraham's voice over the radio, Baczkowski knew he'd made the right decision.

He listened in as his teams reported that the area around Colonel Barry's position was enveloped by fire. Judging from the sheer volume of rounds, he assumed that Barry and his crew had perished, but in one of those sickly humorous moments so common in war, he heard Ingraham and Lentz report seeing the convoy race out of the city balls to the wall. Baczkowski recalls, "It was a strange feeling, like, 'Okay, Barry got out, but where does that leave my guys?' "

To Baczkowski it was clear that the Iraqis would soon claim the city and his teams would be cut off. He'd been a little uneasy when Colonel John Admire and the regimental staff had first cooked up the idea to send them in after the first waves of rockets impacted. It just seemed so ad hoc, and the proper assets were never made available to support the teams once they were deployed into the heart of the city. There were no artillery batteries in place. Every aircraft in theater was already earmarked for the deep fight. Baczkowski didn't even have enough Humvees to fully support two active patrols, which meant that one team was always in-

STORM ON THE HORIZON

serted by vehicle and then left to maneuver in town on foot. On one occasion they'd been forced to borrow the regimental chaplain's Humvee to insert the teams. As the tenor of the evening deepened, Baczkowski began to get a sinking feeling about things.

In his mind, Baczkowski referred back to the original operations order he'd written for Khafji: *If the Iraqis come, then the teams will egress by whatever means available.* Because he couldn't protect the teams or influence the action, he'd long ago decided that extraction was the only sane option. *What else could he do?*

As he was formulating what he was going to say to Ingraham and Lentz, Baczkowski, being the dutiful Captain of Marines, elected to inform Colonel Admire of his decision. He told him that Colonel Barry had already exited the scene post haste and that it was only a matter of time before the city fell, effectively shutting the door on the thirteen Marines hiding out in town. He told him that due to the utter lack of air or artillery support, his specific instructions to his team leaders had always been to leave town if the Iraqis came.

While Colonel Admire—a thoughtful, gentleman-officer who exuded an almost regal bearing—considered this, his second-in-command, who had been standing in the wings, blurted out one of the stupidest things Baczkowski had ever heard: "But if the teams leave, then we won't be able to see what's going on up there!"

It was the biggest DUH! moment Baczkowski had ever been party to. *Why hadn't they given him the air and artillery support he'd requested weeks ago?* He'd been particularly put off by the staff air officer whose job it was to facilitate whatever air requests that were forwarded to him. He'd given Baczkowski the frequencies of a few squadrons in the area— a pittance, a skeletal gesture that fell just short of a slap in the face. None of these people understood or had really counted the cost of this deal. Those were *his* Marines up there, and although in his mind he had long since departed from the elect caste of officers who served the Corps with an austere, almost Samurai-like sense of duty, Baczkowski felt this gauntlet as directly as if he himself were cut off in Khafji. In the words of another officer present at the time, "It was like Dan aged ten years right there."

After thinking on the matter for a few moments, Colonel Admire spoke. "Leave the teams in."

Baczkowski knew what he was expected to do. He was supposed to salute smartly, do an about-face, and tell his teams to stay put. But he couldn't reconcile his commander's seeming absence of compassion for his team's predicament. Baczkowski assumed that Lentz and Ingraham were on the verge of being overrun and that by ordering them to remain, there existed the very real possibility that he would be ordering them to their deaths.

He thought back to the endless procession of stern-faced leadership lectures he'd endured at Quantico about officers being paid to make the tough calls and how for so long the Marine Corps had seemed to him to be the only possible life worth leading. He'd followed his older brother to the Naval Academy and into the infantry and he'd relished his days as a recon platoon commander in Hawaii. He had had a good run so far.

Then he thought about what he was going to tell his Marines, lost up some street in a forgotten Saudi town: He was going to leave it up to them; they could stay and keep reporting on the Iraqis, hoping against hope that they'd be rescued at some point or they could come out now, knowing that he alone would deal with the consequences of their premature departure. It was an enormous decision, one that he knew might cost him his career, not to mention the lives of thirteen men.

Baczkowski walked the short distance to the tailgate of the Humvee that served as the platoon headquarters and picked up the radio handset.

17

Morning, January 30, 1991,
Khafji

The time was just before daybreak, an hour when the uneasiness of the air affected trees and animals, and made even sleepers turn over sighingly. Mohammed, who wanted to see the fight, awoke. To get me up he came over and cried the morning prayer-call in my ear, the raucous voice sounding battle, murder, and sudden death across my dreams.

       —T. E. LAWRENCE, *Seven Pillars of Wisdom*

SHORTLY AFTER dawn broke, Lentz was awoken by Lance Corporal Alan Cooper, one of the team's radio operators: "Dude, they're rolling into town like it's the fucking circus!"

Lentz and the rest of the team scrambled up topside again and took it all in. It was like one of those old Soviet May Day parades: A long convoy of armored vehicles was crawling bumper-to-bumper toward their position like a gigantic iron centipede. The only thing missing was the superannuated Premier figure peering down from a lofty balcony. Gazing through binoculars, Lentz could tell these guys were veterans. The soldiers jutting out of the backs of the armored personnel carriers sported dirty, scraggly beards. Bundles of equipment hung off the sides of the advancing vehicles.

They rolled along the coastal road, but instead of hanging a right to go over the causeway, they hugged the waterline as far east as the land would allow them. They seemed to know exactly where they were going. None of the Marines noticed any outrider vehicles covering their flanks, which struck them as odd, as though they weren't concerned about getting plugged from the sides. These guys acted like they owned the town, like it had been conquered already and they had arrived merely to sign for it. Having circumvented the cause-

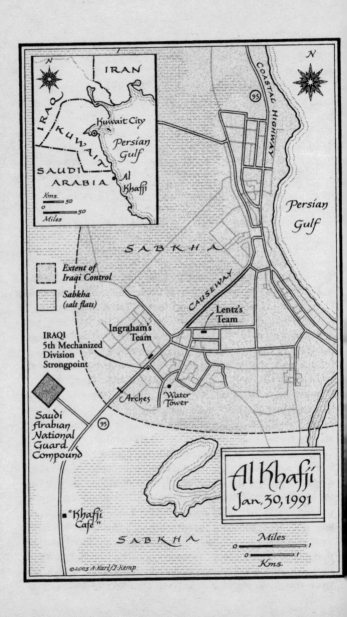

way, the convoy hung a sharp right and bore west toward the downtown area, toward Ingraham, along a hard surface road one block south of Lentz's house.

As the Iraqis drew near, Lentz mentally reviewed his team's disposition. He had worked hard to ensure that their pos would be as well hidden as a bear's den. The team's two Humvees had been parked in the lee of the ten-foot-high cinderblock wall surrounding the house. The vehicles' antennas had been removed, and Lentz had made sure that none of the team's gear or weapons were visible from the street. There were no tall nearby houses that would allow the enemy to peer down into the yard.

If it came down to it, however, the team was prepared to slug it out Alamo-style and Lentz had taken all the standard precautions for dismounted infantry in the defense. All the main avenues of approach were covered; Slavenas was down behind the squad automatic weapon aimed out the front door of the house. A Marine with an M-203 grenade launcher was stationed in the second-story stairwell prepared to support any position that came under attack. All the machine-gun ammunition had been linked together to ensure a steady hail of outgoing fire should the situation call for it. Lentz didn't want anyone fumbling around for ammo when the heat was on.

Lentz's final instruction to everyone was, "Don't fire until you see the Iraqis coming over the wall," figuring this whites-of-their-eyes tactic might stave off a fight until it was absolutely unavoidable.

Despite these extensive measures, Lentz hoped that it wouldn't come down to a straight fight. He knew that seven well-armed men didn't stand a rabbit's chance at a rodeo against an Iraqi mechanized brigade. The time-honored recon mantra of "If you have to fire your weapon, then you've failed" had never seemed more true. If the Marines were discovered the best they could hope for was a quick firefight to break contact followed by a hasty Humvee exit. However, the ten-foot-high wall that enclosed their position limited that option, since the only way in or out of the cinderblock compound was through a single metal gate that faced the water. In this contest, stealth was their best and only weapon.

Corporal Scott Wagner, the team's communications chief, remembers seeing the Iraqis coming and experiencing a distinct sinking feeling in his stomach. Determined to stay focused as the reality of their predicament sank in, Wagner fidgeted with his comm gear, taking down one of his handcrafted field expedient antennas and triple-checking the rig, making certain that it wouldn't be visible to their pursuers. Lentz, now down on the second story, was sending up spot reports to Wagner on the roof over a pair of Radio Shack headsets that Slavenas had mail-ordered when they'd first arrived in the desert. Wagner in turn was entering this data, including vehicle types, numbers, and locations into a Marine-issue digital handset that broadcast back to Mishab in small, encrypted bursts. This patrol had run long—they had already been in town for several days—and in addition to being out of chow and water, they were running low on radio batteries, which meant that Wagner would soon have to start sifting through the swelling stack of used batteries to suck out whatever remaining juice he could find. It wasn't exactly ringing news given their current lot, but Wagner, with a grease monkey's demented imagination for all things related to radio communication, figured he'd find a way.

He also started relaying the whole mad spectacle to Ingraham's team, who, cloistered in a more southerly neighborhood, had yet to see the ominous Iraqi parade.

Ingraham got the call from Lentz's team, and as the Iraqi vehicles rolled into view, he began to count them. He had always been taught to pay scrupulous attention to numbers and types of enemy, and although in reality it made no immediate difference exactly how many vehicles there were— they were vastly outnumbered and outgunned one way or the other—he took notes and relayed his tally back to Lentz.

There were eleven boxy armored personnel carriers, likely

of Chinese origin, in the advance waves, led by a single odd Volkswagen-like utility van.

Point man Pat Sterling recalls seeing the armored column halted in the middle of the wide boulevard, pausing for some indiscernible reason. Soldiers in assorted uniforms and weapons were hanging all over the vehicles like a grizzled band of gypsies. He thought, *Who are these guys?* After observing the Iraqis idling for some time, he noticed a mustachioed Saddam lookalike emerge from somewhere within the column. The man was visibly angry and began gesturing wildly, ordering the vehicles to disperse out into the city. The column quickly deployed, vehicles splitting off in various directions, angling down the alleys and side streets of the town.

This fearsome rumble soon echoed down the avenues, ringing round the hunkered Marines. The men, now fully caged in, were scared.

Doc Callahan recalls grabbing Corporal Jeffrey Brown, the assistant team leader, and telling him that they needed him to identify some armored vehicles that were loitering near the foot of their building. The consummate military geek, Brown had long since passed from being a basically trained Marine and could best be described as an armor fanatic. He'd spent the listless days of the fall when they were fresh in-theater memorizing the Iraqi armor booklets that they'd been issued, committing the shapes, armament, and capabilities of every known armored vehicle type to memory. Like some military Mr. Spock, he was the team's walking tank encyclopedia, with data at the ready 24/7.

The awful sound of grinding tank treads rebounding off of the street was all to be heard as Brown crept across the span of the open roof to look over. Carefully easing his head over the lip of the parapet, he peered down, and there she was, bigger than Dallas: a Chinese-manufactured Type 531C armored personnel carrier, painted in the ubiquitous dull tan that the Arabs used for all their vehicles. Scanning down to the nose of the battered thirteen-ton beast, he noted a small scarlet unit identification plate, which told him the vehicle was from the 5th Mechanized Division, veterans of the Iran war and generally considered to be one of the best units the Iraqis had short of the Republican Guard. The vehicle commander was outfitted in his best Saddam costume, complete with a black beret.*

Brown counted eight Type 531s and watched as they worked their way south to the arches of town, seeming to move in overlapping squares of four apiece. Observing this peculiar mode of maneuver, Brown surmised that they were searching for something, possibly the Marines. The vehicle commander seemed particularly alert, his head on a swivel, scanning up and down the thoroughfare for any signs of trouble.

As the noisy seconds ticked by, the Type 531s rolled right past the Marines' building, to all appearances totally unaware of their presence. It wasn't long before the Iraqis had secured the southern perimeter of town. There could be no doubt or speculation: The Marines were completely surrounded.

At this point, an argument broke out within the team. Doc Callahan recalls that Ingraham, overcome by the stark reality of being enveloped by the Iraqis, began talking about attempting an escape through town on foot, every man for himself. Members of both teams remember frantically discussing the possibility of escape using Lentz's two Humvees. As the discord mounted, Doc pulled Ingraham into a corner and said, "Hey, Chuck, we're not going anywhere. Get your team together." Doc added later, "You have to understand, this was a super young team. Ingraham was the only experienced recon Marine in the bunch. Not that they weren't good Marines, because they were. But they were the young Turks of Alpha Company, just boat drivers really, and they'd just seen a battalion's worth of enemy vehicles roll right by. At this point I guess I just figured I'm the oldest guy here and that I'd better tell everybody, 'Hey, we're gonna be okay.' I

---

*The lead Iraqi unit into Khafji was the 15th Brigade of the 5th Mechanized Division. The 5th Mech, outfitted almost exclusively with Chinese gear, was described by Dr. Kenneth M. Pollack, author of *Arabs at War,* as "the best mechanized division in the Iraqi army." It was the vanguard of the multi-brigade force tasked with seizing the town.

knew that if we just ran out into the streets of Khafji and tried to make it out to the desert with no friendlies within twenty-five miles of us, we'd be fucked."

Ingraham recalls radioing back to Mishab for fire support, praying that they could drop a few artillery rounds somewhere inside Khafji to keep the Iraqis buttoned up inside their vehicles and away from their building. "I just told 'em, 'Hey, fire something!' And the rear would come back with, 'What's your target?' 'The city is! Fire!' " However, because of higher headquarters' concerns about friendly fire, his requests were denied. Mishab wasn't going to fire for the Marines unless they had a specific target under observation.*

Caught off guard by the momentary wave of panic, Chuck Ingraham lashed out at himself for allowing his men to see the fear, to see him overcome by the moment. As a young team leader he'd always taken the ideals of leadership and command presence seriously. He was a child of the Corps—his father was an active-duty colonel; both of his grandfathers were Marine veterans of the Pacific campaign of World War II—and he'd always known that he would go in and that he would be a leader. He was no stranger to the gung-ho posing and bullshit jarhead bravado, but as he tried to get a hold on himself in the roil of the moment, he seemed to realize that something more, something different and strange, was required of him now. He had risen to his current position by dint of his precocious intelligence and attention to duty. All these things—these bromides of duty, honor, and country and the boy's dream of war that he had known firsthand—

---

*It remains unclear whether the artillery battery attached to 3rd Marines was even prepared to fire yet. Phillip Thompson, a former captain and fire-direction officer with the battery, recalls in his excellent memoir *Into the Storm,* "In the early morning hours before sunup on the 30th, the situation was incredibly screwed up. Utter chaos reigned on the radios, and the Fire Direction Center was alive with radio traffic and Marines, all talking excitedly, most passing on rumors" (Thompson, 135). Additionally, the battery was in the throes of staging a border raid; firing on targets inside Saudi Arabia was probably the last thing on their minds.

Additionally, there is no evidence to suggest that Mishab was aware of the events at Observation Post 4. Fratricide has long been a primary concern of the U.S. military and it is plausible that Ingraham's requests were being denied in the absence of solid information as to the whereabouts of a number of missing Coalition units.

seemed painfully distant now. Now there was only this dirty business at hand: getting his men out alive and being able to look Doc Callahan straight in the face at the end of it.

After some debate, Ingraham decided that they needed to move to a better vantage point in the city so that they could more fully observe the Iraqis. The mid-block building they currently occupied afforded them only a limited view of one of the side streets, and from where they were, it was exceedingly difficult to get a feel for the larger developing situation. After plying about for some minutes, one of the Marines remembered that on an earlier mission they'd worked from atop a taller three-story apartment building, which had a commanding view of downtown Khafji and the wide boulevard that ran through the middle of town. Why didn't they go to that one? he asked. They broke out a map of town and quickly located it. It was a few blocks south along a small side street from their current enclave. After a hasty team poll, the Marines decided that relocating was the thing to do.

McNamee remembers the disarray continuing. "We were all trying to talk Ingraham out of moving, saying 'Let's wait until nightfall and then move.' But Ingraham said, 'The rear needs to know what's up. We gotta go now.'" To McNamee, the situation looked grim. He thought they were on the verge of being overrun. He'd never really considered being taken prisoner, "It was sort of this unspoken thing: Save the last round for yourself."

Anticipating that they might be overwhelmed out on the street, Ingraham instructed the team to burn any personal letters or sensitive documents that they might have on them.

Lance Corporal Pat Sterling, an exceptionally poised former coxswain who served as the team's point man, wondered if his team leader had gone off the deep end. "I don't know if Ingraham had seen too many movies or if he was just excited or what. I mean technically we shouldn't have had anything personal out on patrol in the first place, but burning it?"

Nevertheless, Ingraham, secure in the belief that he had rid his team of exploitable material, girded himself for the move and the uncertainty that lay beyond it. He had the team assemble downstairs in their traditional patrol order, ready to merge into the menacing streetscape and dash to their new hide. Ingraham, seemingly intent upon correcting his earlier lapse, had decided that he would be the first man out the door. "I wasn't gonna make anyone do anything that I wouldn't do, and I wanted to be in a position to decide about our direction of movement. If we were caught out in the open by the Iraqis, we were just gonna split up into two-man teams and try and make our way south." It was a dodgy plan, but given the extremity of the situation, it seemed like a reasonable course of action.

Around midnight on the 29th, as reports of the Iraqi advance filtered up the chain of command, Prince Khalid bin Sultan al Saud, the commander of Arab coalition whose area of responsibility included Khafji, anxiously phoned General Horner's headquarters demanding that the U.S. Air Force level the city with B-52s. The bullish Horner fired back, "—Don't tell me how to do the job. Tell me what you want done." It seemed to Horner that whenever ground commanders got panicky be they American or Saudi they always thought that B-52s would solve all their problems. Horner promised Khalid that he would support him 100 percent and then oddly joked, "By the way Khalid, remember you are in a bunker at Khafji. I am in a bunker in Riyadh." The burly prince, grandson of King Abdulaziz ibn Saud, the founder of Saudi Arabia, failed to laugh.

Khalid was in no mood to jest in part because he was feeling intense pressure from above. His boss, King Fahd, the ruler of Saudi Arabia, considered the Iraqi seizure of Khafji a personal slap in the face from Saddam and demanded that forceful action be taken immediately. As Khalid recounted in his memoir *Desert Warrior,* "King Fahd wanted quick results and rightly so. He wanted the enemy force expelled at once. He wished to deny Saddam the chance of showing the world that he could invade Saudi Arabia and get away with it . . . He wanted me to recover Al Khafji with all possible speed . . . to be decisive at any cost." Arab culture is obsessed with saving face and it was clear to American observers that the careers and reputations and perhaps even the lives of the Saudi commanders in the Khafji sector were on the line. As Captain Joe Molofsky, a First Marine Division Arab liaison officer, relates, "When the Iraqis crossed the border into Saudi Arabia, they violated a very deeply-held Arab sense of infringement upon territory, doubly so because Saudi Arabia is the Islamic Holy Land, the site of the Two Holy Mosques. This was very serious business." While Khafji itself was of only modest tactical value, its rapid seizure by the Iraqis shone as a symbol of Saddam's defiance throughout the Arab world.

Khalid did not yet know about the trapped recon teams nor was he in a position to appreciate how their presence in town would complicate the recapture effort. The initial Saudi reaction, signified by Khalid's B-52 request, was to simply level the city or lay siege to it and wait for the Iraqi invaders to surrender. This crude response to the situation was due in part to the nature of the force that Khalid commanded. While passable at most conventional modes of combat, the Saudi troops in sector had never trained at high-intensity urban operations. The last thing Khalid or any of his subordinates wanted to do was waltz into Khafji and punch it out house-to-house with the vaunted Iraqis.

The full depth and complexity of the recapture equation would only become clear as the Arab coalition and the Marines began redeploying their forces to retake the town mid-morning of the 30th. It was at this juncture that Colonel John Admire was forced to admit to his Arab counterpart, Colonel Turki al Firmi, that he had two reconnaissance teams stuck in town, a fact which greatly limited the Saudis' tactical options. Sacrificing the thirteen trapped Marines was clearly not a possibility and thus the siege plan went out the window. To Marine liaison officer Captain Jim Braden, who watched the parlay in Turki's command bunker, it reminded him of his days as a second lieutenant when he'd foul something up and one of his superiors would look at him incredulously and say, "What do you mean, lieutenant?"

Admire's surprise announcement was met by a full minute

of icy silence after which Turki boldly declared, "I will get them out."

Throughout this process Prince Khalid remained bitter that the sparsely-defended city had been allowed to fall into enemy hands and blamed the American preoccupation with the battles out near the elbow. In *Desert Warrior* he writes:

> "I believe the main reason for the delay in providing us air support was that the Marines were fighting their own battles farther west—battles which in their eyes at the time of greater significance than the crisis we faced . . . The U.S. Marines had set up a major logistics base at Al-Kibrit about 70 miles west of R'as Al Mishab, where they had stockpiled all the supplies they needed for the coming attack into Kuwait. The prime concern of Lieutenant General Boomer was the security of this logistics base . . . But by committing their air force to the battles in their sector, the Marines starved us of the air support we needed and had expected to get."

Regardless of his initial emotionalism, Khalid's assessment was correct and it would take almost a full day before Marine air and the U.S. Air Force woke up to the Khafji situation and several more days before the full weight of the Coalition's air armada made itself felt.

18

Mid-Morning, January 30, 1991,
Khafji

And that is not the way to think, he told himself, and there is not you, and there are no people that things must not happen to. Neither you nor this old man is anything. You are instruments to do your duty. There are necessary orders that are no fault of yours and there is a bridge and that bridge can be the point on which the future of the human race can turn. As it can turn on everything that happens in this war. You have only one thing to do and you must do it.
—ERNEST HEMINGWAY, *For Whom the Bell Tolls*

WITH INGRAHAM leading the charge, the Marines broke out into the open city at a dead sprint, abandoning any pretense of overwatch or mutual support. The men were weighted down with nearly 100 pounds of gear apiece, making for an awkward race, but somehow they were able to reach their newfound sanctuary without being spotted by the burgeoning Iraqi force circulating about the southern half of town. McNamee, for one, was amazed. "It was a pretty long movement, and you gotta figure that with at least eight enemy vehicles and all those troops in the vicinity, we were taking our chances. It was probably just our dumb luck that they had paused to set up their defenses."*

Bursting into the new building, Ingraham immediately ordered all the rooms cleared and secured, a tall order given the sheer size of the structure. *Who the hell knows how many rooms there are in this place?* McNamee thought.

---

*McNamee's rucksack contained a twenty-pound PRC-104 high-frequency radio with several extra batteries, 500 rounds of 5.56-mm ball ammunition, 12 hand grenades, one claymore command-detonated mine, one 66-mm light anti-armor weapon, or LAW, a field expedient antenna kit, in addition to cold-weather clothing and enough chow and water for a four-day patrol.

The building itself was a broad-beamed, spartan dormitory most likely employed to house the expatriate oil workers who toiled at the local ARAMCO facility on the northern side of town. An arcade with recessed and very out-of-business storefronts ran around the perimeter at ground level. A large stairwell with two wide landings rose up the center of the structure to a capacious open roof area. The roof wall, four feet high and circumscribing the entire space, was composed of rough-hewn concrete, forming a nearly flawless parapet, an unusual circumstance the Marines were quick to take advantage of.

The edifice, while conspicuously utilitarian and providing precious little protection from the penetrating cold, looked to be an ideal base of operations for the team, providing both excellent observation over the southern portion of town and outstanding concealment from the increasingly busy streets below. In less bellicose times, one could gaze out from the rooftop, taking in wide swaths of the bristling concrete maze of town, from the signature green arches to the south, complete with ornamental Arabic scrawled across the twin spans, to the concrete causeway bowing over the mysterious *sabkha,* which effectively cut the town in half to the north.

Taking stock of their new hideout, Ingraham had every reason to be satisfied with his decision to move.

There was, however, little time to revel in this minor victory, and the Marines, working with little direction from Ingraham, began prepping the space for combat. Moving up to the roof, Sterling emplaced two claymore mines in the stairwell to cover their rear, leaving the clacker-actuaters in a defensible position at the head of the stairs beneath the covered house that led to the actual rooftop. Next he worked rapidly with his buddy David McNamee in establishing communications with Mishab, both fully aware of the fact that as a recon team they were functionally worthless until they got comm up. After trying unsuccessfully for several minutes, they began rummaging around the roof area in search of the building's antenna farm, which they hoped to plug into as they had done in their previous hideout. In the course of their search they came upon a dilapidated boxspring mattress in one corner and on a lark, hooked the radio antenna into it. Presto! They had Mishab loud and clear. Both Marines cracked up.

At this point, McNamee began to feel increasingly paranoid about the team's new position and, according to some team members, was crouching down on the rooftop, unwilling to move. McNamee reported, "I was very concerned about defending our position and thought we might be overrun at any minute."

The unflappable Pat Sterling, whose temperament Ingraham once described as being "like ice," was more sanguine about the team's predicament: "I felt like we could stay there for a while and that we were safe. Plus, there was reinforced concrete all around us. If the Iraqis tried to come up the stairs, they were gonna get totally wasted. In the end I knew we would be able to defend ourselves, at least for a short period anyway."

About this time Doc Callahan noticed to his dismay that across the broad main boulevard, little more than 100 yards to the southeast, the Iraqis were creating a major strongpoint in their defense. A scrum of utility buses and antenna-studded command-type vehicles could be seen clustering around a large unfinished hotel. Soldiers hustled in and out of the cinderblock structure ferrying what appeared to be ant-tank missiles and heavy machine-gun components. The position was so clearly the focus of the Iraqi effort that Callahan wondered if it was becoming their command post in town.

Learning of this burgeoning Iraqi concentration so close to their new home, Ingraham began working the radios in an attempt to bring some firepower to bear on the problem. Ingraham, while relatively fresh in his billet, had had a fair bit of practice calling close air support and artillery and remembered well the long, sun-flecked training days atop a steep hill in the Pohakuloa Training Area on the big island of Hawaii calling in mock air strikes. He recalled watching with childlike fascination as the screaming gray jets came on-line to do their runs over a wide lava flow, responding as though by remote control to his radio instructions, and looking on awestruck as the bombs pickled, sailing straight as fastballs, detonating with a crisp, visceral roar that shook his insides like a small earthquake.

It was an intense feeling of almost cosmic power watching these deadly birds at work and knowing that unless his calculations were correct and his instructions true, the ordnance, deadly beyond compare, would sail off harmlessly or, worse still, strike his own position. A rough symbiosis must be struck in these fleeting moments between the pilot and ground controller—an air strike usually occurs in the space of only three or four minutes—and Ingraham knew that his fledgling skills were about to be measured in detail.

While Air Force records show that dozens of Allied aircraft of all types were flying over the Khafji region on the morning of the 30th, owing perhaps to the thick, suffocating fog of war that had descended over the battlefield, curiously little American airpower seemed to have made it into town yet. After some minutes scanning the airwaves, Ingraham managed to gain control of a single F-18 Hornet strike fighter. Catching sight of the bird, Ingraham established a time hack with the pilot and passed him the regulation nine-line close-air-support brief, assuming that the flier would be able to quickly decipher it and begin his run-in on the Iraqi position. Ingraham recalls, "This knucklehead comes in, shoots straight up over the city, saying lamely, 'I can't see your target!' "

After this abortive run the pilot proceeded to egress from the scene, releasing his bombs over an abandoned antenna farm on the outskirts of the city, essentially wasting the desperately needed ordnance.

Ingraham was appalled. Here they were, a forlorn recon team cut off in town, and nobody seemed able to help them. The artillery wouldn't fire, and now he had some jet jockey who was too busy doing aerobatics to get bombs on target. "I just wanted someone to do something, because what higher headquarters didn't seem to realize is that there was nothing opposing the Iraqis at this point. I mean *nothing*. I figured

some artillery rounds or some bombs going off in the city
would halt their movement and take some of the pressure
off us."

Some time passed, and eventually Ingraham was able to
get hold of a flight of two Hornets. After quickly briefing the
pilots, the first plane began his run-in, went wings level, acquired the Iraqi-occupied building, and released a 500-pound
dumb bomb that erupted terrifically right at the front
doorstep of the building. "It was unbelievable, right on the
money," Doc Callahan recalls. Ingraham quickly relayed his
wingman's success to the second airplane, saying, "On Dash
One's hits," indicating to the pilot to drop his bombs in the
exact same location. The second F-18 performed as requested, engulfing the street in an enormous fireball. Ingraham saw several Iraqi soldiers enveloped in the flames.

Amazingly, after conducting a second run on another
target north of their position, the Hornet flight leader radioed
back to Ingraham asking if he had any other targets for him.
Confused, Ingraham called back, "But sir, you don't have
any bombs left." (Traditionally, close-air-support strikes
are conducted utilizing one-half of the ordnance on one run
and the second half on another.) *What was this guy talking
about?*

The pilot, evidently sensing the depth of their predicament, replied, "I still got my guns!"

After some fumbling around trying to assemble a mission
for him, the Hornets whipped back around for a spectacular
strafing run right across the front of the Marines' building. It
was like their own personal Blue Angels airshow, the gray
birds streaking in and laying down a solid stream of lead
along the axis of the main boulevard. The sound alone was
impressive, both birds emitting an otherworldly growl as
their 20-mm Gatling guns came to life.

It was a formidable performance that couldn't have come
at a better time. And while the strafing run was of question-
able tactical value, the Marines, anxious to land a blow on
their pursuers, were ecstatic to have that awesome amount of
firepower in their corner. They felt as if the pilots had saved

their lives. The Iraqis seemed in sudden disarray. Medical personnel streamed into the target building carrying their wounded with them. The bombs, while not demolishing the structure, had clearly put a hurt on the Iraqis.*

However, it wasn't long before Iraqis could be seen circling the building and reinforcing the position again. The air strike, while just what the doctor ordered, evidently was not enough to turn the tide. More vehicles prowled the town, the Iraqis continuing their defensive preparations in earnest.

---

*One is reminded of a passage from J. Glenn Gray's classic treatise on the philosophy of soldiering, *The Warriors: Reflections on Men in Battle:* "War is now fought in the air as well on land and sea, and the expanse of vision and spectacle afforded by combat planes is hard to exaggerate. Because these powerful new weapons usually remove those who use them further from the gruesome consequences of their firing, they afford more opportunity for aesthetic satisfaction. Combat in the skies is seldom devoid of the form, grace, and harmony that ground fighting lacks . . . It is true that the roar of fighting planes can be terror-inspiring. But the combatant who is relieved from participation and given the spectator's role can nearly sate the eye with all the elements of fearful beauty"(32).

19

2nd Saudi Arabian National Guard Brigade Headquarters, Five Miles West of Mishab

*You will be like an actor in a foreign theatre, playing a part day and
night for months, without rest, and for an anxious stake. Complete
success, which is when the Arabs forget your strangeness and speak
naturally to you, counting you as one of themselves, is perhaps only
attainable in character.*
— T. E. LAWRENCE, from a confidential British manual,
Handling Hejazi Arabs

IT WAS COMING up on midday on January 30, and Captain
Jim Braden, the ranking ANGLICO advisor attached
to the 2nd Saudi Arabian National Guard Brigade whose sector Khafji was in, hadn't heard from his best friend Doug
Kleinsmith in nearly ten hours. Many of the ANGLICO
Marines who had listened in as the Iraqis came down
from Kuwait and watched as all the observation posts were
overrun, assumed that Kleinsmith and his Marines were
dead. First Lieutenant Bubba Deckert, who was Kleinsmith's
counterpart on Braden's brigade-level team known as Wild
Eagle 3–2, was depressed. He was convinced that Kleinsmith had been killed. He had no reason to believe otherwise. They hadn't had radio contact with him since he left
OP 7 sometime after midnight. *Where else could he be?*

While intensely concerned, Jim Braden somehow knew
that the youthful captain was out there somewhere. A lot of
people who first encountered Kleinsmith's sometimes goofy
demeanor assumed that he was just a lightweight, seven-
months-promoted captain and failed to realize that beneath
the affable exterior was a perspicacious young officer who
knew his way around the battlefield. Indeed it was Kleinsmith who first introduced Braden, a Huey pilot, to the whole

concept of how their highly unusual liaison company operated. Braden knew Doug would be back and told Bubba not to worry.

Braden, Kleinsmith, Deckert, and the rest of the ANGLICO crew had been living among the various Arab units of the Coalition known as the Joint Forces Coalition-East for nearly six months by the time Khafji happened and knew the Arabs better than anyone in theater. They all knew that they had a tough road ahead of them and that the Saudi and Qatari units they advised were an unknown quantity. The commander of the brigade they were attached to, Colonel Turki al-Firmi, was an overweight, ineffectual officer who seemed to have ascended to his current position by virtue of his tribal connections rather than by any discernible gift for command. Behind his back Braden referred to him as "Jabba the Hut." Turki was so large that when Braden had some of his pilot buddies land a section of Cobra attack helicopters in the SANG compound for a hands-on static display, Turki couldn't fit into the bird's modestly sized cockpit. Needless to say, the man did not engender great confidence among his American counterparts.

Turki's force reflected its commander. The Saudi Arabian National Guard, originally formed from the Bedouin tribal elements most loyal to KingAbdulaziz Ibn Saud, the founder of modern-day Saudi Arabia, was a light motorized force that served primarily as the royal family's house guard. Outfitted with the latest equipment and staffed by officers with only the best family connections, the SANG functioned much as did Saddam's Republican Guard: as a counterweight to the regular army and as an instrument for quelling internal dissent. The only action the SANG had seen up to this point was the recapture of the Grand Mosque in Mecca from Shiite terrorists who had seized the holy site in 1979, and it was rumored that this feat had only been achieved with the extensive advice and support of French mercenaries. They were in many ways a glorified militia, with next to no experience in high-intensity armored operations.

Infected with a childlike penchant for wishful thinking,

the SANG officers repeatedly brushed off the Marines' attempts to prepare them for the coming conflict. The numerous entreaties made by Braden and his men were unerringly met with a classic Saudi dismissal: "Oh, Captain Jim, you are too offensive. We will not fight. Arabs will not fight other Arabs. We will reach a political solution with Saddam." This same ostrich-like attitude prevailed in their training philosophy as well. The Saudis almost never fired their weapons, and their armored personnel carriers often sat in place for weeks at a time. The brigade's four battalions were rarely at more than 50 percent strength because their officers were constantly rotating home to spend time with their families, dashing any hopes of ever getting the Saudis to launch any large-scale training exercises. The Arabs avoided training so assiduously and were so dubious in field operations that most of the American advisors attached to them felt compelled to establish their own internal security watches at night, resulting in a perimeter within a perimeter. When push came to shove, no one expected the Arabs to perform.

ANGLICO, which was composed primarily of reassigned pilots and artillery officers, had initially been attached to the pan-Arab force merely to provide fire support, but Jim Braden, along with ANGLICO's commanding officer, Colonel Clay Grubb, quickly perceived that the unorthodox unit could play a pivotal role in the coming war, buttressing the Saudis' anemic fire-support structure and transforming a weak, marginally trained combat organization into a force that could hold its own against the vaunted Iraqis. The ANGLICO Marines realized that due to geographic happenstance the Arab Coalition had been left guarding the Marines' eastern flank in Saudi Arabia and saw themselves as the major guarantors of the unproven Arab force. No one in the Marine hierarchy trusted the Arabs, but Grubb and Braden hoped to prove them wrong. At one point during a briefing with Marine air commanders, a cobra squadron commander approached a map of Saudi Arabia and, looking over toward Khafji, asked, "Who's over here?" When told that that area belonged to the Saudis, he'd responded, "Oh. Well, fuck the

Saudis." Braden and his colleagues, who were sitting in the back of the room, just shook their heads. The ANGLICO Marines had been forging bonds with the Arabs for months, promising them that they wouldn't leave them hanging when the hour of battle came, but there was precious little concern for the Arabs in the higher echelons.

Nevertheless, Braden, who had left the flight line little more than a year prior, was able to exploit his connections in the Marine air wing and coax his buddies into training with the Arabs, who would never have even seen an American airplane otherwise. Along with several other ANGLICO officers, Braden arranged to fly on the U.S. Air Force's AWACS and airborne command-and-control aircraft to familiarize the pilots with ANGLICO's mission and capabilities. They embarked on several tours of the region, briefing generals and aircrews throughout the theater on what their company could do and where they were located. They wanted everyone in theater to know who ANGLICO was, so that when they went into battle and they called for air support, pilots would remember them. As the Desert Shield portion of the deployment continued through the fall months, Braden and Grubb managed to reach many of their colleagues and let them know that they would need their help when the shooting started. The Marine pilots, sensing their buddies' vulnerability, banished among the Arabs as they were, began promising that they would fly for ANGLICO when the time came.

At first, living among the haughty Arabs was hell. The chow, for starters, was the worst the troops had ever seen. The Marines were so far removed from American supply lines that even the freeze-dried MRE (meals ready to eat) rations became a rare delicacy. The enlisted men were subjected to a daily routine of whole boiled goat or chicken served up on a large metal platter. Mixed in the gruel were all the entrails, including beaks, hoofs, feet, and eyeballs. Mealtime was a sight to behold. All hands would gather round and pick at the boiled meat with their right hand until the meal was consumed. As many an ANGLICO Marine learned, eating with your left hand was strictly forbidden and if used would herald a quick halt to the repast. Chowtime soon became known as "The Goat Grab."

Eventually the substandard chow and exposure to the local Arabian bacteria, coupled with the blatant Saudi disregard for field sanitation (they maintained open, rat-infested trash pits in the middle of their compound), resulted in a wave of chronic diarrhea and dysentery sweeping through the company. These twin plagues took their toll on the men and soon nearly everyone in the widely dispersed unit was sick and rapidly losing weight. The average man shed around 40 pounds. Entire four-man teams went down, unfit for duty for days at a time. Captain Kris Elliot, a team leader advising a Saudi regular army brigade to the west of Khafji, was preparing to medevac an already rail-thin Marine named Myers until the man begged to be allowed to remain with his unit. Throughout the month of October 1990 many of the Marines subsisted on care packages of Halloween candy that had been shipped from home by their wives.

The gastrointestinal ailments and bad Saudi water affected each man differently. Bubba Deckert hilariously recalled, "I could shit through a screen door and not leave a trace!" Nearly everyone withered away, cursing the loss of muscle mass won in garrison weight rooms. Disgusted by the grievous living conditions, groups of ANGLICO Marines began filtering down to American airbases on the coast to engage in a time-honored Marine Corps tradition: stealing food and supplies from the United States Air Force. On one occasion, Kris Elliot chatted up a young female supply sergeant to distract her while one of his corporals made off with several crates of MREs. Elliot even managed to finagle a package of genuine stateside toilet paper from the starry-eyed airman before making his exit. Eventually, after pilfering provisions and making special arrangements with the Arab cooks, the teams were gradually able to improve their diet and regain some of the muscle mass, but it was a rite of passage that none of them would soon forget.

Adding to the advisors' difficulties, the Arab soldiery was

intensely skeptical of the American infidels in their midst and assumed—in line with the traditional Saudi love of intrigue—that the Marines were spies sent by the American high command. The Arab officers would frequently remark, "You Americans don't care about us. You just want our oil." However, as the weeks passed and the Marines remained true to their calling, the Saudis began to see that along with the ANGLICO teams came massive amounts of airpower and a influential connection to the vast American war apparatus. The Saudis, who instinctively mistrusted officially distributed intelligence reports, learned to take heed when an ANGLICO officer took them aside and told them, "I am telling you this as a friend . . ." Whatever the Marines passed became gospel to the Saudis. As Doug Kleinsmith put it, "At first there was sort of this weird posturing going on, but after a while it became a point of pride to have an ANGLICO team attached to you. If you were a Saudi commander and you didn't have your ANGLICO team, you'd been snubbed."

Braden and Kleinsmith both knew that they'd crossed the line from suspicious outsider to trusted advisor when the Saudis began dispatching Muslim holy men to convert them. The Saudis were worried for their friends' souls. Around Christmastime, one of the Saudi lieutenants cornered Braden, saying, "We have someone we'd like you to meet." Shortly thereafter, an imam, complete with a stomach-length ZZ Top beard, approached, besieging him with a battery of pointed religious questions. After discoursing with the holy man for an hour and a half, Braden was informed that the imam could turn him into a good Muslim in eighteen months.

"Why so long?" Braden inquired.

"It would take you that long to unlearn all your bad American habits."

It was clear to all the ANGLICO officers that a major threshold had been crossed. They had gained the Arabs' trust and the Coalition and thus the Marine Corps was the stronger for it. By the time Khafji happened in late January, the ANGLICO Marines had forged the tightest bonds between Arab and non-Arab forces since T. E. Lawrence.

As Captain Joe Molofsky, a 1st Marine Division Arab liaison officer with a U.N. Middle Eastern tour under his belt, recalls, "ANGLICO was the single unifying element that brought it all together. With a mixed Coalition force the likes of which we had in northeastern Saudi Arabia you must, without question, have American advisors with common radio equipment permanently cross-attached throughout the force. The fact that the ANGLICO guys were also fire-support gurus only sweetened the deal."

It was a brilliant arrangement, one that had somehow escaped the attention of the generals in the rear, who seemed to look upon ANGLICO as an exotic band of desert gypsies, which in one sense they were. It was also a highly unusual situation—the Marine Corps were typically content to leave the foreign liaison work to the Army's Special Forces—one that had been arrived at only at the personal behest of Colonel Grubb. However, what had begun as a bleak and thankless assignment became the mission of a lifetime for many of the Marines. Living on the outer ring of the realm, the ANGLICO Marines, already an independent-minded bunch, thrived on the experience. The four-man teams, dispersed across the wide desert, were with few exceptions authorities unto themselves, commanding the reverence of native troops, in serene command of the deadliest weapons in human history.

11:00 A.M., January 30, 1991, Saudi Arabian National Guard 2nd Brigade Headquarters, 15 Miles South of Khafji

KLEINSMITH WAS ALIVE. Having navigated the labyrinth of the *sabkha* and cleared friendly lines, the stringy artilleryman walked back into the 2nd SANG brigade headquarters to the extreme relief of his boss and mentor, Jim Braden. Corporal John Calhoun recalled, "It was like a family reunion. We were pretty happy to be there and they were pretty happy that we were alive." Braden, who in truth had long worried about the incredibly young-looking Kleinsmith and had made sure to assign him his three strongest corporals (including Calhoun), was now simply comforted to see that he had indeed made it out alive and unharmed. Kleinsmith's ordeal, however, was far from complete.

Since Kleinsmith's exodus from OP 7, the situation had grown infinitely more complex. Joe Molofsky had checked in with Braden at the brigade headquarters bunker, informing him that the line of the Iraqi offensive stretched all the way to the far west, covering the entirety of the Marine sector out to Observation Post 6. Further, The Iraqis appeared to have excellent intelligence about the American defenses. All along the border they had managed to strike at the vulnerable seams between major units. (The fight out at OP 4 had for example struck on the boundary between the First and Second Marine Divisions' sectors.) While Braden had no reason to think that the Iraqis' intelligence services were all that effective, he thought, *nobody gets that lucky.*

Compounding the spiraling situation were the 3rd Marines recon teams trapped inside Khafji. To Braden, it looked as if they were putting together a raid plan to retrieve the Marines until Colonel Admire stopped by to inform Colonel Turki. After the awkward Turki-Admire parley, Turki had departed for his division headquarters to visit with his boss, Major General Sultan 'Adi al-Mutairi. Braden wanted to go with him but knew that he had his own piece of the fight to fight, his own teams to coordinate. As he left the command bunker, Turki turned to Braden and said in his ragged English, "Captain Jim, you are my communications. I am trusting you with my brigade. All fire support goes through you."

Braden's day in the spotlight had clearly arrived, and in-between working the radios for his various teams and marshaling fire support for the brewing fight, he briefed Kleinsmith on all that had transpired in his absence.

The update complete and figuring that the day owed him some rest before the battle royale was joined, Kleinsmith elected to try and grab some zzz's before heading back into the fray. He had just lain down, when as at OP 7, he was again woken prematurely, this time by Jim Braden. Braden needed him to go up to the north of the city to coordinate the fight in the sector between the city and the Kuwaiti border. For simplicity's sake, Braden had chosen to split their portion of the fight into two halves. Braden would take the southern half of Khafji, where a hasty Saudi counterassault was taking shape. Kleinsmith's job was to ride herd on the various teams in the north. Braden had already launched Bubba Deckert northward to prod the 5th Battalion of the SANG into action. The 8th Regular Saudi Land Force Brigade had launched an armored company to the north and was on its way to link up with Bubba's battalion.

The Saudi plan at this point, as Kleinsmith understood it, was to cut off the city and hopefully talk the Iraqis into surrendering. With the northern end of town still open to reinforcement along the coastal highway, Kleinsmith's piece of the fight was crucial. If the Saudis and the ANGLICO advisors failed to shut down the northern approaches, the Iraqis could continue to pour reinforcements into the city from Kuwait. It wouldn't be long before the Arab Coalition and their Marine partners would be overwhelmed. Although Braden might have had mixed feelings about his Arab brothers-in-arms, he had labored hard to make this marriage work and was determined to see it through to victory. Braden needed Kleinsmith to sortie as soon as possible.

In the fading afternoon light of January 30, Doc Callahan watched with disbelieving eyes as two U.S. Army cargo trucks approached the city up the coastal highway from the south. They were enormous tractor-trailers towing empty flatbeds used to ferry M-1 main battle tanks. Doc, who had been operating in town for weeks, had seen this drama play out at least three times previously: The empty trucks would meander up the highway and roll right into Khafji like lost children at an amusement park, totally unaware of the fact that they had blundered into the border zone. The Marines, thus forced to come out of hiding, would whip out their maps and redirect the wayward drivers, pointing out to them the western turnoff they'd missed on the other side of Mishab. On one occasion Callahan had stopped a truck and was appalled to see a lone female soldier behind the wheel. She had no map, no weapon, and no written directions, and when they told her where she was, immediately began crying.

Doc looked on in horror as the present convoy rolled toward Khafji. The two trucks were quickly taken under fire by the Iraqis across the boulevard from the Marines' hideout. The first truck absorbed the brunt of the fusillade and rambled out of control off the highway, slamming full-force into a cinderblock retaining wall. The driver of the second truck in the column, seeing this calamity unfold, executed what Doc described as "the fastest U-turn in history, like he was a VW Bug," leaving only a trail of dust and a memory.

Iraqi soldiers quickly descended upon the two occupants of the first truck, collecting them up as if the entire evolution had been rehearsed. A small fleet of command trucks joined the scene, and it wasn't long before the Marines saw several of these vehicles racing through town toward the Kuwait border with two American soldiers inside. The Marines relayed the drama in its entirety to Mishab.

Specialist Melissa Rathbun-Nealy of the U.S. Army's 233rd Transportation Company could tell that something wasn't right. She, along with her comrade behind the wheel, Specialist David Lockett, were piloting their 22½-ton heavy equipment transporter from the Saudi Arabian port of Dhahran to their austere forward base in the western desert when Rathbun-Nealy noticed the glimmering expanse of the Persian Gulf off to their right side. They had been traveling in a long convoy of trucks and had lost sight of their column on the rolling desert roads. She knew they were supposed to be heading west, into the lonely heart of the desert, and that they shouldn't be seeing the water now. Protesting to Lockett, she told him to pull over. "I stopped the trucks and told them we needed to take the exit we'd just passed. They refused to listen to me, said I didn't know where I was going, that I hadn't been on any missions before." It was like that age-old story: a husband-driver is lost, his wife insisting that he pull over to inquire about directions. The man, confident in his own innate sense of direction, is dismissive and keeps on driving.

Rathbun-Nealy's colleagues would soon wish they'd heeded her complaints. Proceeding northward along the coastal highway, they passed several platoons of Marines in Humvees on the right, driving right up to the gates of Ra's al-Khafji. Rathbun-Nealy remembers, "The Iraqis got off a lucky shot and hit our steering box and we rolled into a wall. They came up from our left, so we started to run up the inside of the wall. There was a huge, mansion-like house that we were trying to get to, but they surrounded us with AK-47s and pistols and told us to get down. I was in a hysterical state, heaving like I was crying, but there were no tears."

Lockett recalls that the Iraqis snapped them up and dragged them to a gas station 100 yards away. They threw him and Rathbun-Nealy into a crawlspace underneath the station, and both anxiously waited while their captors decided their fate. Eventually, the soldiers pulled them out from under the gas station and tossed them into a waiting utility van. According to Rathbun-Nealy, "As they were walking us back, an air raid began and we heard a large explosion. We thought our truck had been blown up, but we found out afterward that it had been the large house we had been trying to reach." A flight of Cobra attack helicopters, dispatched by the Marines the soldiers had bypassed, were loitering over the southern neighborhoods of Khafji searching for Lockett and Rathbun-Nealy when they began engaging the very column the two prisoners were set to join.

In the course of their capture and subsequent journey both Lockett and Rathbun-Nealy were wounded, although neither seriously. Lockett caught some shrapnel in his abdomen and Rathbun-Nealy had a bullet lodged in her right forearm, although she wouldn't notice it for some time.

Major Craig Huddleston, executive officer of the 3rd Battalion of the 3rd Marine Regiment, had just returned from a cursory reconnaissance of the captured town when he got the word that an army truck had gone missing inside Khafji. Huddleston was stunned. *What the hell was an army transport truck doing up near Khafji? Didn't they realize it had just been seized by the Iraqis?*

Huddleston had been dispatched from Mishab with a reinforced rifle company late on the 29th to establish a blocking position five kilometers south of Khafji. The town rested squarely within the Arab Coalition Forces' area of operations, and despite the fact that the 3rd Marines had been sending teams into town for weeks now, it had always been understood that defense of the town was exclusively an Arab responsibility. The apparent error of this division of labor was highlighted when shortly after the Iraqi attack began, long lines of Saudi vehicles could be seen streaming out of town like ants from a hole in the earth. After several instances of near-fratricide between parties of Marines and fleeing SANG vehicles, Colonel Admire decided that a combat outpost was needed to keep tabs on the situation to the north and to provide an advanced guard against any further Iraqi incursions.

There was an element of simple distrust involved in this move as well. Watching the obviously flustered Saudis racing about had tested the Marines' confidence in their fledgling allies. One officer from Admire's staff took it upon himself to double-check on the Saudi special forces team manning the cratering charge that had been emplaced in a culvert just up the coastal highway from the 3rd Marines encampment. Blowing the road was their last resort should the Iraqis make a lunge for them, and at this point the hard-bitten captain wasn't comfortable trusting his fate to unsteady Arab hands.

On the afternoon of the 30th, Huddleston was having trouble reaching Mishab over the radio. Having completed his hasty patrol up to the city gates, he was slowly plying his way south, testing the VHF signal every few hundred meters in his Humvee, praying all the while to the fickle gods of radio comm that they might grant him this reprieve. After several minutes of this, he was able to regain radio contact. It was then that he received a report from the forwardmost elements of the 3/3 outpost that a pair of soldiers in a truck had disappeared. Huddleston immediately glanced back at the battalion sergeant major who was seated behind him in the Humvee, asking, "What do you think we oughta do?"

The sergeant major was unable to utter a complete answer, as hard on the heels of the first message the news came that a female soldier had been on the first truck and was now missing in action. Huddleston recalls, "I'll never forget it— it was clear as day what we needed to do. I turned around and looked at the sergeant major. He was glaring back at me and I said, 'I think we gotta go get 'em.' " Huddleston got back on the radio and told the company commander at the northern outpost to assemble a patrol of volunteers to go up into Khafji and recover the lost soldiers.

When Huddleston regained the outpost, he discovered to his surprise that all of the 128 Marines at the outpost wanted to be a part of the rescue squad. It was one of those unexpectedly poignant moments in war when out of the sound and fury an unaffected, crystalline camaraderie makes its presence known, as if to say, "I've been here all along, waiting for you." Despite this unforgettable outpouring of concern, Huddleston hardly wanted to drag a full company into town only to get decisively engaged, which would merely turn into another sordid case of the rescuers needing to be rescued. Instead, he grabbed the outpost's TOW platoon commander, Captain John Borth, an artillery forward observer, and a forward air controller, along with a handful of heavy machine-gun and TOW Humvees. After briefly sketching out a scheme of maneuver in the sand, the small force struck out from their hasty bastion toward the gates of town.

The 3/3 Marines, who were all familiar with the southern stretches of town, having been stationed in the vicinity since New Year's, watched nervously as the myriad recognizable landmarks along the highway slid by at high speed. Once they were in sight of the green arches, everything went like clockwork. The Humvees established a hasty half-moon facing north as Borth's team of TOWs punched out toward Khafji proper to locate the missing pair.

As they assumed their position, Huddleston recognized a French-made Qatari tank that had been posted on the coastal road from his earlier expedition. He'd briefly conversed with the sergeant vehicle commander at the time, advising him that in his current position he was exposed and well within range of the Iraqi guns to the north. The Qatari, in his failing English, didn't seem to grasp the concept, and after several minutes of awkward gesturing, Huddleston had given up, reasoning that the tank didn't belong to him anyway. The major saw now that the tank was all blacked over, its exterior ravaged by fire.

Everyone aboard was dead. In the space of time that it had taken him to move south past the outpost and then return northward to within sight of the gates, these men had been annihilated, as if by some brooding invisible force. Just like that. Extending out from Huddleston's Humvee in wide, staggered arcs were scores of artillery craters, pocking the dead land like a moonscape. His mind snapped back to the missing Americans. He thought, *What the hell were those guys thinking driving up here? Couldn't they see the burned-out tank and the craters everywhere? Why didn't they just turn around?*

As these thoughts coursed through his head, Borth's squad raced by, giving him a hasty thumbs-up in passing. Overcome with relief, Huddleston assumed that they'd managed to recover their miscreant comrades. The remainder of the patrol beat a quick retreat, and Huddleston noted as they returned south that a pair of Iraqi Type 531 APCs had taken up position just north of the gates as if to bid them a menacing farewell.

Circling the wagons at a gas station a mile south of town, Huddleston asked Borth what had happened. In fact, the soldiers had not been recovered. Having pushed up to the gates, Borth and his team had located the wrecked truck. The heavy loader was riddled with bullet holes, the rear wheels of the rig still spinning. As if to mock the tragic scene, the

truck's hazard lights had blinked on and off like a broken-
down semi on the side of the interstate. There were no
bloodstains, although the Marines managed to locate the
soldiers' deuce gear and canteens. After rummaging around
the area yelling, "U.S. Marines! U.S. Marines! Come out!
We're here to rescue you!" the team had come up dry. Noting the approach of several Iraqi armored vehicles, the
Marines had beat feet, having no desire to trade sporting
fire, given that they had little bite to match their bark.

Huddleston was happy with his subordinate's decision,
noting that he was under no orders to seek out an engagement with the Iraqis at this stage. In the midst of composing
himself from this unsettling encounter, he was set upon by
an errant NBC television news reporter who had managed to
finagle his way up to the forward gas station. It was a post-
modern moment, the major mere seconds out of the heat of
battle and having a camera jammed in his face. Keenly
aware of the gravity of the situation, Huddleston announced
that a pair of U.S. Army soldiers were missing in action, deliberately omitting any mention of Rathbun-Nealy. It would
take thirteen days for the Pentagon to confirm that an American woman had become an Iraqi prisoner.*

Morale in the 3rd Marines command post plummeted
when the news reached them that Rathbun-Nealy had been
captured, all hands automatically assuming that she would be
exploited and abused by her captors. Upon hearing these ill
tidings, Colonel Admire immediately deployed his forward
command post farther northward in an attempt to get a better
feel for the spiraling situation made worse by the uncertain

---

*Despite numerous reports that the two had been taken prisoner, including one from a
captured Iraqi soldier who claimed to have been one of their captors, nearly two weeks
passed before the Pentagon began listing Rathbun-Nealy and Lockett as missing in action. On February 12, 1991, responding to "conflicting information," officials announced, "We are reasonably confident that they are prisoners of war. Where they are,
precisely what shape they're in, we don't know."

The cause of this startling information gap remains unclear, although some Pentagon critics have suggested that officials were slow to announce that the pair had been
captured because of the incident's incredible propaganda potential. Rathbun-Nealy
was the first female American soldier captured since World War II.

fortunes of the lost Americans. As time went on, the disappearance of the two became even more problematic as Admire's staff and other officers became increasingly hesitant to fire into the city, knowing that Americans might be incarcerated somewhere in its environs.

Doug Kleinsmith—with his three trusty corporals, Calhoun, Foss, and Simons, in tow—departed from the SANG brigade headquarters west of Mishab at around 2:30 on the afternoon of the 13th, bound for the northwestern edge of the city to set up a blocking position. Owing to the narrow escape at OP 7 or perhaps to the searing six-month prelude to the war, the ANGLICO team, known on the radio as Wild Eagle 3–2 Forward, was strangely ecstatic about getting a chance to rejoin the battle. Lying down to rest in the compound down south, the men had encountered the ageless paradox of war: Having had a brief taste of the deadly affair, they were drawn back to the fatal beauty and excitement of it all like moths to the flame. It could have been the death of them, but they lusted after the experience anyhow. After being roused, the team excitedly repacked their modified Humvee and rambled northward, the well-tattooed "Tigger" Foss behind the wheel, the crew singing like a busload of schoolchildren bound for Sea World: "We're goin' *no-orth!* We're goin' *no-orth!* We're goin' *no-orth!*"

Kleinsmith, who while reveling in the intoxicating abandon and the odd freedom that modern battlefield produces, was at the moment deeply concerned that he might unwittingly get his men killed and felt that perhaps he ought to tamp down the team's revelry. Looking to his left at Foss, he told the spirited corporal, "Hey, Foss, man, you're goin' way the fuck too fast."

As the chorus of "We're goin' north" continued, the Humvee crested a small rise in the desert. Suddenly the ground gave way and the Humvee was airborne. Aghast, Kleinsmith thought, *This is it. We're done. We're out of the fight.* Smashing back down into mother earth, the vehicle was a sea of hollering, pissed-off Marines. Corporal Simons, seated di-

rectly behind Foss started smacking him in the head, screaming, "You idiot!" Calhoun, who was originally a motor transport specialist, was leaning out the side of the vehicle to
ensure that the frame hadn't cracked in half. Still in command of the vehicle, Foss laughed maniacally, totally unfazed by the ruckus.

Kleinsmith couldn't believe the mischief he seemed to
find himself in with his team and thanked God that while
they were all clowns, they were, to a man, extremely intelli-
gent and committed to the profane crafts of war. They
switched drivers, Kleinsmith informing Corporal Foss that
he had been forever relieved of his driving duties. The team
continued their northward trek, dodging scattered mortar
barrages along the way.

It took more than two hours to complete the lengthy journey north, and by the time Kleinsmith linked up with one of
the Saudi battalions in the unfettered plains ten kilometers
west of the city, the shortened winter day was nearing its end.
He'd hoped to begin sealing off the northern edge of town
before nightfall, but owing to the confusion in the Saudi
ranks and the late arrival of several of the 5th Battalion's subunits, it was clear that the movement to contact would have
to wait until the following morning. The 5th Battalion,
whose job it was to screen the border region in the Khafji
area, had been scattered to the four winds when the Iraqis
came, and it was going to take them some time to reconsti-
tute themselves.

Wandering among the widely dispersed Saudi vehicles,
Kleinsmith found Bubba Deckert.

Deckert had only a few hours prior concluded a full day's
journey himself, having been dispatched by Braden to locate
and assist the 5th Battalion of the SANG in its blocking mission up north. He'd begun his expedition on the southwestern
edge of the city and slowly made a northward arc, bumping
into other ANGLICO teams scattered along the way. Everyone he encountered seemed engaged, fighting their piece of
the fight. Everyone had an Arab unit that they were trying to
coax into position or that they were calling in air strikes for.

To the ANGLICO Marines it seemed as if the Saudis would make the calls about what units went where, and then the Marine teams, dispersed throughout the battlefield, would ensure that the big blue arrows that they'd drawn on the map inside the command bunker were actually executed. They didn't make any of the major tactical decisions, but because the many of the Arab units lacked common radio equipment and had never been a part of a brigade-size deployment before, the ANGLICOs were usually the ones coordinating the moves of the various players on the ground. As he wandered around the fringes of the city, Bubba ran into Captain Kris Elliot, who was advising a Saudi regular army tank unit. Elliot, who was a Supporting Arms Liaison Team leader like Jim Braden and thus his superior, asked him, "What are you supposed to be doing?"

"I'm trying to find fucking 5th Battalion. Have you seen anything of them?"

Elliot, whose unit was supposed to working in conjunction with 5th, pointed him off to the east, where he eventually ran into what he thought was the ghost of Doug Kleinsmith.

Bubba couldn't believe that Kleinsmith was alive, and after a round of hugs and thank-God-you're-alives, Kleinsmith told him that they needed to get their battalion organized and ready for the coming fight. Deckert was stunned; after all that had transpired, he didn't want to let Kleinsmith out of his sight, and yet he knew that they had to get to work. Deckert remembers, "I was like, 'Wait a minute, motherfucker, you've been dead for the last day and a half . . .' "

Deckert spent the remainder of the night trying to get the scores of errant Saudi armored personnel carriers pointed in the right direction. Originally, the idea had been to get the Saudis oriented to the north to engage whatever Iraqis might be coming down the coastal corridor, but after seeing the gross disarray of the Saudi formation, he had satisfied himself with merely getting the Arab V-150s pointed away from each other. It seemed like every driver in the entire battalion had decided to face his vehicle inward as if to prepare for a mass duel with itself. It was dicey work. Bubba was trying to safely approach the Arab vehicles in the inky darkness, and the crews, who usually spoke no English, were on Stress Factor 11. Mortar rounds were crunching in the desert all around them. Deckert's men kept asking him, "Sir, those rounds are getting close. Do we have to do this right now?"

At the moment, Deckert thought it paramount to provide positive direction to the unbloodied Saudis and told his men, "Don't get nervous, because if we get jumpy, then the Arabs are gonna shit the bed and fucking boogie again and I don't know about you, but I'm not driving through their fucking lines a second time." He kept driving around for several more hours, corralling the scattered Saudi vehicles that had been dispersed over an eight-kilometer area and talking with the English-speaking Saudi officers. Most of the officers were so frightened that they wouldn't even emerge from the safety of their vehicles. Deckert had to talk to them through a two-inch slit cut into the shell of the tall armored vehicles.

Kleinsmith, although disappointed with the Saudi performance that evening, was hardly surprised. He knew the full depth of the SANG's incompetence. Previously, he'd witnessed an Army Special Forces team pouring diesel fuel into a Saudi .50-caliber machine gun just to free up the bolt enough to pull it to the rear. The rank-and-file Saudi failed to perform even the most basic of soldierly tasks: cleaning his weapon. Despite the half-year of ANGLICO admonitions and on the eve of their baptism by fire, the Saudis remained tragically unprepared for the battle to come.

As the full weight of the situation began weighing down on Captain Baczkowski, he came to the realization that he was going to have to get his guys out himself. Although it appeared that for the moment his teams were passably secure, he knew it was only a matter of time before the Iraqis found them out and either killed them or shipped them off to Baghdad. Baczkowski was not yet aware of the Rathbun-Nealy saga, but on balance the episode confirmed the idea that, given the right circumstances, the Iraqis could do damage to the Americans.

Baczkowski, near-stricken with trepidation over the potential loss of his men, was encouraged by their conduct, given the extremity of the circumstances. They continued to provide detailed reports on the Iraqis' activities in town, which not only aided in the burgeoning recapture effort but also served as an ongoing reminder of their defiant survival in the face of ever-lengthening odds. A siege atmosphere took hold in the 3rd Marines command post, and over the hours of the long night that began the crisis, Baczkowski, along with the platoon's senior team leader, Sergeant Bill Iiams, and a few of the nearby radio operators, began cooking up some rescue ideas for the two beleaguered teams.

Other larger wheels could be seen turning as well. The 1st Battalion, 12th Marines, the 3rd Marine Regiment's organic artillery unit, began deploying its Alpha and Charlie batteries, maneuvering them into hasty firing positions up the coastal highway. Colonel Admire, who habitually haunted the four-Humvee perimeter that comprised the command post area, was gone, lighting out on an extended liaison tour to the various Arab units in the 3rd Marines sector. In light of this, it remained far from clear who would retake the town, the seasoned and composed Hawaii Marines or the Arab Coalition Forces, which looked, even to the untrained eye, to be in profound disarray.

Late on the afternoon of the 30th, Baczkowski, along with Sergeant Iiams, two radio operators from the head shed, and a nervous Kuwaiti army translator, Lieutenant Naif, struck out in the regimental chaplain's Humvee, which had the words "Amazing Grace" scrawled in chalk across its thin fiberglass body.

Naif, a poor discomfited soul, had been a foreign exchange student in London three weeks prior and had been drafted by the Kuwaiti government in exile to serve in the liberation of his homeland. He didn't look as if he'd ever fired a weapon in his life. The captain was less than ecstatic about the Kuwaiti's inclusion in the patrol and felt as if the conspicuously awkward former student was being forced upon him by certain members of the regimental staff.

Having roughly sketched out a plan for getting the boys out of town, Baczkowski bade farewell to his newly acquired brother-in-law, Captain Kent Bradford, who happened to be the assistant operations officer for the regiment. Said Bradford of the Baczkowski expedition, "No one authorized or encouraged his plan. Overcome with concern for the welfare of his Marines, Dan just thought it up and did it." Bradford had a stake in the looming tragedy as well: He'd commanded Alpha company for several years. He, along with nearly every other unoccupied soul at Mishab, had been listening to the drama over a radio speaker set up in the command post.

With Iiams behind the wheel, they quickly reached the small service station that only hours before had played host to Major Huddleston's crew. Over the course of the battle it would become the major southern stopping-off point for the battle, referred to as either "Checkpoint 67" or, more commonly, the "Khafji Café." Strewn throughout the surrounding area were scores of thin-skinned Saudi National Guard vehicles bolstered by two companies of French-made Qatari tanks.*

At the Khafji Café, Baczkowski encountered Captain Joe Molofsky, the 1st Marine Division's Arab liaison officer, who'd originally been assigned to the 3rd Marines. Molofsky, an uncommonly seasoned officer with extensive experience throughout the Middle East, had traveled far afield with the Arab forces over the course of the war, becoming a rare sight at Mishab in the process. It was a huge comfort for Baczkowski, already careworn and bedraggled by the ordeal, to see Molofsky's familiar face. Also present was U.S. Army Lieutenant Colonel Michael "Coyote" Taylor, the SANG battalion's American advisor.

While he was solely concerned with the recovery of his besieged teams, Baczkowski noted with some mystification

---

*This was the 7th Saudi Arabian National Guard battalion, commanded by Lieutenant Colonel Matar. The SANG were outfitted with Cadillac Gage V-150s, essentially a crude, taller version of the Marines' LAV. The Qataris, longstanding allies of the Saudis and members of the larger Arab Coalition, were more heavily equipped with 1960s-vintage AMX-30 main battle tanks of French manufacture.

that the political issues seemed to have been sorted out, leaving the Arab Coalition Forces to liberate Khafji. There were a few nominal Marine vehicles seasoning the Arab ranks, but otherwise the burden to recapture the Saudi Arabian town appeared to rest squarely in Arab hands. This fact was of only passing concern to Baczkowski, who considered himself merely along for the ride; however, the pitfalls inherent in such an arrangement soon began to emerge.

In the lee of the Khafji Café, nearly a dozen Arab officers of varying stature clustered around a Humvee apparently in the throes of determining exactly how the recapture was to be conducted. These officers, who had been jabbering away in Arabic in the absence of any real intelligence or maps, stood back in awe as Baczkowski sauntered up, producing a detailed, 1:50,000-scale topographic of the city he had acquired from the regimental intel shop. A raucous "Aaahhh . . ." emerged from everyone's lips, as if the Prophet himself had arrived. After this numinous moment passed, the aimless confab continued, the participants appearing to pick up from where they'd left off a minute earlier. Standing around in a large circle, the Arabs yelled across at each other with varying degrees of passion, not a soul appearing to exercise an ounce of authority or control over the orders group.

As Lieutenant Colonel Taylor later noted, the Saudi National Guard, which is composed of Bedouin tribesmen loyal to the Saudi family, practice a form of tribal democracy in their military operations: "The privates and corporals feel that their opinions are just as valid as anybody else's; Allah is going to take care of them." This process seemed like pure anarchy to Baczkowski, who after several hours of this circular yakking retired to Amazing Grace to rest, telling Sergeant Iiams, "Wake me up if the Saudis decide to do anything."*

---

*Doug Kleinsmith experienced a similar phenomenon when he went on an artillery shoot with the Saudis. After firing an initial adjustment round, the Saudi gun crew would confer for several minutes before beginning another mission, dragging out a process that an American firing battery would have taken mere seconds to perform. It was, in the words of Bubba Deckert, "adjust fire by committee."

* * *

Captain Joe Molofsky, watched the evening scene developing at the Khafji Café with a similar, if somewhat more seasoned, sense of dismay as Dan Baczkowski. He'd just come up from the division headquarters, where he'd lain down for a catnap and had been roused by a staff colonel, telling him, "Captain, your unit's in action up at Khafji." It was the first he'd heard of the Iraqi invasion.

Molofsky was that all-too-rare breed of American military man: an urbane warrior-poet with a deep abiding interest and experience in Middle Eastern affairs and a fierce, first-person engagement in world events and the muddy, often imperceptible division between the sword and the diplomat's pen. He was a latter-day, cammie-clad Lawrence of Arabia (although he would have vehemently denied this), a foul-mouthed trigger puller who read Homer. A Romantic who "wasn't afraid of whacking people." A tanned, well-muscled riot of contradictions. As a budding Arabist with a U.N. tour in the Middle East under his belt, he was passionately committed to the Arab cause and yet was under no illusions about the Saudis' true military capabilities.

Without his John Lennon–style granny glasses, Molofsky looked every bit the knuckle-dragging Neanderthal. A few inches over six feet, he projected a raw, physical presence that was felt as much as seen. He had entered the Marine Corps late in life after playing semiprofessional football and had spent a year in the merchant marine, tramping across the Atlantic on freighters of various nationalities. That he was often the only English-speaker aboard the rolling traders only heightened the experience, and Molofsky found himself glorying in his newfound nomadic existence, bunking among savages, leading the life that T. E. Lawrence had mythologized; luxuriating in the sympathies and passions of alien cultures.

His father was a twice-decorated Army medic from World War II, so it was only a matter of time before the strains of the martial life reached Molofsky's ears. Like so many young men before him, he instinctively turned to the institution that so luridly embodied the American lust for action and foreign adventure: the U.S. Marine Corps. Commissioned as an infantry officer, Molofsky later took the recon indoc and commanded a Deep Reconnaissance Platoon at Camp Pendleton. While posted to Officer Candidate School at Quantico, he peeled himself away from the parade deck, earning a master's degree in Western thought from Johns Hopkins in night school. After completing Amphibious Warfare School, a course reserved for the Corps's most promising junior captains, he took the unusual step of putting his name in for a United Nations observer tour in the Middle East. It was hardly a career-building move.

The Marines' officer corps, which resembles a small Southern town where everyone knows everyone else, has long placed a premium upon command time, preferably in a frequently deploying combat unit. It is often said that an officer should either be "teaching it, learning it, or doing it," the *it* being infantry operations. Any other type of tour, while not forbidden, is looked upon as deviating from the straight gospel of the Corps. Most of Molofsky's peers from amphibious warfare school were heading off to prized company commander slots, the billet considered by many to embody the purest form of infantry leadership. Launched far afield, lost among the effete blue-bereted U.N., Molofsky's lust for adventure would seem to have taken him off the fast track.

However, this was the late-1980s, a time of immense change in American attitudes toward the Middle East, and Molofsky found himself irresistibly attracted to the embattled region. After reading about Lieutenant Colonel Richard Higgins, the Marine U.N. observer who'd gone rogue in Beirut and been kidnapped by Hezbollah terrorists, Molofsky decided to throw his hat in the ring. "I don't know what it was exactly, but when I was a student at Amphibious Warfare School in '89, Colonel Higgins had just been captured and that intrigued me for some reason, so I worked my bolt and got a job on his old team."

Assigned to the U.N. troop supervision organization of Palestine, Molofsky spent the first few months of his tour living in a lizard-infested villa in Cairo and patrolling the Sinai Peninsula, working on multinational teams monitoring troop movements, coursing the haunted wastes from Ismailia to Sharm El-Sheikh. It was a formative period for the burly, tractable captain, one of those rare moments when those in uniform are afforded a front-row seat at the shuddering pageant of history. The patrols were often staffed by Russian special forces officers, and together they watched as Gorbachev's budding *perestroika* movement took hold and the Soviet Union began its inexorable decline. Molofsky took a copy of Chaim Herzog's *The Arab-Israeli Wars* along on their week-long expeditions and traced the campaigns of '56, '67 and '73, reliving Ariel Sharon's quixotic drives into the wadis of the Negev and walking the ground at Mitla Pass, place-names that hold as much meaning for modern-day Israelis as do Guadalcanal and Normandy for Americans. It wasn't long before he had driven every hard-surface road in the Sinai.

Sent next to Jerusalem and then to Gaza, Molofsky observed the first Intifada uprising up close and watched as the Israelis fought their first full-blown insurgency. The Palestinians, savvy street fighters, would often rush his patrol vehicle, knowing that the Israelis would be hesitant to fire upon the observers, and use it for cover while hurling rocks at the soldiers. On one occasion, while he was driving with his daughter, his car was stoned by Palestinians. For an impressionable young officer, a character raised and cultivated in the ways of warrior-ship, versed in the currents of history, this was heady stuff.

His year-long tour complete, Molofsky began his long journey homeward back into the mainstream Marine Corps. Assigned to the 3rd Marine Regiment in Kaneohe Bay, Hawaii, Molofsky was anxious to begin his long-delayed company commander tour. As fate would have it, he reported on August 2, 1990, the day Saddam Hussein invaded Kuwait. In the flurry of activity that followed, Molofsky was tasked as the local Middle Eastern specialist to teach a bevy of classes on desert survival and Arab culture to the Marines of the regiment, at one point teaching to audiences of a thousand at a clip. Colonel Admire, unwilling to make a last-minute roster change in any of his line companies, kept Molofsky on as a regimental assistant operations officer. Molofsky was crushed. "I was absolutely unhappy. I had that company commander slot in my heart," he recalls.

Nevertheless, destiny seemed to have drawn a bead on Molofsky. Not long after he arrived in theater, the Arab Coalition requested a liaison officer from the 1st Marine Division. Dying to escape the staid environs of the regimental staff tent, Molofsky pounced on the assignment. Dispatched with a diamond-rare satellite radio and an acne-scarred Corporal radio operator named Tom Cruise, Molofsky found himself dropped off at the doorstep of the only other Marines working with the Arabs, the 1st Air-Naval Gunfire Liaison Company. The only guidance he got from the lieutenant colonel who dropped him off was, "This is where ANGLICO sleeps. You might wanna check in with them."

Molofsky knew a little bit about ANGLICO and was aware of their reputation as a recon-wannabe outfit, a parachuting club with occasional artillery spotting duties. After meeting Jim Braden, the local officer-in-charge, he quickly discerned that this brood of ANGLICO captains were up to something different. They appeared to be the only Westerners with their finger on the pulse of the Arab Coalition. Unlike the Saudis' regular U.S. Army advisors, who would roll into camp, dole out a few weapons classes, and then make for the rear, the ANGLICO Marines were doing it wholehog: living with the Arabs week after week, sleeping on the sand, eating their atrocious chow, and demonstrating for them the myriad uses of American close air support.

Molofsky was particularly impressed with Jim Braden. While he lacked Molofsky's hard-won insights into Arab culture and military affairs, Braden was an unusually foresighted officer who correctly perceived the synthesizing role that ANGLICO could play in the pan-Arab coalition and worked hard to foster relations between the Marines and the Arabs. It was unusual to see a Marine officer—and a Huey pilot at that—interfacing so productively with the Saudi leadership. All too often he'd seen his peers lay on the hard-edged leatherneck vibe, which only made the Saudis nervous. Braden wasn't an Arabist and was at best merely uninterested in Saudi culture, but as Molofsky observed, "They responded to him because he was just so obviously competent." In addition to the intangibles of leadership and operational coordination, Braden provided an invaluable commodity in short supply with the Arabs: American airplanes. Watching Braden at work, Molofsky saw a new and yet strangely familiar mode of warfare emerging.*

While still nominally a division liaison officer, Molofsky aligned himself with the ANGLICO crowd, swapping intelligence, tapping into their Arab logistical hook-ups, and hootching in Braden's tent. Relations were a bit awkward at first. Braden wondered about this intellectual grunt who'd wandered into his tea party, but as time went by, he saw that they both wanted the same thing: to find a way to make the dubious Arab force a viable, combat-capable part of the Coalition against Saddam. The Marine high command might have had little faith in the pan-Arab force protecting their right flank, but Molofsky and his ANGLICO counterparts were going to try their level best to bring their Arab brothers up to speed.

Both Braden and Molofsky agreed that the Saudi leadership left plenty to be desired. Molofsky was convinced that Colonel Turki would never have accomplished anything had it not been for Jim Braden and his ANGLICO cohorts. Even to Molofsky, an officer familiar with the pervasive fatalism and passivity endemic to Arab society, the Saudis were conspicuously incompetent and resistant to American attempts to instill field discipline and the rigors of regular training. He knew that this was in part due to the Saudis' peculiar perception of themselves as God's chosen people, the elect among all Arabs. This feeling that "Allah will take care of us" influ-

---

*One is reminded of Lawrence's dictum, "Arabs believe in persons, not in institutions."

enced all aspects of Saudi military culture and rendered fruitless any attempts at planning operations or training. The Saudis in many ways behaved like spoiled children who expected to purchase the finest tactical advice that money could buy along with first-rate weapon systems that they procured from the West. They had no desire to train, because they were convinced that they would never fight, and even if they did, the Americans with all their airplanes would come to their rescue.

The sad scene at the Khafji Café on the evening of January 30 demonstrated the full depth of the Saudis' incompetence. Surveying this misguided war council, it looked to Joe Molofsky as if their recalcitrance and pig-headedness might now cost him his life.

Before heading to the café, Molofsky had checked in with Braden at the 2nd SANG brigade headquarters. He could tell that Jim's blood was up, although he didn't seem rattled. Braden told him that the Iraqis were coming full force, that Doug Kleinsmith's position had been overrun, and that he and his team were missing in action. Jim didn't seem to have much else to offer him at that point, and since Molofsky's orders from Division were to support whatever counterattack effort the Saudis mounted, he hopped on the coastal highway and linked up with the gaggle of V-150s and Qatari tanks clustered around the café. As he pulled up to the café, he thought that the ragged lines of Arab vehicles parked bumper-to-bumper was the juiciest artillery target he'd ever seen. He didn't understand why the Iraqis hadn't already blasted them all to kingdom come, as they were well within artillery range of the city.

As the hours slipped away at the Khafji Café waiting for the Saudis to arrive at a decision, Molofsky began piecing the situation together. Apparently, a U.S. Army truck with a female on board had gone missing. The soldiers were presumed captured and being held somewhere inside the city. Two reconnaissance teams from 3rd Marines were trapped inside Khafji, a fact that greatly complicated the overall tactical picture. Molofsky had met up with a contingent from

3rd Battalion, 3rd Marines, at the café, and the consensus among the officers he spoke with was that this was a very bad situation. Comm with the teams was spotty, and no one seemed to have a good handle on the teams' location, which meant that firing into the city was a no-go. *If they couldn't fire into the city, how could they be expected to launch a co-ordinated attack into town?* No fire support equaled no maneuver, which equaled no attack plan. As a former recon officer, this frustrated him even further: "That's the bane of the reconnaissance man. You gotta know where you are so you can protect yourself and so you don't shut down maneuver. Nobody was willing at the moment to whack the two reconnaissance teams just to slap at the Iraqis."

Timeless and infinite, the pervasive fog of war, that human element which renders mental clarity in battle a lost dream, had descended like a theater curtain over Khafji. Somehow, Ingraham's and Lentz's locations in town—locations that had been dictated over the radio from the teams to the 3rd Marines headquarters several hours prior—hadn't been circulated to the people who needed to know the most. Had Molofsky or Lieutenant Colonel Taylor or Lieutenant Colonel Matar been given the grid coordinates for the two teams, they could have relayed this information to the waiting Marine artillery batteries, which could have developed an in-depth fire-support plan for the impending assault into town. As it stood, the teams were presumed to be in the center of town, which effectively made the entirety of Khafji a no-fire area.

It was a real goat-fuck of a situation, and Molofsky was shocked that his home regiment had been launching patrols into Khafji without letting him, the Saudis, or ANGLICO know about it. The city of Khafji had always belonged to the Saudis and/or Colonel Barry. Now that push had come to shove, the unlicensed Marines were at the mercy of the Arabs, as now it appeared as if Colonel Admire had been ordered to stand aside and let the Saudis lead the rescue/recapture effort.

The exact process by which it was decided that the Saudis

and not the Marines would recapture the city remains unclear. However, given the Saudis' sudden uncharacteristic aggressiveness and deployments up to the city gates, it was obvious that the Iraqi attack had knocked them out of their months-long torpor.*

The message to *attack and attack now,* conveyed from Fahd to Khalid to Turki, clearly showed on the face of Lieutenant Colonel Matar, commander of the 7th SANG battalion assembled south of town at the Khafji Café. To Molofsky, who was standing right next to him, it was clear that Matar had absolutely no idea what to do, and his complete lack of self-confidence rippled outward to the assembled force like a stone thrown into a still pond. As the disjointed parley continued on the hood of Molofsky's Humvee, Matar grew more and more agitated. It seemed to Molofsky that the only instructions Matar had been given were to attack with everything he had as soon as possible. It seemed as if in response to the king's dictum the Saudis felt compelled to take decisive action however rash or premature it might be. As Jim Braden, monitoring the big picture back at the brigade headquarters recalls, "It was just too soon. All the pieces just weren't in place yet."

Molofsky, Lieutenant Colonel Mike Taylor, Captain John Borth, and the commander of 3/3, Lieutenant Colonel J. J. Garrett, watched as Matar paced back and forth, consuming innumerable cigarettes, a dark expression on his face. Molof-

---

*The command relationship between the 3rd Marines and the Arab Coalition remains the subject of some debate. Colonel Admire, in an article in the *Marine Corps Gazette* after the war, recalled, "For me, the battle of Khafji involved one of the most difficult decisions I've ever had to make. . . . As a leader of Marines, one waits a career for such an opportunity to execute a major counterattack, to recapture an enemy-seized objective. . . . But it was also an opportunity for us as Americans to demonstrate our belief, our trust, our confidence in the Arab Coalition Forces. . . . Khafji was in the Arab area of operations, and for us to preempt the Arabs with an American-dominated attack would have been, at least in my opinion, counterproductive."

Admire's explanation, however eloquent, omits the fact that the decision to step aside and allow the Arabs to lead the counterattack was never his to make. Admire's authority effectively ended north of Mishab. To defy King Fahd's wishes and launch a unilateral Marine charge into town would have been an affront to Saudi sovereignty and caused irreparable harm to the larger Coalition.

sky could see the panic rising in Matar's face, as if to say, "Holy shit, we're gonna have to fight somebody tonight."

It was a classic tactical drama, one that would have been jarringly familiar to American advisory veterans of Vietnam and Afghanistan. The Marines felt like they knew exactly what needed to be done, but their hands were tied. The mantle of leadership in the battle had been handed over to the Saudis. To attempt to exert control over the Arab force would have been unthinkable. Yet Molofsky, as a warrior and a trusted advisor who had long promised his Saudi brothers that he would never desert them in battle, knew that to personally weasel out of this attack, to not go, would have dealt a devastating blow to the Coalition liaison effort. "Backing out there would have demolished my credibility with the Saudis, which would have directly impacted on Colonel Admire's credibility and by extension, America's credibility," he recalled.

Given that there didn't appear to be any airplanes available to do bombing runs and that Cobras weren't well equipped to operate at night, the best thing Molofsky could think to do was arrange for a hasty artillery barrage before the Saudi counterattack commenced. However, because he didn't know where Ingraham and Lentz were, even this meager gesture had to be greatly curtailed.

Molofsky called over to 3/3's fire-support center and tried to coax them into firing an artillery prep for the attack, twisting the arm of a buddy in 3/3. His friend, also in the dark about recon's locations, didn't like the idea on the face of it. *If they didn't know where the teams were, how could they fire a decent prep?* Right around this time, the never-ending tactical conference came to an abrupt halt, and Matar announced to Molofsky, "Whether you shoot a prep or not, we attack in ten minutes." Molofsky finally had to plead with his 3/3 friend, "Hey, man, this thing is gonna happen, and we're all gonna get killed unless you shoot a prep up here."

The whole idea of this hasty counterattack violated every cardinal tactical principle Molofsky had ever learned. There was absolutely no cover or concealment to employ. The

Saudis were poised to attack along the most obvious avenue of approach imaginable. No preliminary reconnaissance had been conducted. Next to no fire support was available. Molofsky assumed that they would drive into the teeth of the Iraqi defenses and be slaughtered. Any idiot, even the Iraqis, would have laid down the bulk of his defenses along the southern approach to town. The only other way into town was around the sucking *sabkha* several miles to the far northwest where Kleinsmith and Deckert were currently attempting to forestall a mass Saudi fratricide. Molofsky recalls, "I was just resigned to my fate. I just didn't see any way out of it. It was our job. We had to do it. But it all just seemed so unfair, so *unreasonable*. As Marines we train so hard, we plan so thoroughly, we rehearse, we inspect. This, man, this flew in the face of all that."

Idling behind Matar's V-150, waiting for the go order in their Humvee with Cruise at the wheel, an artillery observer and an air controller in the back seat, Molofsky had a final chance to mull over the situation with Colonel Garrett. In a rare moment of familiarity, he asked if he could have a slug of the colonel's coffee. Handing his mug over, Garrett offered, "You know, you don't have to go up there."

"Actually, I do, sir."

The prep, a quick rolling barrage that thudded ineffectually into the *sabkha,* came and went. Then at approximately 11:00 P.M., without a discernible order given, the column took off, shuddering up the road toward the emerald gates.

A few hours later Bill Iiams was shaking Captain Baczkowski awake; the Saudis had a plan. Iiams spelled out what he knew to the captain (Naif had proved worthless in this exchange): The Qatari tanks would lead into the city, followed by the Saudi armored vehicles. The Marines would run tailend Charlie in this affair, hoping that as the Arabs gained a foothold in the city, they could dash in and grab Ingraham's team. It seemed like a simple, straightforward plan, and for the life of him Baczkowski failed to understand why it had taken three hours to come up with it. *Well, at least we're moving now.*

As they began to roll, Baczkowski occasioned their tardy advance with a look skyward, noticing a full and lonesome moon illuminating the evening. It was sometime after 11:00 P.M. and the young captain could see the moon-driven shadow of the Humvee jutting thinly across the sand of the roadside.

Chuck Ingraham and the recon Marines up on the roof could see the Saudis, with their tan 4X4 armored vehicles and Toyota-type trucks, collecting south of town. It was a great feeling for the men, like watching the cavalry riding in, and they thought how great it was that someone was here to fight and to get them out. As Ingraham watched, more and more vehicles and tanks rolled in. Lentz, on the northern part of downtown, couldn't see the gathering storm, and Ingraham radioed over to him, telling him simply, "Hey, man, they're here."

The Marines called down to Mishab to tell them to tell the Saudis not to come up the main drag, which the Iraqis had covered like a shooting gallery.

20

11:00 P.M., January 30, 1991,
on the Coastal Highway Just South of Khafji

*In some sense, the counterpart of the soldier-adventurer is the more
serious professional soldier whose relation to death is governed by
the feeling of fate. Death will come to him, he reasons, when the
time is ripe and will, he hopes, afford him the opportunity to show
himself worthy and unafraid. Sometimes he hopes that death will
come to him in full career, that he can die with his boots on, as the
phrase has it, for the fatalistic soldier wants to face death as he has
faced danger so many times, with a calm, matter-of-fact air. The
proper discipline in the event of leaving one's life is, for him, no
other than the discipline needed to master life itself.*
—J. GLENN GRAY, *The Warriors: Reflections on Men in Battle*

WHEELING NORTHWARD in the dark, ensconced in the
canvas-sided Humvee, Joe Molofsky's overriding concern at the moment was to avoid being crushed by the advancing company of V-150 mech vehicles, all of which
towered a good four feet higher than his Humvee. The entire
way up toward Khafji, he was yelling at Corporal Cruise,
"Go left! Go left!" and "Jesus, watch out for that tank!" It
was nerve-racking.

The jolting race northward didn't last long. Soon Molofsky noticed that the Qatari tanks were pulling off to the right
side of the road. Matar and his gang were still rolling to the
fight, but as the advance continued, the formation morphed
into an ill-shaped flying wedge of intermixed Saudi and Marine vehicles. He assumed that at least a quarter of Matar's
vehicles were ahead of him.

Inside the unarmored Humvee, the Marines were crouching lower and lower in their seats, anticipating where the
Iraqi kill zone would begin. "It was an ugly, ugly scene," re-

calls Molofsky. Everyone on board knew what was about to happen.

As they crossed the invisible line, it was as if someone had turned a spigot on. The night was suddenly aflame, a swirling kaleidoscope of Iraqi tracer fire hammering right at them. It looked like the Iraqis were launching fireworks at the oncoming column. Just before the fire started, Molofsky noticed that several V-150s had passed underneath the gates and were now inside the city. Reacting to the heavy fire, the remainder of the column south of the arches hit the brakes in unison, the attack skidding like a dog on the kitchen rug. It was hard to believe that anyone had survived the first few seconds. Fifty meters to his left Molofsky saw a Saudi vehicle explode and thought, *Fuck me, we're next.* Amid the jumble of fire, he saw a flare or an RPG round skip wildly underneath one of Borth's heavy machine-gun Humvees. Looking to see Matar's next move, it was like a boxer being called over to the side of the ring. Matar's V-150 stopped and then almost bashfully eased over to the left shoulder of the road and came to a stop. Molofsky told Cruise to pull in behind him. He saw that Dan Baczkowski and Sergeant Bill Iiams' vehicle had pulled over to the right across the road.

After the initial wall of lead, a strange lull developed. Then, without any apparent control or organization, vehicles began jockeying around the periphery of the corridor, vying for cover and firing independently back at the Iraqi defenses. It was a difficult position to negotiate: To the left of the road was nothing but the quagmire of the *sabkha,* to the right a few dozen yards of loose sand, which tumbled down to the waters of the Gulf. To Molofsky, it appeared to be every man for himself. He noticed the blinking lights of Melissa Rathbun-Nealy's truck switching on and off in the murky distance and watched as somebody cranked off a TOW missile at it, which missed. The two Marine heavy machine-gun vehicles that had followed Molofsky and were led by one of Borth's staff sergeants began engaging the Iraqis. They appeared to be having some suppressive effect on the buildings.

Still, without any effective leadership, the shambling assault had turned into a Mexican standoff, with neither antagonist willing to maneuver against the other. It was like two blindfolded heavyweights jabbing awkwardly at each other, both unwilling or unable to close or try a hook shot. Molofsky began relaying the action back to Colonel Garrett at the café. He just hoped that someone, maybe John Borth, would take good notes and record this debacle for history's sake. And to make sure that it was never repeated. Molofsky was certain that he wouldn't live long enough to write such an account.

Nevertheless, having survived the opening salvoes, Molofsky decided to check in with Colonel Matar and Coyote. Climbing up onto Matar's V-150, he first saw Taylor. The two clasped arms, exchanging so-you're-still-alive greetings. Gazing over at Matar, it seemed to Molofsky that the man wasn't in command of himself let alone his unit. Staring off into space, his hands urgently gripping the sides of the vehicle, he was practically catatonic.

Off across the road he heard the unmistakable sound of U.S.-style small-arms fire and a hand grenade go off. Molofsky thought, *Shit, the Iraqis are already intermixed with us.*

The fire rose again, the Saudis and Qataris slinging lead wildly in every direction. Molofsky could see fire being exchanged north to south, east to west and west to east. It looked like the Saudis were simply hammering away at anything that moved until they ran out of ammunition. The fire would slacken, ammunition would be redistributed, and then the fusillade would start right up again. This cycle repeated itself at varying intervals for several hours. Molofsky and his crew were frozen in place, praying on luck that they would not be struck by the unruly exchange. They couldn't move for fear of being hit by one of their own. Even during the lulls occasional tank rounds would sing out. They were helpless. Later, somewhere in the early morning hours, a resupply convoy came up from the south to replenish the Saudi TOW vehicles, which had been firing almost continuously for several hours. However, because the Saudis had established no checkpoints and had deployed no pickets or road-

guards to their rear, the Saudi trucks rolled right under the
arches and were slaughtered.

Baczkowski, Iiams, Lance Corporals Radcliffe and Baron
with Lieutenant Naif in tow began the near-midnight attack
rolling along in Amazing Grace, maintaining a cautious pace
behind the long ribbon of Saudi armored personnel carriers.
They had begun the fitful movement to contact a mere mile
away, and after a few minutes of the accordion-like, stop-
and-go rhythm common to all vehicle convoys, Baczkowski
and Iiams noted with mounting dread the familiar outskirts
of the city approaching. Both noticed as they reached the
halfway point of the journey that the Qatari tanks had begun
peeling away from the column. Baczkowski thought, *Well,
that's smart. They're leaving somebody in reserve.*

After seeing several more like-minded vehicles replicate
this maneuver, it occurred to Baczkowski to count the tanks
as they halted. It wasn't long before he'd tallied 24 tanks, and
still more were seen arcing away from the convoy, stopping
in the sand off the highway. Slowly, he began to realize that
this was no planned conservation of combat power, no deliberate redeployment of Arab armor; the Qatari branch of the
plan was a bust.

Their Humvee continued rolling in trace of a Saudi V-150
for several more seconds, everyone aboard assuming that the
Saudi column rolling ahead of them was pressing on with the
attack. All of a sudden the armored vehicle ahead of them
peeled off as well, revealing the brightly decorated gates of
Khafji looming like a beacon a few hundred yards in front of
them. The Saudis had balked, leaving the Humvee to lead the
ill-organized charge.

After several pregnant seconds with the thin-skinned
Amazing Grace drifting alone on the wide coastal highway,
the night was suddenly bright with heavy Iraqi machine-gun
fire, the fight emerging from the heavily garrisoned strongpoint with a full-voiced roar. All hell broke loose with Amazing Grace astride it as the Saudis and Qataris returned fire. A

blazing umbrella of tracers descended upon the Marines like a deadly laser light show.

Iiams, momentarily stunned behind the wheel, somehow retained the presence of mind to veer their track off to the right, terminating their journey miraculously unscathed in front of an abandoned gas station on the eastern shoulder of the highway, the Humvee bumping awkwardly against the curb at the foot of the station. In awe of the sheer volume of fire being traded (Lieutenant Colonel "Coyote" Taylor, an infantry veteran of Vietnam, called it "flabbergasting"), the Marines piled out of Amazing Grace, Baczkowski and Iiams groping around the building for cover. The five found refuge in the open dugout of a conveniently located oil-changing bay in front of the gas station. Baczkowski called over to Coyote, still with the command group, saying, "I don't know what's going on but we're in the middle of it. We're at this gas station over to the east."

Coyote, under no small amount of duress himself, replied, "Okay, stay where you are. Let things cool down a bit and then we'll work on getting you back with the headquarters element." Overwhelmed by the Fourth of July–like display coursing before him, Baczkowski had little sense of the bigger picture and was simply hoping to see the Saudis press on with their attack, which at the moment seemed fatally stalled. He knew full well that the fate of both his current patrol and the cut-off Marines lay in the unsteady hands of the pan-Arab force currently wilting under the Iraqi barrage. He hoped that somehow this temporary disarray could be counteracted.

As they waited out the tumult in their hasty safe harbor, Iiams and Baczkowski began hearing suspicious noises coming from inside the service station. Thinking that they ought to at least explore the remainder of the large cinderblock structure, the pair emerged from the oil pits and began poking around the large junkyard area surrounding the station. Proceeding around to the left of the structure, they encountered a four-foot-high brick wall. Peeking over this convenient bulwark, they spotted an Iraqi armored personnel carrier looming a handful of meters away.

Ducking down, Baczkowski hissed over at Iiams, "What do we do?" They were surrounded by fire on all sides, and now they had an enemy APC staring them down at point-blank range. They had literally nowhere to run to, and unless they could suppress the APC, it would soon make mincemeat of them. Fortunately, before abandoning Amazing Grace, the two had thought to grab a few light antitank weapons, several handfuls of ammunition, and some hand grenades.

Composing himself, Baczkowski shrugged a LAW off his back and prepared to fire the disposable rocket. The last time he'd fired one was at The Basic School in Quantico, Virginia, and he rewound briefly to that distant, wooded vision of a place, hoping that the muscle memory gained there would come to his aid now. He shouldered the weapon, rose to fire, and to his supreme disgust, depressed the wrong button on the rocket, causing it to collapse down as if for storage.

"Shit!"

Knowing full well that someone on the far side of the thin wall was trying to kill him, Baczkowski crouched again, resetting the tubular weapon. Popping up again, he repeated his blunder, again collapsing the LAW. In the heat of the moment he'd worked himself into a paralyzing frenzy, which Iiams, the eternal smart-ass, was somehow able to capitalize on, bursting out in laughter at his struggling superior. The third time turned out to be the charm, and Baczkowski managed to get off a fatal shot into the metal side of the Iraqi vehicle.

Exiting this embarrassing scene, the Baczkowski and Iiams worked their way around the other side of the gas station with the intention of clearing the remainder of the building. Furthering their shame, they discovered that the Iraqi APC had been killed already—presumably by a Marine Cobra—and was Swiss-cheesed with a number of large bullet holes. Spying a single corpse in the interior, Iiams indulged the ubiquitous impulse of fighting men the world over, grabbing a souvenir Kalashnikov rifle from inside the charred vehicle.

Presently, they again heard noises emerging from inside the gas station. The muffled and unrecognizable sounds were coming from a back room of the building, which was sealed with a large metal door. After their previous encounter they were in no mood to play SWAT team games. After locating a series of windows, which served the back room, they elected to pitch in some hand grenades and be done with it.

Baczkowski wanted to let Coyote know what was about to transpire and radioed over to him, informing him that they were about to set off some hand grenades. The main event between the Saudis and the Iraqis seemed to have trailed off for a moment, and Coyote came back, saying, "Okay, I've told everybody what's up. Go ahead and clear the building."

Both men tossed their grenades through the windows, crouching down against the cinderblock wall. After the standard, seemingly interminable five-second delay, both bombs detonated simultaneously with an ear-splitting concussion, powderizing every window in the room. Then, as if keying off the blast, every Saudi and Qatari vehicle across the road began blasting away furiously. The hellacious fire seemed split in two: Some of it was going toward the Iraqis; some of it was aimed at the Marines, the rounds skidding across the metal roof of the gas station. For the second time that night they were caught in the crossfire, paying again the weighty price for their too-quick trust in their fledgling allies. Baczkowski knew that green troops tended to be trigger-happy, and it was this fact that motivated his preemptive radio call over to Coyote, but this was absurd. It was a damn good thing that these idiots were also indulging the rookie habit of aiming way high during nighttime engagements, he thought.

The pale night sky, lit up again with smoke and the thunder of the exchange, spanned over their gas station refuge, which seemed for the moment like the eye of a hurricane; both antagonists groping madly at each other around the knot of Marines stuck in the middle. Baczkowski and Iiams, already crouching, slowly inched their way down the wall looking at each other, the look in their eyes stating the obvious in unison: *That's the last time we're gonna do something like that!**

Radioing back to Coyote, pleading with him to call the dogs off, Dan Baczkowski, full of all the impatience and irritability of a man under intense fire, thought hotly, *It was such a simple fucking plan, why couldn't the damn Saudis just stick to it?* He was furious. There were lives at stake here, he had guys in the city depending on him to get them out, and his efforts were being catastrophically stymied by the Saudis, who at this point in the game were more dangerous than the Iraqis. At least the Iraqis were predictable.

After lying in the dirt for several minutes while the firing slackened, Iiams and Baczkowski decided that rather than tremble out in the no-man's-land between the two combatants, they ought to brave the gauntlet and try to get back to Coyote and the safety of the SANG command group. Yelling over to Naif, Radcliffe, and Baron, they told them that they were coming around the building and not to shoot them. As they were dusting themselves off, an errant gunshot rang out from the oil pits.

Baczkowski yelled over, "What the hell was that?"

Radcliffe, like a child caught with his hand in the cookie jar, replied, "Aw, nuthin."

Answering in his comrade's stead, Baron hollered, "Radcliffe just shot a pole!"

Iiams snarled back, "Way to go, Rady-Oakley!"

The young Marine had had his weapon off safe and in the midst of climbing out of the subterranean oil pits had accidentally jerked the trigger, the round singing off harmlessly.

Baczkowski, amazed at Iiams's ability to somehow retain his sense of humor through all this, was glad he'd brought the

---

*Numerous observers of Arab military culture have noted the exceptionally poor marksmanship and fire discipline of Arab troops of all types. In Arab armies it is often considered disgraceful to return from battle with any ammunition, resulting in troops often launching long streams of automatic fire into the air for no readily apparent reason.

trusty sergeant with him. He had a good habit of making himself indispensable wherever he went.

Rejoining their comrades at the front of the station, Baczkowski looked down and saw Naif retching his guts out down in the oil pits. The erstwhile student was in shock, the fire and turmoil clearly having taken its toll on him. Baczkowski, who in less tumultuous times might have felt some compassion for the poor fellow, was disgusted. The young Kuwaiti was simply another Arab millstone around his neck, preventing him from retrieving his Marines. He hadn't aided their efforts a bit so far and now was a drain on resources, unable to even stand up on his own.

Coyote radioed back, advising Baczkowski that it was not safe for him to attempt the highway crossing back to the command element at the moment. The Saudis, unsettled by the clumsy assault, were still perilously trigger-happy. If they attempted the crossover, they ran the chance of being shot up by their own people.

Huddled around the oil pits, thinking of what to do next, the Marines heard the raucous KLINK KLINK KLINK KLINK of Iraqi tanks shifting about inside the city. Overcome with frustration and desperate to take action, Baczkowski and Iiams began snatching up AT-4 rockets and rechecking their gear. Before the pair realized what they were doing, they found themselves under fire and running the hundred-odd yards up to the gates of Khafji.

They quickly covered the distance, sprinting up the open four-lane highway to the two small kiosks that adorned the bases of the yawning arches. The arches served not only as a dramatic entrance to the city, but also created an artificial chokepoint for any party wishing to set foot in the town, with walls limiting access on both ends of the structure. If they were going to make it in to where Ingraham and the boys were, they were going to have to cross under the arches to an even broader and deadlier killing field than the one they'd just traversed.

Each man was alone. Baczkowski had run straight to the center kiosk, which was only a few feet wide; Iiams, seeing no further cover there, had veered to the kiosk across the road to the right. Poised like schoolchildren playing hide-and-seek, the Marines waited for a break in the action, hoping to take out a passing tank with their AT-4s.

After a few moments up at the arches, things seemed to settle down a bit. Pausing briefly to reflect on their situation, Baczkowski was suddenly struck by an overwhelming urge to move his bowels. It was totally unbelievable. He later mused, "Here I am in the middle of the fight, I haven't taken a dump in probably three days and then WHAM!" In all the turmoil and excitement of the past twenty-four hours, he simply hadn't had a chance to go. So debilitating was the urge to heed the call of nature that he considered going right then and there. He even talked it over with Iiams, saying, "Dude, if I get killed in the act, would you at least pull my pants up?"

Miraculously, the stalwart young officer was able to hold it in, and as the impulse passed, both he and Iiams began to think better of their wild scheme. The offending tank had evidently disappeared and they both began thinking, *What the hell are we doing up here?* They were two lone Marines with only the lightest of armaments caught between two rattled Arab armies. It was a recipe for disaster. Iiams reflected, "I don't know exactly why we went up there. I just loved those guys so much. We had been living in the desert together for so long and we had become brothers. I would've done anything to get those guys out." Both men decided that the rescue would have to wait and began loping back to the gas station

En route they ran into two Saudi supply trucks racing up the highway, hell-bent on delivering supplies to the now-scattered assault forces. Stopping the convoy, the Marines gestured vigorously, attempting to indicate to the two non-English-speaking drivers that Khafji was not a place they wanted to be. Baczkowski knew, based on Ingraham's reports and his own hard-won experience that the Iraqis had established a commanding defensive position overlooking the main avenue on the southern edge of town. The ailing sign language continued for several minutes out on the expanse of the highway. Eventually the two drivers decided they'd heard enough and abruptly took off. Hoping that they somehow had gotten through to the drivers, Iiams and Baczkowski continued their trek south, meandering their way back to the shelter of the service station. As they continued walking, they heard the sounds of the trucks picking up speed. Then, as if on cue, the Iraqis positioned inside the hotel blasted them. The trucks never stood a chance. Absorbing the full impact of the 40-mm fire, the lead truck exploded, sparks spraying upward in a shower visible to the Marines over 500 meters away. In a sickly denouement, the two Marines heard the trucks' large rubber tires rolling to a permanent halt, the distinctive RRRRRRRRRR hum echoing in the shattered streets of town.

This entire sequence of events hit the young officer like a ton of bricks. They had been talking to these guys less than a minute earlier, trying mightily to make them understand. Impatient to complete their mission, the drivers had gone on ahead, crossed under the gates, and been slaughtered. Dan Baczkowski was appalled and touched by the incredible futility of it all. These men had not understood them and they'd died, and there was nothing anyone could do about it.

Trying in vain to shake off the effect of this foul episode, the two turned south again. Upon reaching the station, they got word that Coyote was finally ready for the Marines to return to friendly lines. Loading Naif, who by this point was practically catatonic, into the Humvee, the patrol began heading back to the main Saudi line, hoping against hope that the SANG wouldn't accidentally blast them to smithereens.

As they made their way south on the blacktop, the men heard the Qatari tanks rumbling back to life, apparently preparing for another lunge at the gates. Baczkowski noticed a single Qatari tank no more than 50 meters away bearing down on them. Suddenly a sharp crack rang out from the maze of town, and with a fiery shower a tank round smacked into the 30-ton vehicle, rocking it violently upward onto one of its tracks. Teetering back down, the damaged behemoth came to rest. No survivors emerged. Baczkowski didn't see how anyone could have survived the hit.

The cool night air came alive with fire as the Saudis and Qataris launched headlong into yet another unbridled exchange. Strewn across the southern approaches of town, the confused pan-Arab force shot at anything and everything. The Saudis fired into Khafji. The Qataris, jarred by the sudden loss of one of their own, began shooting at the Saudis. The Iraqis chimed in as well, returning the poorly aimed fire with cannon and tank rounds. It seemed for a time as if everyone were fighting everyone else.

The deadly clamor grew, tracers arcing across the night sky, the fire quickly reaching all-time heights of intensity and futility. Caught in the middle of this stunning rush of violence was Amazing Grace, with its five-fold human cargo, desperate to get out of the way. It seemed beyond miraculous that the Humvee had survived even a moment of the fusillade.

Baczkowski watched tracers skipping on the pavement off the right side of the Humvee as Iiams piloted them off the crown of the highway into an open stretch of sand. Passing a lone chain-link fence line, one of the Marines in the rear of the vehicle cried out that an antitank missile was coming right at them. The men watched awestruck as the missile shot toward the Humvee and glanced into the fence, disintegrating brightly, the remnants tumbling in midair toward the Marines. Iiams kept right on going, careening the truck through the rippled sand out of the path of the hurtling debris.

Speeding away from the blacktop, Iiams spied a pitcher's mound–size hillock and angled toward it. The vehicle rolled to a halt, and the Marines dove behind the undersized mound, overjoyed to have located some semblance of cover. It was a confusing situation, and although the group was within sight of Saudi lines, the fight seemed to find them anyway. The consensus after the missile close call seemed to be to seek cover as soon as possible. Baczkowski recalls lying on his stomach and having to fend off Naif, who, desperate for comfort in the sprawling nightmare that his life had become, kept crawling up his leg. Baczkowski, in a rare outburst, yelled, "Quit crawling up my ass, Naif!"

It was now close to three in the morning. After some time the firefight tapered off, the Saudis and Qataris seeming to succumb to their exhaustion and confusion. To Baczkowski it seemed like "everyone had decided 'we're not gonna do anything else tonight,' which given the situation was probably very wise." Taking advantage of this lull, the Marines picked their way back to Coyote and the command element.

Arriving finally at this place of relative shelter, Baczkowski was happy to once again see Joe Molofsky's familiar face, thinking, *You won't believe what we've just been through!* Safely back in the fold, a silent decision was made by the Americans embedded in the pan-Arab force to strike out on their own and set up camp until dawn somewhere away from their rattled allies.*

This impromptu crew meandered through the wastes west of town for about a mile or so until they came upon an odd complex of open warehouses in the middle of nowhere. After finally relieving himself, Baczkowski and his Marines grabbed a few desperately needed hours of shuteye.

Before hitting the rack himself, Molofsky mulled over their situation and for a moment considered putting a patrol together to infiltrate into Khafji and extract the two recon teams. He knew the city fairly well. In the months leading up to the air war, he and several ANGLICO officers had against orders been lunching at the Khafji Beach Hotel. He figured if he grabbed Iiams and a couple of other Marines and some AT-4s, Baczkowski and he might be able to get his boys out.

Molofsky thought back to some advice he'd picked up from some Vietnam vets when he'd been coming up through the ranks. He remembered what one of them had said: "Pick

*This was a common sentiment among American advisors to the Saudis. Sergeant M. E. Garcia, an ANGLICO Marine, recalls setting up a separate perimeter inside the Arab perimeter every evening. "We never knew if they were gonna fight or run," he argued.

the ditch you're gonna die in. Don't get killed the first night."
Molofsky realized that this was going to be a long war, and
if the sad spectacle he'd just emerged from was any indica-
tion, it was going to go on for years. He wisely dismissed his
scheme.

Before the American group had defected, Molofsky had
taken a look around the Saudi force sprawled over the highway. They appeared worn and thoroughly shaken. He wasn't
sure how many of the men had been in the Grand Mosque
siege of '79, but as far as he could tell, this was their first
combat experience and it had not gone well. They had
obeyed the King's orders, and it had resulted in a complete
rout. Not an inch of territory had been won, the Iraqis still
commanded the town, the recon teams were still isolated,
and the Coalition had been handed a resounding defeat in its
first encounter with the Iraqis. Not a thing had been done to
reverse the Iraqi tide that had swept through the border forts,
ejected Barry's, Lang's, and Kleinsmith's teams, and seized
the largest Saudi town within 100 miles. The idea of Iraqi
battlefield dominance was very much alive in Molofsky's
mind. There was nothing to suggest that the Iraqis weren't a
capable, potent force. It was going to be a long war indeed.

Sometime during the initial Saudi counterattack, Corporal
Jeffrey Brown, Ingraham's assistant team leader, pulled out a
microcassette recorder that he used to maintain a patrol log
and began recording a comedic play-by-play of the firefight
raging around them.

"The Liberation of Khafji, Take One."

Thick machine-gun fire thumped in the background, followed immediately by a cascade of all calibers, automatic
fire mixing in with crisp single shots. The products of these
discharges, while mostly invisible in the darkness, could be
felt striking all about the lower reaches of the Marines'
building.

Continuing the riff, Doc Callahan broke in, "It's a lovely
moonlit night here in the Saudi."

"Get some!" Brown exulted.

As the firing continued, Doc added, "There are no more combat virgins in Third Platoon, Alpha Company."

A lull in the fighting opened up and Brown, outfitted with the uniquely Marine talent to make a sexual reference out of practically anything, began feigning near-orgasm into the recorder, "Oh, come on, don't stop now. I'm almost there!" Sometime later, the gods of war complied, unleashing an epic wall of lead, which overwhelmed the recorder's microphone. The strange, disjointed fight shambled on.

While the mood of the team had lightened considerably, the initial optimism accrued by watching the rescue force gathering on the horizon was quickly undercut by the staggering disarray of the Saudi forces. It looked as if the Saudis didn't realize that there was a serious, brigade-size Iraqi force in town. The Marines watched as tracers zipped steeply upward into the sky like old World War II footage. It was as if the Saudi guardsmen were just holding their triggers down and firing wildly into the air. In contrast, the Iraqi fire was focused and professional; Doc Callahan remembers, "The Iraqi fire coming from town was perfect grazing fire, three feet off the deck."

Ingraham called back to Mishab, begging them, "You gotta tell the Saudis to quit coming in from the south!" It was agonizing watching the Saudis take it on the chin, but there was precious little the Marines could do to influence the action: None of them spoke any Arabic, nor did they have the SANG radio frequencies. Artillery still wouldn't fire. They had none of the requisite equipment for calling in air strikes at night. They watched helplessly as their rescue squad was pummeled into submission.

Doc Callahan remembers, "By this point our building was like Swiss cheese, having been hit by every type of round, SANG, Qatari, Marine. You could feel every impact. This was one of those points where we thought that we weren't gonna get out of Khafji alive. Things were getting pretty scary. However, I personally was confident that the Marines were gonna do something."

*   *   *

Over to the north, distanced somewhat from the action, a strange air of mischief hung over Lentz's team. The Marines watched the fire boiling up from the south from inside their house. It was unlike any combined arms exercise the men had ever seen. Tracers and all kinds of ordnance were going everywhere.

Marcus Slavenas piped in, "Y'know, guys, we're only seeing every sixth shot. Imagine how many of those rounds are grazing the house."* They all piled over to the northern side of the building to watch the show from a safer distance. Soon afterward a TOW missile howled right by the house with a deafening roar, slamming into a building down the block.

Slavenas spoke up again. "Can you imagine what would happen if one of those things hit the house?"

"Don't tell me, please!" Lentz snapped, knowing that Slavenas, a former TOW gunner, was about to launch into a detailed lecture on the subject.

Slavenas remembers the sounds of the counterattack reaching an unsettling volume: "There's no way to replicate being enveloped by that level of chaos. There's shrapnel and stuff whizzing by and it's just so loud and so real. You don't even hear where the explosions are coming from anymore, you just feel them rattling in your ears, overloading your eardrums with dense static, like KKKKHHHH. It's not a distinct sound you can zone in on or directionalize."

The men watched in awe as the disjointed battle raged on. It looked to them like the Saudis were getting their asses handed to them. A few hours passed and Lentz received a radio call from Coyote saying, "We're gonna have to retrograde. We'll try again in the morning." Things got real quiet after that.

After taking all this in, some of the Marines began to get antsy. Everyone knew that Captain Baczkowski and Sergeant Iiams had been mixed up in the Saudi fiasco, and here they were just sitting on their asses doing nothing. Corporal Wag-

---

*Machine-gun bullets are belted with a tracer every sixth round to help gunners aim during periods of darkness.

ner, whose buddies Radcliffe and Baron were also in the first wave of the attack, leaped up and began collecting all the team's AT-4s and LAWs and heading up to the roof of the house with a furrowed look on his face. To Lentz he looked like a little kid, with all the rockets and gear hanging off him. He half-expected Wagner to say, "I'm taking my toys and I'm going home!"

"Where the fuck are you going?" Lentz asked.

Wagner spat out, "I'm gonna do something! I'm gonna take care of this shit!"

"Dude, if you go up there and start cranking off rounds, then we'll all be fried! There's seven of us and a thousand of them. What are the odds?" Lentz added, "Are you a gambling man?"

His ire dissipating, Wagner admitted, "Yeah, yeah, you're probably right."

While the Saudis had been dealt a stinging defeat in the south, General Chuck Horner had his attack jets going full blast. The air-war commanders had been slow to react to the unexpected offensive, but now fleets of U.S. Air Force jets were roaming up and down the stretch of coastline north of Khafji and across southern Kuwait, hunting down the Iraqi invasion force. Khafji was still firmly in the Iraqis' grasp, but north of the Saudi border they were taking a savage beating from the air.

Directed by an experimental radar surveillance plane, known as a JSTARS, which scanned deep into enemy territory, sections of A-10s waded into the reinforcing Iraqi columns like hounds on a fox.* The pilots, accustomed to trying to ferret out camouflaged tanks deep inside Kuwait,

---

*Two E-8A JSTARS, or Joint Surveillance Target Attack Radar System aircraft, essentially converted Boeing 707 jetliners, were in theater at the time. The JSTARS uses a phased-array radar system to produce a photo-like image of a selected geographic region. With a reported range in excess of 155 miles, the JSTARS can cover an estimated 386,100 square miles in a single eight-hour sortie. Unfortunately, this valuable information was almost never disseminated to the frontline troops who needed it the most.

found the Iraqi armored vehicles easy to identify once they were on the move out in the open desert. Air Force A-10 pilot Rob Givens described one such mission over the sparsely-wooded al-Wafra forest: "The adrenaline obviously was very high. We understood the significance of an Iraqi attack. It was something straight out of a textbook. . . . As I proceeded in, I couldn't really believe what I was seeing. It was something that you're taught from A-10 school—what you want to see. And there they were, no kidding, a column of vehicles on the road." Because of the full moon, Givens could clearly see a dark road contrasted against the tan desert floor and a miles-long column of Iraqi armored vehicles snaking forward.

Givens and his wingman set up to attack the convoy with a combination of infrared Maverick missiles, cluster bombs, and 30-mm cannon fire. In attacking a long armored column, the idea is to destroy both the first and last vehicles in the convoy to trap the remaining targets in-between the burning hulks. The surviving vehicles caught in this pickle are then easily dispatched as they scramble to get away. Both planes had a full tank of gas and made run after run on the Iraqi column, quickly destroying the vehicles on both ends of the line. The pilots had plenty of ammunition remaining and pressed on with their attack. One plane would hold in high cover searching for surface-to-air missiles while the other swooped down and shot up the convoy. The turkey shoot continued for 45 minutes.

Givens recalls, "That night when we left—and it's a sight I will remember forever—there was at least a couple miles of road on fire with vehicle hulks. A vehicle burning at night is an image you never forget, especially with all the secondary explosions. If an armored vehicle has ammunition on board, which they all did, and it's blown up or catches fire, then all that ammunition starts going off. The explosions continued on long after the initial impact of our weapons. You could see the entire road outlined for 50 to 60 miles away as we were going back home into Saudi Arabia."

One Iraqi mechanized brigade (the 26th from the 5th Mechanized Division), moving south through Kuwait to reinforce the units at Khafji, was caught moving through a narrow lane in one of their own minefields when its lead tank was struck by a missile from a Saudi multiple-rocket launcher. American aircraft pounced on the trapped brigade and chopped it to pieces.*

As the response to the Iraqi offensive widened, Horner ordered his special operations wing to launch their AC-130 Spectre gunships into the fray. A combat variant of a conventional cargo aircraft, the AC-130 is outfitted with an awe-inspiring array of 20-mm and 40-mm cannons and, amazingly, a 105-mm howitzer. Such a fearsome weapons platform was beloved by ground troops for its sheer shock power. Watching a Spectre at work was like having a front-row seat for The Apocalypse. With no other weapon system was dominant American firepower grossly evident and its effects so directly observable. However, the Spectre, while legendarily potent, was also extremely vulnerable to ground fire because of its size and slow speed. During the first few weeks of the air war, Spectre aircrews had become increasingly concerned that they were being misused by being ordered into highly defended areas by the Air Force brass. One Spectre gunship had maneuvered so violently to avoid an Iraqi surface-to-air missile that it suffered significant structural damage and had to be sent to Germany for repairs. Some crews began refusing to go on certain missions. Concerned for his men's safety, the head of Air Force special operations contingent in theater, Colonel George Gray, finally decided that all missions needed to be personally cleared by him before launching.

Khafji was the first time Gray had authorized any Spectre missions in over a week. Two of the aircraft were launched into the battle and destroyed numerous armored personnel

---

*One survivor of the 26th Brigade who was later captured told his interrogators that he had fought in every major engagement of the Iran-Iraq War and that his unit sustained more damage in thirty minutes of U.S. air attacks than from eight years of war with the Iranians.

carriers before returning to base. A third Spectre gunship, piloted by Major Paul J. Weaver, was sortied just before daybreak.

It was common knowledge among Spectre aircrews that flying during daytime was a gamble, and with each passing minute, the crew of Weaver's aircraft, known as *Spirit 03,* were pushing their luck. At 5:30 on the morning of January 31, Gray's headquarters began asking for the plane to be recalled. Despite the risks of antiaircraft fire and the even greater danger of sunlight glinting off of the circling gunship, the crew of *Spirit 03* elected to stay on a few extra minutes to try and suppress an Iraqi Astro rocket battery that had been reported near OP 8. At 6:23, *Spirit 03* was ordered to break off its attack. Co-pilot Captain Clifford Bland radioed back nonchalantly, "Roger, roger."

As the dawn grew, the Spectre's silhouette became visible against the rising sun, making it a tempting target. At 6:35, *Spirit 03* sent out a frantic Mayday distress call. An Iraqi portable surface-to-air missile had struck the Spectre between the fuselage and the inboard left engine, ripping the wing off. Pitching to the left, the aircraft spiraled down and crashed into the Persian Gulf a mile east of the desalinization plant in waters scarcely ten feet deep. All fourteen crew members were killed. It was the largest single air loss of the entire war.

As Rob Givens noted of his own mission, "We were two weeks into the war and were really starting to get a feeling of invincibility. We were naive about that. The threat of being shot down was not in your brain as much as you might think."

The loss of the Spectre was a bitter pill, but the continuing air attacks were rapidly depleting the Iraqi force coming down through Kuwait. Every hour they grew weaker. The Iraqi grand scheme called for a rapid exploitation of their early gains inside Saudi Arabia, but as the punishing air campaign picked up steam, the Iraqis discovered that it was almost impossible to move on the battlefield without incurring the wrath of the U.S. Air Force.

According to classified intercepts of radio conversations between Baghdad and the Iraqi III Corps headquarters on the Kuwaiti coast, Major General Mahmoud, the Iraqi commander in charge of the offensive, knew that his plan had been demolished by the air strikes and that the already-moving reinforcements would never arrive at their intended destination. Late on January 30, the prudent Mahmoud requested permission from Baghdad to break off the attack but was informed that he was engaged in the "Mother of all Battles" and to press on with the invasion. He repeated his request twice more and each time was denied. Saddam was so intent upon poking the Americans in the eye that he refused to face the fact that his army was walking into a killing field. He allowed thousands of men to be sacrificed on the roads of southern Kuwait and inside the gates of Khafji.

21

Nighttime, January 30, 1991,
Five Miles Northwest of Khafji

The bullets from the .50-caliber machine guns and 20-mm cannons churned the water in the strafing runs. The rockets exploded on the sampans, breaking them apart. The shiny aluminum canisters of napalm tumbled end over end and burst on the reed fields, engulfing a group of guerrillas in a great orange flower. From the air the scene had beauty to it. In the cool clarity of the midmorning sky there was no consciousness of the sweat and terror in the heat below. Instead there was the sensation of grace as the planes responded to the controls and the intoxication of omnipotence in the power of these weapons. The pilots had rarely seen such good shooting.
——NEIL SHEEHAN, *A Bright Shining Lie,* describing one of
the first battles of the Vietnam War

U P IN THE northwest of the city, the tardiness of the 5th Battalion's advance to seal off the northern front turned out to be a boon to this distant half of the Coalition effort. As Captains Deckert and Kleinsmith worked in the night to reorient the armored unit's many V-150s, another Saudi regular army tank company outfitted with American M-60s migrated in from the west, providing a much-needed heavy punch to deal with the tank-heavy Iraqi formations. Following in trace of the M-60s were two more ANGLICO teams led by Captain Kris Elliot and First Lieutenant Andy Hewitt. With the appearance of the M-60 company, there was now a sizable enough Coalition force to stanch the border area north of town and contend with whatever Iraqi forces might turn up. Before the recon teams could be rescued and before the city could be picked clean of Iraqis, the Saudis and their ANGLICO advisors had to close down the border region to ensure that no Iraqis could get in or out of the beleaguered town.

As dawn broke on the 31st, the Saudis and their American advisors moved out to the east, ostensibly to establish a blocking position across the coastal highway. Soon after the advance began, the force encountered the better part of an Iraqi brigade, the Iraqis, like their opponents, seeming to have taken their cue from the rising sun. The Iraqis, like their brethren already inside the city, were outfitted with T-55 main battle tanks and Chinese Type 531 armored personnel carriers. Having crossed the breach near OP 7, the armored column swung east to surmount the coastal road and reinforce the brigade-size garrison already in town.

Spotting the Iraqi advance, the Saudis, still several kilometers away, charged headlong at them, rapidly closing the distance between the two opposing forces. Kleinsmith recalled, "It was like *Lawrence of Arabia*—everybody's screaming and riding like mad into battle, except that instead of camels, the Saudis were all in fucking armored vehicles." The charge continued, and as the Saudis began to take fire, their line began to falter. Kleinsmith recollected, "The situation was so fluid, like kids in a snowball fight behind the schoolhouse. One group would charge forward and then the other would run away."

As the lead element of the Iraqi column passed south of the desalinization plant that Lieutenant Colonel Barry had evacuated not 36 hours prior, the Saudi TOW gunners, who were now just within range, unleashed a punishing guided-missile barrage, dispatching several enemy reconnaissance vehicles. The intensity of the sudden Arab fusillade was stunning. Kleinsmith recalls, "They were perfectly content to engage the Iraqis at maximum range, shooting at the cyclic rate. They were just pissing rounds away, using TOWs like artillery." It reminded him of the soccer matches they'd had with the Saudis before the air war had begun. The Saudis were much better ball handlers than the apish Marines, but once the Americans began to get physical with the Arabs, they would crumble. The Arabs as a people seemed to shrink from physical confrontation, and it showed in their self-selected mode of combat. They showed no desire to close with and destroy the enemy. The burning Iraqi hulks from this initial barrage served as beacons for the remainder of the fight.

This first cannonade continuing, Deckert looked over and saw Kleinsmith leap out of his Humvee with his M-16 and begin popping off rounds toward the Iraqis. He couldn't believe it—they were still at least three kilometers away from the Iraqis, well outside of small-arms range, and his buddy was firing away as if he were at the rifle range. Deckert yelled over at him, "What the hell are you doing? Your rounds are gonna fall short, man."

"Yeah, but how often do you get to shoot in combat?" Kleinsmith replied excitedly.

The Marines from the two ANGLICO teams present seemed in accord with this logic, and before long all hands were squirting lead into the air toward the enemy. Deckert, who'd been neglecting his rifle for months, managed to get off two rounds before his weapon seized up, a victim of the insidious Saudi sand. As the Saudis pursued what looked to be the first Coalition victory in the new war, Bubba Deckert sat sprawled in the dirt, strenuously field-stripping his service rifle to the amusement of his comrades.

As the Marines watched, one of the regular army M-60 companies advanced, squaring off against the Iraqis less than 1,500 meters distant. The other tank company soon joined them to cover their left flank, facing north toward Kuwait. On the right flank, stretching southeast toward the coast, was a company from the 5th Battalion augmented with numerous V-150 TOW variants. Lieutenant Hewitt stuck close with the leftmost tank company as it redeployed. Deckert moved to the right to support the eastern flank, while Kleinsmith remained in overall control in the center between the two Saudi wings.

As a result of the longer range of the Saudi TOWs, the front stabilized somewhat, with the Saudis standing back uneasily and delivering salvo after salvo of deadly missiles into the Iraqi column. The Iraqis, short-armed with their

Chinese-made recoilless rifles, absorbed the Saudi blows without response while still somehow holding their ground.

At about this time a section of Marine Harriers checked in with Kleinsmith, who promptly turned control of them over to Captain Kurt Horney, who had rolled in behind the tardy M-60 company early that morning. Horney, who had been stationed out west along the border, had just navigated the same labyrinth of *sabkha* that had been Kleinsmith's salvation the night before. While tired from the long journey, he brought the Harriers to bear on the Iraqi vehicles that had been fixed by the Saudi TOW gunners out in the open. Working together, the two jets destroyed several Iraqi armored personnel carriers and disabled a tank with some 500-pounders and their 25-mm Gatling guns. This impressive raid seem to break the back of the Iraqi effort, and those vehicles not already destroyed by the M-60s and the TOW barrages were unceremoniously abandoned by their crews or took flight to the north.

Dozens of enemy soldiers, fleeing from their stricken vehicles, scattered like sheep across the desert, running for the hasty cover of an abandoned Kuwaiti refugee camp that had been erected by the Saudis prior to the onset of the air war. This sanctuary was quickly obliterated by a pair of Air Force A-10 Thunderbolts, which, under Horney's direction, pocked the area with several 500-pound bombs and conducted gun runs with their ominous 30-mm cannons. The American air arm was beginning to sink its teeth into the problem, and because the ANGLICO teams had managed to fix the Iraqis out in the open desert, making the problem of directing the aircrews onto target relatively easy, sections of attack aircraft began stacking up high into the sky. Kleinsmith, attempting to manage the slaughter, had at one point eighteen separate sections of jets awaiting taskings from their ANGLICO controllers.

In the rear, air-traffic controllers at the Marine Direct Air Support center in Safaniya recalled running out of space on their tracking boards for all the various divisions of A-10s, Harriers, F-18s, and A-6s responding to the call.

The rout seemed to be nearing fruition, and the Saudi M-60s, comfortable with their early winnings, retired to rearm and refuel, taking Horney and Lieutenant Hewitt with them. Sensing that a threshold had been crossed and that the exploitation phase of the battle had begun, Kleinsmith transited east and linked up with Deckert's team. The two teams followed behind a company of V-150s as they descended upon the remnants of the Iraqi position. As the party approached to within 500 meters, scores of dispirited Iraqi soldiers materialized from the wreckage of the battlefield, emerging from charred vehicles, bomb craters, white refugee tents, and hastily dug foxholes. In all, approximately 75 Iraqis surrendered to the 5th Battalion, leaving behind 7 destroyed T-55 main battle tanks and 11 Type 531 armored personnel carriers.

After halting briefly to process these prisoners, the Saudi guardsmen continued their advance into the killing ground, which sloped gently downward toward the coast. Kleinsmith and Deckert both assumed that the Saudis, having been bloodied, were now responding to the soldier's instinctive need to assure that his enemy was dead and were in the process of mopping up the battlefield and collecting whatever stragglers might have remained behind. To their surprise and disgust the Saudis raced down to the smoke-wreathed scene and began looting the fallen Iraqis, snatching up watches, jewelry, and whatever other booty could be located. The Marines couldn't believe it. *You gotta be shitting me,* Kleinsmith thought. The Saudi guardsmen, mimicking their Bedouin ancestors, had won the day and in their eyes it was now time to collect their justly earned war trophies.*

Deckert, meanwhile, could see several Type 531 APCs exiting Khafji toward Kuwait along the coastal road. He ran over to a nearby Saudi TOW vehicle and, screaming in his

---

*The practice of looting, while anathema to the Marines, was common among the Bedouin tribes whose descendents comprise the Saudi Arabian National Guard. Indeed T. E. Lawrence lured many Arab tribes into British service with the promise of war booty.

pidgin Arabic, told the gunner to engage the Iraqis coming up the road. The gunner emitted a full-voiced, "Ahhhh" and after traversing his turret toward the approaching enemy, fired off a single missile. Deckert, who had expected the traditional "Is the backblast area clear?" warning before the missile launch, was right underneath the turret as the TOW screamed out of the tube. His eardrums took the full brunt of the launch. Practically the only thing his ears would register afterward was a ringing *neeeeeee*.

Meanwhile, Kleinsmith began to notice that tiny pieces of jagged metal had begun to drizzle down around him. Scanning around behind him, he saw to his horror that two Saudi V-150s and an ambulance, not fifty meters from the Marines, had just been cleaved in two by what he assumed to be Iraqi missile shots. *It was fucking debris that was raining down on them!* To Kleinsmith it appeared as if someone had taken a giant knife to the vehicles, and he could see large pink strips of meat hanging off the sides of the vehicles which from a distance looked disturbingly like Spam.

Deckert looked back and saw a Saudi soldier sticking halfway out of the ambulance. The man was on fire and trying to extricate himself from the burning vehicle.

Kleinsmith wasn't sure what had hit the Saudi vehicles, but just then four Cobras appeared over the horizon. *Man, those fuckers just lit us up!* His corporals began popping red smoke canisters to ward off the Cobras. One of the men jumped on the radio and after raising the Cobras asked, "Did you guys just fire?"

The Cobra flight leader responded, "No."

Slowly it dawned on Kleinsmith: *Oh, fuck, the Iraqis are still in the fight!* It looked to him as if the Marines were now caught in a crossfire from Iraqi positions east of the coastal road and from a gas station in the vicinity of the desal plant. The Saudis caught in the killing zone wasted no time in beating a hasty retreat. Only Kleinsmith's and Deckert's teams— eight Marines total—were left in the open. The ANGLICO Marines stood their ground and scanned the area for targets. Kleinsmith thought to himself how lucky they were that they were only driving Humvees, as the Iraqi gunners always seemed to zero in on the bigger-gunned vehicles. In their ignorance of the American order of battle, they failed to realize that the unarmored Humvees were, by virtue of their influence over the American aircraft, far and away the most powerful vehicles on the battlefield.

Kleinsmith summoned the flight of four Cobras back around. The clangorous birds came right over the top of the eight Marines and began hosing the whole area down with 2.75-inch rockets and 20-mm cannon fire. The gunships hovered directly over the Marines for several minutes. As they continued to engage targets, the spent brass casings from their cannons began pelting the men struggling in the roaring propwash below. Kleinsmith had to put on his Kevlar helmet to protect his head from the showering brass. He couldn't remember the last time he'd worn his helmet.

The Iraqis began launching rocket-propelled grenades at the Cobras. The Marines underneath the loud helicopters were confused because all they saw were airbursts appearing in the air to their front, like antiaircraft artillery. Kleinsmith figured that the Iraqi RPGs were hitting their 800-meter limit and self-destructing. He took this as a good sign. Wherever the Iraqis were, they weren't very close.

As the RPG bursts continued, Kleinsmith figured that the Cobras had by this point covered the Saudis' escape and decided to egress from the situation with his team. Moving south about a kilometer, the Marines regrouped in a revetment they located in the otherwise uncluttered plain. After taking a quick breather, they began redirecting the air they had on-station. Kleinsmith called the Cobras back around for another pass. Meanwhile, Bubba Deckert erected his team's MULE laser designator to set up some Hellfire missile shots from the Cobras toward the Iraqi muzzle flashes. After a few passes the Cobras were out of ammo and returned to base to rearm and refuel. Shortly after the Cobras departed, a section of Harriers checked in, and Deckert's Marines directed them onto a building near the desal plant that had been the Iraqi base of fire for the counterattack.

Using the MULE again, the Marines guided the Harriers' 500-pounders for several resounding direct hits. The Harriers came back up after completing the pass, saying that they had spotted several Iraqis running along the beach. Kleinsmith cleared them hot, saying simply, "Gun 'em."

It was now noon on the third day of the battle.

At this point there was a great deal of confusion over the radio about who exactly had killed the Saudi V-150s and the ambulance. Several SANG commanders had angrily concluded that the four-ship section of Marine Cobras had committed the apparent fratricide. It wasn't long after breaking off the fight that Kleinsmith received a call from Kurt Horney, who was attached to another SANG battalion. The Saudi battalion commander was blaming the Cobras for shooting his men up. Kleinsmith vehemently denied this. Having observed the scene firsthand and questioned the pilots directly after the strike, he had concluded that Iraqi Sagger missiles had destroyed the Saudi V-150s. Deckert agreed. Both felt as if the Saudis, in their lust for war trophies, had completely stopped thinking about security and looking to their front. Deckert and Kleinsmith felt that the Cobras had saved their skins. Kleinsmith added, "Maybe if the motherfuckers hadn't been looting dead Iraqis and were paying attention to where the gunfire was coming from, they would know that it wasn't the Cobras who did it."

Because ANGLICO's communications resources had long since been maxed out, resulting in all the radio traffic for the battle being passed over a single frequency, practically every American team in Khafji overheard this heated exchange as it was going on. As a result, the word that a Cobra might have just killed some Saudis spread like wildfire throughout the theater. The air controllers back at the Marine direct air support center in Safaniya also latched on to the story, which led to an even wider distribution of the apparently erroneous report.

Kleinsmith was disgusted by the Saudis' inexcusable conduct and was incensed that they would try to dodge the blame for a lamentable situation that they had caused. Kurt

Horney, trying to diffuse his comrade's rising ire, came back up, saying, "Okay, Doug, I got it. I'm just trying to figure out what happened. Everything's cool."*

Having driven the Iraqis from the field, Kleinsmith retired rearward to try and locate the Saudi guardsmen who had retreated behind them, leaving Deckert in place to maintain a watch over the northern sector of the city. As they drove back toward Saudi lines, seven unarmed Iraqi soldiers appeared, running across the open desert, waving the Marines down. Once the Marines came close enough for the Iraqis to see that they were Americans, they stopped dead in their tracks. When the Marines exited their vehicles to search and cuff their newfound prisoners, the Iraqis all fell to their knees, slipping into what seemed to Kleinsmith to be the "execution stance," with their heads bent down. It was clear they assumed that the Americans would kill them on the spot. One of the Iraqis stood up and identified himself as an officer, saying, "Please, you no kill me."

The Marines responded that they weren't about to kill anyone. The others, sensing the success of their officer's plea, all began petitioning loudly for the Marines to spare their own lives, "Please no kill me! Please no kill me!" After the Marines informed them that no one was going to die, the Iraqis immediately broke into celebration of their new leases

---

*In *Desert Warrior,* Khalid bin Sultan relates, "Air and artillery support from friendly forces was vital and welcome, but to the men on the ground it often seemed to come too late or too close. For example, after destroying an Iraqi tank that morning, a U.S. helicopter gunship fired by mistake at a Saudi National Guard armored car, killing the driver and badly wounding some of the crew. Although U.S. forward air controllers assigned to Saudi units generally did a good job, not all aircrews were familiar with National Guard vehicles and there was evidently some confusion over identification" (382).

Kleinsmith's observations about the apparent fratricide somehow never reached the aircrews involved and it was several years later before Jim Braden, who knew the Cobra pilots on scene (who I have chosen to leave anonymous here), was able to relay the word to them. No official investigation of the incident was ever conducted and Saudi officers have since suggested that the situation was downplayed so as not to appear ungrateful and endanger the American air support they hoped to receive in the coming invasion of Kuwait. It was yet another example of the shocking prevalence of friendly fire on the modern battlefield. As Kleinsmith later remarked, the prevention of friendly fire was a primary duty of the ANGLICO teams.

on life, laughing and joking around with each other, joyously leaping up to be searched by the now irritated Marines.

Just then Bubba Deckert rolled up with six more prisoners on the hood of his Humvee. Deckert was positioned on top of the team's Humvee in a sitting firing position with a fitted loop sling around his biceps, fully zeroed in on the captives. According to Deckert, "I had just cleaned this goddamn thing and I was locked in. I know that if I think Bang! someone's going down." Both batches of Iraqis were freshly turned out in brand-new winter field jackets, and Deckert noted that they appeared to be in far better condition than his Marines, who were grossly unshaven and whose filthy uniforms hadn't been washed in more than six weeks.

Leading the thirteen prisoners back to Saudi lines, the now outnumbered Marines slowly made their way west. About four kilometers northwest of the city limits they happened upon the regular Saudi armored battalion that had retired early from the previous engagement in a horseshoe-shaped formation facing to the north. Soon vehicles from the 5th Battalion of the SANG rolled in to reinforce the armored line to the southwest. Safe for the moment, the Marines began to decompress from the battle and review the day's events. An order came down from Marine higher headquarters to change out the cryptographic data in all their radios, a move necessitated by the loss of the valuable gear at both the desal plant and at Observation Post 8. All four of the adjacent ANGLICO teams rendezvoused with Kris Elliot five kilometers south of the horseshoe, where new crypto fills were distributed.

The fighting seemed to have died down, and as the sun neared the sandy horizon, the Marines circled the wagons inside the Saudi horseshoe to wait out the night. The evening of the 31st was surprisingly quiet. The Marines heard the rumblings of the jumbo-size strike packages working the road networks north of town in an effort to discourage any further Iraqi moves near the border. The only action the Marines saw that evening was dealing with a lone Iraqi Astro rocket launcher that had managed to leak through and launch several of its rockets toward Saudi lines. The Saudis suffered no casualties, and the launches were quickly detected by the ANGLICO teams, who forwarded the report to an orbiting OV-10. The spotter plane soon vectored in a section of F-18s, which blasted the ill-fated launcher.

Inside the command bunker at the SANG's 2nd Brigade compound, Jim Braden tracked the various ANGLICO teams in contact with the enemy. He wasn't in charge of the recapture effort, but because of the Saudis' often weak decision-making skills, he felt an extra measure of responsibility to ensure that the operation ran smoothly and that all the various Arab units worked in conjunction. He recalls, "It was not a coordinated fight. It was done with Coalition forces that ANGLICO teams coordinated." It was an extremely unusual command arrangement. Braden was, in reality, merely a helicopter pilot who'd been to a few extra fire-support coordination schools, but because he was accustomed to assuming responsibility for things and had found himself in a unit that desperately needed leadership, he ended up playing an enormous role in the fluid Coalition effort such as it was. The operation itself reminded him of his days as a Huey pilot carting infantry battalion commanders around during exercises. He'd been able to learn a surprising amount just by listening in on all the various radio conversations. He saw Khafji as merely an extension of this. He tried to place teams where they needed to be and ensure that Marines didn't shoot up Arabs and vice versa.

Employing this uncluttered logic as the situation developed, he found himself making decisions far above his pay grade. If he had been back in a Marine unit, he would have been tracking the sorties of a handful of aircraft. Currently, he was the primary advisor for the Arab commander assigned to reverse a major Iraqi offensive. As he looked over the ANGLICO teams now in contact, he realized that the entire American side of the battle was being run by a bunch of captains. His boss, Colonel Grubb, had shown up early on the morning of the 31st to see how the battle was progressing and had mentioned almost as an aside, "Well, let me know if anything exciting happens."

"Sir, I have six teams in contact with the enemy right now. What's your definition of exciting?"

Grubb's reply was stunning. "Jim, I'm not gonna get involved in your business, because you're only doing what I would be doing. I can't do anything but interfere."

Braden was blown away. Marine officers wait their entire careers to command troops in battle. By all rights, Colonel Grubb should have been running the entire ANGLICO effort. It was, after all, *his* company and yet somehow he was clearheaded and unassuming enough to let his subordinates manage the battle. Grubb and his predecessor at 1st ANGLICO, Colonel Lindaro, had trained them to be the best fire-support experts around and now they were being given free rein. Braden felt that he had a firm grasp of the situation and was thankful for his boss's generosity, but it struck him and other ANGLICO officers as very peculiar.

As grateful as Braden was, he had a battle to run and numerous players in the Coalition to keep in their various lanes. Before the Saudi counterattacks had started, Colonel Turki had told Colonel Admire directly, "No one fires a round unless Captain Jim says it's okay." However, this directive didn't seem to have filtered down to the lower levels of the chain of command. Not long after Turki said that to Admire, the 3rd Marines' artillery battery began lobbing clusterbomb artillery rounds into the city. Braden, who was already disgusted at 3rd Marines' disregard for the Saudis' operational boundaries, was livid and immediately called over to the regiment's fire-support coordination center and ordered them to cease fire. He had no idea what they were firing at. The Saudis certainly hadn't requested the barrage. After completing the mission that was under way, 3rd Marines ceased fire. Because of their history of maverick behavior, Braden didn't trust 3rd Marines and took steps to ensure that they didn't fire anymore. Colonel Grubb agreed and thought that Admire's reconnaissance teams (Lentz and Ingraham) had no business being inside Khafji, which was squarely within the eastern Arab Coalition sector, at one point saying, "If 3rd Marines would've stayed out of our way, we could have done our job quicker, easier and cleaner."

Soon after the battle had begun, Braden switched into overdrive, and as the ebb and flow of the command bunker continued, he incessantly issued orders to the Marines on his team, trying to anticipate what might happen next. Every night he would grab two hours of near-sleep where he would close his eyes and listen to only the wavetops of the numerous radio conversations as they pattered roughly around him. His mind would drift during these twilight hours, but in truth he never really left the fight. There was just too much to do, too much to think of, too many players to brief and coordinate and coax into this crazy quilt of a battle.

22

Dawn, January 31, 1991,
Khafji

*In any war story, but especially a true one, it's difficult to separate
what happened from what seemed to happen. What seems to happen
becomes its own happening and has to be told that way. The angles
of vision are skewed. When a booby trap explodes, you close your
eyes and duck and float outside yourself. When a guy dies, like Curt
Lemon, you look away and then look back for a moment and then
look away again. The pictures get jumbled; you tend to miss a lot.
And then afterward, when you go to tell about it, there is always
that surreal seemingness, which makes the story seem untrue, but
which in fact represents the hard and exact truth as it seemed.*
— TIM O'BRIEN, *The Things They Carried*

THE SUN rose over the beleaguered city, marking the beginning of another cold and anxious day for the recon
Marines of 3rd Platoon. They had been caged inside the town
for well over 36 hours now, and the unrelieved tension was
beginning to show on the men as time and their perception of
it began to waver, events bleeding over into one another,
empty seconds sometimes taking on the vastness of the
desert that encircled them. As David McNamee, who would
go on to work at the Marine Corps's Amphibious Reconnaissance School, put it, "I never rested the whole time we were
in the city. At ARS we figure you can go about 72 hours without any sleep and still be 50 percent effective." Given that
the Iraqi offensive had begun after the teams had already
been on patrol (and sleeping little) in the city for several
days, it is safe to assume that the Marines were beginning
the inevitable downward spiral into exhaustion and mental
oblivion.

In combat, time takes on an entirely new and erratic dimension, formed only by the flood of images and emotions in the minds of its participants. A man under fire often moves breathlessly, oblivious to all but that which is saving his life, his mind unexpectedly cleansed and unfettered by the non-real madness streaming around him. His existence in relation to clocks and calendars seems utterly trivial.

To portray the events that follow as somehow simple and discrete and knowable, like some well-lit theatrical production, would be to overlook the major characteristic of war, namely, that it is the province of unbridled uncertainty where the mystical hunch and the calculated shot in the dark often carry the day. A foot soldier in extended combat struggles for mental clarity against the tide of confusion like a drowning man, certain of little except that his buddies are nearby and that other equally befuddled men are attempting to kill him. What remain for the writer and the historian trying to record the event are merely the wavetops of this storm-tossed sea, the dozen "Dear God" moments recorded indelibly in gray matter. The linkages between these fearsome scenes often fade into obscurity, leaving the survivor with only the recollection that his nightmares are true and that some time ago, in his youth, other men unknown to him in life were trying desperately to bring about his death.

Pat Sterling had been manning the pair of Claymore mines at the top of the dormitory stairwell ever since Ingraham had ordered them to the building 24 hours prior. He lay on his stomach, a handful of fragmentation grenades and both of the Claymore actuaters set neatly before him. The wide, two-landing stairwell, illuminated by a series of tinted glass windows, two at each level, afforded him a surprisingly complete view of the side street to the north of their position. For hours on end he had scanned up and down the street for signs of trouble. McNamee had tried to relieve him once to allow him to go grab some chow, but Sterling, switched on and unwilling to quit his post, had refused.

Sometime on the morning of the 31st, amid the rising

sounds of a second Saudi counterattack, Sterling noticed through the darkened panes a cluster of 30 or so disheveled Iraqi soldiers emerging from around the corner of a building across the way. The soldiers were crouched and looking around as if in anticipation of a move to another position. Sterling noticed to his utter bewilderment that many of the soldiers didn't have rifles. As before, the Iraqis' identity and intentions remained an enigma to the Marine.

As the Marines watched, the mysterious group of soldiers suddenly strode across the street toward the Marines' position. Although he didn't show it, Sterling felt a little bit shaky as he realized that he and his buddies were going to have to fight their way out of the city now. Frantically he whispered over to Doc Callahan, "Hey, they're coming toward the building!"

In a rush Sterling and Callahan agreed on a plan of action should the Iraqis come for them: They would wait until the soldiers were two flights up the stairs, and then they would drop a single grenade down the gap that ran down the stair flights, bolting out to the open roof and slamming the large outer door shut while simultaneously depressing the actuaters. They figured the shrapnel from both of the deadly Claymores and the grenade would ricochet all over the inside of the corridor, annihilating anyone inside.

Standing tensed at his post with only the top of his head peeking out over the handrail, Sterling heard the soldiers enter the building, their voices echoing distinctly in the cavernous enclosure. Carefully edging his head out a inch further, Sterling caught sight of three or four figures with distinctive World War II–style steel pots darkening the ground floor.

To Sterling it seemed like they were rehashing the old Chip 'n Dale cartoon argument. "You go up the stairs and see if they're up there!"

"No, *you* go up there!"

"No, *you* go!"

David McNamee remembers running back and forth be-

tween Sterling and Ingraham, telling his team leader out on
the roof that the Iraqis were inside the building. Ingraham in
turn was working the radio trying to get the artillery battery,
which was setting in south of town, to fire for them. Several
Iraqi combat vehicles were stopped on the boulevard in front
of the building, and Ingraham figured if he could squeeze in
a quick volley, it would disperse the Iraqis and drive the
troops out of the dormitory. The world seemed to halt for a
moment, the various members of the team having snapped
out of the intoxicating fatigue and moving forcefully, totally
in command of the seconds as they rolled into view. McNamee
recalls, "It was one of those rare moments when I felt that I
could concentrate fully on several things at once."

Ingraham whispered into the radio handset, passing fire
directions to the artillery battery. At one point in the radio
exchange the bustling artillerymen told him to "wait one,"
which in Marine radiospeak roughly translates to "Y'know,
I got other things to do than just sit here and talk to you."

Overhearing this abrupt dismissal, Doc Callahan picked
up the handset, snarling, "Gentlemen, we *can't* wait one."

All hands were poised on the precipice, waiting for the
figures to rush up the stairs, waiting for the signal to unleash
all that they had learned and soaked up in training: the awful
movement, the focused release of the will to survive: weapons
up, fingers in trigger wells now, sight alignment, sight picture, the slow steady squeeze, the surprising report of the
weapon, seek cover, get up, move again, watch your back.
The endless idiotic drills and procedures, committed to
memory, stored for posterity on laminated green cards and
in dog-eared crew books and prized beyond reason like
magic spells. Things that whispered to them in sleep in
booming drill instructor voices, never seeming so vital, so
essential, so lifesaving as now, now, now.

The men were trapped like a pack of animals and they
knew it. Once Sterling dropped that grenade, it would be an
open fight, and they would have to run and shoot their way
out the gates of town.

Then, like a breath exhaled, the soldiers who had been arguing in the stairwell—the thick Arabic dancing upward to
the landing that supported the weight of Pat Sterling, a
grenade with his finger through the pin in one hand, the
Claymore actuater in the other—mysteriously exited the
building, their sudden departure as baffling as their arrival.

The moment had passed.

Sometime later that morning as the combined Marine-Arab
force set to retake the city grew, the artillery was increasingly able to field Ingraham's calls for fire. After the initial
confusing delays the cannoneers began responding to his requests with impressive quickness.

Captain Phillip Thompson, a fire-direction officer with
1st Battalion, 12th Marines, the 3rd Marine Regiment's organic artillery unit, recalls moving north to begin coordinating the howitzers for the impending assault and learning that
part of the unit had already begun hurling shells into the city.
The Hawaii-based Marine unit had fired a hasty fifteen-
minute barrage prior to the initial abortive Saudi counterattack and sometime during the evening had scored a direct hit
on an Iraqi armored personnel carrier inside the city. The artillerymen were elated, having apparently destroyed the vehicle with the first adjusting round.

He, along with his assistant, Gunnery Sergeant Quint
Avenetti, had ambled up the coastal road from Mishab in their
radio-laden Humvee and set up shop in the sand right off the
shoulder of the blacktop. It was an unorthodox arrangement.
The only thing between the Iraqis and Mishab were a few
scattered combat patrols and parts of 1/12, who, outside of
their howitzers, which could with some labor be dropped
down into direct fire mode, were armed only with a couple of
light machine guns.

Thompson remembers talking to Ingraham as the Iraqi
soldiers milled downstairs. "I remember at one point I
couldn't hear him because he was whispering and I kept
fussing with him and telling him to speak up and he said, 'It's

kinda hard to speak up right now because the Iraqis are downstairs.' Oh, okay, roger that."

Later that morning Thompson received another urgent fire request from Ingraham. An enormous Iraqi armored column was idling right below the Marines' building.

23

7:00 A.M., January 31, 1991,
Khafji

If he had known how many men in history have had to use a hill to die on it would not have cheered him any for, in the moment he was passing through, men are not impressed by what has happened to other men in similar circumstances any more than a widow of one day is helped by the knowledge that other loved husbands have died. Whether one has fear of it or not, one's death is difficult to accept. Sordo had accepted it but there was no sweetness in its acceptance even at fifty-two, with three wounds and him surrounded on a hill.

—ERNEST HEMINGWAY, *For Whom the Bell Tolls*

LENTZ HAD seen the armored column building up from the north for some time. Ingraham could see only seven Type 531s in front of his building and called over to him to ask if he could see the rest of the column. Lentz could. It was a very long line of Chinese Type 531s. He stopped counting after seventeen vehicles. He could see the bearded men jutting out of the vehicle hatches and the infantry milling about and thought about what a fat target they all were.

Owing in part to his team's worsening battery shortage, Lentz was having trouble communicating with the rear, and Ingraham had to relay this information back to Phil Thompson at the forward fire-direction center. Thompson immediately began preparing to fire the mission.

Thompson could tell Ingraham was good with a map. He was giving the artillery officer some of the best target locations and descriptions he'd ever heard. It was always frustrating working with a shaky guy at the other end who was scrambling to get his act together on the radio. It was embarrassing at times, because normally at such firing positions, a small speaker was set up so that everyone working could hear the fumbled transmissions loud and clear as they went about making their calculations for the firing. But this one was different, and he was glad for it.

This one was going to be a nail-biter. Like the rest of the artillery missions that Ingraham had called in thus far, this one was so near to their building that it was considered "danger close," meaning that his team was actually located inside of the standard envelope of error for artillery rounds. The mission had to be executed perfectly or the consequences would be tragic. Faulty arithmetic, a transposed numeral entered into the firing computer, a shoddily manufactured powder bag, or an ill-timed burst of wind and the Marines would die at the hands of their own comrades.

Thompson began assembling his fire orders for the strike. The Iraqi column was long and had a lot of vehicles in it, and he knew that in order to hit the entire column and ensure that rounds didn't fall harmlessly between the vehicles, he was going to have to fire a lot of rounds. Further, because the target included both armored vehicles and troops in the open, he knew that he had to use the new ammunition— known as Dual-Purpose Improved Conventional Munition rounds—that they had started firing in this war. Each of these new shotgun shell–type rounds contained 88 golf ball–size bomblets, all of them capable of piercing the metal skin of an armored personnel carrier. However deadly effective these new rounds might be, they also added to the complexity of the already formidable gunnery equation, as every extra bomblet shot downrange only increased the likelihood that the trapped Marines might be hurt or killed by a stray piece of ordnance.

Laboring alongside Gunnery Sergeant Avenetti, Thompson was stunned to hear the senior enlisted man ask for the target's attitude and length, indicating that he was going to organize the fire mission so that the rounds would rain down in a single file along the main boulevard to inflict maximum damage. It was a tricky method of fire, one not often employed because of the extra calculations required. Thompson recalled, "I couldn't believe he was actually trying to do this in the middle of combat." Without pausing, the pair completed their complex tabulations and sent the data via digital network down to the gunline. The first volley was set at four rounds per tube for a grand total of 64 rounds.

Unbeknownst to either Ingraham or Lentz, the cannoneers were literally going to thread the needle between the two trapped teams, hurling over 5,000 deadly bomblets to within feet of the Marines.

Chuck Ingraham lay beneath the parapet of the rooftop waiting for the rounds to come. Doc and Corporal Brown were out on the roof with him, but he had sent the rest of the team inside the blockhouse that covered the stairs to protect them from the incoming. He had called the mission in as best he knew how, as he had been trained, using the city map he had to give the artillerymen a good map spot and a target description. After all that he had reminded Thompson again of the gravity of the situation, completing the radio request as he had been instructed, with the words "danger close." Now it was just a waiting game, waiting to see where the rounds would fall. If they fell on the Iraqis then they would be safe for a time. If the rounds fell on him, he would never even know it.

As the rounds exited the tubes of the guns, the crews radioed, announcing, "Shot, over." Ingraham knew from experience the time of flight for the rounds and every time they told him "shot, over," he would hit the start button on his Casio G-Shock stopwatch and watch the black liquid numbers grow until they reached 40 seconds. Then the rounds would hit. This time, however, he didn't have a good feeling about things, and as the black numbers grew, he compressed himself against the roof parapet, squeezing his elbows in, trying to make himself as tiny as he possibly could. In the back of his mind he thought sinkingly, *Game over, man.*

It sounded just like lightning. A horrendous, cracking peal. A moment of ominous silence as the bomblets were kicked out of the back of the first wave of still-airborne rounds. A queer raining spiderweb of small explosions that came and rolled unbelievably fast, enveloping the Iraqis totally.

Everyone saw Brown go down. To Ingraham it looked like someone had tackled him like in a football game. One second he was up trying to make it to the blockhouse. Then he was flat on his stomach, a horrified look sprawled across his face. The bomblets, cast across the city like a tight fistful of ball bearings, were bouncing everywhere, peppering the roof like a strafing fighter plane. Each individual bomblet left a small hole a few inches deep in the thick concrete of the roof.

Ingraham ran across the span of the roof toward the blockhouse, dragging the fifteen-pound radio by its handset, screaming all the while to Thompson, "Check fire! Check fire! Check fire!"

Brown was up now and hopping like a three-legged dog to the safety of the blockhouse, howling, "I'm hit! I'm hit!" Springing into action, Doc Callahan darted inside as the deluge continued and began looking him over. The look on the faces of every Marine was one of sheer fright. They had a man down.

It was a strange wound. Despite Brown's vigorous protests that he had been hit in the leg, Doc couldn't find any blood. He finally had to ask Brown to reach down into his trousers and pull some out. Brown drew his shaking hand out and showed Doc a pin-size crimson dot, like he'd popped a zit. It was a hilarious moment, one lost on the men for the moment, who in the middle of the furious barrage failed to chuckle.

Packed in the blockhouse like sardines, it seemed to Doc like the entire building was going to come down. The fire rolled on and on, like a never-ending metal cloudburst as all four waves of rounds detonated over their heads.

Meanwhile, over at Lentz's position, the Marines saw the whole show. Shortly after hearing the "shot, over" call, Lentz watched as the air suddenly became electric with ringing popcorn-like snaps. He could see thousands of little bombs exploding in midair, hitting the ground and bouncing all over the place. The area around the Iraqi convoy was instantly awash in smoke, dust, and confusion.

The Marines were standing in one of the second-floor rooms looking out over the destruction they had caused when some of the shrapnel started coming in through the open windows. One of the men looked over, a piece of metal in his hand saying, "Look what just hit me in the chest!" The men quickly ducked for cover. Lentz recalled, "We were a bunch of typical dumb-ass Marines who wanted to see a light show."

Lentz began to worry that whatever Iraqis had survived the barrage might soon try to come over the wall surrounding their house in search of cover. He ordered everyone back to their defensive positions.

Just minutes earlier, his assistant team leader, Lance Corporal Scott Uskoski, had pulled the team's Corpsman, a dangerously inexperienced aid station worker, out from under one of the team's Humvees. Lentz—who had worked as a trainer for the Atlanta Falcons for several seasons and usually performed the corpsman role himself, and had had the young doc forced upon him just days earlier by higher-ups—was in disbelief. *What the hell was this guy doing?* Apparently, the Corpsman was so green that he'd never even been on a patrol before and thought that hiding underneath a Humvee would afford him the best protection. Lentz credited Uskoski with saving the corpsman's life, as later they discovered that the exterior of the building and the area around the Humvees was pitted with dozens of bomblet impacts.*

Finally, after they had spent a seeming eternity huddled in the blockhouse, the fire abruptly halted. Ingraham, trying to

*Although no one on Lentz's team knew it at the time, the barrage landed so close to their position that the oilpan and two tires on one of the Humvees had been punctured. Uskoski had indeed saved the young corpsman's life.

assess the results out on the roof, was frustrated as the intense cannonade had produced a vast, impenetrable cloud of dust. After blinking into it for several minutes, trying to discern the damage, the dust didn't show any signs of dissipating. Thompson, back at fire center, desperate to know the results of his labors, began hectoring Ingraham for a report.

He kept pushing. Ingraham eventually snapped, "Gimme a damn minute to let the dust settle!"

Thompson took this as a good sign. If there was that much dust and smoke, they must have hit something.

Sterling, still at his post in the stairwell, was looking out over the street as the smoke cleared and spied a lone figure dart into the road, hop into a mysteriously unhurt Type 531, and do three or four 360s before zipping off to the north. Somehow a few Iraqis had survived the onslaught.

Ingraham saw burning vehicles and some survivors racing away from the killing zone and quickly called some adjustments for another mission back to Thompson.

Huddled around their Humvee, screaming instructions back and forth, Thompson and Avenetti quickly recomputed Ingraham's data and launched it back down to the gunline.

Within seconds this subsequent volley was downrange and raining more death down upon the survivors. This same stunning pyrotechnic process repeated itself: an initial thunderclap followed by a smothering hail of bomblets, the sequence iterating itself four times in the space of thirty seconds as each battery heaved another volley on top of the last one. It was a blistering, deadly display that none of the Marines would forget.

Soon after the second cannonade, two Harrier attack jets appeared asking for targets in town. Ingraham, wanting to capitalize on the available aircraft, radioed back to Thompson for a white phosphorous spotting round to aid in orienting the pilots. Ingraham had gotten a grid coordinate on two new Iraqi tanks from Lentz, and shortly after the spotting round appeared, he began directing the jets onto them.

The tanks were off the side of the main boulevard behind a building, and although Ingraham couldn't see them, he figured he could at least get the Harriers close. Lentz's comm was still spotty, so it was up to Ingraham to make it happen. The two jump jets began their first run-in, dropping a series of 500-pound dumb bombs. Ingraham was in the process of assessing the damage and trying to bring the Harriers around for a second pass when a telephone pole–size missile suddenly shot up out of the labyrinth of the city, arcing toward the jets. Apparently, the Iraqis had brought some surface-to-air missiles with them. The Harrier pilots, after deftly evading the missile, quickly egressed from the scene, surrendering the city to the Marines once again.

The missile was a shocking sight, coming on the heels of what had already been an eventful morning for the Marines. Nevertheless, Ingraham was jubilant. After the nerve-racking close call in the stairwell it felt awesome to finally land some blows on the Iraqis. Ingraham recalled, "It was like you're getting beat up by the neighborhood bully and then your big brother comes over and he's the biggest bad-ass on the block and he comes down the street and kicks the living crap out of the bully. That's exactly what it felt like. Just minutes earlier we'd been whispering so that the Iraqis downstairs wouldn't hear us and now we were yelling like Jim Carrey. It was awesome."

His elation persisted even after the cries of a mortally wounded Iraqi drifted up to rooftop. Judging from the sound, it seemed like he was inside another building. The screaming continued for several minutes before drifting off. To Ingraham it seemed clear that the Iraqi had died.

Doc noticed that the twin barrages had also killed a camel that had chosen this unfortunate moment to wander in from the desert. According to Callahan, the beast "keeled over like an elephant at the circus" in the face of the first artillery strike, collapsing at the foot of a stop sign directly below the dormitory. *Poor thing,* he thought. It was a strange moment, one that affirmed the observations of some that men in combat frequently reserve more compassion for lost animals than for their fellow men who happen to be wearing the wrong uniform.

* * *

For Thompson, the pair of artillery strikes into the city turned out to be contentious ones. Soon after the missions were completed, the 3rd Marine Regiment's fire-coordination center called over to Thompson instructing him to cease any fire missions into the city. In the confusion of having so many Arab and Marine units roaming around, some higher-ups thought that Thompson might have just destroyed a Qatari armored column. For a few moments after this call Thompson felt sick, believing that he may have just killed friendlies. After some intense reflection, the dilemma passed; Thompson knew inside that he'd done the right thing. He'd fired upon a target that had been clearly identified by Marines with "eyes on." He couldn't have asked for a clearer, more professionally executed fire mission.

The regimental fire-coordination people came back up a few minutes later confirming that the strike had been on the money. They had killed Iraqis, not Qataris. Thompson could breathe easy. These glad tidings were immediately followed by uncommonly stern instructions that he was not to fire any missions that hadn't been cleared by ANGLICO. Conversely, any mission originating from ANGLICO was automatically cleared. The fight was shifting now, and more units were piling in to take the city back. Lentz and Ingraham's teams weren't the only ones with "eyes on" anymore. They were still in the thick of it, but a new phase of the battle had begun, a phase belonging almost exclusively to the Arab Coalition Forces and their American advisors.*

---

*Several ANGLICO Marines assert that Ingraham had called artillery in on the Qataris on the afternoon of January 30. Jim Braden remembers receiving a call from one of his team leaders saying that he had artillery improved-conventional munition rounds impacting near his position. Realizing that the ICM barrage was almost certainly American in origin, Braden called over to the 3rd Marines fire-support center and told them to cease fire.

There have been a surprising number of accusations traded over the years between the recon and ANGLICO groups, with both sides proclaiming the incompetence of the other. Because of the emotions involved and the lack of any artillery firing unit logs or fire-support coordination center message books, not to mention the pervasive fog of war, it is frequently impossible to determine which artillery mission was called in by whom. However, the large artillery mission called in by the recon Marines on the

Dawn, January 31, 1991,
Just South of Khafji

A NEW DAY had dawned and Dan Baczkowski could tell that the sun had brought more than just light and heat with it. Pacing around the chaplain's Humvee in the growing radiance and taking in the full sweep of the gathering Arab host, he sensed a newfound determination in the ragged crew. Baczkowski recalled, "At this point, they weren't seasoned veterans, but they at least had a night's worth of shooting under their belts, and a new confidence pervaded the daylight. It seemed that somehow the momentum had shifted."

As Joe Molofsky watched, the Saudi soldiers pulled themselves from their vehicles. A chill still hung in the air and some of the Arab soldiers put on their heavy Bedouin robes over their cammies. Others were bent down, kneeling and brewing the traditional pungent Arab coffee. Taking in the scene, it seemed to Molofsky as if nothing had changed since Lawrence's time, as if you could have taken the armored vehicles away and replaced them with camels and that the men would have remained unaltered, unfazed. The crisp desert air throbbing past, the unrestrained horizon, the invisible connection to time immemorial, to the inscrutable eternity that only the desert knows was imminent and irresistible. All was as it was, as it used to be.

Recomposing himself to the pressing concerns of the new day, Molofsky departed the southern edge of town to begin coordinating other aspects of the Arab counterattack.

Shaking themselves out of their all-too-brief repose, Baczkowski and Iiams shoved off from their warehouse refuge, having sent both Radcliffe and Baron rearward to free up space in the Humvee for the load of Marines they hoped to soon recover. Baczkowski was consumed as never

---

morning of the 31st was corroborated by numerous eyewitnesses at both 1/12's firing position and from positions within Khafji.

before with getting his men out. He and Iiams had enjoyed a brief respite from the fray, but the young captain knew that if he didn't get Ingraham and Lentz out soon that they would be going in only to recover their dead bodies. For the time being, at least, he knew his men to be alive and vigilant. They maintained positive radio contact with the two teams throughout the young day and overheard the nerve-racking artillery barrage as it rained down around the men. The Marines, in turn, were reciprocally aware that help was on the way. Baczkowski had told Ingraham that he would be coming in with the first waves of Saudi troops with an empty Humvee to pick them up. He didn't know exactly how they were going to effect the running link-up amid the deadly furor, but he figured they'd find a way. It seemed as if, across the gulf of culture and religion, Baczkowski had taken on a measure of the new Saudi courage as well.

The sounds of battle grew as Amazing Grace quickly covered the open distance from the warehouse complex to the contested southwestern outskirts of town, the proposed extraction now proceeding on a more solid footing. Having been advised at length by Ingraham of the Iraqi position dominating the main drag, Baczkowski decided to veer his and Iiams's advance to the west, hoping to link up with the team in a quieter side neighborhood away from the fire-riven downtown business district.

The SANG had already established a toehold in one of the southern residential areas of town. As they watched, the Saudis took the fight to the streets, the steel-helmeted soldiers squirting wild streams of lead into the blocks of brown concrete houses. As nearly every Marine observer of the battle has noted, the Saudi soldiers were short on technique but long on valor and it showed in their brash daylight assaults rife with extended bursts of automatic fire and hasty charges into the teeth of the enemy's defenses. Their tactic for clearing buildings seemed to be a modified version of the lamentable "spray and pray" technique. These latter-day Bedouin would simply riddle a given structure with bullets for several minutes, issue a demand for surrender over a loudspeaker system, and then push deeper into the city. It was a far cry from the methodical American style and one that left much doubt as to whether a particular building had actually been cleared of Iraqis or not.

As Baczkowski observed these fiery proceedings, he felt a strange sense developing within him of the ebb and flow of the deadly contest. The Saudis would appear to advance momentarily, and then without explanation he would sense resistance, the tide shifting back toward him like the backwash of a collapsing ocean wave. Soon afterward retreating Saudi vehicles would appear. The battle danced about him without explanation and yet responding to an inner music that the captain could not articulate but distinctly comprehended. Nevertheless, in the midst of this maelstrom, he was surprised to see a long line of Iraqi prisoners being led out from behind a building by their Saudi captors.

Synchronizing this surprising intuition with Ingraham's persistent radio reports, Baczkowski felt as if he were able to develop a remarkably accurate picture of the seesaw battle. He and Iiams were only a few blocks into the town, the various Saudi penetrations into Khafji describing a jagged line across the southwestern quarter of the city. It seemed as if he and Iiams were presently located in one of the shallower of the Saudi penetrations and that they were within a few blocks of Ingraham's last known position.

Sensing that the tide was shifting and that another prime opportunity to grab his men might not come again, Baczkowski got on the radio and told Ingraham, "I think this is about as far in as we're gonna get. If you have an opening to come out, then now is the time."

To Ingraham and Doc Callahan, it felt as if the time to act was near. Nevertheless, the exact timing of their impending egress remained as unclear as ever. They knew that Captain Baczkowski and Iiams were coming for them and that they were going to have to make a move soon, but as they waited for a clean moment to present itself, more and more Iraqi tanks and Type 531s seemed to keep appearing out of nowhere.

The Marines could tell from the heavy gunfire that a serious Saudi attack was under way, but having observed the previous night's fiasco up close, they were hardly trusting in the Arab Coalition's ability to pull them out of the fire and the coordination between the two Allied forces remained poor. Ingraham had had a few run-ins with the Saudi guardsmen in town and thought them a "ragtag, undisciplined bunch," even before viewing their amateurish midnight charge.

Ingraham peered anxiously over the roof wall, spying a mixed group of tanks appearing from the north. Straining to determine their identity, Ingraham could have sworn that an American-made M-60 tank was in the approaching armored formation. He could have sworn that the Saudis or the Qataris didn't have any M-60s and puzzled over the mysterious appearance of this combat vehicle. Deciding to consult with the local expert, he quickly summoned Brown and motioned him over to the wall.

Brown carefully looked over the parapet and confirmed Ingraham's intuition. The tank was indeed an M-60, presumably commandeered during the Iraqi conquest of Kuwait six months prior. Accompanying the 1960s-era behemoth were four Russian-produced heavy tanks of varying types. It was the strangest conglomeration of armor he'd ever observed. He watched as the lone American tank inside the box formation created by the four Russian vehicles hurled round after round into the attacking Saudis and Qataris.

Overhearing his teammates' lingering bewilderment, the injured Brown ambled over to the roof wall and rashly poked his head over the parapet, trying to get an eye on the tank. To Ingraham it appeared as if the commander of the M-60 had spotted Brown's head jutting out over the roof wall and cranked off a quick machine-gun burst at him. The rounds thumped roughly into the low roof wall, missing Brown by inches and spraying the area with cinderblock chips. Some of this violently ejected debris became superficially lodged in the corporal's head, furthering his string of ill fortune.

If the tank commander had seen the Marines, he seemed sufficiently distracted by the press of the Saudi assault to leave it at that. The turncoat tank broke off its attack shortly after the machine-gun burst.

Thinking that the tank officer had spotted the Marines, Ingraham became convinced that the team's position had been compromised. Doc Callahan disagreed, adding that if the Iraqis had thought an American spotter team was nearby, why hadn't they continued their attack? Still, the lone barrage and Brown's misfortune added to the extremity of their predicament, ratcheting up the intrateam tension even further.

In an effort to prevent a replay of the "the-Iraqis-are-in-building" drama earlier that morning, Ingraham began working up an artillery mission to shoo away the misshapen tank formation. His brief formulations were interrupted by radio calls from Coyote, who was advising the present SANG assault. Describing the scene playing out beneath their hideout, Ingraham informed the instrumental lieutenant colonel of the tank formation menacing their position.

After conferring briefly with his Arab charges, a fusillade of TOW missiles detonated near the ground floor of the dormitory. One of the deadly rockets struck home, loudly exploding an antenna-studded Type 531 command-and-control variant right underneath the Marines. Choking black smoke soon poured out of the stricken vehicle, enshrouding the building and the Marines and cutting down visibility to mere feet.

Exchanging a heavy glance, both Ingraham and Doc decided that the appointed hour had arrived. To Callahan it seemed like the tide was turning and that the Marines might be able to take advantage of the lull in the fighting created by the spectacular destruction of the Type 531. Moreover, Ingraham thought that the smoke and secondary explosions from the burning vehicle would help cover their escape. He recalled, "The hardest decision I had to make the whole time we were in the city was choosing what time to leave the safety of the rooftop and expose ourselves out in the street. We had no idea if the enemy was in our area. Only minutes before, we'd been hearing Iraqi voices on the bottom floor."

Encouraged by Doc Callahan, Ingraham decided that they were going to sprint out of the city and instructed everyone to begin shedding all their nonessential gear to lighten their load. They would leave their rucksacks, their cold-weather gear, and the antitank rockets and make the run with only their weapons and radios. The Claymores would be left in place.

McNamee thought this was the stupidest thing he'd ever heard and wondered if the pressure had gotten to Ingraham. "Chuck, why don't we take everything out of our rucks and put all the mission essential gear in there. That way we'll be able to run and have both hands free to fire our weapons," he protested.

Driven to the point of inflexibility by the extended strain of the past 48 hours, Ingraham wasn't hearing any of this and ordered the men to strip down their gear and move down-stairs in patrol order, ready to hit the streets. Ingraham then radioed Baczkowski and told him they were coming out and to be on the lookout for them. They would be carrying the bright orange air panels they'd been issued to distinguish their Humvees to Coalition aircraft, Ingraham thinking that displaying such a bright marker would forestall the crazy Saudis from firing up the sprinting men. He was unspeakably glad that he'd chosen, some days ago, to include the shining square of nylon on the patrol packing list. They'd never really used them before, but at the moment the panels were about their only hope against being rudely dispatched by the Saudis.

Ingraham didn't know exactly where Baczkowski and Iiams were but thought them to be close enough to their building to make the dash. Moving clumsily down the stair-well where the Iraqis had been less than an hour before, the men bunched together, abandoning any pretense of a calm, orchestrated movement.

After peeking anxiously around to ensure that there weren't any Iraqis lingering on the hollows of the ground floor, the six Marines burst out the front door with an awk-ward, "Go!" Out on the street there seemed to be machine-gun rounds snapping everywhere. As the patrol transited the first side street to the west of their former refuge, they began taking sporadic fire. McNamee remembers, "I swear it was like a movie. There were rounds bouncing all around our feet. I have never run a faster fifty meters in my life."

Reaching the fleeting safety of the buildings across the way, the men were out of breath. McNamee recalls, "I was exhausted. It's impossible to explain how tired you get when you're exposed to that extended level of stress. We were all breathing like we'd just run three miles." At this point, McNamee came to the conclusion that hand-carrying the heavy radios out was endangering their lives and thought, *Do I really want to die for this damn PRC-104?* Realizing that the digital handset he had in his leg pocket was a far more valuable piece of intelligence, he dropped the twenty-pound radio set onto the concrete.

After catching their breath, the team moved out again, and Ingraham, his biceps cramping from lugging his own radio, glanced back and spied Sterling trailing far behind the pack with the lost PRC-104 in tow. Spotting the abandoned radio set, Sterling had instinctively jogged back and retrieved it, returning it to his stunned comrade without a word.

"Damn it, dude, what are you doing?" McNamee sputtered. He just wanted to get out of town.

After hurriedly traversing several more blocks, the men relaxed a bit. So far they hadn't been pinned down or taken heavy fire. The gamble seemed to be working. They knew that they hadn't been too deep inside town and that the safe open desert was close. Rounding a corner, McNamee spotted an Iraqi Type 531 idling in the street. Seeing that the vehicle was pointing in the other direction, McNamee hoped that they would be able to slip by. It looked like the team had hit a roadblock. They had nothing with them that could put so much as a dent on the idling behemoth.

Iiams also saw the Iraqi armored personnel carrier. Just moments earlier, Baczkowski, having heard from Ingraham that they were starting their sprint, raced down a line of nearby Saudi armored vehicles screaming "Ameriki! Ameriki!

Ameriki!" hoping to prevent the trigger-happy Saudis from ripping his men apart when they finally emerged from around the corner. Iiams and Baczkowski had been inching their way closer to where they presumed Ingraham and the boys would come out, and as they rolled into an open area sealed off by a platoon of Saudi vehicles, Iiams saw a floppy-hatted head poke out from a distant corner off to the right and then duck back again.

Iiams floored the Humvee, rapidly moving up to Ingra-ham, and whipped the empty truck around in a J-turn, which left him facing the back of the Iraqi armored vehicle, half-hidden down a side alley. Miraculously, no one on board the Iraqi vehicle seemed to notice the sudden appearance of the motley-attired group of Marines. Within seconds the six men with all their gear and Captain Baczkowski were loaded up in the bed of the Humvee and rushing away from the mad scene. Iiams didn't stop until they were well outside the city limits, and even then the Marines jumbled in back yelled, "Keep going!"

Gloriously tangled in the back of Amazing Grace, the men were soon in tears, overwhelmed by their sudden salvation. Somehow, they had won the gamble and escaped from Khafji practically unscathed. However, their rising elation was swiftly undercut when, after inquiring as to the status of Lentz's team, the Marines learned that seven of their close comrades were still hemmed in to the north. Ingraham and company had managed somehow to squeeze out from their hideout, but Lentz's team was easily twice as deep inside the beleaguered city and it was unlikely that Iiams and Bacz-kowski, now encumbered, would be able to facilitate their egress in the near term. For 3rd Platoon, the day was only half done.

Meanwhile, over in Lentz's neck of the woods the odds for survival seemed to be lengthening by the hour. To Scott Wagner, the team's radio guru, whose battery supply had been stretched beyond all reasonable limits, the situation was looking grim indeed. The bearishly built communicator had always been supremely confident in his ability to solve practically any radio problem he encountered, but after more than a week in Khafji, he had simply run out of juice for the team's radios and digital equipment. The physics involved were nonnegotiable. "I had pulled out every trick in the book . . . trying and retrying all the old batteries and trading 'em out but all of them were just dead." Without their radios, the team was dead in the water, scarcely able to even defend themselves let alone remain combat-effective.

The team's lone remaining lifeline was a short-range PRC-77 radio currently being used by Lentz, functioning in defiance of all physics. With the radio Lentz had been able to relay updates and status reports through Ingraham, who was better connected with the rear, but with Ingraham's team now gone, their options were even further curtailed. For Lentz, being able to hear another human voice over the snapping static of the radio—be it Coyote or Ingraham or Captain Baczkowski or an anonymous pilot overhead—had been a continuing wellspring of comfort throughout the ordeal. Now even this luxury was being unceremoniously ripped away.

As any hope of keeping the team's radios alive dribbled away, Wagner found himself without a job. He had essentially nothing to do but wait. Spotting the idled Marine, Lentz handed him an AT-4, instructing him to go over to a distant corner of the building and keep a lookout for any approaching Iraqis, repeating to him the team mantra, "Don't open up until they come over the wall."

Alone and discouraged, Wagner peered out into the bleak afternoon light, unsure of what lay ahead. Just then an Iraqi armored personnel carrier packed with soldiers rambled westward down a side street in full view. "That's when it hit me. I was flat out alone, an Iraqi APC had just rolled past and our comm was dying. That was probably the only time when I thought to myself, This is bad. This is really, really bad."

The moment didn't linger. Soon after posting Wagner and in counterpoint to the APC Wagner had just seen, Lentz received the long-awaited "it's clear" call from Coyote. It was one in the afternoon. Lentz remembers, "Finally, Coyote comes up and says, 'We still have isolated pockets of Iraqis near you, but if y'all are planning on coming out, now is the time.'"

The Marines, who had made a point of not becoming too settled into their hideout over the course of the long patrol, began hustling about the commandeered residence collecting up what little stray gear remained. Wagner turned to breaking down the omnidirectional antenna he'd lovingly rigged out of twigs, slash wire, and spare pipes he'd found lying around Mishab. He then remembered that because he'd had to leave much of the group's cryptographic gear in the Humvees, he'd booby-trapped both of the vehicles with hand grenades lest the codes fall into enemy hands. The antenna finished, he quickly set about dismantling these handmade traps.

Amid the bustle, the long-pent-up tension expressing itself with a vengeance of sudden activity, Alan Cooper realized that something major was amiss. As he and his comrades readied themselves for the impending movement, he noticed that every time he ascended the stairwell leading to the second floor, he heard a strange noise. Cooper called some of his teammates over, and as they looked on, he passed his camouflage hat over a cinderblock-size hole in the building wall. As his hat darkened the aperture, a shot slapped against the outside of the building. They had a sniper on their hands. It was only a matter of time before the shooter alerted his comrades and called them down upon the loitering Marines.

Lentz knew that they were going to have to eliminate this threat if they hoped to get out of the city in one piece. The sniper appeared to be less than 100 yards away in an elevated position overlooking their hide and would most likely enjoy a grand, Lee Harvey Oswald–like shot at their convoy when they attempted to decamp. Whoever this guy was, he'd selected an excellent position; the Marines were practically immobilized until they took him out.

Despite the gravity of their predicament, Lentz recalls making a game out of the sniper pickle as if unable or unwilling to give up his childlike fascination with the brutality of the whole scene. Everyone took turns putting his hat over the opening just to see what would happen. Like clockwork, every time the hole was covered over, a single well-aimed shot rang out.

The Marines assembled a hasty plan. One of them would move his floppy hat over the hole while the others scanned across the way for a telling muzzle blast. Once they determined the sniper's position, they would all engage the position simultaneously, virtually ensuring that the shooter wouldn't be able to turn the same find-the-muzzle-blast trick back onto the Marines. Lentz would hit the upper right of the sniper's position, while two other Marines would hit below and left. The fourth man would pop a few M-203 grenades through whatever opening the man was firing from.

After repeating the hat move, Lentz spotted the shooter on the roof of a three-story building underneath a tin corrugated roof house to the west. He appeared to be at the head of an open stairwell and was grievously backlit by the reflected afternoon sun. As the Marines studied the position, his outline grew even more distinct. Lentz could tell that he was wearing some sort of camouflage pattern different from the traditional Iraqi forest-green uniform.

The Marines covered over the hole a final time and after confirming their prey, savagely stitched the area surrounding the sniper's position with a hail of bullets and fragmentation grenades. With this resounding fusillade, the Marines' course of action was thus sealed. They had been forced to fire their weapons and had announced their position to anyone within earshot. They would now have to abandon the very position that had for so many trying hours been their primary source of comfort and protection.

As this sniper drama played itself out, in a distant back room of the house a dialogue of a decidedly different sort was in progress. The young Doc Dayrit, overwhelmed by the chaos swirling around him, had become paralyzed with fear.

Marcus Slavenas recalls trying to talk the medic down and prepare him for the coming action. "He was really, really scared, saying things like, 'If we make it out of this thing I'm gonna get myself reassigned. I'm not doing any more of this.' "

Slavenas continued to encourage Dayrit, telling him that he had to keep going. Suddenly the young aidman seem to have an epiphany, saying, "Yeah, you're right. My dad and my grandfather were both in the Navy and they managed to make it through." None of this curious scene was lost on the perspicacious Slavenas. "It was almost this clichéd World War II story. We're taking fire and then the new guy gets freaked out."

Despite this touching exchange, Slavenas, who while capable of sympathy was at heart a hard-bitten young warrior, was aghast at the naiveté of the man. "He just wasn't mentally prepared. He'd been working at a desk in a hospital or something right up until the patrol began. I have no idea why they assigned him to our team. It was dangerous and no one on the team was happy with Dayrit. Most of our corpsman were hard-core but Dayrit was no Doc Callahan."

The sniper threat thus suppressed and their spirits bolstered, the men jumped in the team's two Humvees and wheeled out of the compound, Lentz leading the caravan through the front gate in an unarmored troop-carrier variant. Hard behind in a slightly better armored model with Slavenas at the wheel were Wagner and Scott Uskoski, the second-ranking member of the team manning a roof-mounted .50-caliber machine gun. As they slipped past the sniper's building, Uskoski kept the .50 trained on the roof in case their stalker decided to put in a final appearance. No shots rang out, and they rolled by unscathed.

Soon after they began their hegira, Wagner noticed that at least one of his Humvee's tires had been destroyed by the numerous artillery raids that they had called in. He could feel the shredded rubber slapping violently against the floorboard beneath his feet. While not a showstopping setback because of the Humvee's built-in "run-flat" system, the deflated tire caused the entire vehicle to ride at an awkward angle and greatly limited the truck's speed and maneuverability. Up top Uskoski was jostled around violently as the two homeward Humvees rambled heartily over curbs as fast the vehicles would carry them. It wasn't long before Wagner noticed a thick, oily smoke leaking out from under the hood as well.

Lentz, acting upon the instructions of Coyote, had selected a circuitous route through town that, while relatively direct, kept them far away from the hotly contested main boulevard. Initially, the convoy headed due west before making a beeline to the south, and as Lentz's lead Humvee continued to zigzag, the following Marines began to wonder where exactly their fearless leader was taking them. Uskoski, with the best view of things from the turret, recalled, "The exfiltration seemed to take forever and we kept taking turn after turn."

The anxious men rambled by several burning Saudi and Iraqi vehicles. The city seemed transformed; what had once been a sleepy Arab town was now an urban hellscape littered with concrete rubble, garbage, spent brass, twisted streetlamps, and burning armored vehicles. Virtually every building they passed was riddled with bullet holes.

As the two Humvees continued to race southward, the lead vehicle hit the brakes and zoomed in reverse back toward Wagner and Slavenas. Poking his head out the Humvee, Lentz yelled over to Slavenas that there was a tank around the bend that he wanted him to identify. Slavenas, a trained TOW gunner, was the team's leading anti-armor authority, and Lentz needed to know if the tank in question might be Saudi or Qatari. Inching up to see around the corner of the building, Slavenas and Wagner decided that the tank, which was only a few blocks away and traversing its turret toward the Marines, was definitely Iraqi and they weren't gonna wait to stick around to discover exactly what exact type of armored vehicle it was. They quickly evacuated the scene, threading their way southward again.

Uskoski remembers that he began to feel safe when, as he looked out over the Humvee, he began to see unfamiliar tan-colored vehicles to his direct front. Noticing that the tall 4×4s were sporting bright orange panels on their fronts, he quickly deduced that they were Arab Coalition vehicles. They were almost out. The Marines continued to push south, and before they knew it, they were out on the southeastern outskirts of the built-up area. With his radio still fading in and out, Lentz was somehow able to raise Coyote a final time. Coyote directed him over to the far western edge of town, where he was situated with his small command group near the local Saudi National Guard armory.

When the convoy was a mere 200 meters from Coyote's position, Slavenas's Humvee seized up. Unbeknownst to the Marines, the vehicle's crankcase had been shattered by an errant American artillery bomblet that morning, causing the engine oil to leak steadily out over the course of their winding exfiltration. It was an awkward denouement to their trek; they had come so far and lasted for so long under pressure where they shouldn't have, and Coyote—Lieutenant Colonel Mike Taylor—was forced to hop into a nearby Humvee to complete the final few feet of their emotional reunion.

Lentz felt like a long-lost son returning home when he finally met up with Taylor, a man whose voice had kept him alive and in good spirits for so very long. After a rare embrace and handshakes all around, all Taylor could manage was, "Man, are we glad to see you guys!"

While the counterattack in the southern outskirts of the city had gained the recon teams their freedom, it also cost some Saudi guardsmen their lives. At approximately 7:30 A.M., after an intense ANGLICO-organized artillery barrage, the counterattack was relaunched, and much as before, the combined Arab force, which included armored vehicles from both the 7th Battalion of the SANG and two cross-attached Qatari tank companies, ran straight into a blistering wall of Iraqi fire. The Arab vehicles barreled through the streets of town, pouring tank rounds, TOW missiles, and small-arms fire into the surrounding buildings. Soon after passing under the city arches, two thin-skinned SANG V-150s fell prey to Iraqi RPG and Sagger missile fire. Both vehicles erupted catastrophically, killing all aboard. These two kills accounted for most of the Saudi casualties in the entire battle.

The recon-initiated artillery barrage, along with the two Harrier air strikes, had done significant damage to the Iraqi defenses inside the city, and it wasn't long before the Saudis' hard-won lodgment inside the city began to expand outward. As the Saudis continued to press northward, the forces became intermixed, making it difficult to impossible to distinguish friendly from enemy. As frequently happens in urban warfare, the melee became a haphazard block-by-block affair. The Saudis would take neighborhoods only to retreat moments later under a spirited Iraqi countercharge. Blocks changed hands several times over the course of an hour, the Saudis often retreating as brazenly as they had advanced only minutes prior. It quickly became impossible for the fast-moving American attack jets to tell Iraqi vehicles from Saudi ones. The senior ANGLICO officer present, Captain Mark Dillard, began waving off the jets checking in to fight, instead dispatching them to the meeting engagement in the north where Doug Kleinsmith's team was in heavy contact with Iraqis trying to reinforce the embattled Khafji garrison.

At 10:00 A.M. a division of Cobra gunships flew up from the south, came on line, and began raking the tall water tower that Captain Jon Fleming had used as a vantagepoint the night of the twenty-ninth. The tower was such an obvious lookout that seemingly every unit passing through the southern part of Khafji felt compelled to light it up. Earlier that morning, Sergeant Elisio Lozano, attempting to coax the Qatari tank unit he was supporting into the attack, had watched as the Qatari tanks elevated their muzzles and blasted the tower repeatedly. The Qataris, convinced that the Iraqis had stationed observers high in the tower, had refused to roll into town until it was suppressed.

After engaging the tower with Hellfire missiles, the Cobras proceeded northward into the heart of the city, their raucous rotor noise echoing off the walls of the buildings, to engage several Iraqi APCs that had been spotted. After the helicopters fired on the Iraqis, an ANGLICO controller in the streets in the southern part of town came up on the radio, complaining that the Cobras' 20-mm rounds were beginning to ricochet toward his position. Once Jim Braden at the brigade headquarters got wind of this, he called the Cobras off. Although the fire had not been terribly close, Braden and the others felt happy to have prevented what could have been a tragic encounter.

Coalition casualties continued to mount, however, as by 1:00 P.M. on the 31st, the 7th Battalion had suffered seven dead V-150s; ten Saudis had been killed in action and forty-five others were seriously wounded. The battalion was heavily fatigued and out of ammo. Most of the southern half of town had been secured, and the recon teams had been freed, but responding to the deep exhaustion, the battalion commander sounded a recall and the Saudi vehicles limped southward through town. The retrograde from the city was somewhat helter-skelter. The neighborhoods the Saudis had attacked through were not entirely clear of Iraqis, and they continued to receive fire until they reached the vicinity of the SANG compound to the southwest of town.

The 8th Battalion of the SANG, which had been ordered by their brigade to move north at 10:00 A.M., replaced their sister battalion on the line at around 1:30 and continued clearing out the southern half of town. The 7th Battalion had taken the brunt of the fighting that day, and while the town was far from clean of Iraqis, their defenses had clearly been broken. At 4:00 P.M., the 7th Battalion, having rearmed and refueled, rejoined 8th Battalion on the line. By dusk the attack was halted for the night, with both units settling into a loose defensive perimeter for the evening. Although their position could be at best described as tenuous, it appeared as if the Coalition now owned the better half of Khafji. The situation was by no means resolved. Victory had not yet been achieved, but there was at least a sizeable Coalition force holding ground inside the city gates.

Approximately twelve hours after Major General Mahmoud was denied permission from Baghdad to call off the attack, he defied his superiors and instructed his forwardmost brigades to break contact and return to central Kuwait. An intercepted radio transmission later that day reported that two Iraqi divisions bound for Saudi Arabia had been recalled, having lost 2,000 men and 300 vehicles, mostly to Coalition air strikes.

The following morning, February 1, the 7th and 8th Battalions of the SANG were in position and ready to sweep through the city. The 7th would take the western half of town and push northward up the main drag over the wide causeway toward the desalinization plant. Eighth Battalion would drive through the southeastern quarter toward the coastline and then hang a left, rejoining its sister battalion in the north. A Saudi regular army tank company was set up overlooking the northern edge of the city waiting to blast any Iraqi vehicles trying to escape from the city toward Kuwait. It was a classic hammer-and-anvil maneuver, lacking in only one respect: The two converging arms couldn't talk to each other.

In its paranoia over an internal coup, the Saudi royal family had taken extensive measures to ensure that the national guard and the regular Ministry of Defense and Aviation (MODA) forces could never work in conjunction, including outfitting them with incompatible radio and combat equipment. The officers of the two antagonistic units reported to two separate chains of command and rarely if ever spoke to each other. The SANG officers, who considered themselves the elite of the kingdom, looked down their noses at the regular troops and generally thought it unnecessary to coordinate anything with them. To the ANGLICO officers on the scene, the situation seemed ripe for calamity. The SANG's

V-150s would roll through the southern half of town, and as they emerged from the tangle of buildings, would be slaughtered by the trigger-happy M-60 gunners, who had been waiting anxiously all morning for the dreaded Iraqis to appear. The SANG's cries to cease fire would never be heard by their Saudi brothers-in-arms.

To prevent this tragedy from occurring, Braden ordered Kleinsmith to detach his team from the northern sector of the battlefield, move south through the desert to the west of the city, and link up with the northbound SANG troops. Mulling this tasking over, Kleinsmith reasoned that if he could position himself near the head of the SANG column, he would be able to warn Kris Elliot and Bubba Deckert, who remained in the north, that they were drawing near. In turn, Deckert, stationed with the Saudi M-60s closest to the coastal road, would be on the lookout for the approach of his good friend. Further, Kleinsmith figured that if he could coordinate with the other ANGLICO teams in the area, led by Captain Mark Dillard (7th Battalion) and Captain John Bley (8th Battalion), keeping them spread as far out as possible, he could exercise some form of control over the movement and hopefully prevent the type of fratricide that had been the bane of the Marines throughout the battle.

It was a long journey south for Kleinsmith and his tired crew, and in their exhaustion they managed to run smack into a downed power line that lay draped across their Humvee's path. Fortunately, the line wasn't charged, and the Marines were uninjured. Despite the gravity of the situation, the men were able to laugh at the thought of dying by electrocution, having already survived two extended armored engagements. The men at this stage were living on pure adrenaline, reacting to the needs of the moment, going from place to place, doing what needed to be done but not with the full power of their minds at the ready. As Bubba Deckert recalls, "At this point, we were in a reality that created itself. I didn't always know where we were exactly or what time it was. Everything was relative to where you were last." It was a dangerous time for the men, especially for the young officers who were charged with orchestrating the movements of large foreign armored units and controlling deadly high-performance aircraft. One false command and dozens of men could die.

Reaching the southern outskirts of town, the Marines were immediately besieged by a throng of reporters who had been escorted to the front by a Marine public affairs master sergeant. A correspondent from *Time* approached Kleinsmith and pleaded with him, "Please take me into the city. I can ride right on the back of your Humvee!"

Preoccupied with the life-and-death tactical problems facing him and with getting all his men home alive, the last thing Kleinsmith wanted to do was babysit a bunch of tenderfoot newsies. He told the reporter that he wasn't taking anyone anywhere. The master sergeant came up and asked, "Captain, can you take us into the city? I'll accept responsibility for the reporters."

"You got your own vehicle?" Kleinsmith inquired.

"Yeah."

"All right, then, let's go."

Happily the menagerie of safari-shirted reporters loaded up in their vehicles. *Finally they were getting a piece of the action!* As this strange cortege wheeled northward, Kleinsmith noticed that the Saudis had established a checkpoint going into the city. As they pulled up, he noticed that the post was being run by a lieutenant friend of his named Mohammed. The two shared a quick embrace, the lieutenant exclaiming, "Oh, Captain Doug, it is so good to see you! We all thought you were dead. Praise Allah! Surely we shall win the war now!"

Heartened by the friendly reception, Kleinsmith took him aside and, pointing to the truck full of reporters, said, "Do you see those guys? Whatever you do, do *not* let them inside the city."

"I got it, Captain Doug. You go on. I have this."

As Kleinsmith departed, he watched in the Humvee's rearview mirror as Mohammed leaped out into the middle of the road and began reading the reporters the riot act. Mohammed turned and waved knowingly at him as the Humvee pulled away.*

The Marines linked up with the SANG forces pushing through town. Soon the Marines found themselves surrounded on all sides by the tall Saudi V-150s. All the Saudis who saw the Marines spotted the back-from-the-dead Captain Kleinsmith in the passenger seat and whooped at him, "Hey, it's Captain Doug! How are you? Yes, yes, you go forward too!"

"How much further?" Kleinsmith would yell.

"You keep going!" came the reply.

As the Humvee continued to press to the head of the column, the other Marines inside the vehicle began yelling instructions at Corporal Calhoun to stop or speed up, as a sniper seemed to have zeroed in on their Humvee. Kleinsmith recalls, "The guy had a bead on us and was shooting over the top of us. To this day, I don't know why he didn't get us. I don't know where it was coming from, but I could hear it crack right over us."

---

*The battle of Khafji makes for a fascinating case study of military-media relations. The Kleinsmith incident and others like it led to charges by the press that they had been prevented from adequately covering the battle. As reporter David Mould argued in a 1996 article, "The battle of Khafji severely tested the Coalition's elaborate media management system of press pools and military briefings. Under the pressure of fast-moving events on the ground, the system proved unequal to the task of providing quick, accurate information; the best coverage of the battle of Khafji came from journalists who, by choice or force of circumstance, were working outside the system. The Americans did not allow press pool into Khafji until after the town was retaken, so the only reporters who saw the fighting were these 'pool busters' or unilaterals—several print reporters, two French television crews and a team from Britain's Visnews" ("Press Pools and Military-Media Relations in the Gulf War. A Case Study of the Battle of Khafji, January 1991." *Historical Journal of Film, Radio & Television*, June 1996.).

Other journalists thought the military's pool system pitted CENTCOM-approved journalists against the so-called unilaterals. Robert Fisk of London's *The Independent*, who refused to join any pool, recalls being confronted by an NBC news reporter on the outskirts of Khafji. The reporter allegedly shouted, "Get out of here you arsehole. You'll prevent us from working. You're not allowed here. Get out. Go back to Dhahran." The NBC reporter then sicced a Marine public affairs officer on the British journalist. According to Fisk, the Marine yelled, "You're not allowed to talk to U.S. Marines and they're not allowed to talk to you" (Knightley, Phillip. *The First Casualty: The War Correspondent as Hero and Myth-Maker from Crimea to Kosovo.* Johns Hopkins, 2002. 492.).

Seeking cover behind a Saudi vehicle, the Marines discovered to their horror that they had pulled in behind a TOW variant, which immediately cranked off a missile with them squarely in the deadly backblast area. The Humvee's windshield absorbed the full force of the furious launch, which somehow didn't crack or blast back at the men. The Marines quickly abandoned the cover of the TOW vehicle, fleeing behind another more heavily armored Saudi V-150. Unbelievably, Calhoun had managed to select another TOW vehicle to hide behind, and the same hellish process repeated itself. Finally Kleinsmith yelled, "Fuck it, Calhoun, stay away from everyone. We'll just take our chances."

The crew finally reached the front of the SANG column, which was halted for the moment. The Saudis, piloting the thin-skinned Cadillac Gage V-150 vehicles, which were perilously vulnerable to RPG strikes and even well-aimed heavy machine-gun fire, were creeping forward at a snail's pace. If they suspected that a building was occupied, they blasted it with a flurry of TOW missiles. After one such fusillade, the V-150s began to advance again. Eventually, the column reached a wide stretch of road with a palm tree–lined median running down the middle of it. As the Marines watched in amazement, the lead Saudi TOW gunner fired a missile down the road. After the missile had traveled 1,000 meters, the gunner curve-balled it around a wide bend in the road, deftly avoiding the many palm trees, blindsiding a lone Iraqi armored personnel carrier. The Saudis knew a good deal when they saw it, and the Marines noticed that wherever this gunner went, the column was sure to follow. It was one of the most amazing combat performances Kleinsmith had ever witnessed. He was later told that the gunner, whose name he never learned, had already killed seven Iraqi vehicles.

As the southern columns began poking through the city, Kleinsmith called up to his buddy Deckert, saying, "You gotta get those MODA guys turned." Recalls Kleinsmith, "We were about to pop out, and I knew they were gonna whack us. No doubt in my mind."

With the help of Kris Elliot, Deckert managed to convince the commander of the tank force, which by this point had grown to a full-strength battalion, to reorient his vehicles to the north and west, 90 degrees away from the approaching national guardsmen.

As soon as the 7th and 8th Battalions emerged from the southern enclave, they began engaging the already-dead tanks near the desalinization plant, leftovers from the battle that Kleinsmith had witnessed the day before. It was completely ridiculous. The nervous Saudi gunners, spying the charred hulks, which had long since stopped smoking, assumed that they were still alive and shot them repeatedly. Amazingly, the barrage rolled on even after the initial first volleys, almost as if the Saudis sensed that the sweep through town had been too easy and wanted one last swipe at their enemies, even if they were just kicking corpses around. The ANGLICO Marines, after attempting numerous times to dissuade the Saudis of their folly, threw up their hands and allowed them to waste their precious ammunition. Northern progress was halted for nearly two hours while the Saudis blasted away at the wreckage. Finally, the Saudis, content with the carnage, began inching forward toward the desalinization plant.

Soon after reaching the desal plant, a group of Army Special Forces soldiers raced up the coastal road, hell-bent on recovering the precious cryptographic equipment they'd abandoned three days earlier. The compound was occupied by a group of Iraqi holdouts, and a Green Beret major approached the Marines to see if they wanted to help retake the cluster of buildings. Kleinsmith declined. After a hasty Saudi artillery barrage, the compound was easily seized by a combined force of MODA tanks and vehicles from the 8th SANG. The Special Forces soldiers retrieved their lost gear. The fight had clearly gone out of the Iraqis.

With the fall of the desalinization plant, the battle of Khafji was, for all intents and purposes, over. However, owing to the Saudis' haphazard building-clearing techniques, it would take weeks to mop up the pockets of snipers and dead-enders strung out across the city. As night fell on February 1, the combined Arab force stretched over a nearly perfect defensive arc from the coastline inland to the wide and now silent desert. Kleinsmith noted that for once the Arab vehicles were all pointed in the right direction.

EPILOGUE

This is a strange new kind of war where you learn just as much as you are able to believe.

—ERNEST HEMINGWAY, in a dispatch from the
Spanish Civil War, April 14, 1937

THE BATTLE of Khafji, however life-altering for the men who fought in it, was for the most part forgotten or overlooked by the American military leadership in theater and was treated mostly as an inconsequential skirmish carried out in a distant corner of Saudi Arabia. After an initial flurry of newspaper and broadcast news reports on the engagement, any remembrance of the battle was quickly washed away, lost in the tidal wave of coverage preceding the much-anticipated ground offensive into the belly of Kuwait. The best records of Khafji remained, as all battles, preserved however imperfectly in the memories of the men who were there. Absorbed in the preparations for the impending attack, the American high command gave lip service to the engagement but didn't allow it to disrupt their intricate invasion plans. Some officers at the U.S. Central Command seemed to take it as a point of pride to dismiss the conflagration that had so dominated the Saudi frontier region for four days. General Schwarzkopf himself characterized the Iraqi offensive as being "about as significant as a pinprick on the hide of an elephant."

Nevertheless, the battle was a watershed in ways that are only now beginning to become clear. The Iraqis had been resoundingly defeated by a vastly outnumbered but lethal group of dedicated American professionals employing a brand-new class of military weaponry. The sheer disparity of the forces and the lack of American casualties spoke volumes about the coming ground war and the poor fighting quality of the Iraqi fighting man, and yet no major changes were made in the overall offensive set to roll two weeks after Khafji. Indeed, the battle was largely ignored by most of the American military establishment for several years. The explanation for this apparent oversight can in part be chalked up to the fact that through sheer happenstance, no major U.S. Army units were engaged at Khafji, and as the lead service in the Coalition effort, the Army and Schwarzkopf, himself an Army man, felt no compunction to alter the carefully scripted Hail Mary end run to the far west. The Iraqis had been thwarted, and thus the Americans saw no need to pay the battle any mind.

That the battle's finale was fought by foreign troops and was at the end of the day an Arab victory only furthered this uniquely American process of forgetting. Some military analysts, including retired Marine Lieutenant General Bernard Trainor and Michael Gordon, authors of the authoritative account of the conflict, *The Generals' War,* have concluded that Schwarzkopf's ignorance of the rout and his subsequent misapprehension of the Iraqis led to the incomplete conclusion of the war and thus to the continued survival of Saddam Hussein's regime, arguing that if CENTCOM had heeded the lessons of Khafji, they could have more fully demolished the Republican Guard and thus taken away Saddam's main instrument for survival.

For the Marines who had done the lion's share of the fighting on the American side, however, the battle was viewed as an omen, a vital scrimmage, and a rude wake-up call all rolled into one. First and foremost, they had learned that the Iraqis couldn't mount coordinated multi-divisional operations and thus could be beaten. As the first major engagement since the Vietnam War, it proved that American boys still had the right stuff and that the frequently draconian Marine training worked. They had, however humbly, held up the standard set for them by their ancestors at Guadalcanal, Iwo Jima, and Khe Sanh.

In the early hours of the fight, the battle had seemed like an extended skirmish to the Marine high command, but as the detailed after-action reports began filtering in and the full measure of the action was taken, Khafji was seen as undeniable proof that the Iraqis had been vastly overrated. The battle served to confirm General Boomer's suspicions about the abysmal quality of the Iraqi fighting man. The Iraqis lacked the nerve of the North Vietnamese he'd fought two decades earlier and couldn't seem to hit anything with their artillery. And while the Iraqis had undertaken an audacious plan with the Khafji offensive, they clearly lacked the skill to execute it. As one Marine put it, "Get in the first shot at him and the rest will run away."

After conferring extensively with his two division commanders, Boomer decided to launch a much more aggressive invasion of Kuwait. Both divisions would attack simultaneously, attempting a risky dual breach of the Iraqi obstacle belts. General Mike Myatt, commander of the 1st Marine Division, anticipating a wide-scale capitulation, set aside an entire 1,000-man battalion just to manage the expected flood of Iraqi prisoners.

Despite this newfound optimism high up in the Marine food chain, many in the ranks expected a deadly slugfest in Kuwait. More than a few of the men who survived the ordeal at Khafji, including Chuck Ingraham and Joe Molofsky, took the battle to be a prelude of the slaughter to come, a brief, searing episode that prefigured a horrific struggle in the sands of Kuwait. Despite the Iraqis' poor showing, most Marines assumed that the liberation of Kuwait would take months if not years. For the light-armored vehicle crews and the recon men who had been thoroughly briefed on their dim prospects for survival, the ominous run-up to the invasion took on an alien sort of fatalism. It is difficult to fully convey the emotional impact that such portents of doom can have on a young man about to walk into the battle of his life: the echoes of wasted youth, the unshakable feeling you are condemned, that all you've ever known, loved, shared, and dreamed is about to come to a violent end.

To the American public, watching a systematically sanitized version of the war safely ensconced at home, this conflict, this passing storm, which was to become indelibly fixed in the popular imagination as "the easy war," such a feeling of sure doom is impossible to understand. However, it was just this type of fatalism that motivated Chuck Ingraham, preparing for a risky pre-invasion patrol into Kuwait, to call home and inform his parents that the only way he would be returning from the Gulf was in a body bag.

To the Saudis and their national guard contingent in particular, Khafji came to be viewed as a heroic endeavor, a classic victory against the minions of Saddam—their finest hour. They had engaged a feared enemy on their own soil, been bloodied, and emerged victorious. Their losses, while far from trivial, were comparatively light: They suffered 10 dead and 32 wounded. Their hard-won success at Khafji led the Saudi royal family to reconsider its role within the Coalition. In an elaborate victory dinner conducted at the SANG compound on February 2, 1991, Jim Braden, Bubba Deckert, and Joe Molofsky looked on as one of the crown princes grandly proclaimed that a great victory had been achieved and that the Saudis would be joining in the Allied liberation of Kuwait, a move they had long resisted. Owing in large part to the efforts of a few American advisors, the Coalition emerged from the fires of Khafji newly tempered and almost completely transformed.

For the Iraqis, Khafji was the high-water mark for the war, the last gasp of their dying army. It was the last time they ever held the initiative, the last time they handed the Coalition a defeat. They never launched a major offensive again. Estimates of the Iraqi casualties during the battle vary widely. U.S. Air Force tallies run upward of 2,000 men killed in action. The 1st ANGLICO after-action report lists 75 vehicles destroyed, 48 dead, and over 400 prisoners taken in the immediate vicinity of Khafji. A broad, theater-wide accounting of the battle, given its proximity to the wreckage incurred by the huge offensive into Kuwait, seems highly unlikely.

A large portion of Khafji's legacy revolves around the myriad questions of fratricide, or so-called friendly fire.

Shortly after the city was recaptured, the Marine high command ordered an investigation into the causes of the death of Blaze of Glory at Observation Post 4. The report, in 21 terse pages, manages to dissipate blame fingering no single event or individual but noting briefly that an A-10 pilot attached to the 354th Tactical Fighter Wing reported firing a Maverick missile that "went stupid" near the Kuwait border on January 29, 1991. The death of the Marine TOW vehicle known as Green 2 was erroneously attributed in several reports to enemy tank fire and was largely swept under the rug by Marine leaders. No independent investigation of the event was ever conducted. One officer on the 1st Marine Division staff later suggested that an inquiry was never undertaken for fear of the negative impact that it might have on the troops' morale on the eve of the Kuwait offensive, the reasoning being that no one wants to start doubting their buddies' judgment right before launching a major invasion.

Meanwhile, the U.S. Air Force investigation into the A-10-LAV incident has gone missing in action. Numerous inquiries made by this author to the Air Force's safety center and to the Air Force's public affairs office have gone unacknowledged. One staff member at the Air Force archives was able to locate the file, which mysteriously disappeared before being photocopied. According to sources familiar with the report, the Air Force version of events blames the seven deaths in Blaze of Glory on a malfunctioning Maverick missile. (This "stupid missile" theory flies in the face of virtually every eyewitness account of the battle that has been recorded.) Needless to say, numerous questions raised by the tragedy at OP 4 remain unanswered. Sadly, the search for some sort of final meaning and resolution from the horror of war is often a futile exercise.

After the war, a debate raged in the pages of the *Marine Corps Gazette,* the Corps's professional journal, about the implications of tragedies such as Observation Post 4 and the increasing incidence of fratricide in modern conflict. One such letter, written by a World War II veteran, admonished:

Much has been made of the casualties caused by friendly fire in Desert Storm. One can deeply sympathize with families mourning their dead killed by accident rather than by enemy action. I believe a large percentage of our casualties have been caused by errors or mistakes in all our wars. . . . And what if we did not employ the heavy firepower we use in battle to protect our troops and to offset the numerically superior enemy forces? Would the casualties be lesser or greater? War is a brutal and dangerous endeavor in which men—and now women—are exposed to death and horrible wounds. Every leader worthy of the name keeps his casualties to the irreducible minimum but the simple fact is that war is death and destruction. Lest I be judged too harshly for these observations, let me assure the reader that one of the high points of my life was during one of my World War II battalion's reunions, when several wives thanked me for bringing their husbands safely home.

The most amazing and mind-boggling testimony regarding the calamity of fratricide comes from the man in the best position to speak about it: Ronald Tull, the lone survivor of Blaze of Glory. Of the incident he recalled, "I don't blame the pilot of the A-10 one bit. Sure he messed up, but he was just trying to do his job. I mean could you imagine if those A-10s hadn't been there? I made it out alive, so you could say that those pilots saved my life."

Tull's staggeringly gracious response to the horror of his experience transcends normal human reason. That he is able to express such forgiveness is perhaps best taken as a testament to the redemptive qualities of the human spirit and to Tull's abiding Christian faith, which remained unaltered by his monstrous trial.

For Ron Tull's comrades who died at OP 4 and their loved ones, the legacy of the battle is a bitter and ambiguous one. Dying at the hands of one's own comrades is perhaps the most tragic form of passing, because it not only seems to diminish the sacrifice of the fallen in the eyes of the public but somehow reduces the entire incident to something that seems despairingly preventable and unnecessary. At least one of the widows of the fallen has described being treated as a second-class citizen among the survivors, as if her loss were somehow less real and devastating than those whose loved ones died at the hands of the enemy. Their deaths are treated by many as an embarrassment, a grim asterisk, something not easily fathomed and thus ripe to be looked past. The sense of emptiness and irresolution echoes like stone-made circles in a pond; a tragedy doubled by the shame of being associated with events that our culture as a whole clamors to forget.

Fratricide occupies a strange place in the horrific panoply of war because it not only snuffs out the precious flicker of life but also creates a potential villain where before there was only a beloved comrade. And who can account for the dark, obscure nights out on the line where even your own shadow seems worthy of doubt? Who, reading the face of facts that this book presents, would judge the men involved by an absolute standard of conduct without consideration for the moral vertigo that war creates? To search for a merciful excuse or some ethical back door in such affairs is to delude oneself. War reduces us all with its grim report on the status of the human condition: soldier, civilian observer, correspondent, all must cope with war's soul-crushing revelations, fratricide being but one species of the plague. Nevertheless, fratricide remains, in a sense, the perfect metaphor for the evil of war as a whole: We are, in essence, killing ourselves.

In the final analysis, Khafji can be seen as the first clash of the new American empire, a lopsided, ironic, mediated battle between an outnumbered but vastly superior American force and an obsolete Third World army, a preview of the conflicts to come in Kosovo, Afghanistan, and Iraq proper. A battle that subtly but irrevocably changed the calculus of war, where few U.S. casualties were taken but an enemy was overwhelmingly defeated. It birthed a new American military tradition: the mismatched, high-technology rout. It defined a previously unheralded battlespace, a near-perfect Cartesian plain where American war technology, fueled by a vast military-industrial complex, exerted the full measure of its might for the first time. Where massive enemy casualties were surgically inflicted at a distance, casualties that would remain for all intents and purposes anonymous, kept from Western eyes by a skittish media establishment and the sheer geography of the Arabian desert.

With the exception of the egregious fratricides at Observation Post 4, there was precious little tragedy on the Coalition side at Khafji. The Iraqis inflicted no casualties on the Marines, making the profane business of modern war seem somehow palatable to a dangerously sheltered public, a new form of mass entertainment paid with the lives of faceless peoples who live far away. And there is, to be perfectly truthful, a discernible disappointment among the Marines that the Iraqis weren't able to put up a better fight than they did. Indeed, how can one hope to measure up to one's grandfather if there is no splash of blood, no hero-generating Bastogne-like siege, no Chosin Reservoir, no Hue City? Where does one go to experience the camaraderie, the sacrifice, the adrenaline, to wrestle with Hemingway, if not the battlefield? As Marcus Slavenas, whose father was a Army Special Forces veteran, relates, "I didn't feel as if I experienced that true feeling of shooting and moving against an enemy and I'll confess that I've wanted to experience combat again just to know." And although there were in numerous instances genuine danger and imminent death, the risks were experienced by only a select few. These few, in particular the recon men at Observation Post 4 and those trapped in Khafji, were by virtue of their rare combat experience destined to become minor celebrities back in their home units.

This hugely unequal distribution of danger seems to defy the very definition of war. As Michael Ignatieff writes in *Virtual War*, his treatise about the Kosovo campaign, "War without death—to our side—is war that ceases to be fully real to us: virtual war." Put simply, there were to be no bloodshot bayonet charges in this new kind of war, no made-for-Hollywood scenes, no golden myth-making moment to capture the imagination, no Audie Murphy, no Sergeant Stryker.

One is forced to wonder in sum of events whether such un-
even victories aren't in some strange way dangerous to the
body politic, whether they defy the wisdom imparted by
Robert E. Lee after the slaughter of Fredericksburg: "It is
well that war is so terrible, or we should grow too fond of it."

The writer and historian grappling to record and remember these events is left at the end with a dim assemblage of
impressions and recollections, maps with no clear feeling
topography and little transcendent meaning. War, as the extreme outer ring of human existence, would seem to promise
us prime insight into the nature of humanity and consciousness, and yet after all has passed, one retains precious little
that is certain except that human life is frail and that men die,
often horrifically. The awful machinery of war grinds on,
mocking the survivors with its endurance. The man, the combat veteran, graying in the weak light of that which passes
for history, remains an enigma, trapped across an unfordable
moat of experience, alone and inscrutable. And yet one of us.

WHERE ARE THEY NOW?

Dan Baczkowski left the Marine Corps shortly after the war and lives on his aptly named Semper Fi farm, outside Lexington, Kentucky, with his wife and son.

Jim Braden continues to distinguish himself as a Marine officer. The Cobra squadron he commands (HMLA-169) was recognized as the Corps's Squadron of the Year shortly before deploying to the Middle East in support of Operation Iraqi Freedom.

The Marine that I have dubbed **"Joshua Brierly"** was immediately transferred out of Vitale's TOW Group and shipped back to the United States. He was honorably discharged shortly after the war and currently serves as vice president of a major investment management firm in Chicago.

Jason Brown, along with several of his TOW compadres, served in Somalia before leaving the Corps. He works as an software developer in St. Louis, Missouri.

Kevin "Doc" Callahan retired from the Navy in June 1998 and currently resides in Wailua, on the north shore of Hawaii, near his favorite surf break.

Gregory Gillispie, now a Master Gunnery Sergeant, is currently serving in the Marines' First Force Reconnaissance Company and has completed two tours in Iraq. He is one of the most experienced reconnaissance Marines in active duty and is always on the hunt for a good boondoggle.

Bill Iiams led one of the hairy pre-invasion patrols into the Iraqi obstacle belts inside Kuwait. He, along with Lentz and Doc Callahan, was nearly killed when an American F-18 dropped a 1,000-pound bomb near their observation post. Bill runs an air-conditioning company in Los Angeles.

Chuck Ingraham, unlike his father and grandfather, chose not to make the Marine Corps a career. After leaving the service, he earned a degree in finance from the University of New Orleans in 1995 and lives with his wife in Metairie, Louisiana. He has a son.

Douglas Kleinsmith has gone on to a distinguished career in the Marines. He was decorated for his service at Khafji and served on a joint task force in Bosnia. He was at the Pentagon on September 11, 2001, when American Airlines Flight 77 crashed into the building. He escaped unharmed. In April 1997, for political reasons beyond the scope of this book, the Air-Naval Gunfire Liaison Companies were disbanded. Lieutenant Colonel Kleinsmith is heading up the effort to re-establish ANGLICO.

Lawrence Lentz was honorably discharged from the Marine Corps in 1993 and works as a narcotics officer in Concord, North Carolina.

Lentz's Humvee, damaged by American artillery fire in Khafji, never ran again and had to be towed into Kuwait.

Joseph Molofsky completed an advisory tour with the Saudi Arabian Marine Corps in 2002 and was transferred to the U.S. Navy's Fifth Fleet headquarters in Bahrain prior to the launch of Operation Iraqi Freedom. While in Saudi Arabia, he continued to indulge his passion for Middle Eastern history, retracing the movements of T. E. Lawrence and visiting numerous battlegrounds made famous in David Lean's classic film *Lawrence of Arabia*.

Roger "Rock" Pollard commanded Delta Company until September 1993. He later served as a military advisor to the Saudi Arabian National Guard, teaching light-armored vehicle gunnery and tactics. He retired from the Corps in August 2000. He lives with his wife in Butler, Tennessee.

Melissa Rathbun-Nealy and **David Lockett** spent the remainder of the war in a Baghdad prison. Rathbun-Nealy had to fend off a sexual assault during the pair's two-day journey to the Iraqi capital. She recalls, "An Iraqi soldier attempted to fondle me, and I made the decision then that I would rather die than be violated. He continued to bother me and I reached across with my uninjured arm and punched him. He pulled out a gun, but his superiors who were in the front seat, turned around and told him 'no.' "

Once in Baghdad the pair were separated and kept in adjacent cells at a one-story prison. They wouldn't see each other for the remainder of their time in captivity.

Rathbun-Nealy's cell consisted of a 12-foot square room with a foam mattress on a tile floor. Confused and terrified, the young soldier cried and screamed nonstop for several hours. Eventually she was able to calm herself down and then realized to her horror that she had been shot in the arm. "I prayed to God, asking him for strength, although I knew I would get out alive. I figured that if I was supposed to die, I would have died during the gunfire." Sometime later the Iraqis sent a doctor to tend to her arm.

Kept in solitary confinement for the entire month of February 1991, Rathbun-Nealy tried to fend off boredom by counting the tiles in the hallway the led to her cell. "There were 644 tiles in the hallway and 230 in my room. I even tried to count the holes in my wall," she recalled.

The Iraqis fed Lockett and Rathbun-Nealy a disgusting amalgam of soup and porridge for breakfast, lunch and dinner. Trapped inside Baghdad, the pair endured regular Allied bombing runs. Rathbun-Nealy recalls, "I remember one night I was coming from the restroom. I guess I had a brain lapse, I forgot where I was, I forgot that I was in a middle of a war, I forgot that I was prisoner. I just remember looking through a window and seeing those real pretty lights going up into the sky. Then it dawned on me that there were tracers coming from antiaircraft artillery. That the Iraqis were shooting at the Allied planes. There were a lot of air raids that hit close by. It was scary."

On February 28, Rathbun-Nealy was informed by the Iraqi officer in charge of her imprisonment that she had been given 48 hours to live. "He told me that if the war didn't end in the next 48 hours, he had been ordered to kill me. I said, 'Well, let's hope that it does.' " Whether by accident or design, a cease-fire was declared later that day. She and Lockett were released in a group of six American POWs on March 4, 1991. Since the war's conclusion, Rathbun-Nealy, who is now married and goes by Melissa Coleman, has complained of symptoms associated with Gulf War Syndrome.

Steven Ross went to flight school after the war and serves as the executive officer of a Cobra attack helicopter squadron (HMLA-367). **Max Morton** was his commanding officer. Currently a lieutenant colonel, he serves on the First Marine Expeditionary Force staff at Camp Pendleton, California.

Pat Sterling, who stayed in the reserves and is currently deployed to Iraq, lives with his wife and children just up the road from Doc Callahan at Haleiwa, Hawaii.

Ron Tull returned to Delta Company after the war and served out the remainder of his enlistment under Captain Pollard. He works as a computer programmer in Dallas.

ROSTER OF THE FALLEN

LIGHT-ARMORED VEHICLE-TOW "GREEN 2"
CORPORAL ISMAEL COTTO
PRIVATE FIRST CLASS SCOTT A. SCHROEDER
LANCE CORPORAL DAVID T. SNYDER
LANCE CORPORAL DANIEL B. WALKER

LIGHT-ARMORED VEHICLE "BLAZE OF GLORY" OR "RED 2"
LANCE CORPORAL FRANK C. ALLEN
CORPORAL STEPHEN E. BENTZLIN
LANCE CORPORAL THOMAS A. JENKINS
LANCE CORPORAL MICHAEL E. LINDERMAN, JR.
LANCE CORPORAL JAMES H. LUMPKINS
SERGEANT GARETT A. MONGRELLA
LANCE CORPORAL DION J. STEPHENSON

AC-130 SPECTRE GUNSHIP "SPIRIT 03"
CAPTAIN CLIFFORD BLAND, JR.
STAFF SERGEANT JOHN P. BLESSINGER
SENIOR MASTER SERGEANT PAUL G. BUEGE
SERGEANT BARRY M. CLARK
CAPTAIN ARTHUR GALVAN
CAPTAIN WILLIAM D. GRIMM
STAFF SERGEANT TIMOTHY R. HARRISON
TECHNICAL SERGEANT ROBERT K. HODGES
STAFF SERGEANT DAMON J. KANUHA
SENIOR MASTER SERGEANT JAMES B. MAY II
TECHNICAL SERGEANT JOHN L. OELSCHLAGER
STAFF SERGEANT MARK J. SCHMAUSS
CAPTAIN DIXON L. WALTERS
MAJOR PAUL J. WEAVER

U.S. MARINE CORPS KEY WORDS AND ACRONYMS

A-6 Marine attack aircraft, a.k.a. Intruder

A-10 U.S. Air Force attack aircraft

AMX-30 main battle tank used by the Qatari forces

ANGLICO Air-Naval Gunfire Liaison Company

APC Armored Personnel Carrier

AT-4 a light, disposable antitank rocket

AWACS Airborne Warning and Control System, an air force surveillance and command and control aircraft.

BDA bomb-damage assessment, usually conducted after an air strike has been completed

CAS close air support

CENTCOM Central Command, General Schwarzkopf's headquarters

CO commanding officer

Cobras Marine attack helicopters

CP command post

DPICM dual-purpose improved conventional munition, an artillery-delivered cluster bomb

E&E escape and evasion; when the mission breaks down and it's every man for himself

EPAC Eastern Pan-Arab Command, the conglomeration of Saudi and Qatari units that retook Khafji

FIC team fire control team: the basic operating ANGLICO team

FSCC fire support coordination center, a headquarters-type unit that coordinates air and artillery strikes

GPS Global Positioning System

LAV Light-Armored Vehicle

LAW Light Antitank Weapon

M-60 a medium machine gun; the same designation is also used for a U.S.-produced main battle tank

M-203 a shotgun-style grenade launcher mounted underneath the M-16

MEF Marine Expeditionary Force, the Marine high command in theater

MODA Saudi Ministry of Defense and Aviation, distinguished from the SANG

MRE meals ready to eat, field rations

MULE Modular Universal Laser Equipment, a laser unit used to designate targets for air strikes

NCO Non-Commissioned Officer, a serviceman who holds the rank of corporal or above

NVGs night-vision goggles

OP observation post, e.g., OP 7, OP 4.

OpsO operations officer, a commanding officer's right-hand man and primary planning assistant

OV-10 propeller-driven Marine spotter plane

POW prisoner of war

PRC-77 a.k.a. "Prick-77," the standard Marine radio of the time

Recon generic term for Marine reconnaissance units

RPG rocket-propelled grenade

SALT Supporting Arms Liaison Team, the headquarters agency for ANGLICO FIC teams

SANG Saudi Arabian National Guard

SAW squad automatic weapon, a light machine gun

SEALs sea, air, land (teams), U.S. Navy special operations forces

SINCGARS Single Channel Ground and Airborne Radio System, the newer Marine short-range radio set of the time

SRIG Surveillance, Reconnaissance, and Intelligence Group, ANGLICO's higher headquarters

SOP standard operating procedure

TOW tube-launched, optically tracked, wire-guided missile, the heaviest antitank missile in the U.S. inventory

Type 531 a Chinese-made armored personnel carrier

V-150 the main armored personnel carrier used by the Saudis

XO the executive officer of a given unit, the second-in-command

SOURCES

Acts have their being in the witness. Without him who can speak of it? In the end one could even say that the act is nothing, the witness all.

—CORMAC MCCARTHY, *The Crossing*

THE JOURNEY that this book represents began for me the day I stepped off the bus in Quantico, Virginia, to begin Officer Candidates School. For better or worse, my brief time in the Corps shapes and informs the perceptions recorded herein. After leaving the service in 1998, I found myself wondering long and often how to reconcile my searing experiences with my new life on the outside. I'd served in the infantry, and while I had never tasted combat, I felt as if I'd done a lot of living in those four years, and as I tried to explain myself and my experiences to my civilian friends, I consistently found myself coming up short. I had met some pretty strange characters in the infantry. Killers. Snipers who had watched men die in their spotting scopes. Guys who needed the pain and exertion of the field to feel alive. For whom no order remained in the world save what Death and the Corps had put there. At the end of it I knew that inside of them was something that was not inside of me. I had met the killers of men and I was not one of them.

And yet, like many of my peers, I was strangely disappointed that I had never been shot at and was still curious what it was like. I had read all the manuals, I had been to all the schools, I'd heard an earful of late night yarns. But I still didn't know. I needed a story to tell to find out. One afternoon in the library I happened upon an old *Marine Corps Gazette* article about Khafji by Major General Admire. The product of this chance encounter is what you are currently holding in your hands.

As I began investigating this opening action of the Persian

Gulf War, I was repeatedly struck by the lack of surviving documentation about the conflict as a whole. Several excellent books have been written about the war, but almost all of the extant literature recycles the same anecdotes, strip-mining the original primary sources until the stories nearly reach the point of cliché. Sadly, the Marine Corps archives offered little more. There were precious few radio logs or oral histories or after-action reports to draw upon. However, as I began interviewing veterans of OP 4 and Khafji, the story quickly came to life. Times, dates, and places poured out of these men like water from a burst dam. Much of what they told me took me completely by surprise. So many of them told me how long they had waited for someone to ask them about what they had seen. They were shocked at what they had been through, but they were even more shocked that no one back home seemed to care. That it took twelve years for someone to interview these veterans does not speak well of our current literary establishment. I shouldn't have written this book. Someone else more quali-fied than I, with a better command of historiography and in touch with the alchemy of the written word, should have written it ten years ago.

INTERVIEWS

Major General John H. Admire USMC, ret.; Master Sergeant Luis Adrianzen USMC (formerly Luis Bench); Marion Alcorn; Dan Baczkowski; Colonel Rick Barry USMC, ret.; Lieutenant General Walt Boomer USMC, ret.; Paul Bowen; Lieutenant Colonel Jim Braden USMC; Jason P. Brown; Staff Sergeant John D. Calhoun USMC; Chief Kevin Callahan, USN, ret.; Master Sergeant Evan J. Chang USMC; Bill Covington; Gunnery Sergeant Mike Davis USMC; Scott Davis; Lieutenant Colonel Paul "Bubba" Deckert USMCR; Lieutenant Colonel Kris Elliot USMCR; Michael Eroshevich; Stephen Franke; Gunnery Sergeant Michael E. Garcia USMC; Captain Kenneth C. Gardner USMC; Joe E. Garza, Jr.; Master Gunnery Sergeant Gregory Gillispie USMC; Colonel Clay Grubb USMC ret.; Lieutenant Colonel Craig Huddleston USMC; Bill Iiams; Chuck Ingraham; Michael Kies; Lieutenant Colonel Douglas Kleinsmith USMC; Lawrence Lentz; Ken Lieuwen; Gunnery Sergeant Elisio Lozano USMC; Gunnery Sergeant David McNamee USMC; Lieutenant Colonel Joe Molofsky USMC; Lieutenant Colonel Max Morton USMC; Colonel Tom Murray USMC;

Lieutenant Colonel Dave Neely USMCR; Ken Pollack; Major Roger "Rock" Pollard USMC, ret.; Colonel Jeff Powers USMC, ret.; Major Tom Protzeller USMC; Scott Pruett; Derek Puterbaugh; Staff Sergeant Miguel Roche USMCR; Lieutenant Colonel Stephen Ross USMC; Mel Russell; Major Glenn Sadowski USMCR; First Sergeant Scott A. Sampson USMC; Colonel C. O. Skipper USMC, ret.; Major Phillip C. Skuta USMC; Marcus Slavenas; Staff Sergant Pat Sterling USMCR; Lieutenant Colonel Rory Talkington USMC; Gunnery Sergeant Tim Themer USMC; Phil Thompson; Ron Tull; Scott Uskoski; Sergant Major Alfonso Villa USMC, ret.; Chief Warrant Officer-2 Nick Vitale USMC; Scott Wagner; Major General Tom Wilkerson USMC, ret.; Lieutenant Colonel Scott P. Williams USMC; Michael Wissman.

BOOKS AND GOVERNMENT DOCUMENTS

Atkinson, Rick. *Crusade: The Untold Story of the Persian Gulf War.* Houghton Mifflin, 1993.

Barnett, Correlli. *The Desert Generals.* Cassell, 1999.

Blumenson, Martin. *Kasserine Pass: An Epic Saga of Desert War.* Jove, 1983.

Bolger, Daniel P. *Death Ground: Today's American Infantry in Battle.* Presidio Press, 2000.

Caputo, Phillip. *A Rumor of War.* Ballantine, 1977.

Clevenger, Maj. Daniel. *"Battle of Khafji": Air Power Effectiveness in the Desert.* Air Force Studies and Analyses Agency, July 1996.

Cohen, Eliot A., and Thomas Keaney, gen eds. *Gulf War Air Power Survey.* GPO, 1993.

Conrad, Joseph. *Lord Jim.* Oxford, 2000.

Cordesman, Anthony H. *Saudi Arabia: Guarding the Desert Kingdom.* Westview Press, 1997.

———. *The Lessons of Modern War, Volume 2: The Iran-Iraq War.* Westview Press, 1990.

———. *The Lessons of Modern War, Volume 4: The Gulf War.* Westview Press, 1996.

Crane, Stephen. *The Red Badge of Courage.* Modern Library, 2000.

Cureton, Charles H. *U.S. Marines in the Persian Gulf, 1990–1991: With the 1st Marine Division in Desert Shield and Desert Storm.* History and Museums Division, Headquarters, U.S. Marine Corps, 1993.

Foss, Christopher F. *Jane's Tanks and Combat Vehicles Recognition Guide,* 2nd Edition. Harper Collins, 2000.

Fromkin, David. *A Peace to End All Peace: The Fall of the Ottoman Empire and the Creation of the Middle East.* Henry Holt, 1989.

Glubb, Sir John Bagot. *A Short History of the Arab Peoples.* Stein and Day, 1970.

Gordon, Michael, and General Bernard Trainor. *The Generals' War: The Inside Story of the Conflict in the Gulf.* Little, Brown, 1995.

Gray, J. Glenn. *The Warriors: Reflections on Men in Battle.* Harper Torch Books, 1970.

Halberstam, David. *War in a Time of Peace: Bush, Clinton and the Generals.* Scribner, 2001.

Hemingway, Ernest. *By-Line: Ernest Hemingway.* Simon & Schuster, 1998.

Hemingway, Ernest. *For Whom the Bell Tolls.* Scribner, 1940.

Hemingway, Ernest. ed. *Men At War: The Best War Stories of all Time.* Bramhall House, 1979.

Heraclitus of Ephesus. *The Collected Wisdom of Heraclitus.* Trans. Brooks Haxton. Viking, 2001.

Herzog, Chaim. *The Arab-Israeli Wars: War and Peace in the Middle East from the War of Independence Through Lebanon.* Vintage, 1984.

Hiro, Dilip. *Desert Shield to Desert Storm: The Second Gulf War.* Routledge, 1992.

Ignatieff, Michael. *Virtual War: Kosovo and Beyond.* Metropolitan Books, 2000.

Khalid bin Sultan. *Desert Warrior: A Personal View of the Gulf War by the Joint Forces Commander.* Harper Collins, 1995.

Knightley, Phillip. *The First Casualty: The War Correspondent as Hero and Myth-Maker from the Crimea to Kosovo.* Johns Hopkins UP, 2002.

Lawrence, T. E. *Seven Pillars of Wisdom: A Triumph.* Anchor Books, 1991.

Lamb, David. *The Arabs: Journeys Beyond the Mirage.* Vintage, 2002.

Lewis, Bernard. ed. *A Middle East Mosaic: Fragments of Life, Letters and History.* Modern Library, 2001.

Liddell-Hart, B. H. *The Rommel Papers.* Da Capo, 1953.

Lippman, Thomas W. *Understanding Islam: An Introduction to the Muslim World.* Meridian, 1995.

McNabb, Andy. *Bravo Two Zero.* Island Books, 1994.

Melson, Charles D. *U.S. Marines in the Persian Gulf, 1990–1991: Anthology and Annotated Bibliography.* History and Museums Division, Headquarters, U.S. Marine Corps, 1992.

Michaels, G. J. *Tip of the Spear: U.S. Marine Light Armor in the Gulf War.* Naval Institute Press, 1998.

Moskin, J. Robert. *The U.S. Marine Corps Story.* McGraw-Hill, 1987.

Mroczkowski, Dennis P. *U.S. Marines in the Persian Gulf, 1990–1991: With the 2d Marine Division in Desert Shield and Desert Storm.* History and Museums Division, Headquarters, U.S. Marine Corps, 1993.

Norton, Bruce H. *Stingray.* Ballantine Books, 2000.

O'Brien, Tim. *The Things They Carried.* Penguin, 1990.

Pollack, Kenneth. *Arabs at War: Military Effectiveness, 1948–1991.* Nebraska UP, 2002.

Quilter, Charles J. *U.S. Marines in the Persian Gulf, 1990–1991: With the I Marine Expeditionary Force in Desert Shield and Desert Storm.* History and Museums Division, Headquarters, U.S. Marine Corps, 1993.

Reynolds, Colonel Richard. *Heart of the Storm: The Genesis of the Air Campaign Against Iraq.* Air University Press, 1995.

Schwarzkopf, H. Norman. *It Doesn't Take a Hero.* Bantam, 1992.

Shakespeare, William. *The Complete Works of Shakespeare.* Longman, 1997.

Sheehan, Neil. *A Bright Shining Lie: John Paul Vann and America in Vietnam.* Vintage, 1989.

Shrader, Charles R. *Amicicide: The Problem of Friendly Fire in Modern War.* U.S. Army Command and Staff College, 1982.

Simon, Bob. *Forty Days.* Putnam, 1992.

Stearns, LeRoy D. *U.S. Marines in the Persian Gulf, 1990–1991: The 3d Marine Aircraft Wing in Desert Shield and Desert Storm.* History and Museums Division, Headquarters, U.S. Marine Corps, 1999.

Thompson, Phillip. *Into the Storm: A U.S. Marine in the Persian Gulf War.* McFarland, 2001.

Thesiger, Wilfred. *Arabian Sands.* Penguin, 1991.

Tsouras, Peter G., ed. *The Greenhill Dictionary of Military Quotations.* Greenhill Books, 2000.

Underwood, Lamar. ed. *The Quotable Soldier.* Lyons Press, 2000.

Waller, Douglas C. *The Commandos: The Inside Story of America's Secret Soldiers.* Dell, 1994.

Wolff, Tobias. *In Pharaoh's Army.* Vintage, 1994.

Wright, Patrick. *Tank: The Progress of a Monstrous War Machine.* Viking, 2002.

Zimmeck, Steven M. *U.S. Marines in the Persian Gulf, 1990–1991: Combat Service Support in Desert Shield and Desert Storm.* History and Museums Division, Headquarters, U.S. Marine Corps, 1999.

ARTICLES

Admire, Brigadier General John H. "The 3d Marines in Desert Storm." *Marine Corps Gazette,* September 1991.

Apple, R. W., Jr. "Sixty Thousand Iraqis Mass Near Kuwait Town." *New York Times,* February 1, 1991.

Bird, Julie. "Confusion, Limited Air Force-Marine Training Contributed to Mistakes, Analysts Say." *Navy Times,* August 26, 1999, 13.

Bruton, James K. "The Subjective Side of Cross-Cultural Communication." *Special Warfare,* April 1994, 28–31.

Eshel, David. "Fighting Under Desert Conditions." *Marine Corps Gazette,* November 1990, 40–44.

Fuentes, Gidget. "Camp Pendleton Marine Honored for Persian Gulf Heroism." *North County Times,* February 18, 2001.

Granberry, Michael. "Marine Widow's Retreat to Disillusionment." *Los Angeles Times,* June 12, 1994.

Grant, Rebecca. "The Epic Little Battle of Khafji." *Air Force Magazine,* February 1998, 28–34.

Hackworth, David. "Friendly Fire." *Newsweek,* February 11, 1991.

Hedges, Chris. "Iraq Ruse." *New York Times,* January 31, 1991.

———. "Iraq Shells Empty Town." *New York Times,* January 21, 1991.

———. "Town Regained." *New York Times,* February 2, 1991.

Hughes, D. P. "Battle for Khafji." *Army Quarterly and Defence Quarterly,* January 1994.

Ignatieff, Michael. "Handcuffing the Military? Military Judgment, Rules of Engagement and Public Scrutiny." *Military Ethics for the Expeditionary Era.* ed. Patrick Mileham. Royal Institute of International Affairs, 2000, 26–32.

Jones, Robert A. "Firefight at Hamaltyat." *Marine Corps Gazette,* June 1991, 30–32.

Kershaw, Charles W. "Reconnaissance Battalion: Eyes and Ears in the Desert." *Marine Corps Gazette,* March 1992.

Kessler, Robert E. "Friendly Fire: 'Verdict' Long Island Firm Clear in Gulf Deaths, Admits Phony Test." *Newsday,* May 17, 1994.

Kufus, Marty. "Eyewitness to 'Friendly Fire.' " *Command,* April-May 1992, 46–52.

Lindow, Megan. "Marine Get Bronze Star Ten Years After Deed." *San Diego Union-Tribune,* February 18, 2001.

Maxwell, James J. "LAI: Impressions from SWA." *Marine Corps Gazette.* August 1991.

Metzger, Lieutenant General Louis. "Some Thoughts on Combat." *Marine Corps Gazette,* January 1993.

Mould, David, H. "Press Pools and Military-Media Relations in the Gulf War: A Case Study of the Battle of Khafji, January 1991." *Historical Journal of Film, Radio & Television,* June 1996.

Pollard, Roger L. "The Battle of OP-4: Start of the Ground War." *Marine Corps Gazette,* March 1992.

Radigan, Mary. "Former War Prisoner Reveals Iraqi Death Threat." *Grand Rapids Press,* March 2, 1997, A1.

Santoli, Al. "Lessons Learned in the Savage Eastertide Offensive Paid Off at the Battle of Khafji Almost Two Decades Later." *Military History,* February 1996.

Schmitt, Eric. "Five Years Later, the Gulf War Story Is Still Being Told." *New York Times,* May 12, 1996.

Sciolino, Elaine. "Reaction Worries Abused POW." *Austin-American Statesman,* June 30, 1992, A1.

Stanton, Martin N. "Khafji: Trial by Fire for the Saudi National Guard." *Armor,* March-April 1996, 6–11.

Taylor, John M. and Drew A. Bennett. "Word from the Front." *Marine Corps Gazette,* June 1991, 63–70.

Usry, Floyd J. "Stop Killing Each Other." *Marine Corps Gazette,* September 1992, 39–40.

Washabaugh, Bradford, G. "Friendly Fire: Time for Action." *Marine Corps Gazette,* September 1992, 37–39.

Ziv, Laura. "Gulf War Disease Is Slowly Killing Me." *Cosmopolitan,* June 1997, 142–148.

ORAL HISTORIES

Captain Jim Braden, USMC, U.S. Air Force Studies and Analyses Agency (hereafter AFSAA)

Brigadier General Thomas V. Draude, USMC, U.S. Marine Corps Historical Center, Washington, D.C. (hereafter MCHC)

Captain Rob Givens, USAF, AFSAA

General Charles Horner, USAF (ret.), AFSAA

Lieutenant David Kendall, USMC; MCHC

Lieutenant Colonel Cliff Myers, USMC; MCHC

Captain Roger Pollard, USMC; MCHC
Lieutenant Colonel M. L. Rapp, USMC; MCHC

UNPUBLISHED SOURCES

Command Chronology, 1st Reconnaissance Battalion, January-March 1991. MCHC.

Command Chronology, 3d Battalion, 3d Marines, December 1990. MCHC.

Command Chronology, 3d Battalion, 3d Marines, January 1991. MCHC.

Command Chronology, 3d Battalion, 3d Marines, February 1991. MCHC.

Command Chronology, Light-Armored Infantry Battalion, First Marine Division, January 1991. MCHC.

Frag Order 15–90, 1st Reconnaissance Battalion, 30 November 1990. MCHC.

Radio Journal, 1st Reconnaissance Battalion, 28 January–3 February 1991. MCHC.

Radio Journal, 3d Battalion, 3d Marines, 30 January–2 February 1991. MCHC.

1st Air Naval Gunfire Liaison Company, "After-Action Report for the Battle of Khafji, 29 January 1991–1 February 1991." Forwarded to author by former ANGLICO personnel.

Braden, Jim. "The Battle of Khafji: A Coalition Air Ground Task Force Victory." Diss. U.S. Marine Corps Command and Staff College, 1999.

al-Firmi, Turki. "The Battle of Khafji: 29 January–1 February 1991." Slide Presentation, Saudi Arabian National Guard.

Gumpert, C. A. "Trip Report: Division Air/Third MAW Coordination Meeting." October 22, 1990. MCHC.

Hendrickson, Colonel G. D. "Tiger Team Anti-Fratricide Report." February 10, 1991. MCHC.

Newell, John F., III "Airpower and the Battle of Khafji: Setting the Record Straight." Diss. Air University, 1998.

Palmer, Peter J. "Battle of Khafji: A Gulf State Perspective." U.S. Army Center for Lessons Learned. Undated.

Titus, James. "The Battle of Khafji: An Overview and Preliminary Analysis." Airpower Research Institute, 1996.

U.S. Department of Defense. *Conduct of the Persian Gulf War: Final Report to Congress, April 1992.* GPO, 1992.

Womack, Lieutenant Colonel R.J. "Investigation to Inquire into the Deaths of Sergeant G. A. Mongrella, et al. in an Engagement with Iraqi Forces on 29 January, 1991, in the Vicinity of the Saudi-Kuwaiti Border." February 22, 1991. MCHC.

NOTES

PREFACE

xi Epigraph: Conrad, 37.

xi Mystique of Khafji: author's personal experiences.

xxii "The battle of Khafji ushered in a new era in American military history": Titus, 1. Gordon and Trainor, 268, 288.

xii "Ten-foot-tall giants," Admire interview.

xii "They had rolled into the Kuwaiti emirate": Pollack, 236–237.

xiii "There was no reason to expect an easy victory in this first war": Admire, Ingraham, Molofsky, Williams interviews.

xiii "Marine commanders began reshaping their offensive plans": Gordon and Trainor, 288. Boomer interview.

xiv "Leading these men was a graying cadre of Vietnam veterans": Santoli, Admire interview.

xv "War is the father and king": Heraclitus, 29.

PROLOGUE

1 Epigraph: Wilfred Owen quotation from Underwood, 123.

1–7 This section is based on extensive interviews with Gillispie, Ross, Roche, and Adrianzen along with the Kufus *Command* article and Norton's *Stingray,* which includes an interview with then-Staff Sergeant Jeffrey Buffa.

CHAPTER 1

11 Epigraph: Chuikov quotation from Tsouras, 118.

11 "An air campaign the likes of which the world had never seen": Halberstam, 47–56; Gordon and Trainor, 75–102.

12 "Handpicked to fire the opening salvos": Atkinson, 17–19.

12 For more on this notion of "virtual war," see Ignatieff, *Virtual War: Kosovo and Beyond.*

12 "Nevertheless, Saddam was far from defeated": Stearns, 122. For Tawakalna Division figures, see Gordon and Trainor, 329.

12–13 Iraqi III Corps: Pollack interview. See Pollack's *Arabs at War,* 243–245. Also Gordon and Trainor, 268. Mahmoud's preeminence is further underlined by the fact that he was one of two generals selected by Saddam to conduct the Iraqi surrender at Safwan on March 3, 1991.

13 Boomer's dream: Stearns, 140.

14 For information on "the Great Scud Hunt," see Gordon and Trainor, 227–249 and Waller, 396–417. See also McNabb's *Bravo Two Zero,* which describes a famously harrowing and controversial anti-Scud patrol conducted by the British Special Air Service.

14–15 Myatt's "ambiguity operations": Protzeller interview. See also Cureton's now-rare 1st Marine Division history of the war. Also Melson, 134–135, 173–182.

14 Attack on Observation Post 6: Chang interview; Jones *Marine Corps Gazette* article.

16 The Iraqi plan: Gordon and Trainor, 268–269; Titus 3–5; Newell, 13, 15–33; Pollack interview.

16 Kibrit: Skipper interview. See Zimmeck, 106–107; Gordon and Trainor, 276, 295; Melson, 157.

16–17 Coalition's inward focus: Gordon and Trainor, 272; Titus, 6; Newell, 20–21; Sterling interview.

17 85% casualties: Williams, Puterbaugh interviews. The grim casualty expectations were a recurring theme during many of the inteviews I conducted with LAV Marines.

17 Exploitation of American satellite patterns: Gordon and Trainor, 271. Iraqi communications security: Pollack interview.

CHAPTER 2

19 Epigraphs: Bible, King James Version, Thomason quotation from Thomason, John W. *Fix Bayonets!* Scribners, 1926. p. 4.

19–36 The lion's share of this chapter is based on interviews with Gillispie, Ross, Roche, Adrianzen, and Talkington, along with Norton's *Stingray.*

24 "Beautiful lunatics": Adrianzen interview.

25 Leadership style of Captain Bean: Gillispie, Ross, Ingraham interviews.

26 "Indeed, the mythology of the 1990s Marine Corps": author's personal experiences.

30–32 Desert operations: Kershaw, Eshel; Gillispie and Ingraham interviews.

31 "Several units were issued maps formerly used by British Airways pilots": Wissman interview.

32 DRP's deployment along border taken from Buffa interview in Norton.

33 Buffa's recollections of the beginning of the air war: Norton, 319.

34 "One Marine from 3rd Recon who'd always been a tiger in training": McNamee interview.

34 "You just never knew what to expect from one day to the next": Adrianzen interview.

35–36 Bob Simon's capture: Gillispie, Roche, Talkington, Kleinsmith interviews and Simon's *Forty Days.*

35 "What I did was a stupid mistake" Schmitt, *New York Times* article.

CHAPTER 3

37 Epigraph: Lawrence, 29.

37–45 This chapter is primarily based on interviews with Gillispie, Ross, Roche, Adrianzen, and Talkington along with Kufus's *Command* article and *Stingray.*

38 The description of OP 4 is derived from scores of photographs, video, satellite imagery, veterans' descriptions, and maps of the area. Notable among the maps is the British Military Survey 1:50,000 scale K7611 5547-III map sheet.

39 Treaty of Uqair information taken from Fromkin, 17, 510.

41 Information on Claymore mines derived from the Federation of American Scientists website and from the author's personal notes from The Basic School, Quantico, Virginia.

CHAPTER 4

46 Epigraphs: Lawrence, 196; Hemingway, xviii.

46–64 This chapter is based largely upon interviews with the battle's main participants, including Pollard, Tull, Covington, Sadowski, Vitale, Wissman, Pruett, Brown, Williams, and Villa. The timeline was established from Pollard's *Marine Corps Gazette* article and Colonel Womack's investigation of the A-10 fratricide.

48 "Like Ross, Pollard had no reason to expect action this evening": Alpha Company, LAI battalion had conducted a border raid near OP 4 on the twenty-seventh, which failed to provoke an Iraqi response.

48 Pollard, "fucking screening mission," comment taken from Protzeller interview.

48–49 Commentary on the newness of the LAV concept is taken from Protzeller, Garza, Pollard, Powers, James Maxwell's *Marine Corps Gazette* article and the author's personal experiences. I have several good friends who served in LAV units and had an opportunity to drive a "hog" once.

57–60 The Plan Purple episode is based on interviews with Pollard, Sadowski, Tull, Villa, Williams, and Powers and is reflected in the LAI Battalion Command Chronology.

61 Characteristics of the TOW missile system and the A/N-TAS-4A thermal sight were taken from the Federation of American Scientists website and from the author's personal notes from The Basic School.

CHAPTER 5

65 Epigraph: Lawrence, 248.

65–72 Timeline derived from Womack investigation, Pollard article, and Vitale interview. The dialogue for this section is based on Jason Brown's excellent unpublished account "Green One, Red One," and was buttressed with interviews with Nick Vitale Derek Puterbaugh, Scott Pruett, and Michael Wissman. Brown went to great lengths to help me with this chapter and with the entire LAV-TOW group story, answering dozens of e-mails and explaining minutiae relevant to the night in question.

65 "They ain't roller-skating out there": Puterbaugh interview.

70–72 Delta's stand-to taken from Pollard, Tull, and Covington interviews and Womack investigation.

CHAPTER 6

73 Epigraph: Wright, 40–41.

73–79 This chapter is based upon my interviews with Ross, Roche, Gillispie, Adrianzen, Davis, Buffa's account in *Stingray* and the Marty Kufus article in *Command* magazine. The chronology was corroborated by the 1st Reconnaissance Battalion radio logs found in the Marine Corps Historical Center. Gillispie's recollections regarding radio transmissions and situation reports to the rear were accurate down to the minute. It was well known among the Marines that AT-4s and the older 66-mm LAWs were largely ineffective against Warsaw Pact main battle tanks. Nevertheless, many of the Marines spoke of hoping for a lucky "mobility kill" on one of the behemoths by knocking off some tank treads.

79 The atmospheric conditions at OP 4 for January 29 were garnered with the aid of Mr. Marion Alcorn, M.Sc. of the Texas A&M University Meteorology Department.

CHAPTER 7

80 Epigraph: Remarque quotation from Tsouras, 103.

80–82 The first section is based on my interviews with Gillispie, Ross, Roche, and Michael Kies overhead in *Blaze 71*. Kies's and Ross's recollections agree in almost every particular.

82–83 The story of the two recon teams in the police post was based upon my interviews with Master Sergeant Adrianzen, Gunnery Sergeant Mike Davis, *Stingray*, and the Kufus article, which is based on an interview with team leader Sergeant Thomas Manney. Blackwell's miraculous flare shot was recalled by Marines at both positions.

83 Initially, I was skeptical when I heard Marine claims about the strangely effective Iraqi jamming, thinking perhaps that they were making excuses for sloppy radio work. However, as I tracked down other participants of the battle, I discovered that units outfitted with the newer, frequency-hopping SINCGARS radio sets, which are immune to traditional jamming methods, had solid radio communications throughout the fight, a fact that pointed to jamming as the likely cause of the widespread comm failures. The Iraqi jamming is also noted in several 1st Reconnaissance Battalion Team Debriefs found at the MCHC.

85–88 There has been no love lost between Delta Company and the Deep Reconnaissance Platoon over the years. Pollard still can't understand why the recon Marines opened up with their machine guns at the tanks, a move that necessitated Delta's advance upon the police post to extract the pinned-down platoon. Ross and Gillispie both contend that Delta was more of a threat to their safety than anything else and wrote a stinging letter to the editor in response to Pollard's March 1992 *Marine Corps Gazette* piece. In the jointly written missive they argue, "Contrary to the [Pollard] article, the recon platoon forward deployed at OP 4 received no assistance from the LAI company to its rear. Recon was neither rescued nor supported by LAV fire during any part of the action." They go on to say that they remained hunkered down behind the horseshoe because (1) more A-6s were thought to be en route and (2) they wanted to assist in the anticipated battle handover with Delta Company. Ross and Gillispie assert that they only abandoned their position after learning Delta had halted its advance because of the loss of the LAV-TOW to friendly fire.

CHAPTER 8

89 Epigraph: Conrad, 8.

89–92 First section timeline and sequence of events derived from Womack investigation, Kendall oral history, Pollard article and interview, Williams, Tull, Covington interviews.

92–93 Second section dialogue and events taken from Brown account and interview and Vitale interview and checked against Wissman, Pruett, and Puterbaugh interviews.

92–93 Third section based on Pollard article and interview, Sadowski, Tull, Vitale.

93 Lawrence quote: 375. The passage in question bears a striking resemblance to the events of January 29: "Night came down, and the valley became a mind landscape. The invisible cliffs boded as presences; imagination tried to piece out the plan of their battlements by tracing the dark pattern they cut in the canopy of stars. The blackness in the depth was very real—it was a night to despair of movement."

CHAPTER 9

94 Epigraph: Shakespeare, 1054.

94–95 The first section of this chapter is drawn from Gordon and Trainor's *The Generals' War,* 278–279, Titus's USAF study and Major John F. Newell's revisionist thesis, "Airpower and the Battle of Khafji: Setting the Record Straight."

94 Republican Guard 50% attrition goal: Gordon and Trainor, 190.

94–95 Horner's message to Schwarzkopf is taken from Newell, 20.

96–97 The second section is based on my interview with Colonel Jeffrey Powers and Myers' MCHC oral history.

97–98 The Second Marine Division's role in the battle is described in Gordon and Trainor, 274–275 and Mroczkowski, 20–22.

98 The scene at Kibrit is based on my interviews with Colonel C. O. Skipper, Gordon and Trainor, 276, and Zimmeck, 106–110.

CHAPTER 10

99 Epigraph: Steinbeck, 31.

99 Timeline derived from Womack investigation and Vitale, Brown, Wissman, Pruett, and Puterbaugh. Much of the dialogue in this section is based upon Brown's unpublished account.

102–104 The second section of this chapter is based on my interview with Bill Covington and the Kendall MCHC oral history.

104 Pollard's recollections in this chapter are derived from his *Marine Corps Gazette* article and from my interviews with him. Pollard appears to be the only one who still believes that Green 2 was destroyed by enemy fire. In the LAI battalion command chronology for the period January 1 to February 28, 1991, a document that was generated in Saudi Arabia less than a month after the battle for OP4, Green 2 is listed as destroyed by friendly fire. To virtually every other participant in the battle it seemed clear that one LAV-TOW had shot another LAV-TOW. Bill Covington told me that Marine leaders had initially attempted to cover up the fratricide until enlisted men from Delta Company protested. He cited a confrontation between a Delta Marine and General Boomer during a question-and-answer session after the liberation of Kuwait.

Nick Vitale recalls, "The TOW guys never claimed it to be anything other than a fratricide. For awhile there the powers that be were saying that it was a vehicle kill [i.e. enemy-inflicted]. That was the word coming down. The first debrief I gave, when I was OPCON'd [i.e. transferred] back to Alpha Company was that it was a fratricide. There wasn't anyone trying to convince me otherwise but I had heard it from one or two people and I had been around TOWs long enough and I read a blast pattern and I understand things about 'Okay, if one of my gunners shoots a missile and it goes for 2.7 seconds, it's gone 620 meters,' you know, I'm not stupid.

"At that point I'd fired probably 100-plus missiles, I know what they do to things. I know how to read a blast pattern. That vehicle [Green 2] was hit from behind by a TOW."

104–107 The fourth section of this chapter is based upon Brown's excellent account and my interviews with Vitale, Wissman, Pruett, and Puterbaugh. The details about Octol were taken from the Federation of American Scientists website and www.ordnance.org.

107–108 The fifth section is derived from Tull.

108–112 The sixth section is derived from Ross, Roche, Gillispie, and Bench.

112–116 The final section of this chapter is taken from my interviews with Pollard,

Williams, Sadowski, Tull, and the Kendall oral history. "It was strange fighting at night": taken from Pollard's *Marine Corps Gazette* article, 49.

CHAPTER 11

117 Epigraph: Ignatieff, 27–28.

117–127 The foundation for this chapter is the Womack fratricide investigation, which elaborately establishes the overall timeline and major characters in play. Events and details were added by my interviews with Tull, Williams, Pollard, Covington, Gillispie, Bench, Villa, and Roche. Several Delta Marines claimed credit for the idea of directing the A-10s with the LAV's 25-mm Bushmaster cannon.

119 Details regarding the functioning of the A-10 and the Maverick missile system were derived from the Pentagon's *Conduct of the Persian Gulf War* (Appendix T), Raytheon Corporation's website (the current manufacturer of the Maverick), the U.S. Air Force's web-based fact sheets as well as the venerable Federation of American Scientists' website (www.fas.org). In 1993, relatives of six of the Marines who died in *Blaze of Glory* filed a multimillion-dollar negligence lawsuit against Hughes Aircraft (then manufacturer of the Maverick). The lawsuit was later thrown out of federal court in Los Angeles on the grounds that it would compromise national security and the so-called "contractor defense," which protects defense manufacturers working in good faith from litigation. While one of the subcontractors of the Maverick, Lucas Aul of Garden City, New York, was later cleared of any responsibility for the death of the seven Marines it did admit to falsifying test results for defective missile components. One of the plaintiffs, Carol Bentzlin, widow of Corporal Stephen Bentzlin, was particularly outspoken in her dissatisfaction with the outcome of these suits and was quoted in *Newsday* saying, "Nobody's ever held responsible for friendly fire." Dion Stephenson's family notably declined to participate in any litigation against either Hughes Aircraft or Lucas Aul.

119 Air Force A-10 crews earned a mixed reputation during the Gulf War. Among ANGLICO Marines, arguably the most experienced forward air controllers in theater, A-10 crews were often viewed with suspicion. One senior ANGLICO officer told me, "I'd rather have an Iraqi battalion in front of me than an A-10 overhead." Jim Braden was a bit more even-minded on the subject and thought that the problem resided in the relatively green reservist A-10 pilots, who had arrived late in theater and had undergone practically no night training. The identity and experience level of the pilot of *Hitman 75* has never been released by the Air Force.

CHAPTER 12

128 Epigraph: Thesiger, 89.

128–135 This chapter is based on my interviews with the TOW Marines, including Vitale, Brown, Wissman, Pruett, and Puterbaugh. The Alpha Company experience is drawn from G. J. Michaels's excellent memoir *Tip of the Spear*.

131–132 Tull's apparent hallucinations are drawn from my interview with him.

133–134 For an alternative version of events on the morning of January 30, see Captain William H. Weber IV's letter to the editor in the June 1992 issue of the *Marine Corps Gazette* (p. 64). Weber, a platoon commander with Alpha Company, takes issue with the conduct of the battle as a whole, commenting in his Amazon.com review of. Michaels's book that "the author is too kind to some of the leaders of our battalion, men who deserve to be excoriated for their role in the friendly-fire deaths of eleven of our Marines." Owing perhaps to the space limitations intrinsic to a forum such as Amazon.com, Weber never fully explains what he thinks should have been done to prevent the friendly-fire deaths.

CHAPTER 13

136 Epigraph: Vegetius quotation from Caputo, 2.
136–149 This chapter is based upon my interview with Protzeller and Sampson at Camp Pendleton; Powers, Cureton's divisional history, and Gordon and Trainor, 275.

CHAPTER 14

153 Epigraph: This epigraph is a general bromide that has made its way into the Marine canon. Its exact origin is unknown.
153–170 This chapter is based on my interviews with Lozano, Russell, Kleinsmith, Calhoun, Barry, Atkinson's *Crusade*, 201–203, and the Fuentes and Lindow news pieces. Also of great utility were the maps forwarded to me by General Bernard Trainor. Lieutenant Colonel Kleinsmith subsequently briefed me using these maps, which greatly aided my spatial understanding of the events leading to the fall of Khafji.
154, 156–157 The portions dealing with ANGLICO's rotation up to the border forts were informed by my extensive talks with Lieutenant Colonels Jim Braden, Doug Kleinsmith, and Kris Elliot and emails traded with Colonel Grubb. The description of ANGLICO's technical prowess was based on my interviews with over twenty ANGLICO Marines, Lieutenant Colonel Joe Molofsky, my own professional experiences, and the judgment of U.S. Army Special Forces personnel who asked to remain anonymous. See also Melson, 143–144.
155 Passages regarding the odd World War I–like atmosphere in the border region are derived from my interviews with DRP and ANGLICO Marines and from 1st Reconnaissance Battalion Team Debriefs of the period (MCHC). These debriefs describe Iraqi soccer matches going on inside Kuwait. One recon team was "mooned" by several Iraqi soldiers.
159–161 Kurt Lang was later blamed by some for compromising Marine radio communications for the entire theater. While it is true that Lang's men abandoned their radios and other sensitive equipment, they did so under great duress. At one point Kleinsmith addressed Lang's critics, asking, "Have you ever been overrun by a bunch of tanks?" Personally, I'm inclined to agree with Kleinsmith's assessment.
161–170 The OP 7 section is based on my interviews with Kleinsmith, Braden, Deckert, Elliot, Calhoun, Neely, Gordon and Trainor, 276–277 and the excellent 1st ANGLICO after-action report.
161–163 Braden's Marine Corps Command and Staff College thesis presents the most complete discussion of Bley's observations. See pp. 8–9. Also Gordon and Trainor, 271.
162 "This prophecy never reached the men up at OP 7": Braden and Kleinsmith group interview. Kleinsmith let out a good-natured scoff when Bley's near-clairvoyance was recounted.
167 The 5th Battalion of the SANG was charged with screening the northeastern portion of the Kuwait border. By all accounts they evacuated with utmost haste at the first signs of the Iraqi charge. See Gordon and Trainor, 274–275 and Pollack, 436.

CHAPTER 15

171 Epigraph: Wolff, 132–133.
171–177 This section is based on my interviews with Barry, Boomer, Admire, Elliot, Lentz, Lozano, Russell, Kleinsmith. Jon Fleming's recollections are recorded in Atkinson's *Crusade*, 201–203.

172 Barry was not alone in his suspicions of Iraqi defectors. The Marines' experience at OP 6 on January 21–22 was reason enough to be leery of Iraqi "defectors."

172 Barry's account of the Harrier raids near Wafra on the twenty-eighth roughly correlate with Bley's experiences in the same timeframe. See Braden, 8–9.

172 Iraqi attack expected along the Wadi al-Batin, see Gordon and Trainor, 268; Titus, 5.

177–189 The Max Morton section is based upon my interviews with him, Jim Braden, Ross, Gillispie, Marines working in the Direct Air Support Center at Safaniya on January 29, and the Stearns official history, 124–127.

CHAPTER 16

190 Epigraph: Crane, 7.

190–202 This chapter is based on interviews with Ingraham, Callahan, Sterling, Lentz, McNamee, Slavenas, Wagner, Admire, Iiams, Baczkwoski, Thompson's *Into the Storm*, 132–144, the 3/3 Command Chronologies, the Stanton *Armor* article, and a 3rd Marines staff officer who asked to remain anonymous. Lentz's ordeal is described in Atkinson, 204, 208–211. Chuck Ingraham and Doc Callahan aided me immensely with this chapter. All times and occurrences were reviewed via email and telephone. On the rare occasion where there was dissent among the team members, I deferred to the majority opinion.

CHAPTER 17

203 Epigraph: Lawrence, 202.

203–211 This chapter is based upon my interviews with Lentz, Slavenas, Wagner, Ingraham, Sterling, Callahan, McNamee, Baczkowski, and Thompson. The May Day parade simile is drawn from Lentz's and Ingraham's comments. Also of great utility were the maps lent to me by General Trainor and the extensive video footage forwarded by Ingraham. Doc Callahan also sent me dozens of graphic after-battle photographs. For specifications of the Chinese Type 531 and pictures of an abandoned specimen in Khafji, see Foss, 138–139. For notes on the history and characteristics of the 5th Mechanized Division, see Pollack, 243–244.

211–213 The second section of this chapter is taken from Khalid's *Desert Warrior*, 361–390, Gordon and Trainor, 278–279, Braden, Admire, and Molofsky interviews. I should point out that Khalid's chronicle of the battle has been vigorously disputed by several Americans who were at Khafji. However, as it remains the singular full Arab account of the battle, I felt compelled to include limited portions of it. Additionally, Khalid was privy to conversations and events far from the purview of any American in Saudi Arabia at the time and gives readers a rare look into the inner working of the Saudi government and military.

211–213 Khalid "King Fahd wanted quick results" quote, 376; "I believe the main reason for the delay" quote, 369–370.

CHAPTER 18

214 Epigraph: Hemingway, 43.

214–219 This chapter is derived from my interviews with Ingraham, Callahan, Sterling, McNamee, Lentz, Wagner, and Baczkowski, several hours of documentary videotape, scores of veteran photographs, several U.S. NIMA 1:50,000 maps, along with diagrams drawn for me by Ingraham. I was also able to use an edited version of a detailed letter Ingraham wrote to his parents immediately following the battle. The wealth of detail for this portion of the story presented a challenge in the sense that much of the information had to be clarified and deconflicted. I did this by re-interviewing both Ingraham and Callahan, whose slightly differing recollections frequently served to complement each other.

CHAPTER 19

220 Epigraph: Lawrence quotation from Lewis, 305.

220–252 This chapter is based on my interviews with Braden, Elliot, Kleinsmith, Deckert, Molofsky, the Braden oral history, Braden's Command and Staff College thesis and the 1st ANGLICO after-action report. The history of the Saudi Arabian National Guard is drawn from Cordesman's *Saudi Arabia: Guarding the Desert Kingdom*, Fromkin, 326, and Pollack's indispensable *Arabs at War*, 425–446. In reference to the Saudi-U.S. military relationship, Pollack notes, "U.S. military personnel placed little faith in Saudi combat capabilities. Based on the experience many had had with them in training or on joint operations, the Americans largely assessed that the Saudis could contribute little to the Coalition campaign against Iraq. Many, including high-ranking U.S. officers, expected the Saudis to run away en masse when the first shots were fired. In addition, experienced U.S. officers noted the Saudi tendency to dissemble and obfuscate rather than admit a mistake. As a result, U.S. military commanders carefully constructed Coalition operations to minimize the role of the Saudis and to make sure that they only went into battle under optimal conditions. U.S. air and artillery forces were assigned to provide fire support to Saudi units, which were given only supporting missions in less critical sectors of the front, and U.S. military personnel were attached to Saudi forces to provide advice and to make sure that their reporting was accurate," 434. Pollack also notes that in 1979 when rising tensions with neighboring Yemen prompted a Saudi mobilization, nearly all of the SANG's 400 armored cars were nonoperative due to widespread maintenance problems, 642–643.

222 In regards to the Saudi use of Marine close air support, Stearns, in the somewhat sanitized official history of the 3rd Marine Aircraft Wing, writes, "As the artillery raids continued, Marine ANGLICO teams assigned to the Joint Forces Command East north of Mishab worked closely with the 3rd MAW to arrange offensive air support for its drive into Kuwait. Toward this end, General Moore [the head Marine aviator in theater] expected to provide close air support to the Arab force, JFC-E. *Although important from a political perspective, he did not want to over-commit Marine air to the diverse Saudi coalition force.* [italics mine] With no tradition of close air-ground cooperation to speak of, these forces were not fully capable of exploiting the synergy of such a relationship [hence the need for Grubb's ANGLICO teams]," 122–123. Moore's reticence about supporting the Saudis would have ramifications later.

223–226 The passages regarding ANGLICO's experience living among the Arabs were drawn from my extensive talks with Elliot, Murray, Deckert, Grubb, Kleinsmith, Braden, Molofsky, Russell, Lozano, Garcia, and Franke.

226–228 Kleinsmith's escape is based on interviews and map studies with him, Braden, Molofsky, Deckert, Elliot, emails exchanged with Calhoun, Gordon and Trainor, 276–277.

229–235 The sections that address Melissa Coleman (née Rathbun-Nealy) and David Lockett's capture were taken from my interviews with Callahan, Ingraham, Admire, Huddleston, Molofsky, Elliot, a 3rd Marines staff officer who asked to remain anonymous, the Radigan, Sciolino, Ziv articles as well as from information from the non-profit POW Network's website.

235–238 The section that deals with Kleinsmith's redeployment to the north of Khafji was taken from my interviews with Kleinsmith, Braden, Deckert, Elliot, emails traded with Calhoun, in addition to the 1st ANGLICO after-action report and Braden's Command and Staff College thesis.

238–241 The section dealing with Baczkowski's rescue plans for the trapped teams comes from my interviews with him, Iiams, Thompson, Admire, Molofsky, a former 3rd Marines staff officer who asked to remain anonymous, the Stanton article and the Palmer paper available on the U.S. Army's Center for Lessons Learned website.

241 Lieutenant Colonel Taylor quote taken from Palmer, 12.

242–252 The description of Molofsky's arrival at the Khafji Café was derived from my numerous interviews with him, Baczkowski, Iiams, Braden, Kleinsmith, Deckert, Admire, Gillispie (who knew Molofsky before the battle of Khafji occurred) and notes taken by Lieutenant Colonel John Meagher forwarded to me by General Trainor.

CHAPTER 20

253 Epigraph: Gray, 125.

253–267 This chapter is drawn from my interviews with Molofsky, Baczkowski, Admire, Iiams, Braden, Thompson, Gordon and Trainor, 281–282, the Turki al-Firmi briefing, the ANGLICO after-action report, Lieutenant Colonel Stanton's article, 8–9, and Braden's thesis 11–13. I tried to use Khalid's chronicle of this portion of the battle but found it so grossly inaccurate and so intent upon dissembling what was by all accounts a catastrophic counterattack that I had to abandon any attempts at reconciling it with my other sources.

268–271 Members of both trapped teams vividly recalled the failed first counterattack. Ingraham sent me a copy of the microcassette tape made during the battle. It is an amazing peek into the heart of combat.

268–273 For this chapter's final section on the air war, I employed Clevenger's extensive AFSAA study, which is available on CD-ROM. The Givens oral history is included as an appendix on the CD. See also Titus, 10, 15–21, Gordon and Trainor, 283–284. Newell's more recent thesis provides a good balance to the Clevenger and Titus accounts, both of which stop just short of saying that the U.S. Air Force won the battle single-handedly.

272–273 The *Spirit 03* passages were derived from Gordon and Trainor, 283–284, Atkinson, 210. The website www.specialoperations.com also presents an uncorroborated but plausible account. See also "Death at Daylight," *Pensacola News Journal*, February 23, 1992.

CHAPTER 21

274 Epigraph: Sheehan, 84.

274–284 This chapter is drawn from my interviews with Kleinsmith, Braden, Deckert, and Calhoun, Scott Davis at the Marine Direct Air Support Center at Safaniya, the 1st ANGLICO after-action report, and Braden's thesis. See also Pollack's *Arabs at War,* 439, Stanton, 9 and Hughes, 21.

278–279 Lawrence observed numerous instances of looting by Bedouin tribesman during the Arab Revolt. After one of his famous train ambushes he observed, "The valley was a weird sight. The Arabs, gone raving mad, were rushing about at top speed bareheaded and half-naked, screaming, shooting in the air, clawing one another nail and fist, while they burst open trucks and staggered back and forward with immense bales, which they ripped by the rail-side, and tossed through, smashing what they did not want. . . . To one side stood thirty or forty hysterical women, unveiled, tearing their clothes and hair; shrieking themselves distracted. The Arabs without regard to them went on wrecking the household goods; looting their absolute fill. Camels had become common property. Each man frantically loaded the nearest with what it would carry and shooed it westward into the void, while he turned to his next fancy," 369.

284–286 This second section dealing with Braden in the 2nd SANG command bunker was drawn from my interviews with Braden, Kleinsmith, Murray, Thompson, emails traded with Colonel Grubb, the 1st ANGLICO after-action report, Braden's 1999 Command and Staff College thesis, and Thompson's *Into the Storm,* 141.

CHAPTER 22

287 Epigraph: O'Brien, 78.
287–292 This chapter is based on interviews with Ingraham, McNamee, Sterling, Callahan, and Thompson, and Thompson's *Into the Storm,* 134–144.

CHAPTER 23

293 Epigraph: Hemingway, 312.
293–323 Lentz, Ingraham, Callahan, Sterling, and Thompson, and on Thompson, *Into the Storm,* 134–144.
297–299 Several ANGLICO Marines claim that Ingraham was not in fact controlling the Harriers, which appeared shortly after the large artillery strike. This is possible, although Lentz also discussed calling in the Harriers, which makes me think it was a larger team effort. In any event, American Marines of some stripe were calling in these pivotal airstrikes. I should add that these same ANGLICO Marines have been unusually assertive in their opinions about what Ingraham and his Marines did and did not do despite the fact that they were not present in the building. Their arguments appear to be based largely upon rumor and hearsay. The ANGLICO after-action report describes it thus: "As the attack progressed an artillery mission from the recon teams through Wild Eagle 1–2 [Captain Mark Dillard's ANGLICO team] was fired into a group of enemy APCs on a major intersection of the city. Right after, a white phosphorous round was fired as a marking round in the same area. Captain Dillard then brought in two AV-8s [Harriers] with a Rockeye drop. *Many enemy vehicles were caught in this one-two punch* [italics mine]. Other sections began checking in but they had to be passed north to the battle there. By now the fighting had become very intertwined through the city streets. Sifting enemy from friendly became difficult to impossible," 6. Phil Thompson, back at 1/12, didn't recall talking to ANGLICO about any artillery mission until after the two large DPICM missions had been fired.
297–299 The passages describing Ingraham's rescue were derived from my interviews with Baczkowski, Iiams, Molofsky, Ingraham, Callahan, McNamee, Sterling, the 1st ANGLICO after-action report, and diagrams produced by Ingraham for me. Pollack describes this second counterattack: "The Saudis again conducted a frontal assault, without maneuver, covering fire, or combined arms coordination; they just marched forward behind the artillery and air strikes, stopping occasionally to add their own fire to the attack. When they reached the town itself, the Saudis ran helter-skelter through the streets, firing in all directions and mostly abandoning their formations, rather than conducting a determined, block-by-block clearing operation. The Iraqis fought back at first but were simply overwhelmed by the magnitude of the firepower

they faced—'smothered by fire' in the words of one U.S. liaison officer," 440. Pollack's account of the battle is accurate, but as he himself admitted, he had little to no knowledge of ANGLICO's activities during the battle and never interviewed any Marines present at Khafji.

308–314 The section dealing with Lentz's exfiltration is based on my interview with him, Wagner, Slavenas, Uskoski, and Atkinson's *Crusade,* 211.

314–323 My description of the final hours of the battle is drawn from my interviews with Kleinsmith, Braden, Calhoun, Elliot, Deckert, the 1st ANGLICO afteraction report, Braden's thesis, and the Stanton article.

EPILOGUE

324 Epigraph: Hemingway, *By Line: Ernest Hemingway,* 267.

324 Schwarzkopf's elephant comment taken from Gordon and Trainor, 289 & Mould article.

324–325 "No major changes were made in the overall offensive set to roll two weeks after Khafji": Gordon and Trainor, 287–289, 308, 431, 464, 473.

325 Marine perceptions of Khafji: Gordon and Trainor, 294–296, 355; Atkinson, 212; Braden thesis, 18–20.

327 In 1996, the U.S. Air Force commissioned a series of studies on Khafji, which on balance seem aimed to seize credit for the Coalition victory at Khafji. James Titus argues in his study for the Air Force's Air Research Institute, "The battle of Khafji was preeminently an airpower victory," 1. In a concluding section titled "Can Airpower Alone Stop Advancing Ground Forces?" Titus continues [sic], "Indeed, perhaps the question is no longer: Can airpower stop advancing ground forces? But rather more simply: How much airpower is required to do so?" 25–26. A February 1998 *Air Force* magazine article by Rebecca Grant takes the issue a step further: "The conclusion, for some, is that the U.S. should put more emphasis on airpower and less on ground forces," 6. Daniel Clevenger's extensive study is similarly slanted toward this unilateralist Air Force view of Khafji. Taken as a whole, the symphony of Air Force studies, while valuable in their discussion of previously classified events and dialogue, reads more like a carefully scripted lobbying effort than a genuine attempt at history. Without launching into a detailed taxonomy of the inter-service rivalries involved, I think it is fair to say that the Coalition win at Khafji resulted from the efforts of a broad spectrum of players both on the ground and in the air, both Air Force and Marine, Arab and American.

327–328 The SANG interpretation of Khafji: it is rumored that Colonel Turki collects a stipend for his actions at Khafji. I was also informed by Americans who lived in Saudi Arabia after the war that the SANG holds an annual celebration in observance of its victory at Khafji. Owing in part to the suffocating secrecy that pervades Saudi society, my numerous entreaties to the SANG and MODA offices in Washington, D.C., and Riyadh were largely ignored.

329 "Much has been made of the casualties caused by friendly fire in Desert Storm": Lieutenant General Louis Metzger, *Marine Corps Gazette,* January 1993.

329 Tull's response taken from my interview with him.

331 Ignatieff quotation taken from *Virtual War,* 5. Lee quotation: Tsouras, 514.

ACKNOWLEDGMENTS

FIRST AND FOREMOST I must thank the scores of Marines former and otherwise whom I interviewed for this book and who entrusted me with the treasure of the memories. They are the lifeblood of this work. In particular, I would like to thank Jim Braden, Jason Brown, Kevin Callahan, Kris Elliot, Gregory Gillispie, Chuck Ingraham, Doug Kleinsmith, and Joseph Molofsky for their patience and dedication in helping to preserve this important chapter of history.

Lieutenant Colonel Kris Elliot deserves special recognition for turning me on to the ANGLICO story. This crucial aspect of Khafji has long been overlooked and might have been omitted from this volume had not Kris phoned one afternoon saying, "You're missing something big."

I wish to express my sincerest gratitude to my literary agent, the estimable Agnes Birnbaum of Bleecker Street, whose initial encouragements led to this project. Her wise counsel throughout this process has been beyond measure.

Special thanks go out to my family and friends, who provided inexpressible amounts of support and encouragement over the life of this project. I could not have done it without you. My father's early enthusiasm and support for the book when it was little more than a half-baked idea was instrumental. Kudos to Ryan R. Sims, my partner in crime, who always understood, always helped, always saw. To my reading group, the Midnight Philosophy Club: Joe Garza, Ryan Sims, Todd Kiker, Mitchel "Sleepyhead" Zafer, Nathan "YoYo" Phelps, Joel Kiker, Stephen Chupaska, and Jonathan Sims. Thanks to Peter Zafer, whose initial sketches led to the maps for this book. To my great brood of buddies for tolerating my endless grumpiness and absenteeism.

Thanks also go out to Stephen Morrow and Bill Rosen for their foresight and ardor for this project from its inception. It has been an unexpected pleasure working with my editor, Liz Stein, whose dedication to this book has been a tremendous asset especially given its unusual provenance. Similarly, I would like to salute Stephanie Fairyington for her continued assistance and general Johnny-on-the-spot-ness.

Much of the source material for the Khafji story was originally collected by Lieutenant General Bernard Trainor for use in his book *The Generals' War.* He graciously shared these precious papers with me and helped me develop sources that might otherwise have remained unavailable. Thank you and *Semper Fidelis*.

I am indebted to Ken Lieuwen and Chief Warrant Officer-2 B. Sean Fairburn for their assistance in locating the LAV Marines who fought and were bloodied at OP 4. Ken's website (www.1ofthefew.com) was an excellent resource for me throughout the long months of research.

Thanks go out to Amy Eldridge and Marcia Straile for their help in transcribing the scores of interviews for this book. Amy's startling maturity and professionalism were a breath of fresh air.

I have long considered Anita Karl and James Kemp's maps to be works of art, and it is a true joy to present their work as an accompaniment to this volume.

Last, I would be remiss if I failed at this late hour to issue my thanks and gratitude to Dear Old Mom.

INDEX

Abdulaziz Ibn Saud, King of Saudi
    Arabia, 211, 221
Abkins, Lance Corporal, 80, 111
AC-130 Spectre gunships, 271–72
Admire, John, xiv
    and battle for Khafji, 200–202, 212,
        227, 231, 234–35, 239, 248,
        285
    and capture of U.S. soldiers, 234–35
    Molofsky's military career and, 245
    and relations between Marines and
        Arab Coalition Forces, 248, 250
Air Force, U.S., 74, 224
    air campaign and, 11–14, 269–73
    Arab Coalition Forces and, 223
    and battle for Khafji, 162, 211–13,
        217–18, 277, 327
    on friendly-fire incidents, 327–29
    outpost battles and, 96, 117–27,
        130–31, 132–35
All Quiet on the Western Front
    (Remarque), 80
Alpha Company, 3rd Reconnaissance
    Battalion, U.S., 123, 128,
    133–34, 143
Alpha Group, TOW Platoon, 1st Light-
    Armored Infantry (LAI)
    Battalion, U.S.:
    casualties of, 103–13, 115, 122, 124,
        128
    Delta Company's defensive positions
        and, 46, 60–64, 65–70
    outpost battles and, 90–93, 99–112,
        115–16, 120–21, 128–31,
        133–34
al-Wafra, 270
    and battle for Khafji, 162, 172
    oil fields of, 94n, 143
Anderson, Lance Corporal, 81
Apache helicopters, 12
Arab-American Oil Company
    (ARAMCO), 185n, 215
Arab Coalition Forces:
    and battle for Khafji, 211–13,
        220–23, 225–26, 230–33,
        235–41, 253–66, 285–86, 300,
        304, 313
    and escape of Marines from Khafji,
        313–14
    relations between Marines and,
        223–26, 228, 231, 235–41,
        241–42, 245–51, 261, 266,
        281–82
    see also National Guard, Saudi
        Arabian
Arabian Sands (Thesiger), 128
Arab-Israeli Wars, The (Herzog), 244
Arabs at War (Pollack), 208n
armored personnel carriers (APCs), 14,
    221
    and battle for Khafji, 167, 176, 203,
        207, 233, 237, 251, 253–58,
        274–79, 281, 290–91, 294, 298,
        303–7, 309–10, 314–16, 317–19,
        320–21
    V-150, 240n, 247, 251, 253–54, 256,
        274, 276–78, 281
Army, Iraqi, 61–64
    and Army-Marine withdrawal from
        OP 7, 165–69
    and battle for Khafji, 129–70,
        171–77, 192–99, 201–8, 209–13,
        216–19, 222, 226–35, 237, 239,
        248, 251–52, 253–63, 265–69,
        274–85, 287–319, 320–22,
        324–28, 329–31
    casualties of, 131–35, 143, 146,
        147–48, 162, 219, 258, 272, 278,
        282, 316, 327, 331–32
    Coalition air campaign and, 11–12,
        94–95, 228–30
    and Coalition offensive in Kuwait,
        16–17, 326–27
    Delta Company's defensive positions
        and, 62–63, 66–71
    deserters from, 2, 48, 137n, 153–55
    and escape of Marines from Khafji,
        305–8, 309–13
    evaluations of, xii–xiv, 70, 149, 208n,
        325–26

Marines trapped by, 208, 212,
216–17, 227, 262, 265–69, 274,
285–86, 287–306, 308–13,
331–32
media and, 35
misinformation tactics of, 171
Myatt's operation and, 14
OP 4 and, 1–6, 38–41, 43–44, 75,
78–88, 89–92, 93, 95
OP 6 and, 14, 144–49
outpost battles and, 80–88, 89–92, 93,
95–98, 99–104, 107–26, 129–35,
137–49, 172–73, 179–80, 266
prisoners from, 15, 98, 134–35, 149,
153–56, 271*n*, 278, 282, 302–3,
327–28, 333
prisoners taken by, 35, 228–35, 238,
247, 334
snipers and, 310
units of, 13–17, 94–96, 208, 221, 271,
325–26
Army, U.S., 12, 17, 20, 32, 37, 38*n*, 48,
226, 245, 331–32
and battle for Khafji, 154, 161–62,
164–70, 175, 197, 228–35, 238,
247, 321–23, 325–26
cargo truck incident and, 228–35, 247
equipment of, 32
outpost battles and, 133, 164–70
prisoners from, 228–35, 238, 247,
334
relations between Arab Coalition
Forces and, 238
A-6 Intruders:
and battle for Khafji, 162–64, 184,
277
outpost battles and, 80, 83–87,
117–18
Astro rockets, 155, 172, 178, 192–93,
272, 283–84
A-10 Thunderbolts, 270
and battle for Khafji, 162, 277
in friendly-fire incidents, 119, 123,
125
outpost battles and, 114, 117–27,
133–35, 328
AT-4 antitank rockets:
backblast from, 76
and battle for Khafji, 175, 261, 265,
269, 309
at OP 4, 1–2, 7, 77–78

outpost battles and, 81–83, 86–87,
102–3
Avenetti, Quint, 291, 294, 298

B-52s, 4, 114, 211–12
Babski, Lance Corporal, 75, 80
Baczkowski, Dan, 333
background of, 199–200, 201–2
and battle for Khafji, 195, 199–202,
238–41, 242, 251–52, 256–66,
268, 301–3, 306–9
and escape of Marines from Khafji,
306–8
and retreat of Barry, 200–201
Baron, Lance Corporal, 256, 260, 269,
301
Barry, Rick, 161, 266
and battle for Khafji, 163, 171–72,
191–96, 199, 200, 248
retreat from Khafji of, 173–75,
193–94, 199, 200–201, 275
safe house of, 192–93
Baumgardner, Jason, 122, 133
Bean, Mike, 25–26, 30
Bedouin tribes, 34, 38*n*, 221, 241, 278,
301–2
Bench, Luis, 41, 75–78, 81–82, 85, 109
Bioty, John R., ix
Blackwell, Lance Corporal, 82
Bland, Clifford, 272
Bley, John, 161–62, 318
Boileau, Jason, 76, 92
Boomer, Walt, xiv, 326
and battle for Khafji, 158, 172, 213,
326
Coalition air campaign and, 13
and Coalition offensive in Kuwait, 16,
326
Borth, John:
and battle for Khafji, 249, 255
and capture of U.S. soldiers, 232–33
Braden, Jim, 245, 327, 333
Arab Coalition Forces and, 220–25,
228
and battle for Khafji, 170, 212,
220–22, 226–28, 237, 247, 249,
284–86, 316, 318
Molofsky's relationship with, 245–46
suspected fratricides and, 282*n*, 300*n*
and whereabouts of Kleinsmith, 220,
226–27

Bradford, Kent, 240
Bright Shining Lie, A (Sheehan), 274
British Airways, 31
Brown, Jason, 60–61, 63–64, 333
    Delta Company's defensive positions
        and, 65–67
    outpost battles and, 92, 100–108,
        130
    Walker's relationship with, 104–5
Brown, Jeffrey, 207, 266–67, 295–96,
    304
Buffa, Jeffrey, 24, 33, 77, 82
Burrows, Dave, 65–68, 72
Bush, George H. W., xiii

Calhoun, John, 226–27
    and battle for Khafji, 162, 168, 235,
        320–21
Callahan, Kevin "Doc," 207, 312, 333,
    335
    artillery support and, 295–97, 299
    and battle for Khafji, 192, 206–10,
        218, 228–29, 266–67, 290,
        295–96, 299, 303–5
    escape from Khafji of, 306
    on U.S. cargo truck incident, 228–29
Camp 15, 29
Camp Pendleton, 22, 51, 243
Camp Schwab, 20–27, 29–30, 42, 76
CBS, 35
Central Command (CENTCOM), U.S.,
    320*n*, 325
Central Intelligence Agency (CIA),
    137*n*
Charlie Company, 3rd Light-Armored
        Infantry (LAI) Battalion, U.S.,
        136–49
chemical weapons, 13, 17, 178
Chuikov, Vassili I., 11
Civil War, 49, 331
Claymore mines, 41, 215, 288–90, 306
cluster bombs, 270
    and battle for Khafji, 164, 285
    outpost battles and, 85–86
CNN, xi , 12, 16
Cobra attack helicopters, 333, 334–35
    and battle for Khafji, 164–65, 175,
        177–89, 221–22, 230, 250, 258,
        279–81, 282*n*, 316
    outpost battles and, 114, 131, 133,
        179–82

Conner, Staff Sergeant, 47–58
Conrad, Joseph, xi, 89
Cooper, Alan, 203, 310
Cotto, Ismael, 103–6, 128–29, 130*n*
Courtnay, Corporal, 156–57, 160, 176
Covington, Bill, 52–53, 63, 102–3
Crane, Stephen, 190
Crosby, Benz, 67–69, 92
Cruise, Tom, 245, 251, 254
Cruz, Corporal, 174, 176
Cummings, Beaman, 83–85, 108–9

Davis, Mike "Strike," 21
    OP 4 and, 2–6, 44, 77
    outpost battles and, 81–82, 85
Dayrit, Carlos "Doc," 311–12
Deckert, Paul "Bubba," 241*n*, 327
    and battle for Khafji, 162, 220–21,
        228, 236–38, 251, 274–83
    sickness of, 224
Deep Reconnaissance Platoon (DRP),
        Charlie Company, 3rd
        Reconnaissance Battalion, U.S.,
        17, 20–46
    communications of, 73–76, 82,
        85–87, 90, 108, 111, 118
    Delta Company's defensive positions
        and, 46, 68
    desert experience lacked by, 30–31
    equipment of, 26, 29–32, 42–43
    hygiene of, 43
    Iraqi probes and, 43–45
    in Okinawa, 20–26, 30, 42, 76–77
    OP 4 and, 1–6, 37–45, 73–79
    outpost battles and, 80–92, 94–95,
        97–98, 102–3, 107–15, 117–18,
        124–26, 134–35
    in Philippines, 26–27
    reputation of, 76, 112
    in Saudi Arabia, 28–36, 78
    in transit to Saudi Arabia, 27–29
Defense Department, U.S., 15, 234
Dell, Gunnery Sergeant, 126
Delta Company, 3rd Light-Armored
        Infantry (LAI) Battalion, U.S.,
        46–64, 65–72, 104–35
    casualties of, 59, 123, 126, 131–35,
        142–45
    defensive positions of, 46–49, 62–64,
        65–72
    deranged atmosphere in, 57

modified command structure of, 55–56
OP 4 and, 48, 126
outpost battles and, 84–88, 89–93, 96,
    99, 101–3, 104–35, 141, 144–45
predeployment organization of, 50–53
reputation of, 49, 55
in Saudi Arabia, 53–72
TOW antitank vehicles and, 46,
    61–64, 65–72
training of, 49–55, 107, 127
Desert Shield, Operation, 223
Desert Storm, Operation, 27, 167,
    328–29
Desert Warrior (Khalid), 211–13, 282n
Dillard, Mark, 315, 318
Dual-Purpose Improved Conventional
    Munition rounds, 294

East of Eden (Steinbeck), 99
8th Regular Saudi Land Force Brigade,
    228
82nd Airborne Division, U.S., xiii
Elliot, Kris, 224, 283
    and battle for Khafji, 237, 274, 318,
    322
"Exposure" (Owen), 1

Fahd, King of Saudi Arabia, 211, 249,
    249n, 266
F-18 Hornets, 114
    and battle for Khafji, 217, 284
1st Air-Naval Gunfire Liaison Company
    (ANGLICO), U.S.:
    and battle for Khafji, 153–70,
    171–77, 193–94, 220–23,
    225–26, 235–38, 246, 250–51,
    274–86, 300, 314–16, 317–23,
    327
    outpost battles and, 164–70, 235–36,
    247–48
    prisoners taken by, 153–55, 282
    relations between Arabs and, 220–26,
    228, 235–38, 242–47, 265n
    suspected fratricides and, 253n
    training of, 155
1st Battalion, 9th Marines (1/9), U.S.,
    50–53, 118
1st Battalion, 12th Marines (1/12), U.S.,
    239, 291–95, 298, 300
1st Force Reconnaissance Company,
    U.S., 14, 71

1st Marine Division, U.S., 2, 48–49,
    226, 245, 326–29
    and battle for Khafji, 212, 240,
    241–42, 247–50
    Myatt's operations and, 14
    outpost battles and, 136–38, 227
1st Marine Expeditionary Force (MEF),
    U.S., 173
1st Reconnaissance Battalion, U.S., 22,
    29, 32
1st Surveillance, Reconnaissance, and
    Intelligence Group, U.S., 161,
    171–77, 191–95, 199
Fisk, Robert, 320n
Fix Bayonets! (Thomason), 19
Fleming, Jon, 163–64, 174–77, 315
For Whom the Bell Tolls (Hemingway),
    288, 293
Foss, Steve, 167–68, 235–36
fragmentation grenades, 288–91, 311

Garcia, M. E., 265n
Garrett, J. J., 249–51, 255
Generals' War, The (Trainor and
    Gordon), 325
Gillispie, Gregory, 20–29, 78–79, 333
    in Okinawa, 20–27
    OP 4 and, 1–6, 40, 43–44, 78
    outpost battles and, 80, 81n, 83, 85,
    88, 109, 124–26, 134–35
    in Philippines, 27
    in Saudi Arabia, 29, 33–36
    in transit to Saudi Arabia, 26–28
Gilmore, Sergeant, 93
Givens, Rob, 270, 272
Global Positioning System (GPS), 32, 195
Glosson, Buster, 95
Gordon, Michael, 325
Gray, George, 271–72
Gray, J. Glenn, 219n, 253
Great Britain, 16n
    media and, 269n–70n
    OP 4 and, 37–38, 39n
Grubb, Clay:
    Arab Coalition Forces and, 222, 226
    and battle for Khafji, 154, 222,
    284–85

"Handcuffing the Military?" (Ignatieff),
    117
Handling Hejazi Arabs, 220

Haney, Scott, 179, 181–82, 188
Harrier jump jets:
  and battle for Khafji, 156, 164, 172,
    277, 281, 298, 315
  outpost battles and, 108–10, 114, 146
Heartbreak Ridge, 24
Hellfire missiles, 12, 280
Hemingway, Ernest, 46, 214, 293, 324,
    331
Henderson, Lance Corporal, 44
Heraclitus, xv
Hernandez, Sergeant, 148
Herzog, Chaim, 244
Hewitt, Andy, 274, 276–77
Hezbollah, 244
Higgins, Richard, 243
Ho Chi Minh, 15
Holcomb, Keith, 97
Horner, Chuck, ix, 94–95, 211, 269
Horney, Kurt, 277, 281–82
Huddleston, Craig, 230–35, 240
Huey helicopters, 186, 220, 245–46, 284
Humvees, 6, 29–33, 41–45, 51, 76,
    229–30
  and Army-Marine withdrawal from
    OP 7, 167–69, 205, 209
  and battle for Khafji, 156–61,
    167–69, 174, 177, 190–91, 197,
    200–202, 231–32, 235, 239, 241,
    249–58, 263, 276, 280, 283, 291,
    302, 306, 310, 313–14, 318–20,
    334
  and capture of U.S. soldiers, 232
  and escape of Marines from Khafji,
    305–7, 309–10, 311–14
  outpost battles and, 80–82, 91,
    110–11, 125
Hussein, Saddam, *see* Saddam Hussein

Ignatieff, Michael, 117, 331
Iiams, Bill, 199, 333
  and battle for Khafji, 239–41,
    251–52, 254–66, 301–3, 306–8
  and escape of Marines from Khafji,
    305–8
Independent, The, 320n
Ingraham, Chuck, 333
  artillery support and, 291–95, 298,
    304–5
  and battle for Khafji, 191–95,
    198–202, 198–99, 200–202,

206–11, 214–19, 249, 262, 285,
    288–92, 293–95, 298–309, 326
  and burning of documents and
    personal letters, 209–11
  and Coalition offensive in Kuwait,
    207–9
  escape from Khafji of, 305–9
  suspected fratricides and, 300n
In Pharaoh's Army (Wolf), 171
Instant Thunder, Operation, 11
Into the Storm (Thompson), 209n
Iran-Iraq War, xii, 13, 17, 149, 208,
    271n
Iraq:
  Kuwait invaded by, xii–xiv, 50, 94,
    95n, 244, 304
  Saudi Arabia invaded by, xiii, 15–17,
    27, 32, 48, 137, 142, 144, 212,
    272
Israel, 14, 243–44

Jestel, John, 21
  OP 4 and, 2–5, 77
  outpost battles and, 67–68, 70–71
Joint Surveillance Target Attack Radar
    System (JSTARS), 94n, 269n
Jubail, 178–80, 188
Julius Caesar (Shakespeare), 94

Kendall, Dave, 52, 91, 102–3, 112–13
Kershaw, Charles, 29
Keys, Bill, 98
Khafji:
  Barry's retreat from 174, 194,
    199–201, 275
  escape of Marines from, 305–14
  and Iraqi invasion of Saudi Arabia,
    16, 137
  map of, 204
  Marine escape plans in, 198, 209
  Marine observation posts in, 175–77,
    203–8, 210, 214–17, 228, 248,
    267, 293–99, 303–6
  Marines trapped in, 208, 212–13,
    217, 227, 262, 265–69, 274,
    285–86, 287–306, 308–13,
    331–32
  outpost battles and, 96, 136–38,
    140–41
  U.S. Army cargo track incident in,
    228–35, 247

Khafji, battle for, xi–xiv, 13*n*, 153–70,
171–77, 177–89, 190–223,
226–43, 247–52, 253–73,
274–86, 287–332
and air support, 153–60, 162–65, 169,
172, 175, 177–89, 192–93,
195–96, 201, 211–13, 217–19,
221–22, 230, 250, 258, 268–73,
276–82, 282*n*, 283, 297–300,
314–17
and ANGLICO, 153–70, 169–77,
193–94, 220–23, 225–26,
236–38, 246, 250–51, 274–86,
300, 314–16, 317–23, 327
and Arab Coalition Forces, 211–13,
220–23, 226–29, 230–33,
235–41, 253–66, 285–86, 300,
303–5, 313
and Army-Marine withdrawal from
OP 7, 139–70
artillery support in, 251, 284–86,
291–303, 304–5, 314–15
casualties of, 162, 219, 231, 233, 255,
258, 263, 278, 282, 298–300,
314–17, 326–27, 329, 336
end of, 322–23
and 1st Marine Division, 212, 240,
241–43, 247–50
and 1st Surveillance, Reconnaissance,
and Intelligence Group, 161,
171–77, 191–95, 199
and fratricides, 264, 281–82, 282*n*,
300–301*n*
Iraqi defenses in, 216–19, 263
Iraqi retreat in, 278, 282–83, 297–98,
317
and media, 234, 319, 324, 331
prisoners taken in, 228–35, 238, 247,
278, 282, 302–3, 327–28, 334
and SANG, 167–70, 176–77, 194–99,
220–21, 228, 231, 235–41,
247–52, 253–69, 271, 274–86,
288–89, 291, 301–8, 313–23,
327
Saudi counterattacks in, 249–52,
253–69, 274–86, 288–89, 290,
301–5, 314–23
significance of, xii, 324–38, 329–32
sniper problems in, 310–11, 321,
322–23
and 3rd Marines, 192–93, 199, 209*n*,

231, 234, 239, 247–51, 284–86,
291, 300
and 3rd Platoon, Alpha Company, 3rd
Reconnaissance Battalion,
191–202, 203–13, 229, 239–41,
247–52, 254–69, 274, 287–91,
293–309
and 3/3, 230–35, 240, 247–48
urban warfare in, 314–16
warnings before, 153–54, 156,
171–74
Khafji Café, 240–41, 247, 249, 255
Khalid bin Sultan al Saud, Prince, ix,
211–13, 249, 282*n*
Kibrit, 16, 213
and battle for Khafji, 182–85
outpost battles and, 95–98
Kies, Michael, 83–85, 108–9
Kleinsmith, Doug:
Arab Coalition Forces and, 221, 225,
237, 241*n*
and battle for Khafji, 159–70,
227–28, 235–38, 251, 274–82,
315, 318–23, 333
media and, 319
retreat from OP 7 of, 164–70, 220,
225–26, 238, 247, 267, 319–20
sniper problems and, 320–21
suspected fratricides and, 281–82
Krulak, Chuck, 97–98
Kuwait, 11–17, 277–79
and battle for Khafji, 157, 161–63,
171–72, 220, 229, 239, 261, 278,
317
Coalition air campaign and, 11–14,
33, 95, 269–73
Coalition offensive in, 16–17, 32–33,
58*n*, 192, 213, 282*n*, 324,
326–28, 333
Iraqi invasion of, xii–xiii, 50, 94, 95*n*,
244, 304
Myatt's operations and, 14
oil fields of, 95*n*, 137, 143–44

Lang, Kurt:
and battle for Khafji, 155–63, 174–77
outpost battles and, 266
Lawrence, T. E., 37, 46, 65, 93, 203,
220, 225, 242, 246*n*, 275, 278*n*,
301, 334
Lee, Robert E., 332

Lentz, Lawrence, 334
    artillery support and, 296–97
    and battle for Khafji, 161–73, 175,
        182n, 248, 252, 268–69, 285–86,
        293–95, 296–99, 308–14
    escape from Khafji of, 310–14
    escape plan of, 197–98
    sniper threat and, 310
    theater master communications chart
        of, 196–97
light anti-armor weapons (LAWs), 82,
    175, 214n, 258, 269
light-armored vehicles (LAVs), 37–43,
    47–53, 57, 84–86, 203n
    and battle for Khafji, 180–81
    capabilities of, 49, 61
    Delta Company's defensive positions
        and, 46–49, 62–64, 67, 72
    friendly-fire attacks on, 123, 126–27,
        131–35, 143–45, 328
    OP 4 and, 51–53
    outpost battles and, 86–88, 90–93,
        97–98, 101–2, 107–12, 117–20,
        121–27, 129–30, 131–35,
        136–41, 143–49, 180–81,
        327–32
    training with, 55
    see also TOW antitank vehicles
Lindaro, Colonel, 285
Lockett, David, 229–35, 334–35
long-range navigation (Loran), 182–83
Lord Jim (Conrad), xi, 89
Lozano, Elisio, 153–61, 173–77, 315

McAvoy, Mike, 82
McCracken, Corporal, 27
McNamee, David:
    and battle for Khafji, 208, 210,
        214–17, 287–88
    contents of rucksack of, 214n
    escape from Khafji of, 306–7
    hypervigilance of, 215–16
Mahmoud, Salah Aboud, 13, 273, 317
Manney, Thomas, 3, 21
    outpost battles and, 81n, 134–35
    in Saudi Arabia, 30, 32
Manza, John, 143
Marine Corps, U.S.:
    air campaign and, 33–34
    command structure of, 179–80, 189
    media and, 35–36

    in Okinawa, 20–28, 30, 42, 76
    at OP 4, 37–49, 73–79
    in Philippines, 22–23, 27
    relations between Special Forces
        teams and, 32
    in Saudi Arabia, 28–36, 53–72, 78
    in transit to Saudi Arabia, 27–29
Marine Corps Gazette 249n, 328
Markaz az Zabr, 38, 40–43
Matar, Lieutenant Colonel, 240n,
    249–50, 253–56
Matthew, Gospel according to Saint, 19
Maverick missiles:
    Coalition air campaign and, 270
    outpost battles and, 118, 118n, 121,
        123, 133, 328
Men at War (Hemingway), 46
Mercer, Lance Corporal, 81–82
Michaels, G. J., 131, 133–34
Ministry of Defense and Aviation
    (MODA), Saudi Arabian, 317,
    321
Mishab, 170, 310
    and battle for Khafji, 162, 172,
        177–81, 183–84, 188, 192, 195,
        198–99, 199–201, 206, 213, 216,
        228–35, 235, 240, 249n, 252,
        267, 291
Mitchell, Marcus, 112
modular universal laser equipment
    (MULE), 157–59, 280–81
Molofsky, Joe, 240, 241–51, 326–27, 334
    background of, 242–45
    and battle for Khafji, 212, 240–41,
        242, 247, 250, 253–56, 265–66,
        301
    and capture of U.S. soldiers, 247–48
    and relations between Marines and
        Arab Coalition Forces, 220–26,
        228, 245, 248–51
Mongrella, Garett, 108, 123–24
mortars, mortar vehicles, 139, 238
Morton, Max, 335
    and battle for Khafji, 177–89, 198
    on Marine command structure,
        179–80, 189
Mould, David, 320n
M-60 machine guns, 3, 7, 33, 81
    and battle for Khafji, 274, 277, 318
M-203 grenade launchers, 82, 159–60,
    175

M-249 squad automatic weapons
(SAWs), 77, 82, 86, 205
Myatt, Mike, 14, 326
Myers, Cliff, 70

Naif, Lieutenant, 239, 251, 256, 260, 263
National Guard, Saudi Arabian (SANG),
220–23, 327, 334
and Army-Marine withdrawal from
OP 7, 167–70
and battle for Khafji, 136, 167–70,
175, 194, 196–99, 221, 226–28,
230–32, 235–41, 247–52,
253–69, 271–72, 274–86,
288–89, 290–91, 301–8, 313–23,
327
casualties of, 255, 263, 279, 281,
314–16, 326–27
and escape of Marines from Khafji,
305–14
history of, 221
looting of, 279, 281
military incompetence of, 246–47,
249–50, 256, 259–60, 265–66,
284
prisoners taken by, 278
retreat from Khafji of, 198–99
suspected fratricides and, 281
training of, 221–23
units of, 167, 169–70, 198n, 220–21,
226, 229, 236, 240n, 247,
249–50, 274, 277–78, 283–84,
314–19, 321–23
see also Arab Coalition Forces
Navy, U.S., 23, 61, 79n, 312
and battle for Khafji, 155–56, 171,
174, 193–94
sea, air, land (SEAL) teams of, 37,
154–56, 171, 174, 193–94, 333
NBC, 234, 320n
Neely, Dave, 164–68
New People's Army, 27
Noriega, Manuel, 60

O'Brien, Tim, 287
Observation Post 2 (OP 2), 97, 158
Observation Post 3 (OP 3), 34–35
Observation Post 4 (OP 4), 1–2, 59n,
73–79, 80–88
and battle for Khafji, 172–73,
180–83, 209n

communications of, 3–6, 41, 73–76
defenses behind, 46–49, 68
defenses of, 41, 43
DRP at, 1–7, 37–45, 73–79
geography of, 1–2, 37–42
hygiene at, 43
Iraqi attack on, 80–88
Iraqi probes at, 44
location of, 1–2
Marine evacuation of, 127
Marines at, 37–45, 73–79
mission at, 2–5, 41
outpost battles and, 89–92, 93, 95–98,
104–5, 107–8, 109–15, 117–20,
124, 126, 133, 136–37, 140–44,
172–73, 179–83, 227, 327–32,
333
weaponry at, 3, 7, 41, 45
Observation Post 5 (OP 5), 138–44
Observation Post 6 (OP 6), 14, 38n, 39,
143
and battle for Khafji, 227
dislodging Iraqis from, 147–48
outpost battles and, 96–97, 136–37,
139, 141–49
Observation Post 7 (OP 7), 32–33, 235
and battle for Khafji, 158–70, 275
Marine withdrawal from, 164–70,
220, 226–28, 247–48, 266–67,
319–20
Observation Post 8 (OP 8), 38n, 283
and battle for Khafji, 153–64, 172,
176
outpost battles and, 173, 272
Ogden, U.S.S., 28
Okinawa, Marines in, 20–28, 30, 42, 76
outpost battles, 80–149
air support and, 80, 83–87, 91–92, 96,
108–10, 111–27, 131, 133–35,
145, 172, 179–82, 272–73,
327–28
Alpha Group and, 90–93, 99–112,
115–16, 120–21, 128–31,
133–34
ANGLICO and, 164–70, 235, 248
and battle for Khafji, 172–73,
180–83, 247–48
casualties of, 100–113, 115, 119–23,
125–27, 131–35, 143–46,
148–49, 328–32
Charlie Company and, 136–49

outpost battles (*cont'd*)
Delta Company and, 85–88, 89–93,
96, 99, 101–2, 104–35, 141–42,
144–45
DRP and, 80–88, 89–92, 94–95, 98,
103, 107–14, 118, 124–26,
134–35
friendly-fire incidents in, 100–114,
115, 119, 122, 125–27, 131–35,
143–44, 327–32
and Iraqi invasion of Saudi Arabia,
142, 144
OP 4 and, 89–92, 93, 95–97, 105,
107–8, 109–15, 117–20, 124,
126, 133, 136–37, 140–44,
172–73, 180–83, 227–28,
327–32, 333
OP 7 and, 164–70, 220, 226–28,
247–48, 266–67, 319–20
prisoners taken in, 134–35, 149
2nd Marine Division and, 97
standoff tactics in, 91*n*
OV-10 spotter planes, 164–68, 284
Owen, Wilfred, 1

Pacheco, Lance Corporal, 87, 109
Palestinians, 173, 244
Panama, U.S. invasion of, 60
Persian Gulf War:
air campaign of, 4, 11–16, 33–35,
94–95, 144, 171, 199–200,
269–73
casualties of, 15, 57–58, 100–114,
115, 119–23, 126–27, 131–35,
142–46, 148, 162, 180–81, 219,
230, 233, 255, 258, 263, 272,
278, 282, 297–300, 315–16, 324,
326–32, 336
cause of, xiii
end of, xiii, 334
media and, xi , 12, 15, 35–36, 319,
331
prisoners taken in, 12–13, 28–29, 82,
112–13, 124–25, 129–31, 144,
193–98, 202, 209, 229*n*, 234,
238, 255, 276, 281–83
Philippines, 23, 27, 51–52
Pollack, Kenneth M., 208*n*
Pollard, Roger "Rock," 43–60, 334
background of, 53–54
Conner's plan to kill, 57–60

Delta Company's defensive positions
and, 46–48, 63
demeanor of, 53–57, 59, 86
LAV training and, 55
outpost battles and, 86–87, 89–93,
101–4, 107–10, 112–15, 122–27,
130, 136
Sadowski's relationship with, 54,
56–57
TOW antitank vehicles and, 61
Williams's relationship with, 56
Powers, Jeff, 56, 96, 138–43
Protzeller, Thomas:
outpost battles and, 136–49
reprimands received by, 139–40
Pruett, Scott, 66
background of, 61
outpost battles and, 100–102, 104–5,
130
psychological weapons, 15–16
Purple, Plan, 57, 93
Puterbaugh, Derek, 65, 106

Qatar, Qatari military, 97–98
and battle for Khafji, 154, 221, 233,
240, 247, 251–52, 256, 259,
263–65, 267, 300, 304, 313
casualties of, 263–64
and escape of Marines from Khafji,
313–14
and Iraqi invasion of Saudi Arabia, 15

Radcliffe, Lance Corporal, 256, 260,
269, 301
Rapp, Michael, 43–44
Rathbun-Nealy, Melissa, 194–35, 238,
254
imprisonment of, 334–35
Reagan, Ronald, xiii
Red Badge of Courage, The (Crane),
190
Remarque, Erich Maria, 80
Rietsch, Manfred A., 12
Riyadh, 126
and battle for Khafji, 172, 178, 211
Coalition air campaign and, 94–95
Roche, Miguel "Pete," 23–24
OP 4 and, 3–5, 43, 75–76
outpost battles and, 80, 81*n*, 71,
91–94, 105
in Saudi Arabia, 30–33

rocket-propelled grenades (RPGs), 15, 43
  and battle for Khafji, 254, 280, 315, 321
  OP4 and, 4
  outpost battles and, 144
Ross, Steven, 17, 24–28, 77–79, 335
  in Okinawa, 20, 24–28
  OP 4 and, 1–7, 37, 40, 46–48, 73–76, 78–79
  outpost battles and, 80–81, 81n, 82–88, 90–91, 108–11, 114, 133–34
  in Saudi Arabia, 29, 32–35
  in transit to Saudi Arabia, 26–29
Russell, Mel, 153, 156–57, 160, 176

sabkhas, 31, 215, 226
  and Army-Marine withdrawal from OP 7, 166–69
  and battle for Khafji, 251, 254, 277
Sabot ammunition, 89, 121
Saddam Hussein, xiv, 37, 55, 221, 246, 325
  and battle for Khafji, 211
  Coalition air campaign and, 11–15, 33–34, 273
  Iran-Iraq War and, 12, 14
  and Iraqi invasion of Kuwait, 50, 95n, 244
  and Iraqi invasion of Saudi Arabia, 15–18, 48
  Kuwaiti oil field fires and, 144
  physical appearance of, 207
Sadowski, Glenn, 51
  Conner's undermining of, 57
  outpost battles and, 92–93, 114
  Pollard's relationship with, 54, 56–57
Sagger missiles, 112–13, 146, 281, 315
Sampson, Scott, 141–43
Saudi Arabia, xiii, 26–36, 37–39, 100
  and Army-Marine withdrawal from OP 7, 166–70
  and battle for Khafji, 166–70, 172, 179, 191, 194–99, 202, 211, 221–22
  Coalition air campaign and, 12, 94–95
  holy sites in, 221, 266
  Iraqi invasion of, xiii, 12–17, 27, 32, 35, 48, 137, 142, 144, 212, 272

  Marines in, 28–36, 52–64, 65–72
  Marines in transit to, 26–29
  oil fields of, 32, 48, 137
  Okinawa-based Marines and, 21–24
  OP 4 and, 1–2, 37–38, 42, 73
  outpost battles and, 95, 97–98, 124
Schroeder, Scott, 106
Schwarzkopf, H. Norman:
  air campaign and, 94–95
  and battle for Khafji, 325
Scud missiles, 14, 37, 94
2nd Marine Division, U.S., 97, 227
2nd Reconnaissance Battalion, U.S., 21
Seven Pillars of Wisdom (Lawrence), 37, 46, 65, 203
Shakespeare, William, 94
Sharon, Ariel, 244
Shaw, Gary, 178–79, 182–89
Sheehan, Neil, 274
Shupp, Mike, 123, 128, 130
Simon, Bob, 35–36
Slavenas, Marcus:
  and battle for Khafji, 194–95, 206, 268, 312–14, 331
  escape from Khafji of, 312–14
Smith, Bryan, 61, 66, 101, 129–30
Snyder, Dave, 106
Spanish Civil War, 324
Stalingrad, battle of, 11
Steinbeck, John, 99
Stephenson, Dion, 63, 71–72, 133
Sterling, Patrick, 335
  artillery attacks and, 298
  and battle for Khafji, 207, 210–11, 216, 288–91, 298, 307
  escape from Khafji of, 306
Sultan 'Adi al-Mutairi, 277
Sweeny, Sergeant, 133

Talkington, Rory, 29, 33
tank fright, 74
tanks:
  AMX-30, 240n
  M-1, 228
  M1A1, 98
  M-60, 304
  T-55, 159, 176, 275, 278
  T-62, 78, 87, 133, 148
  T-80, 99–100
Task Force Troy, 14

Taylor, Michael "Coyote":
   and battle for Khafji, 198*n*, 240–41,
      249, 255–56, 259–63, 265,
      268–69, 305, 309, 313
   and escape of Marines from Khafji,
      309, 313–14
Thesiger, Wilfred, 128
Things They Carried, The (O'Brien),
   287
3rd Battalion, 3rd Marine Regiment
   (3/3), U.S., 230–35, 240,
   247–48
3rd Marine Regiment "3rd Marines,"
   U.S., xiv, 244
   and battle for Khafji, 192–93, 199,
      209*n*, 231, 234, 239, 247–51,
      284–86, 291, 300
3rd Platoon, Alpha Company, 3rd
   Reconnaissance Battalion, U.S.:
   artillery attacks and, 291–95,
      297–300, 304–5, 314
   and battle for Khafji, 191–202,
      203–13, 214–19, 227–29,
      239–41, 247–52, 254–69, 274,
      287–91, 293–310
   communications of, 191, 195–99,
      202, 206, 209, 215, 217, 252,
      260–63, 268, 290, 291–99,
      301–3, 306, 308–9, 314
   defenses of, 215–16, 288–89, 296–97,
      305–6, 309
   escape from Khafji of, 305–14
   Iraqi envelopment of, 207–8, 212–13,
      217–18, 227, 262, 265–69, 274,
      285–86, 287–306, 308–13,
      331–32
   sniper threat to, 310–11
   training of, 191
Thomason, John W., 19
Thompson, Phillip, 209*n*
   and battle for Khafji, 291–92,
      293–95, 298, 300
   suspected fratricides and, 300
Time, 319
TOW antitank vehicles, 60–72
   and battle for Khafji, 255, 275–79,
      321
   capabilities of, 60–62, 62–64
   and capture of U.S. soldiers, 232
   competition among gunners of, 100
   Delta Company and, 46, 61–72

electrical failures of, 130
friendly-fire attacks on, 100–114,
   115–16, 121–22, 126, 133–34,
   144–45, 327–28
misfires of, 143
outpost battles and, 86–87, 90–93,
   99–112, 115–16, 120–22, 124,
   134, 138–46, 148, 327–28
Trainor, Bernard, ix, 325
tube-launched, optically tracked, wire-
   guided (TOW) missiles, 39, 61,
   278, 313–15
   and battle for Khafji, 179, 188, 254,
      268, 305, 315, 321
Tull, Ron, 59, 335
   Delta Company's defensive positions
      and, 63, 70–72
   injuries of, 131–32
   outpost battles and, 107–8, 115, 122,
      131–32, 329
Turk, Lieutenant, 3, 80
Turki al Firmi, 246
   and battle for Khafji, 212–13, 221,
      227, 249, 285
   physical appearance of, 221
Twentynine Palms training base, xiv, 31,
   51–53, 119, 129

Umm Hjul, 1–2, 37–38
   Delta Company's defensive positions
      and, 62, 67
   outpost battles and, 86, 119
United Nations, 242–44
Uskoski, Scott, 297, 312–13

Vegetius, 136
Vietnam War, xiii, 11, 26, 59, 71, 171,
   178, 250, 257, 265, 274
Villa, Alfonso, 50, 92, 126
Virtual War (Ignatieff), 331
Visnews, 320*n*
Vitale, Nick, 60–64, 53–70
   background of, 59–60
   Delta Company's defensive positions
      and, 46, 62–64, 65–70
   outpost battles and, 90–93, 99–102,
      105–8, 115–16, 120, 124,
      128–31
   popularity of, 60, 62
   in search of missing TOW vehicle,
      128–29

Wadi al-Batin, 172

Wagner, Scott, 206, 268–69, 308–9, 312–13

Wainwright William, 117–19

Walker, Daniel, 105–6

Walsh, Tom, 137, 140, 145

Warden, John, 11

Warriors, The (Gray), 219n, 253

Weaver, Paul J., 272

West, Gary, 184

Williams, Scott, 50, 53–56, 58n
  LAV training and, 45
  leadership philosophy of, 56

outpost battles and, 86–87, 90–92, 107–8, 112–15, 118–22, 126
  Pollard's relationship with, 56

Wissman, Michael, 63, 100–102, 106–7, 130

Wolff, Tobias, 171

World War I, 17, 38–39, 73, 155

World War II, xiii, 11, 16n, 18, 30, 74, 136, 209, 234n, 242, 267, 289, 312, 328–29

Zawalick, Russell, 114, 117–22